FIRST BLUE

Also by Robert K. Wilcox

Black Aces High

Wings of Fury

Scream of Eagles

Japan's Secret War

Fatal Glimpse

Shroud

The Mysterious Deaths at Ann Arbor

FIRST BLUE

➤ THE STORY OF

WORLD WAR II ACE

BUTCH VORIS

AND THE CREATION OF

THE BLUE ANGELS

ROBERT K. WILCOX

Foreword by James Lovell

THOMAS DUNNE BOOKS / ST. MARTIN'S PRESS 〽 NEW YORK

THOMAS DUNNE BOOKS.
An imprint of St. Martin's Press.

FIRST BLUE. Copyright © 2004 by Robert K. Wilcox.
Foreword copyright © 2004 by James Lovell.
All rights reserved. Printed in the United States of America.
No part of this book may be used or reproduced in any
manner whatsoever without written permission except
in the case of brief quotations embodied in critical articles
or reviews. For information, address St. Martin's Press,
175 Fifth Avenue, New York, N.Y. 10010.

Map by James Sinclair

www.stmartins.com

Library of Congress Cataloging-in-Publication Data

Wilcox, Robert K.
    First blue : the story of World War II Ace Butch Voris and the creation of the Blue Angels /
    Robert K. Wilcox.
        p. cm.
    ISBN 0-312-32249-6
    EAN 978-0312-32249-6
    1. Voris, Roy Marlin, 1920– 2. Fighter pilots—United States—Biography. 3. World War,
1939–1945—Campaigns—Pacific Ocean. 4. United States. Naval Flight Demonstration
Squadron—History. 5. United States. Navy—Officers—Biography. I. Title.

V63.V73W54 2004
359.9'4'092—dc22
[B]

                                                                  2004046752

First Edition: October 2004

10   9   8   7   6   5   4   3   2   1

To all who strive to be the best

When I was lucky enough to get the chance to write Butch Voris's biography, I thought it would be relatively simple. Interview Butch, get the general layout and outline, supplement with research, fact checking, and hard actual writing, and voilà, a biography. Of course, it wasn't that simple. But what a great project. I was able to immerse myself in World War II, one of my favorite subjects, and specifically, the Pacific war, the generally lesser known of the two great war theaters. I learned a lot. Meeting Butch and getting to know him was another great benefit. When I first started, I checked almost everything he told me, spending a lot of time verifying. He was almost always right. His memory was extremely good. He never lavished or embellished, never took the chance to make himself look good. How many times did he say to me, "I know what you're after, Bob, but that's all there is." He's a truly honest and unpretentious person yet one who has lived an adventure worthy of the great halls of intrepid achievement. I came away with enormous respect, admiration, and feeling for Butch. As his son-in-law Hank always says, he is a national treasure, and I consider myself privileged to have researched and verified his story and, in the process, became Butch's friend.

My luck started with Admiral Winston W. Copeland Jr., "Mad Dog" or "Cope" to his friends, who, after a distinguished career as an honored naval aviator and warfighter, is now a San Jose–area businessman. We had met when he was running the naval portion of the Kosovo War from the carrier USS *Roosevelt.* He recommended me to Hank Nothhaft, Butch's son-in-law, whose idea it was that Butch put his experiences down for posterity. I suspect that to Butch, having led the life was enough, and he probably would have been satisfied to leave it at that. But Hank, a naval academy graduate, former marine and student of World War II, was looking to interest a writer. He knew Butch's contribution to the war and the navy had been substantial. All of us got together and hit it off. Hank, a California internet entrepreneur and CEO of his own company, became a constant source of information and inspiration. His knowledge of World War II is near encyclopedic, and being as close to Butch as he is, he was always a help when I needed input beyond what Butch could give me or what I could discern on my own. We became good friends and his input was invaluable.

As the work commenced, I needed a small staff of helpers, most notably Ricki Sawyer of Sherman Oaks, California, who did most of the interview transcriptions for me. Ricki was always pleasant and helpful, and her work was excellent. Ralph Platt, who had worked with me on several earlier books, also helped with transcriptions. In the course of the research, I ran into many people who answered questions and gave me valuable information. Those people, beyond those mentioned in the text, included: Doris M. Lama, head of the navy's Privacy Act/Freedom of Information Policy Branch in Washington. She was instrumental at the outset in getting Butch's military records declassified. Ron Williamson, historian at NAS Jacksonville, forwarded archives from the base's records and knew stories about Butch and what he'd done there. Barbara Lewis, a writer herself, graciously opened her research to me regarding some of the early Reaper training in Hawaii. Other research helpers included Jack Conner, Pratt & Whitney Archives; Larry A. Feliu, manager of the Northrup-Grumman History Center; Mike Walker and Sandy Smith, navy archivists; Susanne Dewberry of the National Archives, Southeast Region in East Point, Georgia; Meg Hacker and Christina Hardman of the Ft. Worth, Texas, branch of the National Archives; Patrick Osborn, Modern Military Records Branch of the National Archives at College Park, Maryland; Robert Young of Wright-Patterson Air Force Base, Ohio; and Emily Lisska, Jacksonville, Florida.

As we got enough to sell, my agent Jim Trupin of JET Literary Associates went out and did the hard work of placing the manuscript. Jim and Liz Trupin-Pulli of the agency are both good friends and top professionals. Jim, who largely handles the nonfiction and therefore the nuts and bolts with me, is always insightful, helpful, and encouraging. I am lucky to have both of them representing me. Luckily, Peter Wolverton, associate publisher of Thomas Dunne Books at St. Martin's Press, bought the book in its early stages. Pete was editor on my last book, *Black Aces High,* and I say luckily because his comments and direction helped shape *Black Aces* into a better book. But this time, he really did his job. From top to bottom, he made major and minor suggestions that cut the wheat from the chaff, induced me to add important new aspects, and generally focused the book into a much stronger narrative. I am grateful to Pete for his expertise. *First Blue* is better because of his editing.

My final and deep acknowledgments go to my wife, Bego, and son, Robert. Writing is a solitary, albeit rewarding, profession. You have to do it alone. Moral support is an important part of the process. Whenever I needed a read just to make sure I was on the right track, or just to get support to keep going in the vacuum, Bego would do it, sometimes giving me new ideas or changing my perspective. Robert, a writer himself, turned out to be my working editor. He was the real mainstay. Whenever I'd finish a chapter, he was eager to read it. His continued interest was a factor in keeping me pumped, and with a keen eye for detail and great imagination, he always had helpful, useful suggestions. I hope to do the same for him as his career progresses. My daughter, Amaya, was away at school during most of the writing, but just so she doesn't feel left out, let me state right here that she completes the support team. Everyone needs a papaya.

Onward and upward.

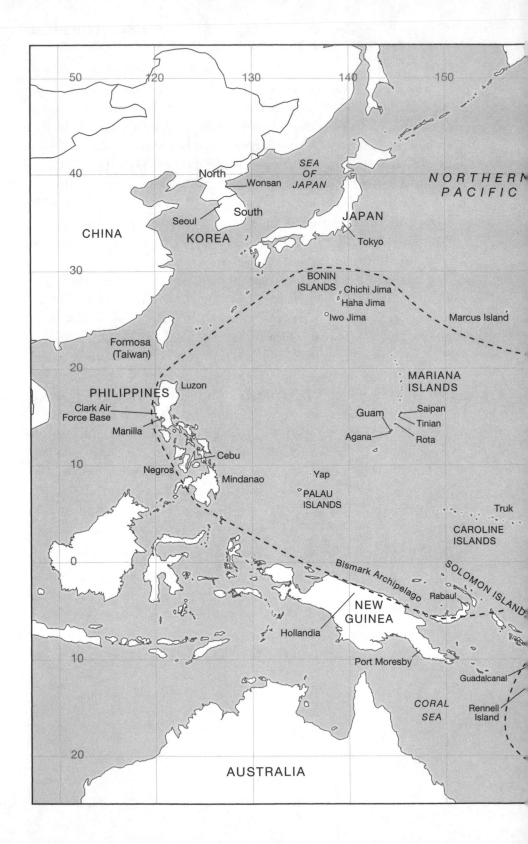

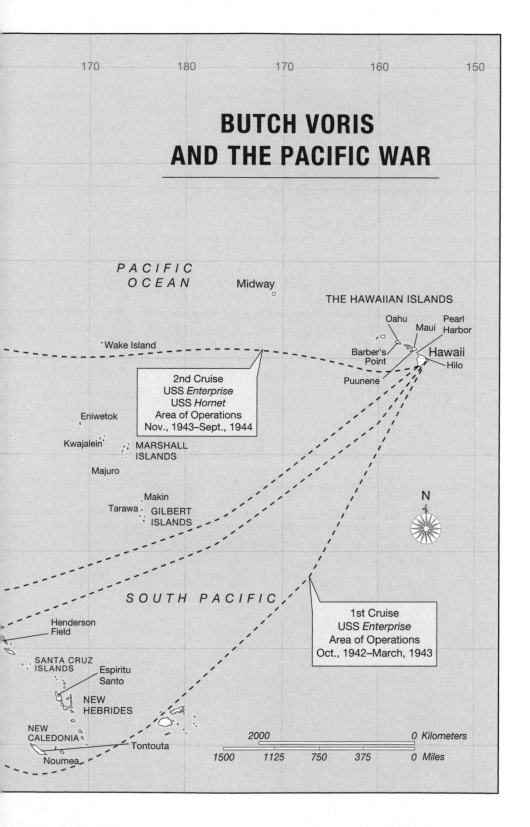

BUTCH VORIS
AND THE PACIFIC WAR

170   180   170   160   150

PACIFIC
OCEAN   Midway

THE HAWAIIAN ISLANDS

Oahu   Pearl
     Maui   Harbor
Barber's
Point   Hawaii
Puunene   Hilo

Wake Island

2nd Cruise
USS *Enterprise*
USS *Hornet*
Area of Operations
Nov., 1943–Sept., 1944

Eniwetok

Kwajalein   MARSHALL
        ISLANDS

Majuro

Makin
Tarawa   GILBERT
        ISLANDS

N

SOUTH PACIFIC

1st Cruise
USS *Enterprise*
Area of Operations
Oct., 1942–March, 1943

Henderson
Field

SANTA CRUZ
ISLANDS   Espiritu
        Santo

NEW
HEBRIDES

NEW
CALEDONIA
        Tontouta

Noumea

2000   0 Kilometers

1500   1125   750   375   0 Miles

The first time I watched the Blue Angels perform, I was a plebe at the United States Naval Academy. They flew overhead in their shiny new Bearcats to put on a show. Wow! So this is what naval aviation is all about. I often wondered how many young men were influenced by the spectacular showmanship of the navy's best aviators to become pilots themselves.

To be a naval aviator is a unique experience. To fly with the Blue Angels is a cherished assignment and a recognition of superb flying skills—but to be the leader of the "Blues" is the ultimate achievement in flying ability: the best of the best. Such a naval aviator was Roy Marlen "Butch" Voris—the First Blue.

This book relates the fascinating aeronautical life of Butch Voris. He was a World War II ace, flying Hellcats against the Japanese. There he learned his acrobatic skills dogfighting with the enemy. He was a natural to head up the navy's first acrobatic flying team. His excellent leadership developed a team of aviators that were the best in the world.

In these pages you will learn about his close calls and crashes; his teammates; the transition from props to jets; Washington politics; his experience at Grumman Aircraft; and finally, finishing his career with NASA.

When you open the pages of this book, you will be flying with the leader of the "Blues." Fasten your seatbelt. The "air show" is about to begin.

James A. Lovell
(Captain, U.S. Navy, Ret.,
and former NASA Astronaut)

PART ONE

ORIGINS

"I'd hang on the fence at the end of the runway and watch as the big Ford trimotors came over at fifty feet in the air."

—*Butch Voris*

CHAPTER 1

Showtime! The four navy F9F-5 "Panther" jets streaked in from the northwest at 450 knots. They were in a tight diamond formation; sleek, bubble-canopied, distinctive bomblike fuel tanks jutting on their wingtips, each plane's dark azure color symbolic of what they were: the Blue Angels, the navy's recently reorganized flight demonstration team.

It was approximately ten a.m., July 7, 1952. The Gulf of Mexico gleamed choppily below the oncoming jets, their wings slicing through turbulent summer air. Up ahead was a crowd of viewers, largely made up of naval academy midshipmen, gathered on the seaplane ramps at Naval Air Station Corpus Christi, the flight team's coastal headquarters. The show, a practice really, was being put on mainly for the benefit of the visiting midshipmen on their summer indoctrination tour. It was hoped that some of them would be sufficiently impressed to opt for naval aviation when they graduated.

It was a clear day, billowy clouds in the sky. Nobody had an inkling of the tragedy that was soon to happen.

The formation was at approximately 4,500 feet and descending rapidly, gathering speed. Leading in "Navy 1" at the front of the diamond was Lieutenant Commander Roy Marlin "Butch" Voris, a thirty-two-year-old World War II ace and veteran of the furious Pacific air wars who had started the Blue Angels, called simply "Blues" by its members, in 1946, and had been asked to restart them again after the team's assignment to the Korean War in 1950 as the core of a new combat unit.

That assignment had halted the team's exhibitions. Now, with the war winding down, the navy wanted its great public relations tool back.

Voris was a big, strapping fighter pilot in the classic Hollywood mold: blond, iron-nerved, square-jawed handsome, but without the Hollywood flair. He disliked pretension and ostentation and wouldn't hesitate to rib those who affected it. Large as an offensive football tackle, which he'd been in college, he had a physical resemblance to the then popular newspaper comic strip hero Joe Palooka, except, unlike the cartoon boxer, he was extremely bright. At six-feet, two-inches tall, and a lean 215 pounds, he could stand up to the toughest in his profession, both physically and mentally. But he was surprisingly even-tempered and good-natured, a smiling recruiting poster officer in his dress whites or simple flight suit who spoke plainly and convincingly and hardly ever got ruffled.

If Voris was anything, he was cool—as in cool under fire.

The flight plan, once the planes had gotten close enough to their audience, was to veer left together in a thirty-degree bank parallel with and facing the shore, revealing their undersides, and streak along in front of the seaplane ramp's entire one mile length so the gathered onlookers could glimpse the large "US Navy" painted in gold on the bottom of their wings. Then, reaching the ramp's end, they'd curl up and back out to sea in a chandelle, a 180-degree revolving slow turn that would rotate them easily around the vertical axis, and then they'd streak back into the airspace in front of the crowd to begin the show's more complicated and startling maneuvers.

It was a proven way to start.

Constituting the rest of the tight diamond were three superb fighter pilots, each handpicked by Voris from the navy's vast aviation pool. Twenty-nine-year-old Lieutenant Commander A. R. "Ray" or "Hawk" Hawkins of Lufkin, Texas, was a World War II and Korean veteran who had shot down fourteen Japanese planes. A Blue Angel before he logged forty combat missions in Korea, Hawkins was on Voris's port, or left, side. The formation was so tight that Hawkins's right wing, stepped down about ten feet from his leader, was actually intruding, had it been at the same altitude, into the small section of airspace directly behind Voris's left wing and forward of his left rear horizontal stabilizer, the small wing-like appendage extending from the jet's upright tail.

That ten-foot difference in altitude, a hiccup in the air, was all that kept the two planes from fitting together like two pieces in a flying jigsaw puzzle.

On Voris's starboard, or right, and, like Hawkins, stepped down, slightly back, and similarly interlocked with the boss, as Voris was called, in the close formation, was Lieutenant Francis J. "Pat" Murphy, a Brookfield, Illinois, native, younger than Voris and Hawkins, who, like Hawkins, had been with the Blues when they were sent to Korea. Flying the "slot," or rear of the diamond, was twenty-seven-year-old Lieutenant (j.g.) Dwight Everett "Bud" Wood Jr., an easygoing, balding Columbus, Ohio-born pilot who had not been part of the team before Korea but had flown combat there and distinguished himself sufficiently that Voris had plucked him from the fleet.

Wood's was the most precarious position in the diamond. The lengthy tubular nose of his Panther actually extended directly under Voris's tail, although it was perhaps fifteen feet below. He was stepped down a little lower than the two wingmen. Woods could look right up through his Plexiglas canopy at the leader's fiery exhaust. Voris's tail was what he flew. When it rolled left, he rolled left. When it rolled right, he did the same. As long as he kept the roughly fifteen-foot interval and stayed directly beneath Voris, he could hold position and escape the dangerous, jostling wind wash that came off the leader. But he had to work perhaps the hardest because he was the only pilot with a good view of the other three. He was counted on to alert them to any detectable problems.

Similarly, the two wingmen flew Voris's right or left wingtip while maintaining their own hair-thin cushions. The leader's wingtip, to their insides, was easy to keep sight of because of the tubular fuel tank attached. The tanks resembled pontoons or small, torpedo-like bombs. They were permanently attached. If the wingman's eyes strayed, which wasn't often, they could follow the thin wing up to see the nose of Voris's Panther, but little else. Neither of the wingmen nor Voris could see Wood. He was alone in the rear slot. Not that they would want to see him. Flying the wingtips, just like flying the slot, demanded intense concentration. Even the slightest deviation could unravel the diamond and possibly cause a collision. Four hundred and fifty or so knots at such close quarters meant that disaster was always just an eyeblink away.

In fact, they'd postponed the show for two days straight because of bad weather, which was always a pilot's enemy with its dangerous winds and often restricted visibility. Instead of flying, they'd allowed the midshipmen to taxi the planes up and down the seaplane ramps, pilots positioned on the wing roots, ready to reach in and grab the controls in case one of the novices got into trouble. It had given the students a taste. But today had dawned clear, with only ten- to fifteen-mile-per-hour winds. There were occasional gusts, but visibility was twelve miles with scattered clouds. Voris in consultation with base officials had determined that the show would go on. Otherwise the midshipmen would have to leave without seeing the Blues.

The oncoming jets encountered no problem until they were just about ready to make their close-to-shore turn. Behind the seaplane ramps were giant airplane hangars evenly spaced. With the ramps and hangars clearly visible, Voris, recalling it nearly fifty years later, said he noticed what he surmised were gusty, individual wind shears bumping them as they descended. "I could see Hawkins's and Murphy's wings moving up and down beside me." The shears, which he thinks were being funneled through the large spaces between the hangars, were hitting each of them separately. "It's amazing how you don't all necessarily bounce together."

He radioed, "Let's ease it out . . . ease it out," meaning the pilots should increase their separation as they readied for the turn.

The gusts seemed to stop, and they went into the thirty-degree bank. They were approximately 200 feet up, maybe 300 feet in front of the ramp, which had bleachers erected to accommodate the crowd. "US Navy" beckoned from each of their underwings as they streaked belly-up down the bay front holding the diamond tight. It was only a two to three G turn, a single G being the force of gravity equivalent roughly to one's own body weight. To the pilots, two to three Gs was mild, not much more than the outward pull a speeding racecar driver might feel negotiating the turns of an oval track. Hawkins, however, because of the tilt, became the low man, and had to work harder to stay "tucked" in.

Beneath and just in front of them midshipmen probably lifted their hats and cheered.

It was the kind of first pass they wanted.

Hawkins later told a navy investigation that he thought they were in good position to continue past the onlookers and back out to sea. Then, as they completed the curving turn in front of the crowd and started up and out in the chandelle, the unexpected happened.

"Hawkins came up or I went down," recalls Voris. "When things go wrong, it happens awfully fast." He heard a loud crashing sound and felt his jet pitch violently nose down and himself lift from his seat and smash up against the top of his canopy—all in a split second. Simultaneously, his jet dived downward and he lost all vision to a surge of blood in the head called redout, the result of a rapid descent in the upright position. Normally, to go down fast, a fighter pilot flips his plane upside down and pulls. The resulting G-force in the dive forces the blood down, toward his seat, and away from the head. It's the most comfortable way to change direction. The pilot struggles to avoid a "blackout," or loss of consciousness, as the blood drains. But this was a sudden "negative G" dive, a painful and scary downward motion without the flip. The blood surged to Voris's head. He didn't lose consciousness but couldn't see anything other than what he later described as a gray-lined and pretty Chinese red.

When he regained his sight, which was probably no more than another second, he was pitched over and roaring toward the shoreside ground, a sure course for a fiery crash and certain death.

Instinctively, he yanked on the control stick between his legs, pulling it as hard toward himself as possible. The action, according to his accelerometer, caused him to pull eight Gs, about as much as a human body can take. The Panther started to shudder its way upward, draining blood from his head. The sudden upward curl was so fast and strong that he lost consciousness momentarily. But he held on. When his consciousness returned, he was rocketing parallel to the ground. On his left, toward the bay side, he was roaring by the tops of tall palm trees that he knew lined a street running along the shore roughly parallel to the line of seaplane ramps. "We called it the Gold Coast Road," he said, because of the admirals' homes fronting the bay there.

On his right he caught flashes of the admirals' porches. He was approximately twenty-five feet above their lawns, streaking like a crazed kamikaze.

Dazed, he wasn't sure what had happened. He figured he'd been in some sort of collision. His first thought was a catastrophic engine explosion. But that couldn't be true, he realized, because the engine was still running. His head and neck and legs, both of which had been under the instrument panel and smashed up against it, hurt, especially his shins. But pain was the least of his worries. The runaway jet was vibrating terribly, his rudder pedals didn't work, meaning he had vastly diminished control, and he was getting an "over temperature" indication from his tailpipe exhaust that signaled the engine might explode any second.

Instantly, with his left hand, he brought the side-mounted throttle back to idle. This reduced the fuel flow and the rising tailpipe temperature. The gauge needle receded. Reduced thrust wasn't an immediate problem because he had tremendous residual speed from the initial pass and the dive he had just been through. Both were propelling him forward. But he had another problem: He could feel the jet pulling to the right and down, which at such a low altitude could kill him in an instant. It took much of his strength to hold the stick to the extreme left in order to counteract the pull.

He probably traversed the entire road in a matter of seconds. At the end of the row of admirals' houses sat the air station's officers' club and pool. He roared over it. "I remember it vividly," he recalls, "even the beach chairs and tables around the pool. It's amazing what sticks in your mind."

Holding the stick hard to the left raised the wing aileron on that side, turning the jet toward the bay and starting its rise, which was his hope. The crowd was now reacting in horror. In his ear, he could hear the show's announcer, Lieutenant Commander Edward L. "Whitey" Feightner, a test pilot and squadron mate from World War II, screaming, "Get out, Butch! Get out!" But it was suicide to eject at that low height. The Panther, by later standards, had a primitive ejection system. Gunpowder blasted the pilot out still strapped in his seat once he'd removed the canopy. But with the other immediate problems occupying him, Voris did not have the time to get the canopy open, and he knew that the explosion and other ejection forces to which he'd be subjected, often resulted in serious injury to the pilot. Most important, the parachute needed at least two thousand feet to deploy properly.

Ejection wasn't really an option.

"I was thinking of getting up to two thousand feet, number one, where I had a chance of getting out."

Still unsure of what had happened, he got on the radio and asked if he'd been hit. Incredibly, the first transmission he heard was no. It was Hawkins, also unaware of what had happened. He had felt no impact. All Hawkins knew, he later testified to the board of inquiry, was that he was alongside Voris one second and the next second Voris was gone. Hawkins, thinking he had somehow gotten out of position, had first thought of try-ing to move back into the formation but then decided it was too danger-ous and had started a standard-procedure rollout to his left to clear the formation. It was sometime during that rollout that he heard Voris's ques-tion and answered in the negative. But then Murphy, who had had an identical experience to Hawkins's, not feeling any impact himself but suddenly missing the leader, had rolled out to his right where there was a different view. There he caught a glimpse of Voris careening downward and saw that his tail was broken and mangled around the exhaust and his left stabilizer was missing. Murphy radioed that they had indeed had a midair.

Climbing, easing on power while keeping the turbine temperature within safe limits, Voris heard the others asking about Bud Wood and glanced over his left shoulder to see the slot man's Panther, minus its nose, hit the water, followed by Wood himself, still strapped into his seat but without his parachute deployed. The frothy impact alone, Voris knew, would have killed him, if he wasn't dead already. The damage to Wood's jet, he later said, was "awful." Hawkins, coming up alongside Voris, now realized that his own right wingtip tank was gone, along with about three feet of the wing. Murphy, coming up along the other side, had a dented left wingtip tank. It was now becoming clear that they'd all been involved in a disastrous collision.

To this day, the exact cause of the accident has never been officially determined. But most agree, and the investigation concluded, that the wind, uncontrollable in such a situation, burbled at least one more fate-ful time. It hit either Voris or Hawkins, or maybe both. As a result, they collided. Hawkins's right wingtip hit Voris's left stabilizer, knocking three feet of Hawkins's wing off and severing the leader's stabilizer. The im-pact, which had tremendous energy, instantly pitched Voris's plane over and down, throwing him up against the canopy, and causing the rear of his jet to hit the nose of Wood's jet, slicing it off at the cockpit. Without its nose, the Panther's center of gravity went to its rear and it became un-flyable, a hunk of metal hurtling through the air. The collision with Wood also smashed Voris's tail, pinching his exhaust, which was the cause of the heat buildup, and permanently jammed the rudder at the back of the tail to the right, which was why the jet was pulling to that side.

Wood, having no options, got out as his disintegrating plane hurtled another nine hundred feet, but he didn't have enough altitude for his parachute to open.

Little of this—except the fate of Wood, which he'd deduced in his quick glance—was clear to Voris or the others at the time.

What they did know was that Voris was in serious trouble.

Now, escorted by his two wingmen, themselves having to deal with their own minor emergencies but giving him momentary accounts of how his crippled plane was handling, Voris reached ejection height.

"Once you pass two thousand, you get a lot braver," he said.

He had more options.

He was still not keen on ejecting. "Probably break an arm at least, if not a hip." As he continued up, the base tower, confused when he didn't exit, began demanding, "What are your intentions! What are your intentions!" He wasn't sure. Without the stabilizing effects of an undamaged tail, it was becoming harder to keep control. In addition to pulling right, the jet, when he slowed down, wanted to go nose up and stall, which would probably flip him over on his back and into an uncontrollable death dive. But when he added power, the forward momentum negated the pitch up and kept the plane going forward and level.

But increasing the speed with more fueled power meant raising the temperature needle.

Luckily, before coming to the Blues for the second time, Voris had spent a tour at the navy's Bureau of Aeronautics in Washington, where he'd been responsible for in-service jet engines. He knew the Panther's J48 turbine engine very well. With his mind racing, he remembered that the engine could handle more heat than the temperature gauge indicated. "We'd done tests and I didn't think the turbine would come apart." So he felt safe with his next move, which was to increase the speed despite the temperature warning. He didn't push it to the limit—but almost. And with Feightner, who was an aeronautical engineer, giving him more pointers, he reached 6,500 feet and an important decision. He was going to try and fly over to NAS Kingsville, an outlying field about twenty miles away, or a few minutes of flying in order to try and land on one of its oversized, 8,000-foot runways.

The long runway was needed because of the speed he'd be landing at. It would be something in the neighborhood of 235 knots, which was about 100 knots faster than the speed at which the Panther normally landed.

"I was hurting. The plane was kind of a mess," he said. "But I could hang on to it at about 240 [knots]."

The pilots involved—maybe everyone watching—knew it would be a miracle if he made it.

The approach was straight in. He could see the field from the height he was at. With Hawkins and Murphy escorting him, he started the long descent. Working the throttle and stick as best he could, he hurtled across the Texas sky in the crippled jet, all the time frantically working the controls. When he dropped below two thousand feet, he knew there was no turning back. That was the last chance he had to eject. "If anything happens now, I'm dead, so we're gonna go."

He continued down, gradually reducing power. At the speed at which he was flying, just touching the runway could blow a tire, and that would send him careening off the runway. "Just before I hit, she started to lose control." The jet was swaying uncontrollably, threatening to crash in multiple ways. He added a little power to keep it up and touched down at approximately 227 knots. His tire treads burned off in a cloud of smoke and screech, but "judicious" and careful touch-braking all along the shortening runway kept them from blowing out. "Just a little wrong pressure could have exploded them and I would have been done for."

He got the jet stopped at the end of the runway. "I did one thing wrong," he said. "I should have shut the engine down. I had all that residual speed. It would have reduced the thrust."

Only after he'd taxied in and tried to lift himself from the cockpit did he collapse.

CHAPTER 2

How does someone have the courage, the cool under fire, and know-how to survive such a life-threatening situation as Voris did that morning in Corpus Christi? Was he born with it? Was it training and preparation? Luck and providence? Probably all those and more. Voris was the founder of the Blue Angels, only one of two of the team's leaders ever to serve as "Boss" twice, and the first to do so. He was a pilot some of the hotshot "right stuff" astronauts, early in their aviation careers at that time, looked up to. But in spite of his talents and temperament, it had really been largely his gut instincts and belief in himself that had been the deciding factors in his miraculous escape. Had he ejected at two thousand feet, he most probably would have survived but ended his career with injury, plus endangered people and houses below. But he'd taken the riskiest option—the one that most probably would kill him but that provided the greatest possibility for a successful conclusion, if one could call it that—a clean chance to save both himself and the damaged plane.

"I was never bothered by risk. I was always between a rock and a hard place. Seizing opportunity is intellectual integrity. To do things better is to attempt to be good," not only in the competitive sense, but in the moral sense. "I've always stuck it out ten percent more. That's how we make progress."

Not surprisingly, the midair collision wasn't Voris's only brush with death. He'd actually had closer calls—and would continue to do so. Who he was, was the product of all that had come before him on that day—his childhood, his upbringing, and the crucible of war where, almost from the very beginning of his aviation training, he'd found himself to be a person superiors counted on to lead.

The war had really fashioned him.

Examining his childhood and war service, therefore, are keys to seeing how he and the Blue Angels are so inextricably bound.

But Voris hadn't planned to be an aviation leader. He'd really not ever considered himself anything more than a ordinary guy who hated repetition and routine, someone who was looking for something better for himself than what he'd trained for in civilian life and wanted to raise the bar when he found it. "I wanted to be the best. That's how you move forward. Sitting on your rear will never get you any opportunity."

Considering that the Blue Angels are regarded as the best in the navy, if not the world, at what they do, it isn't surprising that Voris, their creator, would have such a view. But he hadn't always felt that way, or, at least, he wasn't aware of it early on, in his childhood or schooling. Ironically, given the death-defying work he eventually chose for his career, the man who would become the first Blue Angel had started out thinking he'd probably just lead a comfortable civilian life by becoming a mortician, work he enjoyed, and which he felt was a comfort to those who suffered loss.

★

Born in Los Angeles, California, on September 17, 1919, Butch Voris had been reared in a caring but disciplined home. His father, James Randolf Voris, a physically large and strong man who had labored as a coal miner as a child in New Mexico and a mine elevator operator in Colorado, was a frugal, hardworking dad who demanded that his children be honest and industrious.

Both parents were practicing Seventh-Day Adventists. Butch remembers having to go to church on Saturdays (Adventist Christians celebrate the Sabbath) where his father was choir director. "It was pretty boring." But the basic beliefs, especially those espoused by his mother, Birdie, stuck. He had two younger brothers, fraternal twins, Dick and Bob. There was no television in homes and limited radio in those days. The lack of such distractions may have contributed to his basic calm. While he remembers being enthralled by the radio drama *Chandu the Magician*, after-dinner entertainment was largely supplied by his father playing the violin and his mother accompanying at piano. He remembers classical pieces, especially Franz Liszt's *Liebestraum*. "They enjoyed playing and we enjoyed listening. We had music almost every night in the house." On weekends the family would go to the mountains surrounding Los Angeles for cookouts and picnics. "That's the way my father relaxed." Everybody in the family enjoyed cooking, Butch especially. It would be a hobby that would stay with him the rest of his life.

As the oldest and biggest, he was the sibling leader. The boys were very active, and usually out of doors. In that regard, they took after their father, who stayed in shape by exercising with a car axle and enjoyed, when he wasn't working, auto racing, boxing, and wrestling. He'd wrestled in college. He bought his sons boxing gloves and gave them lessons— sometimes painfully so. When his sons had an argument, he'd usher them to the vacant lot next to their house and have them duke it out. "We'd end up huffing on the ground. It really took the fight out of us." Butch would wrestle his father and always get beat until one day, in his late teens, time and his growth into a powerful high school running guard, shot-putter, and pleasure swimmer finally gave him the edge.

His father was a strong example to the family. "He definitely was the man of the house. He had the last say on anything major. When he spoke, you toed the line. You said, 'Yes, sir.' With my mother, you could discuss [the issue]. Never with my father. That belt would come out. He would unbuckle it and pull it out of his pants and put the lash on us in a split second. One thing he couldn't tolerate was our not telling the truth. Lying, as kids do, I got many lashes. All deserved."

His mother, a smallish woman, was even-tempered—which was perhaps how he acquired the trait—understanding, and affectionate. "Always a smile on her face. Lots of friends . . . I think she paid more attention to us, working with us and doing projects." In his first connection with aviation—although he said he had no inclination to be a pilot then—he made model airplanes and hung many from his bedroom ceiling. Others, lighter and less intricate, he assembled and flew with a toss of his wrist. "She'd take me downtown to buy the balsa wood and would stay close and watch me build them." She tutored the boys when they needed it, helped them with personal problems. "She was the one shepherding us. But she also had her standards. She could be strict." When, as a child, he'd sneak off and get into mischief or go watch race cars at a nearby track without telling his parents, she'd put a line on him and tie it to the pepper tree in their backyard. "That's where I'd spend the day. I didn't know a swear word until I got into the navy."

Although he got into his share of harmless trouble in the neighborhood, he was industrious. By the time he could ride a bicycle, he'd already begun a succession of jobs. He had a route delivering *Collier's,* an illustrated weekly magazine. He was responsible for collections, which taught him a bit about diplomacy. On weekends, he'd go into the city, check out a cart from a dairy company and sell ice cream cups for a nickel apiece. He also sold manure as fertilizer. He liked selling. "I was always looking for ways to get ahead. Everybody was industrious in those days. It was the Depression."

When he was maybe eight years old, his father took him to see his first aircraft carrier. It was anchored in the newly constructed Los Angeles Harbor, which had become a base for the US fleet. The carrier was the USS *Saratoga,* a converted battle cruiser and one of the navy's first flat-tops. Butch was thrilled. "It was Visitors Day. I remember we went out in one of the shore boats. It was going up and down and Dad just reached down [from the sea-level landing] with one hand and pulled me up by my arm. One hand. He was strong." In a little over a decade, he'd make his first carrier landing on the *Saratoga.*

Butch wasn't a very good student in grammar school. Already one of the biggest in his class, he was required, so he wouldn't block the view of others, to sit in the back of the room, where the propensity for mischief was greater. He went to a strict Seventh-Day Adventist school and rather than go home and study after class, he preferred playing sports, exploring on his bicycle, or making things. He was good with his hands, remembers his brother Dick, who starred in school sports and later became a college and National Football League coach. "He could repair things. He'd make fishing poles and model airplanes. I can remember making cars and racing down this big long hill."

He loved speed. Wednesday nights, his dad would take him to the Ascot Speedway in Lincoln Heights and they'd watch the races. "All the big names were there. Wilbur Shaw. Rex Mays. Ernie Triplett." These were the stars of the Indianapolis Speedway. "I used to have all their autographs." With money he'd earned, he'd buy *Flying Ace* magazine, a bulky pulp for its stories about the aces of World War I—Eddie Rickenbacker, the Lafayette Escradrille. He was impressed with the chivalry, the almost gentlemanly way the opposing pilots treated each other before and after a fight. When he could, he'd peddle the four or five miles to the nearest airport and watch planes come winging in. "I'd hang on the fence at the end of the runway and watch as the big Ford trimotors came over at fifty feet in the air."

The Depression eventually took a toll. His father lost money in a savings and loan venture and decided to move the family north to Aptos, a rural redwood forest community south of Santa Cruz. He bought a ranch with fruit trees and a creek full of salmon in spawning season. Butch and his brothers became skilled outdoorsmen, hunting and trapping. In the following years, Butch grew to over six feet and nearly 190 pounds, becoming a well-known Santa Cruz High School football player. He and his buddies caddied at Rio Del Mar Country Club, a lavish 1920s resort near Aptos overlooking the Pacific. After work, in the warmer months, they'd head for the beaches. His brother Dick, who sometimes went along, remembers how impressive his older brother was. "He'd wear these tight little shorts, and did he have a body! Like an Adonis. I'd go next to him because everybody was looking at him, and I thought maybe they also might look at a skinny little guy like me."

Although Voris was physically imposing, he wasn't aggressive or pugnacious. "I was pretty affable. I used up all my energy at practice or the beach." But an incident at the ranch foreshadowed his later penchant for quick action and grit. He was splitting redwood logs for a fence, using a big double-bladed felling ax. A railroad ran through their property. Kids would walk along it to a golf course. A friend passing by yelled his name. He looked up just as the ax came down. He had heavy field shoes on. The blade sliced through the shoe on the side of his left foot peeling back a strip of flesh thicker than a slice of bacon and baring the bone. Blood was everywhere. He was rushed to the doctor, who cleaned and stitched the wound after injecting it with a painkiller.

Later, he was resting the throbbing foot on a pillow in front of the fireplace when a next-door neighbor came running yelling that their house was on fire. He and his mother were the only ones home. "When your house is burning, you forget your foot." He jumped up and ran outside. Smoke billowed from the roof. "It was wood shingle. Very dry. Apparently a cinder from the fireplace had landed on it." His mother went running up the hill to get the fire department. He got a ladder from the shed and climbed up carrying an ax and a hose. "About this time, the stitches are pulling loose and blood is spurting out." He chopped a hole in the roof where the fire was burning, then hosed everything that was smoking. "By the time the fire engine got there, I had the fire out." Then he began feeling his foot. "Oh, it hurt. Oh, my God."

His mother had to call his father again, and they rushed him back to the doctor. But the doctor didn't have any more anesthetic.

The foot couldn't wait.

"They just went ahead and did it."

Even stronger in his memory—in terms of his later decision to become a pilot—was an earlier incident. He was in the school waiting for the bell to signal the next class. Presently, he heard the *vroom vroom* of mighty engines in the sky. He turned and was amazed to see the huge US Navy dirigible *Macon* emerging above him. "We had a tall school building, maybe three stories. All of a sudden this great silver bird appears over the roof. It couldn't have been more than two thousand feet up. It was mammoth. I'd seen dirigibles but not this close. It just kept enlarging as it moved toward me out of the roof."

The *Macon,* one of several Goodyear-Zeppelin-made airships being touted by the navy in those days, was 785 feet long, nearly a football field wide, and filled with helium. Its eight 560-horsepower engines were not synchronized, which was the reason for the distinctive, uneven drone. As he watched, two small biplanes flew up to the giant airship and were "recovered" in its middle. They were Curtis F9C "Sparrowhawk" fighters, miniatures that had been launched from the *Macon*'s internal hangar deck. To retrieve the fighters, a retractable structure called a trapeze was lowered. It had a bar on the bottom. The Sparrowhawk had a hook atop its wing. The plane would engage the bar and be hoisted into the *Macon*'s belly.

"It was fascinating to me. It was aviation." But he still wasn't consciously thinking about a career as a pilot. Occasionally, if he had the money, he'd go over to a little dirt airstrip in nearby Capitola and pay five dollars for a night flight around the field. But it was just for fun. His father, who had been a hospital administrator at one time, wanted him to be a doctor.

He began thinking of medicine as a profession.

After a few years, it became obvious that the farm as a business venture wasn't working out. His father sold it, bought a home on Walnut Avenue in Santa Cruz, and started Voris Realty Company and Insurance.

Butch graduated from high school in 1937, but his grades weren't good enough to get him into a good medical school, and even if they had been, the money wasn't there. "Dad had three boys, and I wasn't going to win any scholarship." He decided to enroll in Salinas Junior College, south of Santa Cruz in scenic Monterey County.

It was to be a turning point.

CHAPTER 3

Up until junior college, Butch had been largely on cruise control, leading a mostly fun-filled life, not taking studies seriously or pushing to make a mark. But something changed in him when he started courses at Salinas. "Maybe it was self-testing or maybe it was ego . . . I realized I couldn't just sit back and expect to get through." He started thinking he'd better do more than he had been if he was going to succeed. "I guess it was the difference between a kid's perspective and an adult's perspective. I began volunteering, getting appointed to things, showing an eagerness to do them."

He took as many premedical courses as he could—"all the toughies"—chemistry, anatomy, bacteriology, trigonometry, German. "I began to learn to study a bit and get better grades." He got involved in student politics and was elected chairman of Lancers, a steering club of student leaders. "I was always starting something new, and I couldn't do that without trying to do it well." He joined the college's football team and made all-conference at tackle. "I'd gotten bigger than a guard—and those were the days when you played both ways." He boxed at field days when they had special events. "I wasn't athletic enough for basketball. I liked contact sports."

Although he wasn't thinking too much about it, this was the beginning of his development of leadership skills—skills he would utilize later in the navy.

Graduating from Salinas—later renamed Hartnell College—in 1939, Butch went up the coast a bit and enrolled in San Francisco's College of Mortuary Science. "I still didn't have the money to go to medical school." Attaining an A-minus average at the college's conclusion nearly a year later, he accepted an apprenticeship at one of San Francisco's largest funeral houses, Gantner and Maison.

"I enjoyed working on cadavers. At school, I'd pull 'em out of the tank and alcohol and put them on the table and do what we had to do." His new job entailed picking up the deceased at homes, hospitals, and morgues, embalming them, applying the makeup for the funerals, which he'd sometimes plan and conduct. "Today they just throw you in the refrigerator. But back then we had to drain all the bodily fluids, the blood and everything, and replace it with formaldehyde. There's a lot of detail in preparing a body for a service."

In a standard procedure, he'd cut a vein in the leg for draining and inject the embalming fluid in an artery in the armpit. "In the case of a woman, you pack the vagina. You have to wire the jaws together to keep them closed . . . It gets pretty gruesome . . . You take the trocar—it's a long, hollow, pointed tube—and suck out all the internal matter from the digestive system, the stomach, the intestines, and then you put in the preservative . . . You had to get rid of all those decaying parts, and you're pretty much left with the skin."

He lived at the mortuary, the bodies on the level below. "I was always good with people, especially in moments of distress. That's the front end of the business. The back end is the operating room or laboratory . . . I enjoyed the work . . . You feel like you're able to help in trying times . . . I could do just about everything pretty well. Whatever I did, I took great care to try and do it better than whoever else was around. It was just my nature."

One of the most memorable cases he worked on was the sad situation of a young girl whose parents were Christian Scientists and wouldn't let her get medical help. "She had an upside-down stomach. She was a pretty little girl, thirteen or fourteen. It was quite widely publicized in the San Francisco papers at the time. I remember going to her home. She couldn't get any food. Her family wouldn't let the doctors correct the thing. She died of malnutrition."

He spent most of 1940 going to wakes and preparing corpses. He probably would have continued in the profession except that in March

1941, at the age of twenty-one, he saw a recruiting poster in a San Francisco post office. It showed a handsome pilot standing by an airplane and said "Fly Navy." The wars being waged by the Nazis in Europe and the Japanese in China had been escalating. "The draft was coming, and you could see we were going to get in it. Slogging my way through the mud in the infantry didn't appeal." The picture of the pilot suddenly beckoned. Even though he'd always been interested in aviation, he'd assumed the cost was prohibitive, the opportunity remote. Recently he'd heard about some high school acquaintances who had signed up for military aviation. Now it all clicked. "I'd always wanted to fly. Here was my chance."

He phoned a recruiter. In short order, he was on a bus to the Naval Reserve Aviation Base at Oakland Airport, across the bay from San Francisco. The base, in a corner of the airport, wasn't much—little more than two hangars and a barracks. A mess hall was still being built. But the physical they put him through was rigorous. "You had to have perfect vision, heart, blood pressure, hearing. Couldn't have a single defect. They'd put you in a damned chair and spin you until you were dizzy, then stop and see how you'd react."

It went on all day.

They were amazed at his perfect teeth. "Must have been the diet we had at home—lots of fruits and vegetables." His final test involved dilating the pupils. "They look inside and check the blood vessels." His eyes were fine. He was a perfect specimen. They told him to go home; they'd be in touch with instructions later. He walked happily outside in the afternoon sun to catch the ride back to San Francisco. Then it hit him. "I couldn't tell a bus from a warehouse. I was blind. They didn't give us dark glasses or anything. Didn't even tell us we were going to have a problem."

He fumbled his way back home by asking people to help him.

CHAPTER 4

Today, a prospective naval aviator goes through what is called Aviation Preflight Indoctrination, a systematic, lengthy, ground syllabus, six weeks or more, that carefully prepares the candidate for what he's about to do. He's in the classroom more than a month before he touches an airplane. And before that, he or she endures a thorough screening. But in 1941, with a shortage of pilots and money and a world war looming, the navy had a different system.

Voris's first stop was a relatively quick do-or-die aviation boot camp aptly named Elimination Flight Training. "Get sick and you were out," recalls Russ Reiserer, a recent Stanford University graduate when he met Voris during that one-day physical. "We were both standing bare-ass naked in the hall waiting to be checked." He and Voris became quick friends and would serve together in the desperate South Pacific fighting, both eventually becoming aces. But when they reported back to the naval air reserve station at Oakland they were lowly entry-level second-class seamen about to undergo ten hours of seat-of-the-pants flying spread out over about a month with minimal instruction and little tolerance for pain or error.

The class of ten candidates arrived April 21, 1941. They called their new home "E-base"—the E standing for elimination. They weren't the first class there in the heightening war buildup, and others soon followed, sometimes two or three a week. They were issued what Voris called "crazy stripped-down marine uniforms"—dark pants, khaki shirts, and neckties. "We couldn't wear them off base." Their barracks was little more than a white wooden building with cots. They started off with classes in a cramped room. It wasn't too long before Voris had second thoughts. "The navy being the way it was, we got lectures on customs and traditions." When they got to the part about what to wear and how many calling cards to leave when visiting a commanding officer, he thought to himself, "Oh, come on." But they soon moved to flying fundamentals like aeronautics, navigation, and propulsion. "Basic stuff. Drag [caused by the air] holds the airplane static. Power pulls it ahead. Lift. Lower pressure on top of the wing combined with higher pressure under, makes it go up. Keep flying speed. That was important. You don't do that, and you're going to fall or crash. Basically, it was here's the theory on the blackboard. Now let's go out and see what you can do in a plane."

Each candidate got an instructor. "He was either going to get you through or wash you out." Voris got a crusty, spit-and-polish marine captain who signed his name H. H. Bullock. "We called him Captain Haus. Officers wore boots and shiny brown belts in those days. He was short. Very proper." They would fly the navy's last biplane, the N3N, nicknamed the "Yellow Peril." It was a single-engine, two-seat, metal-and-fabric aircraft with a fixed landing gear, a large rudder on the tail, and a rubber tube between the front and back open-air cockpits so the instructor and student could communicate amid the considerable noise. "It was quite an airplane. Solid, honest characteristics"—meaning he knew what it would do and it wouldn't deviate or surprise. "A bit noisy, but it didn't stall easily."

He remembers his first flight: "It was a nice clear day . . . [Bullock] sat in the front and I sat in the back . . . We just kinda flew around Alameda and he talked to me . . . You put the stick left, you go left. When it's right, you go to the right. Nothing mysterious about it. You pull back, you go up. You push forward, you go down." Foot pedals controlled the rudder. Turns dip one wing toward the turn, raise the other. "The faster you go, the stiffer the controls get, because you've got more wind force on the control surface"—the movable flaps on the wings and tail that guide the plane's movements.

Bullock let him take the stick.

"It was a great feeling. You say, Hey, this is what I've been looking forward to."

They'd go out in gaggles, eight or ten airplanes bobbing and weaving over the largely unpopulated Northern California countryside as the instructors showed them what to do. Photos of the gaggles show leather-helmeted occupants in the open-air cockpits, at least one of them signaling with his hands.

After a few orientation flights, and some washouts, they started practice takeoffs and landings at a little field near Livermore, California, which is now part of Silicon Valley. "It was just dry hills," recalls Voris. "When we were done, we'd head back to Oakland. [Bullock] loved to flat-hat"—fly so close to the ground, went the talk, that if a person wearing a hat was beneath them, the plane would flatten it. Today, the practice gets a pilot grounded. But back then it was probably the real beginning of what would eventually lead Voris to become First Blue.

"That's where it really started. We'd go through those hills just skimming upside down, feet from the ground. I could almost reach out and touch the dry grass. [Bullock] loved to do that. We were never right side up for very long coming back. He'd let me do it. I'm sure his hands weren't far from the controls, but it was to make me feel comfortable in what we call unusual attitudes. Some didn't like it, but I did. Oh, it was kind of a thrill at first, but then it became routine. You had to control the airplane precisely"—a factor which would become very important when he started the Blues. "Even maybe a half pound of pressure on the stick and she'd pop into the ground on you. [Bullock] was loose and would laugh, 'How do you like that. Fun, isn't it?' It was tremendous. When you are a young kid like I was and you're with a spit-and-polish marine fighter pilot, you feel like you're almost in the hands of God. I learned a lot from that."

Simultaneously, his leadership potential was recognized. He was put in charge of his class. "They called them platoons or details, I think." One day his desire to show prowess got him in trouble. Marching a large group of candidates made up of his own class and others, he spied some pretty girls from the airport watching them. He decided to put on a show. "I'm marching and counting off, 'Left, right, left.' Everybody's together in cadence." He was doing so well, he decided to march the group out of their assigned area and toward the girls, who were near the main airport terminal. An angry officer came running out and herded them back near their hangars.

Called before the commanding officer, he was asked to explain what he thought he was doing? "I was marching, sir, and I thought quite smartly." The CO, concerned about the navy's status as a guest at the airport, didn't agree. He decided to teach Voris and his marchers a lesson. He ordered them to run double time in a large circle with their arms extended holding heavy rifles—run until they dropped.

He mustered everybody out by the hangars.

"It was a challenge. All the instructors came out to watch . . . I said I'm not going to let those bastards beat me."

When the run was finally halted, Voris, although gasping, was among the few still standing.

At the end of the ten hours of instruction, it was time for the final exam—a solo flight. "You passed or you killed yourself." Bullock patted him on the back and said, "You'll do fine. I've got confidence in you." He handed Voris two long strips of cotton cloth, which would function as streamers. They were to be tied to his struts to alert everybody in the vicinity: "Stay clear. This guy's doing it for the first time." Classmates signed the cloth with "Good luck, big fellow," and "Lots of luck, Giant!"

"I remember every minute of it," Voris says now. "These things are indelible. The solo was once around the airport and down. I remember getting in the airplane. They put a big sandbag in the front seat to make up for the weight of the instructor. Strapped it in. It had to do with the balance. You had to have two people in the airplane.

"The takeoff was easy . . . We used a kind of crushed-stone landing and takeoff area, not the main runway . . . Commercial airplanes were taking off, so you're looking out, watching for them . . . You are all by yourself. There's nobody to help you. You don't have any radio . . . I remember climbing to a prescribed eight hundred feet, turn left ninety degrees, and then turn left again . . . You start downwind opposite your landing spot. You come to the landing spot and then you turn left another ninety [degrees] descending. And around until you are complete . . . You come in over the fence and land. I got it down pretty good . . . You taxi over to the hangar. Everybody's out there and clapping. That was it. That solo flight washed out about half of my class."

Voris's final ranking, according to Elimination Training records, was "Above average." He was marked "Qualified: eligible for appointment as aviation cadet." The navy now knew he was worth spending some money on.

It was a milestone for Butch. He was on his way to real flight training.

CHAPTER 5

Corpus Christi was a brand-new naval air station in June 1941 when Butch arrived, the result of Congress's passing emergency legislation to build a new navy flight training facility for pilots in addition to the already existing NAS Pensacola. The legislators had recognized that a lot more navy pilots were going to be needed. "There wasn't any grass growing there, not even a plant." The first flight from the new field had lifted on May 5, just a month prior to Butch's arrival. He had been given charge of perhaps a dozen cadets making the journey from Oakland. They were processed and almost immediately thrown into intensive ground school, including celestial navigation and Morse code. "It was very extensive."

Ground school continued for a month.

In August, he began flying, first in the single-engine N2S, a biplane very similar to the N3N he'd flown at elimination training, and then the SNJ, a North American-built low-wing monoplane still seen in World War II air shows today. Known variously as the T-6, AT-6, "Texan," and "Pilot Maker" because of its role in preparing so many army and navy pilots for combat, the SNJ, with a large canopied two-seat cockpit, was a step up in size and performance for Voris. "I was pretty much a natural. I never got airsick."

But one day during instrument training he thought he was washed out.

Instrument training meant the student was under a hood. He had to fly the plane without seeing outside. Voris had an instructor whose name he remembers as O'Neil. "He was abrupt, terse, not overly blessed with kindness and manners."

O'Neil was in the front seat, Voris in the back. They each had a lengthy metal control stick jutting polelike between their legs. It was connected by a rod running under both seats. So both sticks moved in unison.

They were practicing turns. Voris, watching his instruments, was supposed to keep a little ball in the middle of a dashboard gauge. It told him he was holding his altitude and keeping level during the turn. But he was having trouble, and the little ball kept drifting beneath the line indicating the horizon. O'Neil had warned him several times, but "I got a little too much rudder in. He started screaming at me." Suddenly he felt the metal pole whacking his knees.

The short-tempered instructor was getting violent.

Reacting, Voris whacked him back.

O'Neil grabbed the stick and "just dived that airplane right down. Not a word. I thought, 'Oh, shit. What have I done?'"

They landed and Voris was marched to the hangar in which was the office of the chief flight officer, Eddie Outlaw, soon to become well known in the war as skipper of VF-32, nicknamed "Outlaw's Bandits." In later years, Voris and Outlaw would become good friends and Outlaw would rise to admiral. But on this particular day the chief flight officer was only intimidating—in name, rank, and Voris's particular view.

O'Neil had stood Voris outside Outlaw's glass-enclosed cubicle on the second floor of the hangar. He could see O'Neil "waving his arms and pointing at me . . . and Outlaw nodding his head."

It didn't look good.

"I figured my career was over."

When they were done, O'Neil exited without even a glance at his apprehensive student.

Through the glass, Outlaw motioned Voris in. "I stood there at attention. He didn't look up, just kept me standing there." Finally he acknowledged the student. "Well, Cadet Voris, I've just had a report on your conduct." He asked Voris for an explanation. "I said, 'I'm very sorry, sir. I guess I did it out of reaction, not expecting to be treated as I was. I'm just not of the makeup to take that kind of stuff. I thought officers were supposed to act like gentlemen. I don't think it was proper and my reaction was to take the stick and do unto him as he did to me.' He knew it was insubordination. 'I guess I'm not supposed to do that.'"

Outlaw eyed him silently. "I was just sort of looking at my shoes. Then I noticed he was starting to smile. He said, 'Voris, what am I going to do with you?'" The cadet didn't know. "'I'll tell you what I'm going to do. I'm going to get you a new instructor.'" He smiled broadly. "'Now come on, get out of here.' I don't think he liked O'Neil."

Voris got the new instructor, and it was smooth flying from there. Again tapped for leadership, he was appointed lieutenant commander of his battalion, one of ten in the training regiment. "I was responsible for half the battalion. You had to march them to the airfield, march them back, march them to chow, march them to pay." It was hot and sticky in Corpus Christi, the result of the gulf's humidity. Everywhere they went, they wore flight suits and parachutes with tight harnesses. "Everybody got crotch rot. Oh, jeez, it was awful." The fungus reddened the skin, swelled, and chafed it. "You'd go to sick call in the morning and they'd just line us up. A corpsman would be there with a swab of Merthiolate. He'd just go down the line. It became a daily routine."

But rank had its privileges. He could leave the base at night while others were restricted. "Of course, you don't abuse the privilege because you're pretty tired." Off base uniforms were dress whites, almost identical to regular officer uniforms with raised, stiff collars and shiny buttons. Cadet lieutenant commanders wore a single star on each shoulder board to indicate rank. "We'd go up to San Antonio on the weekends," he remembered. It was the home of Fort Sam Houston, one of the largest army bases in the country at the time. Young soldiers would see the stars and salute them. "They thought we were an admiral or general of some kind."

On Sunday, December 7, almost six months after he'd started flight training, he and several cadet officers were exiting a movie theater playing *Dive Bomber*, a big Errol Flynn actioner of the day about naval aviators, when they learned the Japanese had bombed the American naval base at Pearl Harbor, Hawaii. "We saw a crowd gathered around a cigar shop, like those near every theater in those days. We gravitated over and they gave us the news. Within ten minutes, shore patrol caught us and said get back to base immediately. We were now in a state of war. It got pretty crazy."

His first thought, he said, was "how much more training do I have left before I can get into it?" He was eager to go. They had all been expecting hostilities. "The war clouds had been on the horizon for a long time . . .

At first we were like a bunch of idiots running around in circles. Everybody wanted to get their hands on a war machine. We started flying out over the water to see if there were Japanese submarines in the Gulf. That was kind of fruitless, but we had to do something."

The training command immediately stepped up the tempo. His log book shows a sharp increase in flights. They started flying on Saturdays, which before they'd had off.

Then he had a setback.

After being commissioned an ensign and proudly accepting his wings, he was ordered to report to a dive-bombing squadron.

Dive-bombing?

He'd put in for fighters and was expecting to get them.

"I was upset," he recalled. Fighters "were more of a test of your ability to fight, fly, and win—be the best. It gets back to a challenge." He'd seen the fighter swagger; knew the lore. "I wanted to prove myself. I wanted to be a fighter pilot."

But arguing would do no good. "I knew why I got it. It was a new school. They had to put a batch of students in dive-bombing instruction so I was stuck with this big Curtis Helldiver." It was a two-seat, tanklike biplane with bent top wing—a bomb truck, really—but, ultimately, at least as far as its primary mission went, Butch found it "kind of exciting" once he got into it. "You'd go up to ten thousand feet, push the stick over until you're headed ninety degrees straight down." There was a long scope in the front of the pilot with padding for his eye. "You're watching the target get bigger and bigger. Very impressive as it came up at you. We built up to 240 knots with dive brakes [wing flaps] extended to keep us from going too fast and kissing the ground." When they reached drop altitude, around a thousand feet, they'd "pickle" and "pull like hell" [enduring the force of five or six Gs] to turn back level and exit.

He swallowed his disappointment and reported in early 1942 to the Advanced Carrier Training Group at North Island, San Diego, California. It was the Pacific Fleet's headquarters and must have been impressive. Aircraft carriers. Operational fleet squadrons with names like the Devastators and the Dauntlesses. "There was a different mentality in the fleet squadrons from the training command." The fleet was what naval aviation was all about.

He threw himself into the dive-bombing training, knowing that when he finished the two-month orientation he'd be assigned to Bombing

Squadron 10, one of the hastily put together units that would soon be participating in the frenzied Pacific fight. He had nearly completed the training, had purchased a $10,000 government life insurance policy for which $6.60 would be deducted each month from his ensign pay, and was just about ready to report when he heard an announcement over the hangar loudspeaker that anyone interested in transferring from bombers to fighters should report to the chief flight officer immediately. "Boy, I'll tell you, two of us started on the run for the ladder to get up to his office. We knocked on the door and he said, 'Come in. I hope you're here because you want a transfer.' I said, 'Yes, sir.' I didn't need a very big speech, I'll tell you." As it turned out, the other guy didn't go through with it. "But I got transferred. My orders were modified."

It was right around this time that the Battle of the Coral Sea took place, May 4–8, 1942, the first naval battle in history in which the opposing ships never saw each other. Airplanes from carriers did all the shooting. In the fight the United States stopped the Japanese planned invasion of Port Moresby, New Guinea, but lost the carrier *Lexington* and had another, the *Yorktown,* damaged. Though the battle counted as a U.S. victory, the fleet had reached a crisis. All the US battleships, many destroyers, cruisers, and thousands of men had already been destroyed or killed at Pearl Harbor. And since then, more planes, ships, and men had been lost at Wake Island and the Philippines. America was in pitiful shape in the Pacific. Its navy was scrambling to put together a force—which recent events had proven had to be carrier based—that could stop the formidable, ferocious, and veteran Japanese military machine, which had been fighting in China for ten lesson-learning years.

It had the most experienced, skilled, and brutal military in the world.

But Voris wasn't dwelling on any of this. He was going to be a fighter pilot!

More important, he was about to launch into an experience of war and flying that would ready him for one of the most important jobs of his life: starting the Blue Angels.

PART TWO

WAR

"You had to mature fast or die.
I just sort of clenched down and lost
feelings and went at it."

—Butch Voris

This was it. The decisive test Voris had trained for: carrier qualification. If he couldn't fly from an aircraft carrier, it would be the end of
his career—at least the career he envisioned. He would have to launch
and land on the carrier's moving, pitching, seemingly (from the air) mi-
nuscule deck. Six times he'd have to display the crucial skills that separated navy pilots from the rest.

If he couldn't land on the ship, he couldn't fight from it.

If he was a danger to the ship, they wouldn't have him.

All through his training, all the way up until this very day, the navy had
drilled in him the importance of the skills he was taught. He'd practiced
and practiced on a specially marked-off field. This now was the real
thing, the culmination of all his training. He was nervous, probably as
nervous as he'd ever been since the day he started flying. "In terms of
everything you've done before, this was the big one."

Coincidentally, he was waiting for his turn to launch on the USS
Saratoga, the same ship that over a decade before, when he was just a
boy, his father had one-armed him up on after it had come to Los Angeles. The irony hadn't escaped him. Back then, aircraft carriers were still
in their infancy; battleships were preeminent. Since 1910, when the
Virginia-based cruiser *Birmingham* had launched the first airplane from a
ship—a Curtis biplane—the carrier fleet had been evolving.

In 1914, seaplanes used as scouts had been dropped from the battleship *Mississippi* during a American-Mexican dispute. The British had taken the lead in converting ships to airplane launchers during World War I, bombing German Zeppelin bases with ship-based seaplanes. In 1919, Congress had authorized the construction of the country's first bona fide long-deck aircraft carrier, the *Langley*. In the early 1920s, there had been doubts and fights over the flattop's worth. But gradually a succession of carriers had been commissioned: *Lexington* and *Saratoga* (1927), *Ranger* (1933), *Yorktown* (1937), *Enterprise* (1938), *Wasp* (1940), and *Hornet* (1941). As America's entry into World War II grew imminent, smaller escort carriers had been hastily constructed.

At Taranto in November 1940, in a sneak attack by carrier-based planes, the British destroyed the Italian fleet. Then the Japanese studied Taranto, and did the same to America's major battleships at Pearl Harbor. The carrier, almost by default, became the most important warship in the American naval arsenal, and it had been proving itself in the six months since.

And so on this cloudy but sunny morning, Voris, waiting nervously, knew he was about to become part of that illustrious history. The aging *Saratoga,* one of the few big carriers left, was steaming into the wind one hundred miles off San Diego. It had recently returned from repairs after having been torpedoed by a Japanese submarine five hundred miles southwest of Oahu, Hawaii.

The war in the Pacific was raging.

It was May 26, 1942.

Since about midway in his two-month advanced carrier training and after joining the newly created Fighting 10 Squadron at North Island, Voris had been flying the F4F "Wildcat," the fleet's newest fighter. It had already proven itself in combat. The country's first official World War II ace, Lieutenant Edward "Butch" O'Hare, after whom Chicago's O'Hare Field would later be named, had been flying a Wildcat when he shot down five attacking Japanese bombers that undoubtedly would have sunk his carrier, *Lexington,* had he not been so skillful and courageous. O'Hare's was a stirring story. Voris, like the other young naval aviators, knew it well. He'd been the only fleet defender between the enemy bombers and *Lexington.* Other airborne Wildcats were too far away when the attackers were spotted, and O'Hare's wingman's guns had jammed. He'd had to do it all alone, had been awarded the Medal of Honor. And he'd done it all in the Wildcat, the same plane Voris would be flying for qualification.

Originally conceived as a biplane, the Grumman-built Wildcat had evolved into a stubby, barrel-nosed monoplane. It was the fleet's principal single-winged weapons platform, a rugged, pugnacious-looking fighter with a birdcage cockpit and sturdy, lengthy wings rooted relatively high in the forward section of the fuselage. It was powered by a single 1200 horsepower Pratt and Whitney radial engine. The fuselage was reinforced with armor plate, especially around the cockpit, and had self-sealing fuel tanks which was comforting, said Voris, except for the fact that "you can look down and see this big massive fuel tank right between your legs."

Fire was always a fear.

Primarily because of the extra weight, the Wildcat, with a top speed of approximately 320 miles per hour and a slow climbing rate, wasn't very fast (except in a dive). Or agile. Especially in comparison with its lighter and more nimble adversary, the tight-turning Japanese Zero, which was built for performance and lacked protection for its pilot. The Wildcat's wings were foldable, an innovation to allow more to be stored and handled on the carrier. But a headache for its pilots was the fact that hand-cranking was required to raise and lower the wheels. Twenty-one cranks is the figure Butch remembers. That meant leaning down into the cockpit, taking your eyes away from the sky, often a dangerous and always a tedious and awkward practice in the cramped cockpit space. Some pilots had even been injured by the landing gear crank, which could build up tension and whirl unexpectedly with damaging force. Thankfully, Voris knew, he wouldn't be cranking for the carrier qualification. The wheels would stay down as he circled and momentarily landed for his required six times.

The Wildcat had another pertinent shortcoming. It had caused Voris perhaps his most embarrassing moments in a cockpit up to that point. The plane's two front wheels were relatively close together, only about six feet apart, which was a very narrow spread for landing gear. They were mounted on short, thin, shock-absorbing retractable struts that were adequate for cushioning a crashlike landing on a carrier but not for taxiing. With the relatively big engine and body above the narrow landing gear, "the plane had a tendency to lean either right or left very easily." The large nose and powerful engine would meander the fighter like a big dog dragging its owner.

Earlier, when he'd first arrived in San Diego, Voris had flown the Brewster Buffalo, the navy's first monoplane, a smaller, stubbier fighter with wide landing gear. It didn't have the taxiing problems. When he'd moved to the Wildcat, he'd simply been given a handbook. "You took it home. You read it. You came back the next day and they expected you to fly it. The torque"—the counter rotational force of the spinning propeller—"was terrific." Taxiing out, the Wildcat started veering left. "The only way I could keep it straight was by hitting the right brake [thereby keeping it from going left] and giving it full right rudder until I could get enough airflow over the rudder [vertical tail section] to control the direction."

But on his first takeoff, he'd not known about the need for that correction. "I'm swerving left. I mean really left. Thank God I was on a [huge blacktopped area] and not a [narrow] runway. I'd have been off it in seconds." As it was, he was still aiming to exit even the large blacktop. The veering plane had turned a full ninety degrees, teetering like a bucking bronco as it did, and was heading straight for the base officers' club, a disaster Voris's widening eyes did not want to see. Finally conceding he couldn't cope, he throttled back to idle and, amidst the heckling of the other students waiting their turn behind him, limped the slowed fighter back to its starting point. "It was an experience. The next time I sweated blood, but I got it up there."

Now he had to prove himself again.

★

Voris and his group of pilots had been watching others qualify from an area beneath *Saratoga*'s tiered, middeck island, the towering operations "stack," as they called it, overlooking the 900-foot flight deck. The signal came that it was their turn to qualify. They donned their leather helmets with goggles. The Wildcats were gassed and running, chocked at the wheels for safety. The noise was deafening. He mounted the wing, climbed in, and strapped the lone seatbelt across his waist. There were no shoulder straps.

He left the canopy open. The flights weren't going to be that long and a quick escape was essential if any of them went into the ocean.

The heavy Wildcat would sink fast.

The chocks were removed.

"Things started to happen quickly. You're almost on automatic."

Yellow-shirted plane handlers motioned him to the launch spot approximately a hundred yards from the bow. It was in the middle of the deck. The exact position was determined by wind speed over the deck, which was a combination of the carrier's rapid forward knots and the wind speed. More wind meant a shorter takeoff. "All of a sudden, you see Fly One—he's the guy with the flag, who winds you up and tells you to go."

Also called "plane director" and "flagman," Fly One was to the side. He gestured precisely. Clasping a fist to his chest, he whirled the yellow flag vigorously above his head. The signal meant rev the engine but hold the plane. Voris complied. With a left-handed thrust, he pushed the throttle forward but stood on the brakes. The Wildcat roared with power, surging at the hold.

Voris scanned his systems. Everything looked good. He gave a short, snappy salute, indicating he felt ready. When Fly One, making his own perusal from outside, agreed, the handler turned and pointed the flag toward the bow. It was the signal to commence. Voris released the brakes— but not completely. As he started to roll forward, the Wildcat's powerful torque wanted to pull him to the left, toward the side of the ship and over. But he now knew the correction. He held a little right brake while footing in full right rudder, which caught onrushing air, countering the pull, and kept the plane straight.

As he gathered speed, the wind began to lift the Wildcat, and suddenly it was airborne.

He was off.

Clearing the bow, climbing, a vast sun-kissed ocean boiling beneath him, he made a quick right turn in order to move his slip stream from the path of the next Wildcat that would launch behind him in maybe twenty seconds.

"You want to take off in undisturbed air. That's important."

Now the real test began. He swung back left, making a full 180-degree horseshoe turn until he'd leveled out and was traveling downwind, parallel to the ship but in the opposite direction. He was perhaps a thousand feet out from the carrier, about 150 feet up, which wasn't very high, racing swiftly toward, but out from, its stern, which was approximately 60 feet above the waterline.

When he reached a position roughly abeam—or directly across from—the ship's middeck stack, which obviously occurred very quickly since both were traveling in opposite directions at fairly high speeds, he made his first landing calculation—a split-second reckoning. In order to make sure he was at the precise altitude he needed to correctly accomplish his approach—approximately 150 feet—he visually checked the top of the carrier's stack to his left and made sure its top was aligned with the horizon.

It was. That's all he needed.

He banked, beginning his descent.

Unlike modern jets that sometimes use nearly a mile of rear approach to the back of the boat, the propeller-driven Wildcat hardly used any rear straightaway at all. In that millisecond that he made the visual altitude alignment with the stack, he began a 180-degree descending left turn—another horseshoe really—back to the carrier. If done right, the sweeping turn, gradually dropping him from his 150-foot altitude, was supposed to deposit his fighter wings-level just as it reached the carrier's 60-foot-high rear deck.

That would be a perfect landing. Somewhere in the neighborhood of a 90-foot descent.

But the key words were "if done right."

If done wrong, several things could happen, none of them good:

The plane could come in too low and crash into the carrier's stern, the "spud locker," as the aviators called it.

It could get too slow, stall, and fall into the water. Just before touchdown, maintaining exact speed—approximately 85 knots—was a hairfine balance between what would keep the plane flying and what would let it drop. "You had to watch the speed very carefully."

In normal operations, when the ship would have the barrier up—steel cables erected like a net to stop a badly landed plane from crashing into others parked forward—a fighter hitting the barrier could be dangerously upended. "It can flip you over on your back, and there's always the potential of fire."

If done right, the turn would result in the Wildcat snagging one of several arresting cables stretched tight across the rear deck at the moment of touchdown. A small "tailhook" in the back of the fighter did the snagging.

The reason the Wildcat used the turn to land rather than the straight-on approach was that the fighter's forward fuselage was so big that it was difficult to see over it to the landing signal officer (LSO), the expert on the stern who would direct him in the final stages of the landing. As it was, beginning his turn, he was already looking to his left out of the open, windblown cockpit to locate the LSO's distant yellow paddles as the ship moved rapidly forward on the sea beneath him.

"You're doing a lot of things simultaneously now," he recalled. His hands were constantly moving the throttle and stick, his feet working the rudder. "You're trying to fly as perfectly as you can . . . You're looking at airspeed, altitude, trying to hold your rate of turn. That's not a dial. That's in your head . . . Wheels and flaps are down." He was slowing all the way. "Hook's down. Got to keep the nose up. Slower speed means higher angle of attack."

Raise the nose too high and he'd stall and fall.

At that altitude, he'd be in the drink for sure.

There would be no time or distance to recover.

About halfway into the turn—or "groove," as they called it—he suddenly got a pang of trepidation. "You've got that hollow spot in your stomach. You wonder, how did I ever choose this?" He kept looking for the LSO. "You realize you're really going to have to do this now. You're not playing with kiddy toys anymore. This is the real thing."

The deck looked outrageously small—"impossible," is the word he used. "You're continuing your turn. You're holding that airspeed, which is critical." Steady. Steady. "You're looking for the LSO and pick him up probably about two-thirds of the way through the turn. He'll be giving you signals. If you're in good shape, his arms, the paddles, will be straight out. If you're high, they'll be high. Low, they'll be low. If he gives you like you're rowing the boat, that means you're slow. He'll drop one paddle toward his side if you're fast."

Voris was fast. "I think everybody was. The ship looks like it's speeding away. You're chasing it."

As he concentrated on the final leg, everything became more critical. "Airspeed should go down to about eighty-five knots. Hold it steady. Nose up. Slowing down. If you turn too sharp, you'll end up at an angle to the deck instead of pointing right up it. Take it too wide and you'll be too far behind the ship. Invariably, you'll get a wave-off"—a vigorous crossing of the paddles over the LSO's head.

He didn't want that. Too many wave-offs and he'd be judged unsafe.

End of career.

He slowed almost imperceptibly, only two or three knots, but it made a difference. The deck grew larger. His eyes shot from it to his instruments to the paddles. The LSO was the key. That's where he concentrated. The yellow paddles determined his fate.

At the millisecond he came out of the turn, his wings went level and he saw the LSO sweep a paddle across his throat. It was the "cut," the signal he hoped for. His left hand slammed the throttle back to idle. "Your rear end clenches and you hope it all works." He felt the plane drop and the hook catch a wire.

He was down. He'd done it.

"It was a thrill."

But he didn't have time to dwell. "Everything's frantic. You have the deck hands waving at you. The plane rolls back. The hook disengages the wire." They motioned him to power up again, which he did. Then he taxied back up the deck to the start. He had five more to go. Others were coming in behind him. He launched again. "It became a blur." Each time he did a little better, got a little more confident. "There's a sigh of, I don't know, it's not exuberance. It's relief that you're able to do it."

He now had an important combat skill.

He was going to need it.

CHAPTER 7

Since the attack on Pearl Harbor in early December, the entire world had been engulfed in struggle. It was now truly World War II. While the United States was putting most of its resources and effort into the fight against the Nazis in Europe, the country was waging a lower-priority defensive effort, along with Allied remnants, against the Japanese advances in the Pacific. The battles of Coral Sea, May 4–8, 1942, and Midway, June 3–6, 1942, had slowed the Japanese advance toward Australia and kept them from threatening the US mainland proper. But everywhere else in the Pacific, Japanese forces were bent on conquest. Tokyo already ruled the Philippines, other islands throughout the south and central Pacific, and much of the Asian mainland, especially its coastal areas, including Korea, much of China and points south. Australia, however, a huge prize, was being threatened again, and the US Navy, battered and waiting for reinforcements in the form of new ships and planes, especially aircraft carriers with newly trained pilots, was, along with a smaller force of US Marines and General Douglas MacArthur's depleted army, practically the only barrier to Tokyo's aspirations.

The Pacific was a monster battleground shaping for a showdown.

This was the war situation as Voris joined his first fleet squadron, VF-10, newly formed by Lieutenant Commander James H. "Jimmy" Flatley Jr., a short, charismatic flying leader who, piloting a Wildcat, had shot down two Japanese planes at Coral Sea and won the Silver Star. A native of Green Bay, Wisconsin, Flatley was one of a handful of naval aviators—Butch O'Hare, Jimmy Thach, and Wade McClusky among them—whose name would become synonymous with the titanic, desperate early struggle the US Navy waged in the Pacific. He would also become one of Voris's mentors and teachers, instrumental in shaping young Voris into the kind of aviator who could later successfully meet the challenge of creating the Blue Angels. It wasn't so much what Flatley individually taught Voris, but more Flatley's example—unruffled in action, steadfast, determined—that Voris would emulate. Being Voris's first skipper was influence enough. Flatley, although probably a foot shorter than Butch, was "like a God" to the newly winged "nugget" pilots who arrived at San Diego's North Island to make up the bulk of "Fighting 10." All of them felt privileged to have him as their skipper. Flatley, a Naval Academy graduate, was literally just back from the front and exuded coolness and confidence and stressed knowledge. He'd actually been out there flying and fighting, which was certainly more than they had been doing. He knew of what he spoke. He quickly gave the new squadron a nickname. "The Grim Reapers." And an insignia patch: a winged and savage-faced skeleton wielding a scythe. The motto he penned was "Mow 'em down." Traveling home from the front, he'd written a treatise titled, "The Navy Fighter," about how to defeat the Japanese in the air. It was intended especially for new pilots like Voris.

Basically, the instruction said that the Wildcat should avoid turning with a Zero, or "Zeke" as the Japanese fighter was code-named by the Allies. It was too slow and not as maneuverable as the Zero. But it did have certain advantages. It could dive faster, had more powerful and destructive guns, and its rugged armor and construction could take hits from the Zero's less potent 20-mm cannon and 7.7-mm machine guns and survive. Flatley had been impressed in his own engagements by how easily the Zero had burst into flames or literally disintegrated when hit by the Wildcat's .50-caliber bullets. The wing-mounted machine guns fired tracer, incendiary, and armor-piercing rounds. The way to beat the Zeke, therefore, he coached, was to it fight only on Wildcat terms: Always try and have altitude so you can dive to the attack rather than climb. Slash at the Zero. Don't dogfight. Keep speed. Make sure all shots counted, which meant husbanding ammunition and learning good gunnery. When in trouble, dive. The Zero couldn't follow the Wildcat's power dive. It was so relatively flimsy, it's wings might come off. Even if it kept its wings, the heavier Wildcat could dive faster and thus escape.

Flatley emphasized loyalty and teamwork. "Four eyes are better than two" was a favorite Flatley saying. It referred to the fact that two of them—or three or four, for that matter—could better scan hostile airspace than just one. He wanted his pilots to help and depend on one another. In this regard, by the time the squadron would leave Hawaii for its war cruise in mid-October, Flatley would employ a new defensive tactic labeled the "Thach weave," named after his contemporary and friend, Lieutenant Commander John S. "Jimmy" Thach. Voris remembers attending a briefing on the weave at North Island in late July given by Thach, who, along with his squadron, VF-3, was just back from the Battle of Midway, in which Japan had lost four carriers.

The weave maneuver was a major innovation in fighter tactics. Before it, fighter formations had tended to be large and rigid. The basic formation had been three fighters close together in a V, the two wingmen tight on the leader. The tightness hindered maneuvering because the close elements were in danger of hitting each other. In the weave, the "section," or two-plane grouping, replaced the three. And the two, a leader and wingman, gave each other more space, with the wingman dropped farther behind and out and stepped down. A "division," two sections flying abreast, was the usual formation deploying the weave, although any number of planes could do so. Having maneuvering space between elements was paramount.

The weave itself was simple. Most pilots were shot down when an enemy got on their tail. The victim usually never saw his attacker. To guard against that, the spaced section elements and divisions would position themselves in ways to be able to see the rear of friendlies abreast or across from them. If a pilot saw an enemy on the other's tail, he would instantly turn toward the bandit and begin a head-on pass. Seeing that, the airplane under attack would turn toward his oncoming American defender. That was the "weave": two American fighters curling in and flying at each other, "stitching" their way above or below. As they passed, the oncoming defender would have a shot at the attacker, or could in some other way open up on the trailing enemy. If nothing else, the tactic would brush off the attacker as in a basketball pick play. Sometimes the fighters would weave even if there were no enemies in sight. Turning their fighter planes one way and then the other was a way to keep eyes constantly scanning.

In fighter combat, the pilot who saw his enemy first had a huge advantage.

Moving around also made a plane unpredictable, another advantage.

Offensively, however, the primary advantage was attacking from altitude. Diving. Slashing.

These were just some of the things Voris would learn under Flatley's tutelage, lessons that would build his "bag of tricks," later to be used in starting the Blues.

Throughout June and July, the Reapers took shape under Flatley. They shot at target sleeves, Flatley was seldom satisfied with anything but 100 percent hits. Dyes on the bullets distinguished shooters. Like hunters shooting at fast-flying birds, they had to mentally calculate where the enemy plane would be in the time it took the bullets to reach their traveling targets and aim for that spot. The bullets were sighted to converge at a point perhaps a thousand feet in front of the plane so that impact point had to be taken into account as well.

He preached "smart aggression" and precision timing. Events in the air happened so fast that if timing and movements weren't precise the situation could be completely changed. A position that was safe and dominant in one instant could become dangerous and defensive in the next.

They practiced combat maneuvers—dives, turns, loops, different types of attacks, head-on, diving, lateral—dizzying, body-racking, sometimes blackout-inducing maneuvers they would need to use in order to prevail in the coming battles, moves that later would become staples of Blue Angels shows.

On their own, they hid in the clouds and "jumped" other fighters training in the area to simulate the combat they surely were going to see. There were no restrictions on training then as there are today. "You knew you were going to deploy, you just didn't know when or where. You were building experience that you knew you were going to use."

At the time one of Voris's "greatest enjoyments" was going up by himself and "doing acrobatics for a solid hour or hour and a half. I was always asking, 'Is there a plane available? Is there a plane available?' I'd go up and do loops, slow loops, slow rolls, Immelmanns [a quick way to reverse direction, named for a World War I German fighter pilot]. You pull up as if you are going into a loop. But instead of going around, you roll the plane right side up and heading in the opposite direction. To me it was just kind of stretching the envelope, going a little further, doing a little bit more with the plane. I enjoyed it. That was my core. I was getting comfortable in the airplane."

He'd set tasks. "I'd try to make a perfectly round loop. Set a base at say a thousand feet. Go up and come back around at precisely where I started. Precision. That's what I was trying to achieve. I wanted to do the maneuver as precisely as I could. I wasn't thinking of the Blue Angels then. But that was exactly the kind of thing we would do later [in the Blues]."

Nothing was more "boring" to him than flying straight and level and "punching a hole in the sky. I used to enjoy the snap roll and trying to control it. It's really an uncontrolled maneuver"—a quick way to turn an airplane on its own axis. Think of a pencil with wings. Roll the pencil between two fingers. The wings move but the pencil stays pointed in the same direction. Airplanes do the same. Flying the Wildcat straight and level, "if you want to snap-roll left, you jam full left rudder [with the foot], pull the stick back viciously to the stop and the airplane stalls." That's the uncontrolled part. The Wildcat wouldn't stop going forward, but aerodynamically it wasn't flying anymore. Its surfaces weren't reacting to the air, technically a dangerous situation. The rudder, however, grabs the air, and that pressure rolls the plane like the fingers do a pencil. "Takes less than a second. It's a last-ditch maneuver if you've got somebody on your tail and want to spoil his aim. You do slow down a bit, so he may run into you and get you that way. We didn't do it with each other."

From day one, Flatley emphasized a take-no-prisoners philosophy. Make no mistake, he told his men, the job was killing, and any enemy who escaped could and probably would return to try and kill *them*. "But it wasn't like you were fighting a person. You were fighting a machine. Maybe it was like a video game today. You have to be able to know how to play it, how to fly your machine. You've got to assume everybody is going to be as good as you or better. You underevaluate the guy you're fighting and you're in trouble to start with. The only way you are going to be able to kill him is to fly your machine better than he flies his, get yourself into a firing position and so forth. You don't think of your enemy as a little yellow shit from across the ocean. That never enters your mind."

It was an attitude that could only lead to the sharpening of his aerial skills.

By late July the squadron was beginning to resemble an aggressive fighting unit. Voris was made navigation officer, which meant he had charge of the squadron's flying charts and was responsible for keeping others informed of key coordinates, routes, and flight information. Squadron mates describe him at that time as a "friendly, even-tempered" junior officer with a "teasing" sense of humor. Stanley "Swede" Vejtasa, who had shot down three Zeros at Coral Sea and was one of the squadron's veteran leaders, recalled in a phone interview how the big Californian once playfully put a stool under the wing of Flatley's just-landed Wildcat, ostensibly to aid the diminutive skipper's "considerable jump" to deck. Voris was "green" but "gung ho," said Vejtasa, a lieutenant at the time. "He was always on the job, ready to fly anytime, and he really worked at maneuvering. . . . He was a strong-armed pilot, a big guy who could bend that airplane around pretty good. . . . In the beginning he had a tendency to be very aggressive [in the air]. Too aggressive." Practicing the head-on shot, "he'd hold on too long, the idea being that against the Zero, if you kept coming at him, he'd get you with those twenty-millimeters. They [the guns] were pretty good [at close range]. He'd hold on and try to get a steady shot . . . Well, you don't hold that long. With the fifty-caliber, you give 'em a burst and break . . . But he practiced a lot . . . and got pretty good."

On August 1, Fighting 10 left San Diego for San Francisco and ultimately Pearl Harbor. There, two and a half months later, they would embark on the USS *Enterprise* and sail to war. As they trained, the war in the Pacific had worsened. The Japanese had moved into the East Indies and New Guinea in preparation for an invasion of islands buffering Australia. To counter, the US had begun bombing the Japanese-occupied island of Guadalcanal in the Southern Solomons in hopes of invading and capturing it as a base with which to fight back. The Fighting 10 pilots, viewing the devastation at Pearl, knew they'd soon be thrown into the breech.

Seeing what the Japanese had done to the US ships "was pretty emotional," says Voris. "The battleships on their sides, rolled over, destroyed. What a mess . . . The *Arizona*, all those crew members entrapped inside . . . The bodies were still there, of course, inside the ships. [Workers] were cutting [the ships] up, those that still could be righted. I guess my thoughts were that we didn't have torpedoes like the Japanese. If we'd been doing the bombing, we couldn't have sunk all those ships." American torpedo development before Pearl Harbor was "traitorous. Awful. We had almost entire squadrons wiped out [at Midway] and few torpedos if any, exploded on ships . . . They didn't run at the depth they were set. They went under instead of hitting the hull . . . People should have been court-martialed, but they weren't." Until Pearl Harbor, "we were a Sunday afternoon navy . . . The Japs knew that and were ready." He wasn't angry. "That's something you don't want to do. You don't operate at your best when you're all screwed up being mad . . . I guess I was more like, let's get even. Let's get ready, get out there and fight 'em."

But because *Enterprise,* or *"Big E,"* as it would come to be called, had been damaged by Japanese dive-bombers in a battle near the eastern Solomons in late August, the squadron had to continue training in Hawaii until it was repaired. During that time, Voris was promoted from ensign to lieutenant (junior grade). His log shows close to 450 hours flight time, which wasn't bad for a junior officer but still in crawl mode when compared with the veteran Japanese pilots whom he would face. The squadron spent some initial training time at what became Barbers Point near Honolulu, but the airspace around Oahu was too traveled to allow the kind of extensive combat preparation the Reapers needed, so they had moved to Maui, the archipelago's second largest island, and more spartan facilities. Puunene or NAS Maui, as the field was named after the Pearl Harbor attack, was little more than two runways, two large aviation gas tanks, revetments for planes, and some wooden buildings housing office space, bunk beds, and a combination diner-bar.

Commanding VF-3, a Wildcat fighter squadron based at Puunene, was Butch O'Hare, the same air hero Voris had heard about, back from a grueling publicity tour of the States because of his Medal of Honor. He, too, was a victim of the lack of carriers and was having to wait to get back in the war, which he desperately wanted to do. Flatley had been one of O'Hare's training officers when the young Chicagoan had been a student at Pensacola, and the two renewed old ties. The Reapers and VF-3 lived and trained together for a month, and O'Hare and Voris became friends. Unpretentious and obviously daring, O'Hare would have a positive influence on Voris, who would come to admire him greatly. "He was about five years older than me. But he talked young. We just seemed to hit it off. He was a real nice down-to-earth guy who wore his hero status well." When the field's makeshift bar ran out of liquor, it was Voris whom O'Hare asked to accompany him back to Ford Island to get more. Later, O'Hare would pick Voris for an important and dangerous secret mission.

By mid-October, the squadron had acquired several new pilots, including Edward L. "Whitey" Feightner, a future Blue who would talk Voris through his midair collision at Corpus Christi, and William R. "Killer" Kane, a former U.S. Naval Academy football player who would gain notoriety as a later Reaper skipper and air group commander or CAG. Kane was made executive officer, or XO, second in command. The new acquisitions increased the Reaper roster to approximately thirty-six pilots. The squadron was given O'Hare's VF-3 Wildcats, a small number since VF-3 had already been depleted, and deemed ready to go.

In fact, the Reapers were probably only just beginning to get ready. Today, navy fighter squadrons usually take a year to a year and a half to "work up" to fighting shape; that is to achieve a well-honed edge of preparation, skill, attitude, and teamwork needed for successful carrier battle operations. But this was late 1942. By October, the Japanese had troops on the Aleutian Islands, the bridge to Alaska and North America. From one end of the Pacific to the other, they were massing and threatening.

The Pacific was on fire.

CHAPTER 8

*E*nterprise, onto which the Reapers flew, was one of three new Yorktown-class American flattops built in the late 1930s. The 800-foot-long, nearly 20,000-ton carrier seemed charmed. Had a storm not delayed its scheduled arrival at Pearl Harbor just before the December 7 sneak attack nearly a year earlier, it surely would have been a prime target and probably been sunk by the Japanese. As it was, it had eluded that massacre to later join *Hornet* and *Yorktown* in the surprising June victory at Midway, which unfortunately saw *Yorktown* sunk at the battle's conclusion. Eventually, *"Big E"* would become the most decorated American ship of World War II. But when Voris and the Reapers joined the ship's Air Group 10, which also had torpedo and dive-bomber squadrons, the carrier had just completed rush repairs of major damage received in the Battle of the Eastern Solomons, which had ended in a slight American victory barely a month and half earlier.

The Solomons, a mysterious, remote, largely uninhabited group of ancient volcanic and coral islands halfway across the world from the American mainland were now the focus of the Pacific War. US Marines had landed on Guadalcanal and seized a coastal Japanese airfield, not yet completed, which they quickly finished and named Henderson Field, in honor of a leatherneck SBD dive-bomber pilot killed at Midway. Guadalcanal, a jungled, malaria-and-insect infested island of rugged mountains and ridges, was a rotten place to serve and likely place to die. Large numbers of unsubdued Japanese troops remained right outside Henderson Field's perimeter and throughout the island's coconut grove–potched jungles, not to mention the entire Solomon chain that the Japanese occupied. Angry and concerned over the American landing and capture of the airfield, the Japanese had decided to retake the island as a way to reestablish their dominance. If they could kill all the marines, the issue would be settled. If they couldn't, Henderson Field could become a major thorn in their side. It controlled the southwestern approaches to Australia, which were being used by the Americans to supply their army operations there and in New Guinea, and gave the US a base from which to attack Rabaul, the largest enemy stronghold in the Solomons. From Guadalcanal the Allies would also threaten Truk, further north in the Carolines, which held the major Japanese naval and air base in the South Pacific.

Guadalcanal was key to both sides. But the marines, basically abandoned after their initial victory, had little help or support with which to conduct operations. Allied priority was being given to the war in Europe. They ate Spam and coconut milk, fought mosquitoes, dysentery, mud, and dust, depending on the weather, as well as the Japanese. While the marines were more than giving a good account of themselves under Major General Alexander "Archie" Vandegrift, Japanese dominance of the air and sea around the island had made the few supplies getting through to them an exercise in daring. At night, American surface ships would dash in and out to unload food, gas, and ammunition hoping they wouldn't be attacked, which they often were. Submarines were usually luckier but couldn't carry as much. The marines were constantly being shelled. The sea just east of Guadalcanal would become known as Iron Bottom Sound so many ships would be sunk there.

Once Henderson had been secured, marine Wildcats and bombers had arrived, along with some army planes. But they were greatly outnumbered and the lack of airplane parts, gas, and ordnance, not to mention near constant bombardment of the island, hindered their operations. Guadalcanal and its outnumbered soldiers and air force was code-named "Cactus," which certainly alluded to the prickly conditions. Still, the pilots and their ground counterparts fought on; even began to win small and increasingly sizable land and air battles. If the marines were defeated, not only would those who survived the fighting be killed, but the Japanese, steadily landing more troops on the island and bombing the Cactus stronghold, would own the Pacific Ocean west of Hawaii and would have a perfect place from which to attack Australia, the last Allied stronghold in that part of the world.

The entire Pacific War depended on what happened at Guadalcanal.

That was the situation into which *Enterprise* and its airmen and crew were steaming when they left Pearl Harbor October 16. Guadalcanal had to be defended. *Enterprise,* with only one battleship and some cruisers and destroyers, was to join *Hornet,* the only other US carrier in the South Pacific at the time, and find and destroy the Japanese task force on its way to take back the island. They didn't know how big a force the Japanese would have or where it was, other than somewhere around Guadalcanal. Few of the aviators were aware of how precarious the situation was, but all anticipated a major engagement. "Maybe I just didn't know enough to be scared," said Butch. "I think we were all anxious to get out there. We hadn't started the war. But now we were in it. It was a great national purpose. I would have considered it a shame, were I able, if I had not participated."

★

Entering the war zone, the force, not yet joined with *Hornet,* began an ominous, high-stakes game of cat and mouse. The Japanese knew they'd be coming, and Admiral Isoroku Yamamoto, the Japanese fleet commander in chief and architect of the Pearl Harbor strike, had mustered a much larger armada to meet them—four carriers, several big battleships, destroyers, and attendant support vessels. Rear Admiral Thomas C. Kinkaid, commander of the American force, with headquarters on *Enterprise,* didn't know he was outnumbered. But it wouldn't have mattered. He was spoiling for a showdown. "We didn't know where [the Japanese] were or how many ships they had," said Voris. "We'd lose track of them all the time. The only sightings we would get were if one of our submarines happened to see them or maybe an army air corps Liberator [from Australia] found them." Even then, since such armadas often consisted of separated front, middle, and rear segments stretching beyond the visible horizon, accurate counts based on sightings were seldom available.

Enterprise sent out fighters and bombers to search carefully plotted out sectors projected from the ship. Voris was among the searchers. "You'd fly maybe one hundred, two hundred miles out, use your eyeballs. We didn't have anything else." The carrier was equipped with radar but it was limited in range and meant mainly to detect incoming airplanes.

With radar in its infancy, the equipment often malfunctioned and was frequently vague in what it revealed.

Neither side, for several days, found the other. On October 24, *Enterprise* rendezvoused with *Hornet,* which had launched the stunning Doolittle raid on Tokyo in April, and its support ships, including one battleship and three cruisers. The two groups combined to become Task Force 61, which, with only two carriers, was still only half what the enemy had. But it was the sum total of American naval sea power in the Pacific at the time. The force was south and west of Guadalcanal, approaching the Santa Cruz Islands. Rear Admiral William F. "Bull" Halsey, newly installed as theater commander, a move navy leaders made to put more fight into the South Pacific fleet, ordered the two carriers to swing north and go up above the Santa Cruz Islands, which themselves were approximately 500 miles southwest of Guadalcanal. The Japanese Combined Fleet, circling and hiding, was rightly believed to be in that area.

On the 25th, a PBY Catalina search plane located the advance section of the Japanese ships. They were 150 miles northeast of Guadalcanal and closing fast. The spotted position was in line with what Halsey expected. He wired Kinkaid: "Attack. Repeat. Attack." The distance between the two forces was an extremely long flight for the American warplanes, about 375 miles, which was a 750-mile round trip. Pilots knew they might run out of gas even with extra wing and belly tanks and, because they were leaving after noon, might have to navigate home in darkness, which they didn't like because of the landing problems that presented. Few, if any, had had night-landing training. But in successive waves, Dauntless dive-bombers and Avenger torpedo planes, escorted by eight Reaper-flown Wildcats, launched. Voris wasn't one of them. His ordered turn, along with Flatley's wouldn't come until the next morning. The Japanese, however, had seen the PBY and vacated the area. The *Enterprise* strikers couldn't find them after a lengthy search, and most were lucky to make it back to the carriers, basically on fumes, at night. There were a number of crashes. Several just ran out of gas and had to ditch in the sea.

It was a frustrating prelude.

That night, Commander John Crommelin, *Enterprise*'s Alabama-born air officer, gathered the air group's pilots in the ship's wardroom where the officers ate. "I remember him getting up and saying it appears we could be engaging the enemy force in the morning," said Voris. "It was going to be a major action." Edward P. Stafford, in *The Big E: The Story of the USS Enterprise,* adds that Crommelin, a crack flight instructor and a later admiral, told the aviators they were largely "all that stood between the Japanese and Guadalcanal." They'd trained hard and knew their business. Now the time had come for them to perform. No excuses. He wanted them to get what rest they could before dawn, wake up, and "knock those sons-of-bitches off the face of the earth."

Voris: "I don't remember a lot of emotions, just the realization that now I can see how good I am . . . You're anxious because you're going into something you've never done before . . . It's real . . . You could call it scared. But you're calm, too. It's kinda like pregame jitters until the first hit. I remember it was hot. That was the thing. You'd lie there in your bunk just bathed in sweat. The biggest thing was trying to divert some cold air into your room [from the carrier's limited air-conditioning system] so you'd be cool. Eventually I got to sleep. I slept well."

Up before dawn, Voris was part of the first combat air patrol, or CAP, that was launched. CAP fighters were sent up to orbit nearby as a defense against oncoming enemy planes. It would be the first line of defense, which would include ship's radar and guns. Voris remembers the sun wasn't up, but the sky was beginning to lighten. Details of the ensuing battle are conflicting, but it began exactly ten days after *Enterprise* had left Pearl Harbor. It has been called the most violent carrier-vs.-carrier battle of World War II. The PBYs had again found the elusive Japanese fleet, and this time it was much closer than the day before, only two hundred miles away, which was fully within range of the aircraft of both sides. Task force leaders knew a Japanese aerial attack was imminent. The enemy had searchers out, too. The first order of business was to get the CAP launched and over the force so enemy planes could be repelled. The worst possible situation for a carrier in battle was to be attacked with its fuel-filled, ammunition-laden planes on the deck. Each was a potential bomb. Voris was wingman to Stan Ruehlow, a Midway veteran, and part of a division of four Wildcats which, along with another Reaper division—and Wildcats from *Hornet*—would climb to 10,000 feet, disperse to various areas, and begin patrolling.

Once the CAP was up—and as soon as the carrier could do it—the strike planes were launched. The package consisted of thirteen dive-bombers and torpedo planes protected by eight Wildcats in two divisions under Flatley. *Hornet's* strike package had left earlier. The idea was to have multiple waves of attackers, one after the other, so the second wave could exploit whatever havoc the first planes caused.

Unknown to Task Force 61, but not surprisingly, as they knew they were being hunted, too, the enemy had detected the American carriers and had launched its own morning strike packages earlier. In a strange and perhaps unique few moments in aerial warfare, the two advance strike groups of the opposing fleets, flying at different altitudes and in opposite directions, actually sighted and passed each other on the way to their targets. The respective strike leaders knew their mission was to sink the other's ships, not dogfight. So the opposing pilots and rear gunners in the bombers only eyed each other "warily," writes Eric Hammel in *Carrier Strike*. "Many individual gunners in both forces trained out their machine guns, but no one opened fire, and none of the fighters broke formation to molest the enemy."

But such restraint was too much for the Japanese escort fighters when they encountered the next group of Americans in the broken stream. The initial group they'd passed had been from *Hornet,* the first Americans to launch. The next group, about ten miles behind and still climbing for altitude, was *Enterprise*'s package, barely ten minutes from launch and being escorted by Flatley, who had his fighters in two separate divisions above and flanking the bombers. Because they had wished to maintain radio silence until they reached altitude, according to John Lundstrom in *The First Team and the Guadalcanal Campaign,* the package of twenty-one *Enterprise* planes had not yet turned on their radios and so missed the warning that the first group sent back about the Japanese strike force they were passing.

Dusty Rhodes, who would become a Blue Angel skipper after Voris, who would recruit him in 1946, and one of the four Reapers on the left side of the bombers, remembered: "We were at about 10,000 feet and I saw these Zeros diving into the rear of the TBFs." There were nine of them, cleverly curling out of the blinding, morning sun. "Two of them [*Enterprise* dive-bombers] were hit right off the bat and started for the ocean. Our division [the four left-side Wildcats] immediately turned into the Zeros . . . They had a lot of speed and altitude advantage. They were looping around us."

Division leader John Leppla, with only one gun working, and his wingman, Al Mead, valiantly trying to compensate for Leppla's lack of firepower, were swarmed. Despite the fact that they flamed several of the

Zeros, Leppla was believed to have been killed early in a sandwich attack by the ganging Zeros. Mead's plane was shot up so badly he eventually had to ride it into an ocean landing. Rhodes and his leader, Willis Redding, both had wing tank problems. Redding couldn't get fuel into his engine after jettisoning his tank. The engine quit in the middle of the fight and had to be restarted, which took all his concentration. Rhodes's tank just wouldn't drop, period. The drag made his Wildcat "slow and sluggish." With the violent shooting and maneuvering, the tank caught fire. The Zeros, taking advantage of their adversary's technical problems, swarmed them also, riddling the malfunctioning Wildcats with bullets, shattering cockpits and sending Redding into an escape dive and back to the fleet hugging the water. Rhodes, his engine so mauled it quit in flight and his goggles literally shot off his forehead (miraculously, without injuring him), eventually had to make a last-second, do-or-die parachute jump into the sea.

By the time Flatley and his division, which included Voris's Elimination Training friend, Russ Reiserer, as his wingman, saw what was happening, the attacks on the left-side division had already begun. The Reaper leader immediately led his right-side Wildcats in an arcing attack back on the Zeros and was able to shoot down one of them. But the fight was moving rearward, and he made the battlefield decision that the bombing mission was the priority. He led his fighters back to protect what was left of the shot-up dive and torpedo bombers. "Leaving [Leppla's division] in such peril was one of the hardest things Flatley ever had to do," writes Lundstrom. When the fight was over, five Americans had died and four others were treading water, including Rhodes. Mead and Rhodes were picked up separately by the Japanese after several days of drifting in shark-infested waters. They spent the rest of the war in prison camps enduring starvation and torture.

Back at Task Force 61, Voris, in the first CAP, was enduring what turned out to be an uneventful patrol. "You're on the brink of anxiety waiting to get word they [the enemy bombers] are coming." But the word never came. After several hours, he and the rest of Reaper 3, as his division was call-signed, were running out of gas. They landed. Because VF-10 didn't have enough operational Wildcats for all its pilots, Swede Vejtasa, leading one of the next CAPs to go aloft, took the Reaper 3 planes for his division, Reaper 7, and launched after they were refueled. Meanwhile, Voris went to the ready room directly below the flight deck for what he remembers as baloney and "stale bread" sandwiches, "the day's battle ration," to wait for more planes to come in so he could go back up. The ready room was his "battle station," the place he was required to be during the fight until the next returning CAP planes were refueled and rearmed. "We were to be launched next."

But it was not to be—horribly so. For Voris it was a molding experience.

Not long after he landed, the vanguard of the Japanese strike force entered Task Force 61's defensive perimeter and began an attack on *Hornet*, the first carrier they saw, some twelve miles away. The CAP, reinforced every hour and now numbering over thirty *Enterprise* and *Hornet* fighters, should have met the attackers. But there were problems with fighter direction. Because of vague radar returns and bad positioning by the fighter director, who, himself, had little information, few Wildcats were at the right altitudes or sky positions to intercept the enemy when they arrived. The Japanese bombers pummeled *Hornet* before the CAP, which included Butch's roommate on the cruise, Maurice "Wick" Wickendoll, who would become one of the original Blue Angels with him, Vejtasa, Feightner, and Kane, among others, finally got in position and engaged the bombers. Twenty-five Japanese planes were shot down, mostly by the fleet's antiaircraft gunners, in exchange for a few CAP planes. But the damage was done. *Hornet* was left ablaze, flooded with firefighting water, and adrift without power or propulsion.

In effect, it was dead in the water, out of the fight.

Seeing the distant attack, Admiral Kinkaid, in order to protect the lone remaining operational carrier at that time, ordered the *Enterprise* drivers to start evasive maneuvering at high speed which could be felt in jolts and swerves throughout the ship, said Voris. A hovering rain squall that the carrier ducked into provided protection from aerial detection for a short while and allowed the flattop to recover a good number of returning search planes and CAP fighters, some from *Hornet,* that were nearly out of fuel. But by ten a.m., the *Big E* was back out in the open. Then the second wave of Japanese strikers hit. Again there was confusion in vectoring CAP to the attackers. A nearby destroyer, the USS *Porter,* was so jittery that it fired on two Reaper Wildcat pilots who got close trying to warn the destroyer of a runaway torpedo, which soon hit the ship in its middle and sank it.

Then, in a period of about three minutes, a little after ten a.m., as the carrier wove violently in the water in an attempt to spoil the aim of dive-bombers attacking it, three 250-kilogram bombs rocked *Enterprise,* one of them damaging it severely. The most damaging bomb penetrated the teakwood and steel flight deck near the forward elevator and split in two. One part of the bomb detonated in the hangar deck right below the flight deck where airplanes were being refueled, igniting an inferno, and the other part continued on through to the next deck, where it exploded in the midst of waiting repair crews, killing or severely injuring some forty sailors, officers, and corpsmen and wiping out a largely vacant officers' quarters.

Voris: "We were waiting [in the ready room] to go back out again. The next thing we know, they are announcing [over the ship's PA system], 'Enemy aircraft approaching' then 'Dive-bombers overhead.' I remember it like yesterday. . . . We heard the *brub, brub, brub* of the antiaircraft guns. Then a huge wham!" The bombs "took the ship and shook it like a whip." He felt the enormous carrier literally lifted out of the water. "The bow came up and there was a hell of a *varoomph!*" He and the others in the ready room "couldn't do a thing. We're trapped. The ship's locked down for battle . . . It's a helpless feeling . . . The bomb wrecked the [flight deck] elevator [used to raise and lower airplanes to the hangar deck], killed everybody servicing our planes . . . This is no Sunday stroll . . . The way they were beating us up I thought we were going to lose the ship. You just hope the next bomb doesn't come into the ready room."

When the bombing stopped, he emerged into a scene of destruction and carnage. "There were fires on the ship, firefighting parties going back and forth." He went to the wardroom where a makeshift hospital had been set up. The passageways near it were lined with burned and severely injured men, many of them hideously disfigured, with arms and legs missing. There was no where else to put them. "That was where I ran into Marshall Field," one of the Chicago-based department store heirs, a young ensign who had been battery officer on a bomb-damaged antiair-craft mount. "They were carrying him in. His shirt was ripped open and he's got a gash, God, it went all the way through to the rib cage from his neck to his waist."

He helped carry some litters. The worst scene was the wardroom. Wa-ter from the firefighting was knee deep. The surgeons were having to op-erate in it. "It was awful. They were sloshing around using the dining room tables, not very sanitary, trying to stop the bleeding or whatever."

Outside, "[the wounded] were just laid out in the passageway like logs, on stretchers or sometimes with just a blanket over them, waiting their turn to have a limb cut off. That's when you begin to realize you're really in a war. It's brutal when it gets to that . . . You hated to see those young kids dying, burned, maimed, breathing their last breath."

The carnage probably would have been worse, according to other accounts, if Swede Vejtasa had not shot down five torpedo planes that were threatening the carrier—bringing his kill count for the day to seven and making him the leading naval ace. Torpedoes, which rip gaping holes at the waterline, were the most feared enemy weapons. Wickendoll, even with his guns jammed, dogged attackers until they backed off, and Feightner shot down another Zero. Even so, the horror inside the ship was pervasive. Lundstrom illustrates the scene belowdecks in the blasted hangar with an eyewitness account of an injured sailor seen "with only one arm and no legs and fingers that seemed to dig into the steel deck." The man was trying to drag himself across the charred hangar floor in order to drop out of an open area into the sea—an act of suicide he was allowed to do by corpsmen who, according to the account, told him "he would die anyway."

With only one carrier left and many planes in desperate need of a place to land—a problem that would make *Enterprise* highly vulnerable—Kinkaid decided to exit the battle. "We hauled ass, as they say," Voris recalls. "We needed to get away, open the distance between us and the Jap fleet." While the US strike groups had gone on to damage three Japanese carriers and the Americans had destroyed more enemy planes and killed more enemy pilots and crew than they'd lost, Kinkaid had little left to fight with. In order to keep *Hornet* out of Japanese hands, he ordered it torpedoed and sunk by US ships, and *Enterprise* retreated south at "flank," or full, speed. With the fleeing carrier's massive underwater propeller shafts (three-feet thick) bent by bomb explosions, their furious but out-of-line "wobble" could be felt throughout the ship. "You could see planes bouncing on the deck," Voris recalled. In an amazing recovery operation, the bomb hole in the deck was covered with a huge steel plate, and all the returning planes were landed with minimal mishap, Flatley and his escort Reapers among them. Low on gas because of the Leppla fight, they and their bombers had attacked and sunk a cruiser. At one point in the retreat, late in the day, another incoming Japanese raid was announced. "If they'd hit us with that packed deck, it probably would have been the end of us," said Voris. But the raid, whether unable to find the fleeing flattop or simply a false alarm, didn't materialize. "It was a low start. Gives you a great feeling of helplessness. All those people wounded and the ship out of action. You're not scared. You're numb."

He had lived through hell on earth.

★

The Battle of Santa Cruz, as it became known, was a classic example of the early determination, toughness, and wile shown by both sides in the Pacific. Despite losses and fearsome obstacles, American and Japanese pilots found and attacked their enemy's most important ships. In the beginning of the battle, two lone *Enterprise* scout bombers dived on Japanese carriers and damaged them without protection of escort. They were there, and there wouldn't be another chance. A wounded Japanese pilot in a disabled plane tried to crash into *Hornet* rather than save himself and flee for home. And this was long before the appearance of—or need for on the part of the enemy—Japanese suicide bombers. The Japanese aviators at Santa Cruz were the cream of the enemy's flyers, skilled and experienced from years of war in China before Pearl Harbor. Both sides used intelligence coups to gain advantage. The United States, as at Midway, was forewarned of the enemy approach by deciphering Japanese coded messages. On the other side, a Japanese English-speaker actually posed as a US fighter commander on the aircraft radios and answered an approaching SBD leader's query with "No carriers here. Let's go home." Fortunately, the bomber leader didn't like the retort, and his division went on to find the enemy carriers and bomb them.

Although the Battle of Santa Cruz was considered a US tactical defeat, the truth was that it was a strategic victory. As a result of their losses, the Japanese Combined Fleet, an awesome killing machine, was turned back from its plans of clearing the way for the retaking of Henderson Field. And the Guadalcanal marines who had simultaneously beaten back a large ground assault timed to coincide with the anticipated Japanese fleet victory, were safe to continue their air operations—at least for the time being. From Voris's standpoint, he'd had his first taste of combat in what was only the fourth carrier-vs.-carrier battle in history. It had been sobering, to say the least. "Yeah, we had a moral victory, but we got the shit kicked out of us . . . You're thankful to be alive to fight another day and sorry about the people we had lost . . . But you can't brood over it. You've got to go on. Otherwise, you become a basket case."

But having witnessed *Hornet's* sinking, he wondered, "What was next? We didn't have anything left."

CHAPTER 9

Damaged severely in the Santa Cruz fight, *Enterprise* limped back to Nouméa, New Caledonia, the Allied staging base far enough south—almost a thousand miles from Guadalcanal—to be relatively safe from enemy attack. For the first few days of the retreat, Whitey Feightner said, they didn't even have fresh drinking water, "only enough to run the ship's operations." They had to make do with what they could scrounge. En route, they conducted a service for the dead. "They had [the bodies] up on the flight deck sewed into canvas bags," said Voris. "When the service was over they slid them into the sea." Nouméa, a French possession, had a spectacular harbor. It was a Pacific Eden, a principal stop on the Allied supply route to Brisbane, Australia. Admiral Halsey had set up his headquarters there.

With the cigar-shaped island's little town, pristine beaches, and cooling, tropical mountains, the retreat was a forced rest and recuperation for the ship's personnel. Military construction workers gutted the damaged areas of the carrier and erected a tent city for the approximately three thousand sailors who had returned with the ship. The hard hats labored intensely to repair *Enterprise*. There was no guarantee that the Japanese wouldn't return to Guadalcanal with another assault force. In fact, that's what the navy expected. They had to get ready quickly. The ship's planes went to Tontouta, a small mountain-flanked airfield nearby. The air wing, including the Reapers, followed a schedule of training in order to keep the pilots' fighting edge.

The battle near Santa Cruz had convinced the Japanese that they had destroyed American naval power in the South Pacific, an assumption that was almost correct. Admiral Yamamoto went ahead with his plans for invading Guadalcanal. Two large battleships, *Hiei* and *Kirishima,* would lead the invasion. The enemy force would include destroyers, cruisers, and eleven high-speed transports. The battleships were to first soften Henderson with bombardment from their big guns. The American marines had never encountered such firepower. When the defenses were pulverized and what was left of the Cactus Air Force was destroyed, fresh troops were to be landed as reinforcements for the Japanese already on the island, and a massive ground assault was to commence. Unknown to the Japanese however, American code breakers had intercepted and deciphered the plans—not every detail, but enough to know trouble was coming, and coming fast. Should the plan succeed, Allied leaders knew, there was no way Cactus could survive. So many new enemy troops on the island would overwhelm the Henderson marines. Ready or not, *Enterprise,* the only big US carrier capable of battle in the entire Pacific, would have to fight.

Barely two weeks after they arrived, and with the ship's repairs not completed, the planes at Tontouta were ordered on November 10 back to *Enterprise.* The carrier, workers still hammering and welding throughout it, was leaving Nouméa immediately. Steaming toward Guadalcanal, Air Boss Crommelin again gathered aviators in the wardroom and told them the stakes. "He said, Look around you," Feightner remembers, "Look at each man in this room. You are the only guys in the world who can get there in time to stop the Japanese. You do it, or a lot of marines will die. Now that's motivation."

Voris remembers the briefing, too. This time it had even more meaning. "We were truly the only carrier out there." The *Enterprise* plan was to go full speed toward Guadalcanal. When the carrier got within flying distance of the island, it would start launching searchers and bombers to hunt for the Japanese force, which—because they didn't have complete intelligence about it—was expected to include carriers. Instead of returning to *Enterprise,* which still had a damaged elevator in the middle of the flight deck, the planes would land at Henderson. The carrier then could retreat. It was a way of hedging bets. Get the planes in the fight but save the one operational flattop—if they could.

In the early morning darkness of the thirteenth—which ominously happened to be a Friday—as *Enterprise* sped toward the Solomons, a force of US surface ships delivering supplies to Guadalcanal, including heavy cruisers and destroyers commanded by Rear Admiral Daniel Callaghan, happened upon the Japanese battleships and their protectors getting ready to bombard Henderson. It was in Iron Bottom Sound near Savo Island. The opposing ships were literally at point-blank ranges, some no more than a thousand yards from each other, and a furious surface battle of night-shattering volleys lit up the tropical darkness. Rain squalls and bad radar interpretation had prevented each from seeing the other until the last moment. Marines at Henderson, who had been bombarded nightly for the last few days, scrambled to find vantage points where they could see what was going on. Their fate, they knew, might be settled in the deafening roars and eye-blinding explosions. When the battle ended at daylight, Callaghan was dead, and most of his ships were at the bottom of the sound. But so was a large number of Japanese vessels. And the two big battleships were retreating without having accomplished their mission. That was a victory. *Hiei* was badly damaged and falling behind in the retreat.

More important, the lead elements of the Japanese force had been found. For the first time in the war, American flyers had an enemy battleship within their reach—and knew it. Cactus planes immediately took off and began attacking the stricken *Hiei*. *Enterprise* was approximately 280 miles from Henderson when the air pummeling began. Erroneous reports from the besieged airfield had indicated there were Japanese carriers lurking. Admiral Kinkaid, who'd had a CAP up for protection since shortly after leaving Nouméa, began launching search and bombing aircraft. Within hours, dive and torpedo bombers from *Enterprise*, encountering only light opposition from land-based Zeros, were helping the marine flyers bomb *Hiei*. The Americans pounded the big-gunned Japanese warship all through the day. Sometime after nightfall on the thirteenth, the Japanese dreadnought, "the first battleship to be sunk by Americans in the Second World War," according to Thomas Miller in *The Cactus Air Force*, went to the bottom of the sound.

The sinking of *Hiei* was a great morale booster, but it didn't stop the

Japanese. They still thought they were in the driver's seat. That night, shortly after one a.m on the fourteenth, they returned with some large battle cruisers to do what *Hiei* and sister ship *Kirishima,* damaged the night before and therefore out of the fight, couldn't. The cruisers bombarded Henderson for thirty-one minutes—a long time when screaming fourteen-inch shells are blasting huge holes and spewing white-hot, body-ripping metal. But there was nothing the planes at Henderson could do about it until light came and pilots could see to fly and bomb again. There weren't any more American surface ships available that night to challenge the enemy vessels.

Back on *Enterprise,* the fourteenth dawned for Voris with an order from Flatley. "He got us all in the ready room and said, 'Okay, here's what we're going to do.'" Half the squadron was going to Guadalcanal. Half was staying on the ship to protect it. "He named the divisions that were leaving. Mine was one." Voris was flying in Stan Ruehlow's Reaper 3. "The next thing he said is go to your room and pack an overnight bag, what we called an aviator's bag. You threw in some toothpaste, skivvies, a shaving kit. I think he indicated we'd only be there a couple of days. We launched right away."

The ten Reapers leaving *Enterprise* had two missions. First, they were to escort and protect SBD dive-bombers. Kinkaid, thinking the Japanese had carriers, was launching the bombers as a defensive measure in hopes of attacking the Japanese before they attacked him. Second, when they had finished the escort, the fighters were to go to Guadalcanal and bolster the hard-pressed Cactus Air Force, which figured to be greatly outnumbered during the coming assault. The dive-bombers would return to *Enterprise,* which would already be retreating.

The force of fighters and bombers launched at roughly 7:30 a.m. En route, through no fault of their own, Ruehlow and Voris got separated from the other escorting Reapers when the bombers, at a lower altitude, made an unexpected turn not noticed until too late by Flatley and the majority of fighters out ahead. However, Ruehlow and Voris, closest to the bombers, had followed. The bombers had veered in response to an erroneous report by coast watchers that an enemy carrier had been sighted off New Georgia near Guadalcanal. There was no carrier. Rather than try to find the bombers, Flatley decided to look separately for targets of opportunity. But the mistake took Ruehlow and Voris, with the bombers, closer to Guadalcanal than the other Reapers. And when their Wildcats, which didn't have the range of the dive-bombers, started to run out of gas, they got permission to peel away. Consequently, they were the first Reapers to reach the besieged island.

"I remember coming in because it was the first time I'd seen Guadalcanal. It was a bright, sunny day with a lot of clouds. Finally, it was there ahead of us—the ridge [Bloody Ridge, where a lot of brutal fighting had taken place], the mountains down the back of it. It was a big island." Cactus Control, the air traffic handlers at Henderson, directed them to land on Fighter One, also called "the cow pasture," a new field constructed several miles inland from the main base. They were welcomed by Japanese artillery shooters from nearby hills who lobbed a few shells at them as they taxied in. "They hit the runway, which is pretty good shooting from that distance. But we were moving targets." When he got parked, a marine plane captain jumped up on his wing. "'Where ya' from?' He seemed surprised we were there. I told him *Enterprise* and that we weren't going to be there very long. He smiled like he knew something I didn't. 'Nobody who comes here ever leaves,' he said"—at least not with their planes.

The marine showed him to a tent bunk where he'd sleep. It belonged to a Lieutenant Mass, who'd been shot down over "the Slot," the northern sea-lane between Bougainville and Guadalcanal over which most of the Japanese air and ship traffic traveled. "At the time, nobody knew what happened to him. They assumed he was dead. But I found out later that coast watchers got hold of him and he finally made it back." The plane captain briefed him on security. "The password was 'Lillian' because [commanders thought] the Japs couldn't pronounce the *l*'s. We only owned a few square miles around the fields, and they'd been infiltrating. Passwords were new to us. We didn't need them on the carrier."

Later that afternoon, Flatley and the other Reapers arrived. After separating from the dive-bombers, they'd searched in vain for targets and, being too far from Guadalcanal, returned to *Enterprise*. But they hadn't stayed long. Searchers in the Slot had found the eleven Japanese troop transports which, despite the loss of their battleships, had regrouped and were proceeding with destroyer escorts hell-bent to land their reinforcements. Marine Wildcats had already started bombing these juicy targets, which were teeming with soldiers on their decks, as had a group of other aviators who had arrived at Cactus the day before. When Flatley, back on *Enterprise,* learned about the transports, he immediately volunteered to escort a new launch of dive-bombers to attack them.

Whitey Feightner was one of those who returned with him. "We were at 20,000 feet and had just sighted the [transports] maybe twenty-five miles northwest of Guadalcanal . . . All of a sudden I looked up, about 5,000 feet [above us], and I started counting Zeros going over . . . I'd already counted thirty when Flatley said, 'Okay, I don't think they've seen us . . . I don't want anybody wagging wings [or giving our position away]. Just freeze where you are' . . . The [dive-]bombers were about to push over [onto the transports] so I'm really watching. I knew [the Zeros] were going to come down on us any moment. But [Flatley] very calmly assigned each bomber a different ship so they wouldn't duplicate . . . The bombers shoved over and his last words, as I remember, were, 'Okay fighters, dive and strafe all the [protecting destroyers] Protect the bombers' . . . Talk about cool . . ."

As soon as they dived, said Feightner, the Zeros jumped them but didn't put up much of a fight. Several were shot down, and the bombers devastated the troopships. In Stanley Johnston's *Grim Reapers* Flatley described them as so "packed" with troops "on their open decks" that they resembled "a football crowd in a stadium." The attack turned to carnage as the Wildcats turned from the destroyers, most of which where sunk by the bombers, and began strafing the transports with their .50-caliber machine guns. The big bullets cut through the crowds of Japanese like slicing fan blades and the incendiaries among them started many fires. Marines had been attacking the transports since morning. By the end of the day, more than half were underwater or sinking—another blow to the overconfident Japanese.

But the slaughter didn't extinguish Japanese plans.

That night, bringing the repaired battleship *Kirishima* back with some heavy cruisers, the enemy planned to shell Henderson again and at least land the surviving troops, which were still clustered on the few remaining transports. The Allies, however, suspected as much, and Admiral Halsey ordered the battleships *Washington* and *South Dakota,* screening for *Enterprise,* forward to stop them. Another furious night surface battle ensued in Iron Bottom Sound. While the American ships, which included destroyers and cruisers, suffered heavy losses and had to retreat, *Kirishima* and the big cruisers with her were repulsed. Admiral Yamamoto, determined to carry out his plan, ordered the transports to proceed anyway and beach themselves in order to land the troops. The original Japanese schedule had called for a midnight landing, which would have given the troops time to disembark in darkness and take their supplies with them. But the battle had upset that timetable. By the time the transports had beached and unloaded, the sun was coming up. Henderson CAP fighters quickly spotted them and began attacking. It was another massacre.

It would take one more battle before America could begin to think of victory at Guadalcanal. Voris would get his dogfight initiation in it—a frightening, lesson-learning combat that fittingly, given his coming future with the Blue Angels, would take a wrenching aerobatic maneuver to survive.

CHAPTER 10

Guadalcanal was an eye-opener for the naval aviators who landed there. They'd heard the stories. But nothing sufficed like actual experience. Take the food (when there was any). "Pretty bad," said Voris. "They had butter that tasted like wax. It stuck to the roof of your mouth." Mosquitoes were rife. And big. The flyers had to help service and gas their own planes, something that was always done for them by specialists on the carrier. "We'd borrow a little jeep, go down to the beach and roll some of the fifty-five-gallon drums onto it," remembered Russ Reiserer. "We had to use a little hand pump to get it into the fighters," added Whitey Feightner. Dust or mud, depending on the weather, hampered daily operations. Worst of all, said Voris, was the feeling of helplessness when they got shelled. "It was like an earthquake. You can't control fourteen- or sixteen-inch rounds coming in. You're like a mouse just before the trap slams shut. All you can do is pray or cry." He said the first day they were there a shell came barreling in and landed ten feet from a gasoline tank he and Flatley and some others were leaning against. "You can hear them. All that stuff that you can't is bull. They sound like a freight train. We all dove for the foxhole. Luckily it was a dud."

At 12:30 p.m. on November 15, after the big surface battle of the preceding night—what historians call the Second Naval Battle of Guadalcanal (the first being the action several nights before)—Flatley, according to an after-action report he wrote, took two divisions of Reapers up, including Reiserer and Feightner, to relieve a CAP and protect rescue operations in the sound that were locating survivors of the surface battle. Voris was not one of the eight. Instead, he was on alert duty, meaning, "You're back in the coconut palms, just hanging around, waiting for something to happen." It was casual but they were ready to fly. He had his flight suit and Mae West life preserver on, which had to be uncomfortable in the heat and humidity of Cactus.

Voris wasn't thinking about it then, but years later he reflected on what makes a good pilot: "Confidence. Total confidence. You're not worried or scared to death that you are going to kill yourself, so you can concentrate on what you're doing. I know those who don't. They're lousy pilots. That's what's wrong with them . . . Physical and mental coordination. You're using your arms, your legs, your mind . . . Eye-hand coordination is very important . . . Knowledge and training. You've got to know your machine and be able to pull the most out of it. And think ahead of the machine. Ahead of the game. That's important . . . See the whole picture. Not just focus on one aspect. As a [Blue Angel] leader you have to keep a real big picture because you are not flying one plane. You are flying the whole team . . . Part of it is, you're born with it. Knowing what could happen and being right on top of it mentally. And when it does happen, being able to cope with it."

He was about to get a lesson the hard way.

At three p.m., from a control tent nearby with a telephone, they got word that bogeys were flying down the Slot from the northwest. The unknown airplanes, which no one doubted were Japanese, were at approximately 20,000 feet, said Cactus Control, and sixty-five miles away, which wasn't far. "I remember running for the airplanes." Planes were so scarce on the island that the only one ready for him was a "beat-up marine Wildcat." He had no choice. He jumped in. Four of them, including Stan Ruehlow, the division leader, started down the Fighter One runway. But only three got airborne. The last Wildcat in line got hit by Japanese artillery from the mountainside and couldn't take off.

The pilot survived but it was not a good start.

Rising from Lunga Point, cranking the wheels up right after takeoff, Voris remembers looking down and seeing sharks in the water just off shore. "Lots of them. They stood out against the sandy bottom. It goes through your mind, 'Hey, I'm not going to be your dinner.' It was always a concern." They had repellent called "shark chase" in a packet strapped to their life preservers. Tragically, said Voris—because he later saw at least one horrific scene—after the war, he found out the so-called repellent actually attracted sharks. "But what did we know."

Paramount in their minds as they scrambled was gaining altitude. They wanted to be high in order to dive on the enemy and thus gain a speed advantage. Voris reached down, pulling each T-handle to charge the Wildcat's six machine guns, then flicked the switches that armed the guns. They were ready to fire. He had a gunsight in front of the bullet-proof windscreen. It was made up of small circles and squares arranged inside one another. Each figure had a distance on it. When the target was inside a figure, he knew how far away it was and thus when to shoot. Still, it would take dead reckoning with the target's lead figured in. The trigger was on his control stick, accessible by his gloved finger. Steady was the requirement when firing. Even an eighth of an inch movement of the stick when firing would throw the bullets off as much as a hundred feet. "Smooth is what you want. Jerk the stick and you jerk your guns." Smooth is what they'd call Voris in later years when flying close with the Blue Angels could cause a collision. Shooting guns in a Wildcat was probably how he began developing that control.

They'd barely reached 18,000 feet, he guessed, when they spotted the bogeys—approximately twelve gray-green Val dive-bombers with six or eight escorting brown Zeros. The colors indicated ground-based army planes. "They were forward and to the left about 2,000 feet below us." He believes they were coming to bomb Henderson, but they might have been after the rescue ships. "This was going to be my first hand to hand . . . At that time in the war, their fighter pilots were the best." Reaper 3 was outnumbered at least two to one, not counting the bombers. "You don't freeze, but you've got a pretty good set of pregame jitters."

Flatley and the other two divisions flying CAP had been alerted to the bandits, but they were low on gas and had stationed themselves farther away. They'd taken up a position close to Guadalcanal in order to be the last line of defense in case the bombers got through and also to be within gliding distance of the field because of their dwindling fuel. Another division that had scrambled after Ruehlow's had still not arrived. It was therefore up to Ruehlow, Voris, and the third Wildcat pilot with them to make the first attempt at stopping the raiders.

"[Ruehlow] called 'Tally-ho' and we rolled over [almost inverted] and started down." It was a classic "peeling off." The Zeros saw the three and reared up to meet them. Voris picked the fighter he felt was closest. But the enemy pilot didn't seem to be turning into him hard enough. Either he was going for someone else or, more likely, Voris's steep dive angle was giving him the advantage. With a high-angle-on trajectory that pointed him at the turning Zero's front and side, he squeezed off a burst, perhaps, he later thought, prematurely. "I didn't have the pipper [gun sight] steady. It was my first time." But his instincts were true. The Zero's cockpit exploded. Pieces of its engine cowling began to separate from the nose and loft away. As he sailed past, he saw smoke billowing.

One down.

So far so good.

Converting the dive energy, he twisted up to come back around and saw that the bombers were turning away. It was an elating moment. "They were heading back, so we were successful in that sense."

At the top, he rolled over on his back and applied full power again. Roaring down inverted, he got another Zero in his sights. It was below and at an angle but coming in his direction. To his surprise, the enemy pilot apparently didn't see him and made a turn almost to the opposite direction, giving Voris his rear. It was the classic six o'clock shot from an angle on high. With the Zero's tail and birdcage cockpit growing in his sights, he squeezed the trigger. The enemy fighter rolled awkwardly, and Voris thought he had another score.

But suddenly everything changed. At the exact moment the Zero rolled, Voris's canopy shattered in a shock of noise and splinters, and a projectile from up and behind him slammed into his instrument panel, exploding in the engine. He was engulfed in glass, smoke, and shrapnel. Something ripped into his thigh. "I'd been transfixed [by the second Zero] and hadn't thought about my rear."

Classic mistake.

Instinctively he snap-rolled to spoil his attacker's aim and caught a glimpse of him in one of the rearview mirrors high in his damaged cockpit. There was a dogging Zero dead on his tail. "They'd been up in the sun and we hadn't seen them." Sixteen of them, said the after-action report. Talk about being outnumbered. It was a different group than those protecting the bombers. They'd purposely hung back and above. "They were all over us."

He turned hard, but the Zero hugged behind, its presence a relentless monster in his mind. He knew he couldn't outmaneuver it. Like a doomed man, he resigned himself to the inevitable—the killing shots. And for a fleeting, seemingly interminable, interval he had a strange spiritual experience, a kind of out-of-body vision. It centered on his mother. "How sad she's going to be." Time rocketed down. "A second seemed like an eternity . . . My whole life appeared in front of me. It was almost like an instantaneous picture"—a vivid panorama. Predominant was the sad ending—his mother receiving a telegram from the Navy Department: "I regret to inform you . . ." "The letter was right there . . . I saw her face in the sun . . . the sorrow she had. I wasn't a mother's boy, but that was the key part—how bad she was going to feel that her son got shot down and was killed."

He was sure it was his last instant alive.

But—miraculously, fatefully, however one looks at such things—the shots didn't come. He snapped back to reality. "The last-ditch maneuver," he thought. It was all he had left. (In all probability, the strange vision had lasted no more than a millisecond, the time it took his stressed mind to conjure a possible solution.) Flipping inverted again, he slammed the stick to one side as hard as he could and dived for the ocean. It was a power dive predicated on the fact that they'd been told a Zero couldn't follow. Months before, an almost perfectly intact Zero had been secretly recovered in the Aleutian Islands where the Japanese had flown assaults. Testing it, the Allies had discovered that the nimble fighter's ailerons were too big to allow it to dive with the Wildcat. In a dive the air pressure on them would be too strong. Both the Wildcat and the Zero's maneuvers were largely initiated by cables attached to the slats. A pilot's arm strength on the stick was what moved the ailerons up and down on both fighter's wings.

There was no guarantee that the pilot behind him knew about the problem. Or that he wouldn't follow if he did.

But Voris had to try.

He was at about 14,000 feet when he slammed into the dive. Straight down he went, spinning his fighter on a vertical axis as a way of gaining speed. He remembers seeing Savo Island and then Guadalcanal corkscrewing by as he pushed the plane to its limit. He went as fast as the heavier Wildcat could go—in excess of 300 miles per hour. Suddenly he realized—he doesn't remember how—that the Zero wasn't following. "Thank God," he later reflected. "I don't know why. He had me cold turkey. Maybe he had already marked me up as a victory and went after somebody else."

As soon as he realized he'd escaped, "I started thinking, Well, now, how am I gonna get this little thing down properly." The fear, the anxiety—the superintense concentration and ingenuity to save one's life? "It's all gone . . . You go on to the next thing."

Now he was alone in a crippled plane. It could still do him in. "I didn't want to jump out, because they'd come after me in my parachute."

He was very close to Lunga and Fighter One and could have glided in if he'd had to. But he leveled out of the dive and continued toward home as fast as he could. The battle above him was still raging. His engine was losing oil and overheating. Eventually, he would lose control of the engine. But he made it to the ground before the problems became critical.

"I landed—if you could call it a landing."

Taxiing in and finally halting, two helpers jumped up on his wing. One was a marine captain who "pulled on my flight suit and said 'Are you hurt?' Understand I'm in a state of semishock. I had some blood on my leg, but said, 'Nothing serious.' He pulled out my flight suit so I could see it. There were three holes in the right upper sleeve." Voris hadn't noticed them until then. They'd been made by the Zero's 7.7-millimeter machine gun. The bullets had narrowly missed hitting him. The exploding projectile that had entered the engine had been from the Zero's 20-millimeter cannon.

The other helper—coincidence of coincidences—was an old high school buddy, Leslie Boots, whom Butch had not seen since they double-dated at their graduation prom in Santa Cruz. Boots, a first or second lieutenant, was an army air corps pilot flying P-39 Airacobras which had been sent to Cactus, Voris understood, because of their special abilities to attack the nearby hillside Japanese artillery. "I had no idea he was there and haven't seen him since. But of course we were both surprised to see each other."

Voris was shaking. "When you're up there, it's all business. You can think clear and sharply. It's amazing how concentrated you can be. But when it's over, you begin to realize what you've been through."

What had he learned?

"Watch your six [rear position akin to six o'clock on a clock face]. Standard fighter pilot lesson"—especially the first time out. "The guy that got me I didn't see." Voris had concentrated too long on one aspect, hadn't kept his mind on the bigger picture. "Of course there were so many of them and only three of us. We were overwhelmed. Everything happened so fast. But that's what you have to be prepared for. It's called how to handle an emergency. You're flying right up to the maximum risk and trying not to go over the side. I also learned, I guess, that sometimes it's better to retreat and fight another day. That word 'retreat' had never entered my mind."

They lifted him from the damaged cockpit. He doesn't remember how he got to sick bay—a tent in the dust under the palms—but soon a doctor was sticking a long silver probe into his thigh and retrieving pieces of splintered cannon shell. "The 20-millimeter was the boomer. Just bits and pieces were in me." He remembers it vividly. He didn't have any anesthesia or local painkiller because the doctor had run out. "He'd push it in the hole and come up with one and then push it in again. You just gritted your teeth and let them do it."

When the doctor was done, he opened a packet of sulfanilamide powder, the only antibiotic available, and poured it into the wound. "We were lucky. The Japanese didn't have anything." The *Enterprise* report about his injury says it was "painful but not serious." He would be awarded a Purple Heart, but he had no idea about that in the makeshift sick bay. He'd been bloodied and had shot down two enemy fighters, he believed, although the second Zero, entered by the yeoman in his log, would later be ruled "unconfirmed". You had to have someone else verify the kill to get credit, and those who could have done that, he said, "were fighting for their lives."

Flatley and his planes had eventually joined the battle. All told, the Reapers had "destroyed" six "Nagoya Zeros" with four others "probably damaged" and had lost only one plane and no pilots, a clear victory for the navy flyers. Subsequently, it developed that the November 15 air action was the last daylight raid on Guadalcanal or on the Allied ships and planes around it that the Japanese flew for over a month. Following it, World War II historians write, Yamamoto decided that winning back the island wasn't worth the sacrifice in men, ships, and planes the Cactus fighting was costing them. From that day forward, the issue was never in doubt. The marines and their airfield on Guadalcanal would survive, and the island would soon become recognized as the first Allied conquest in the road leading to Tokyo. As Admirals Halsey and Kinkaid and Brigadier

General L. E. Woods, commander of the First Marine Air Wing on Cactus, would later write in various communiqués, *Enterprise*'s Air Group 10 and the Reapers had come at a crucial time in the struggle for Guadalcanal and were instrumental in turning the tide. "SoPac [the South Pacific force] could scarcely have won the battle without the *Enterprise* and her aviators," wrote Lundstrom.

Of course, the Reapers didn't know this on November 15. Voris, despite his injury, which became infected, continued to fly on various missions, as did others of VF-10 and the air group. "I wasn't disabled. [The leg] was sore and hurt but I could fly." When it became clear that the crisis was over, the pilots began returning to *Enterprise* or Nouméa, depending on the circumstance. Some of the Reapers flew their planes out, but others, like Voris, left them for the marines, whom it was determined needed them more than the navy. He was finally evacuated along with other wounded in an army transport.

★

Enterprise, its crew and pilots, spent Christmas 1942 on Espíritu Santo, a New Hebrides staging island closer to the Solomons than Nouméa. The lush tropical island, part of Melanesia, was a place to regroup and retrain while *Enterprise* finally finished its repairs. Voris's log shows late December and early January training flights for "gunnery," "tactics," and "radar." It also shows an increased number of "night tactics" flights, probably because the Japanese had begun using after-dark air attacks more frequently and US flyers had little experience in night fighting. What his log understandably doesn't show is that during a pickup volleyball game on the island, he went up to the net to make a play opposite tall, mustachioed Lieutenant Leroy "Tex" Harris and came down full weight on Harris's foot, injuring it badly. "We wore those big marine field shoes for flying. I think I broke two of his toes . . . He never did walk the same. I felt so sorry." The accident earned Voris his first navy call sign, "Horse," although Harris, who hobbled but could still fly, was the only Reaper who used it consistently.

On January 28, *Enterprise*, finally fully repaired, left Espíritu Santo on a training-and-looking-for-action patrol. Other ships accompanied her. Reinforcement and evacuation operations had been increased at Guadalcanal, and the Japanese, although beaten back, were still angry and a threat, especially for scaled-down harassing attacks. That night, in what author Stanley Johnston wrote was "the first night torpedo plane attack ever executed by the Japs," *Chicago,* a heavy cruiser involved in resupply operations near the Rennell Islands, south of Guadalcanal, was severely damaged by a raid from Rabaul. By dawn it was in tow at about four miles per hour to Espíritu Santo, pretty much a sitting duck. *Enterprise* was diverted to protect it. Knowing they had a cripple, the Japanese sent more attackers. By the time the enemy planes arrived, Reapers were in the air and fought a defensive battle, claiming twelve Japanese bombers shot down. It became known as the Battle of Rennell Island. Among others, future Blue Angels Wickendoll and Feightner distinguished themselves in the action, beating back the enemy and keeping them from hitting *Enterprise,* which had steamed close. Ultimately, however, *Chicago* took more torpedo hits and sank on January 30. Voris's log notes the fight with a penned-in "combat, Battle of Rennell Island, *Chicago* sunk." The notation indicates he was involved. But he draws a blank on the action. Most probably, either he was in a protective CAP which saw no direct involvement or his participation was in another way peripheral.

In early February, however, the Reapers flew back to Guadalcanal for a few days and Voris clearly remembers strafing enemy transports trying to evacuate the last of the Japanese soldiers on the island. According to his log, it was around February 7. "Brutal" is the way he described it. "You get those six fifty-calibers with their high velocity and high rate of fire and they're deadly . . . I remember the ships . . . Plain old transports, some small and some a bit larger . . . We got a briefing and just took off . . . They were leaving and without air [opposition] we weren't under duress . . . Oh, they had guns and fired back but you just chewed them apart. Put the pipper on the target and squeeze. No mercy . . . zoom up and come back around . . . The worst thing the ground troops have to fear is strafing. Coming down on an open boat or a [troop] front line, you're very accurate . . . almost pinpoint accurate . . . We'd get down there at a couple of hundred feet coming right at them." He remembers ship masts and teeming decks. "You could see them scurrying, splattering, rolling over . . . It was carnage but very effective." He never thought of it "in terms of it being immoral or anything like that . . . It was just another day's work . . . very impersonal . . . Either him or me. That kind of separates everything. If you don't get him, he's going to get you."

According to accounts, there were some ten thousand Japanese left on the island when their high command decided to give it up. The marines, in mop-up operations, killed many of those left. The Allied fighters and bombers dispatched more of them in strafing runs like Voris's. The Reapers left Guadalcanal after several days and their first cruise began winding down. On February 13, Flatley got orders to take over a carrier air group, a reward for fashioning perhaps the best fighter squadron in the navy at the time. Before he left, he appointed Voris a division leader, a key flying post in the squadron, and urged him to apply for a permanent commission in the regular navy, a suggestion Voris jumped at. "I'd wanted to be a regular from day one. The flying, the way of life. It fitted me and I fitted it. I liked the discipline, the smartness, the responsibilities."

By the end of the cruise, March 1943, he and Flatley had become quite close. "I think he thought of me almost as a son." And also as a budding leader, as evidenced by the division appointment. Writing in Voris's fitness reports, Flatley observed, "The fortunes of war and the stress of aerial combat . . . during which he destroyed an enemy fighter although outnumbered 3 to 1 have quickly developed this young officer. His character is of the highest order. His loyalty and initiative have done much to increase the efficiency of VF-10 . . . Voris has been a tower of strength in keeping morale at a high level . . . He has a very strong personality . . . His desire to make the navy his permanent profession is based in a genuine interest in the navy as a whole and naval aviation in particular."

The feeling was mutual. "After serving with Jimmy Flatley, I said to myself, that's what I want to be. I want to be a squadron commander like Jimmy Flatley. That was a big motivation at that stage . . . The flying was priceless. I felt very comfortable in the air. I'd been through combat and felt comfortable there." In regard to his budding leadership qualities mentioned by Flatley, "I was always positive, upbeat, affable, had ideas on what we should be doing, getting people together. Let's go train. Let's go fight. Let's go get a cold beer . . . It wasn't David slaying Goliath. It was day-to-day stuff. You're either a weak component or a strong one."

Not surprisingly—because the navy seldom makes regulars of first-cruise rookies—it would take Voris another year and a half before he'd be awarded a regular commission. But when given the chance in his first cruise, he'd done well. He'd endured terrible bombing and seen up close the horror war could produce. He knew what he was getting into. He'd risen fearlessly in the air and battled courageously and effectively in spite of the odds against him. He'd seen his own death and cheated it at the last second. "You had to mature fast or die. I just sort of clenched down and lost feelings and went at it."

CHAPTER 11

At the end of March 1943, Voris received orders to return home and, as a recognized Fighting 10 leader, help form the veteran nucleus of a new fighter squadron, as yet unconstructed and unnamed. The navy, in a newly initiated rapid buildup program, was creating many new fleet units to fight from the carriers it was increasingly commissioning. The new squadrons required experienced cores for leadership and instruction. Three other higher-ranking Reapers were sent with him: Lieutenant Commander John Eckhardt, a Washington, D.C., native who would become the first XO of the projected squadron; newly promoted Lieutenant Commander Tex Harris, whose foot Voris had mauled and who would succeed Eckhardt as XO; and Lieutenant William "Bill" Blair, a tough-looking, serious-minded aviator from Toledo, Ohio.

The departees flew south from Espíritu Santo to Nouméa in a lumbering twin-engine PBY. The leisurely trip away from the front must have been a welcome break from the tense flying to which they'd become accustomed, a chance finally to take in the beautiful sights and appreciate the exotic area where they'd seen so much fury. From Nouméa, they caught the heavy cruiser *Louisville* to Pearl Harbor. Built in 1930 and on its way to the Aleutians, the big cruiser had several little Curtis Scout Observation biplanes (SOCs) onboard that it could launch from the sides of its gun-bristled decks. Battleships often had them, too. The single-pontooned aircraft, which could land in the water, were used for reconnoitering, rescuing, and depth-charging. The planes themselves were usually launched by an explosive charge that literally shot the aircraft down a short retractable rail. The ship's pilot, George Duncan, was even bigger than Voris. He talked Voris into taking the place of the normal backseater and going for a ride.

"You grabbed handles in the cockpit and held on. Launch was like being fired from a gun." They attacked a towed target with depth charges. Then Duncan told Voris to fly the little plane, which, heavy with some of the undropped ordnance, was no easy task. "I had a stick in the backseat." When they'd finished, Duncan landed, as was procedure, in the "slick" of the cruiser's wake and taxied up close astern so they could be hoisted aboard. The ship's crane lowered a metal hook. It was to be fastened in a sling kept in a hatch on the plane's top wing. "He told me to get out and put the hook in the loop but watch out that it doesn't squash my hand." Voris climbed out of the cockpit and made his way precariously to where he could reach the hatch. Using one hand to take out the sling and the other for the hook, he almost toppled. "George had to hold my legs or I would have fallen in the water." He made the coupling and they were hoisted aboard. "An interesting excursion," he termed it years later.

From Pearl, they took a slow transport to San Francisco. Voris had several weeks' leave granted before reporting to the new squadron on the East Coast and went home to Santa Cruz to see his parents. By this time, his two brothers were also in the service. Dick had enlisted in the marines; Bob was an officer in the navy. Both were away. His mother, he said, as was the custom then, was proud to display three stars on separate cards in a window. It was a way of honoring family members serving their country. They didn't discuss the fighting much, he said. "It was mostly, 'Son, it's good to have you home.'" He told his mother about seeing her when he thought he was going to die but didn't elaborate. She said, "'Oh, my son, I'm so glad you didn't get hurt.' They were always worried about us getting hurt, getting killed. They knew I was going back with the new squadron so it was best to skip the details."

★

Following a near week's train ride across the country, Voris reported to the office of Commander, Atlantic Fleet, in Norfolk, Virginia. From there, he was ordered ultimately to NAS Atlantic City (N.J.) and the reorganization of Fighting Two, an existing squadron formerly made up mainly of enlisted pilots, mostly chiefs. It was being reconstituted as a larger fleet squadron with a full complement of commissioned officers, new and better airplanes, and Lieutenant Commander William A. "Bill" Dean as its commanding officer. Dean was a dark-haired, 1934 graduate of the naval academy. He had been a standout aviator in the training command but had not yet seen combat. "I'd never heard of him. He was nice, didn't say much."

It was early June 1943 and only a few of the new squadron's assigned members had arrived. The bulk of rookie pilots from the training command were still en route. Dean must have been impressed with Voris, or at least seen his size, experience, and manner as an asset for dealing with what would eventually become some forty pilots of varied personality, most of them competing vigorously for flight time. He gave Voris the tough squadron job of air operations officer, meaning he'd be scheduling all the training flights and determining who would fly what airplanes when and where. "It was a big job, inviting argument, and I'm still just a lieutenant (j.g.). But he knew I'd been there and back . . . When you go into a new job and you're an experienced wartime pilot you assume the responsibility." Voris was pretty much on his own from day one, which was Dean's way of doing things, as well as the navy's mostly, and probably the best way to cultivate a prospective leader who, by definition, would be alone and have to handle things by himself anyway.

On June 12, the Rippers, as the new squadron was christened (a play on the success of the Reapers?), received their first Grumman F6F-3 "Hellcat," the new fleet fighter plane that had been designed and rushed into service as an answer to the Zero. In looks, the Hellcat was basically the same barrel-nosed, tank-tough, straight-winged Wildcat the navy and marine pilots had flown with success thus far in the war. But it was bigger, stronger, faster, more protected, and more maneuverable. "Stream-lined" was the word it's designers liked to use. It had a larger, more powerful engine, a 2,000 horsepower Pratt and Whitney air-cooled radial named the R-2800, which was more rugged and dependable and easier to maintain than its predecessor's. It meant few stalls and less maintenance work. It could dive faster and produce a maximum speed of approximately 375 miles per hour in level flight at 17,000 feet. That was faster than the Zero at the same altitude by more than 50 knots! A good advantage. It still couldn't outturn the lighter Japanese fighter at slow speeds, but it could match or slightly exceed it's climb rate and had much greater range than the Zero or Wildcat, as much as 1,500 miles round-trip with extra tanks. It had the same six powerful .50-caliber machine guns in its wings, each packing four hundred rounds, and was better armored and more rugged than the earlier Grumman. Yet it was easier to fly, tighter turning, and more dependable.

Eventually, by war's end, the Hellcat would be so successful that it would earn the nickname "Acemaker." It had half-inch-thick sheet-metal plating behind the pilot's seat. The protection was strong enough to stop a .50-caliber bullet. It had extra armor on the oil and gas tanks. "You lose your oil, you lose your engine," said Voris. It also had hydraulic landing gear and flaps—the first Voris had ever flown. That meant good-bye to bent over hand-cranking of the landing gear. "When I first saw it, I thought, Jesus, this is as big as a DC-3 [a famous twin-engine passenger and cargo plane]. Compared to a little Wildcat, it was a monster. But it had the power and accelerated fast after you tucked in the gear. Climbed well. So I flew around just feeling it and doing chandelle turns [rolls in the horizontal axis, a key maneuver later in the Blues] and finally took it over the top, doing those kinds of rolls, and getting comfortable there. Pretty soon I started fitting into it and liking it. You have to get to know your airplane. That's the first thing. Know it like a brother. Some people never do."

By July the squadron was almost fully manned, and training had started in earnest. Most of the new pilots were from the Advanced Carrier Training Group from which Voris had graduated in 1942. Rushed out, they were "minimally qualified." In addition to his scheduling duties, he instructed. "You hope you can teach them enough to get them through the first few missions. Then they'll be fine." Tactics were based on a simple maxim: "Get into firing position. If you don't, nothing else matters." At the blackboard, he drew Xs and Os. "If he's above you, turn as hard as you can up into him. That takes away the easy side shot. You're beak to beak. Maybe you can shoot him in the face. Turn away, and you give the attacker your behind." Career over. "If he overshoots, you've got a chance to turn onto his rear. But don't bleed too much energy. Keep your speed . . . He's going to want to turn back into you . . . The main thing is don't let him get back into that rear firing position"—the mistake that had almost ended his career.

In practice, they did acrobatic maneuvers—another precursor to his later work with the Blues—routinely "pulling six or seven Gs," which was a pretty good warm-up for a dogfight. It taxed the pilot's strength on the stick and brought them close to blackout as blood tried to drain from their heads. Butch purposely went up alone and pulled high G himself in order to get used to combating the blood drain. They used a grunting and groaning muscle-constricting exercise that forced the blood back up. "You tightened your stomach, similar to what they do now." Unconsciousness wasn't conducive to victory in the air.

The untested aviators learned the weave and "mutual support." Teamwork was emphasized. "If you don't get him on the first pass," he told them, "hopefully your wingman will." To make practice as realistic as possible, the Rippers challenged nearby army fighter pilots to dogfights whenever they could. "They had P-47 'Jugs' [Thunderbolts], the latest army fighters. Pretty good airplane, similar to the Hellcat. We'd fly over and drop rolls of toilet paper as a signal to come up and fight. They'd do the same to us. [The Thunderbolt] had essentially the same engine as the Hellcat except it had a two-stage turbosupercharger which would take it to altitude higher and faster. We had a mechanical blower. It wasn't as good." The Rippers would try to "fend off the Jug" until it dropped to a lower altitude, where "we could outturn them." Eventually, base commanders put a stop to the challenges. "Toilet paper on trees and around the bases got them upset."

The squadron continued to add to its veteran base. For instance, Lieutenant (j.g.) Merriwell W. "Tex" Vineyard, a salty southwesterner who had joined the Canadian Royal Air Force at the war's outbreak and flown RAF Spitfires in the Mediterranean against the Germans. "[Voris] was a big, straightforward type guy," said Vineyard, reached years later in Texas, "He was my kind of person. If he didn't like you, he'd tell you so." Vineyard was the same type. "We got along." Despite the influx, Dean, like Flatley before him, had recognized Voris's prowess in the air and made him one of the squadron's coveted four-plane division leaders despite his relative lower rank and lesser time in service than some of the older pilots. Just prior to leaving the states, Voris was promoted to full lieutenant (the equivalent of captain in the army).

On July 22, while pilots were practicing field carrier landings at Atlantic City, an angry ocean weather front came storming in, catching five of the new pilots helplessly in the air. "These are big, black thunderstorms with lightning and gusty winds. They move fast. Visibility goes to zero . . . I remember being with the skipper in his office looking out over the runway. They put out a recall: 'Everybody on the ground as fast as you can get here.'" Three made it down. But by the time Ensign Earle "Spider" Evans, a young, redheaded pilot from Winnsboro, Louisiana, and Lieutenant (j.g.) John "Obie" O'Brien, a Pennsylvania-born Villanova graduate, got to the field, it was obscured by driving rain and darkness. They tried to skirt the towering tempest by fleeing down the coast to Wildwood, New Jersey, where the weather was better. But O'Brien lost radio contact with Evans en route. "The storm took him [Evans] right out to sea. We never heard from him again. You get swept out like that, you can't get back. The winds are too strong. You don't have the fuel or the instruments . . . Weather's probably your greatest hazard in that type of flying."

At the beginning of October, the squadron, suddenly alerted, left for the West Coast, where, at San Francisco, they boarded a small, unescorted jeep carrier loaded with high octane aviation gasoline, army P-47s and their own thirty-six Hellcats, and made the slow, cramped voyage to Hawaii. Arriving on the eighteenth, they were surprised, according to Tom Morrissey, the squadron's intelligence officer who wrote a privately published book on the cruise, to see in Pearl Harbor a "vast armada poised for the next big strike." Unlike his first arrival at Pearl a year earlier, when he'd encountered mostly twisted and burned-out hulks, Voris now entered a harbor bristling with new ready-to-fight vessels. They included the various-sized carriers *Essex, Yorktown, Monterey, Cowpens, Belleau Wood,* and *Lexington.* Clearly, a major offensive was afoot—different from the desperate, smaller thrusts of Voris's first cruise. These flattops and their attendants were the vanguard of the beginning assaults to retake the Pacific by a strategy that would become known as "island hopping."

In fact, most of the big ships were back from a successful carrier bombing of Japanese installations on Marcus and Wake Islands in the Central Pacific, the initial reconquest foray. But the Rippers' first combat, they were advised, was still a month or so away. They would have to keep honing. They were given residence on Oahu, first at Barber's Point and then at NAS Kaneohe, and resumed training. Now it wasn't only rookies that Voris was having to handle in his ground job as operations officer. He was scheduling for the entire squadron, veterans included, and sometimes having to step on higher-ranking toes. "I was very direct. Never mollycoddled. Had a pretty sharp tongue. Here's who's going to fly and here's who's not. No namby-pamby." It grated on some. "I had people argue and gripe. Why am I doing this? Why can't I do that?" But he strove to be fair, and "none of them ever went to the skipper"—at least as far as he knew—"and the skipper never told me to do anything different than I did." He was learning to handle a diverse and competitive group, not unlike the extremely talented aviators he would have to manage later with the Blues.

For his second section lead, Voris picked a young Ajo, Arizona, native who had gone to junior college in Long Beach, California, near where Voris had spent his early childhood. Lieutenant (j.g.) John "Mike" Wolf was a bright-smiling, fairly tall, and skinny all-American-looking young officer who, in his own words, had been a beach bum and then president of the junior college's student body. Although he had less than perfect eyesight, which probably would have kept him out of the cockpit because of the navy's tough vision requirements, Wolf had managed to elude the eye examination when he and his school buddies with whom he'd volunteered were processed for the flight program. He would become one of the squadron's youngest aces and fly with Voris on almost every mission in the coming combat. "[Voris] was a natural leader," said Wolf years later. "He was big and more experienced than most of us. He seemed older. He could do any of the things he asked anybody else to do . . . He was a real man, and I was proud to follow his orders."

At the end of October, the Rippers, the only available fighter squadron in Hawaii at the time, were assigned to Air Wing 6—not their regular air wing—which was getting ready for the big offensive they'd glimpsed gathering when they'd arrived at Pearl and needed a fighter squadron quickly. Air Wing 6 was headed by "Butch" O'Hare, now promoted to a CAG, or air group commander, and would be flying from *Enterprise,* Voris's former carrier, which had undergone refurbishing at Puget Sound Navy Yard in Bremerton, Washington. It would be arriving soon. Being selected to be "a part of the famous Butch O'Hare's air group" was a "shot in the arm," Morrissey wrote. And no Ripper was happier than Voris, who, because of his admiration of the well-known, unassuming war hero, had recently switched his call sign from Horse to Butch. "We were getting ready for the combat cruise, and you have to have something that's quick to recognize. The skipper [Dean] said, 'Why don't you take Butch? You two were good friends. You're always talking about him.' I said fine."

O'Hare was just back from participating in attacks on Marcus and

Wake Islands where, flying the new Hellcat, the Medal of Honor winner and ace had added numbers six and seven to his score of downed enemy planes. The raids on the two islands, although serious, had been, in part, exploratory. Navy leaders wanted to see how their new carriers and planes would fare. They did fine. They also wanted to probe enemy reaction deep within the ocean territory Japan controlled. The reaction had been limited and not overly threatening, a good sign. There was just too much ocean and island territory for the Japanese to cover decisively with the Allies already thrusting toward Japan from the far South Pacific, where MacArthur was running the show. The stage therefore was set to begin a full-fledged second offensive from the western edge of the Pacific theater. This offensive, in contrast to McArthur's thrust, would concentrate on what was called the Central Pacific, an area, beginning with the Gilbert Islands on the Japanese-held periphery nearest Hawaii (although "near" is perhaps misleading, for Hawaii was some two thousand miles away). The main objectives in the Gilberts were the atolls of Tarawa and Makin—Tarawa because it already had an airfield on it that threatened Allied shipping to the South Pacific and would be a good catch, and Makin, about a hundred miles north of Tarawa, because it was closest to the Marshall Islands, the next objective in the offensive leading to Tokyo through the Central Pacific.

Both atolls were to be taken by amphibious assault, Tarawa by the marines, Makin by the army. *Enterprise,* and thus Air Wing 6 and the Rippers, was assigned to the Makin assault. Its planes would be tasked with bombing and strafing the island's defenses to weaken them for the invasion and then taking command of the surrounding skies. Few in the squadron, if any, were told where they were going until they were under way. Voris remembers that when they were preparing to fly their Hellcats onto the carrier on November 10, Dean called him in. "'Butch O'Hare wants to talk to you. He's in his state room.' He didn't say any more. I went down, knocked on his cabin door, and entered. He was in bed with something like the flu and couldn't fly. He was real sick. Shaking. He said, 'Would you bring my airplane out for me?' It was double zero—'double nuts' as we called it. His special Hellcat. I said, 'Yes, sir. I'd be glad to.'" Voris was flattered. The CAG, one of the pilots he admired most, felt he was good enough to be entrusted with "OO."

For Voris, the favor was the beginning of a heightened involvement in the war, a momentous, historic second cruise, in which he would become an ace and, in the process, hone to maturity already budding flying skills and attitudes, as well as his own maturity as a naval officer, all of which would be needed when the opportunity for him to start the Blue Angels arose.

CHAPTER 12

The cruise, so far, had been relatively uneventful—if a combat cruise, even the beginning of it, could be so described. Task Group 50.2 had steamed the long Pacific route southwest to the Gilberts without incident. Voris and most of the other Rippers had never been in such an oceangoing armada: ships in every direction, as far as the eye could see—carriers, destroyers, battleships, cruisers. The refurbished *Enterprise*, with new quarters, enhanced radar, more and better guns, a longer and wider flight deck, was the leader, flagship for Rear Admiral Arthur W. Radford, commander of 50.2, also known as the Northern Task Group, the ships specifically going to Makin. Radford was an academy graduate, an accomplished aviator. He was aggressive. "This was much better than the first cruise," recalled Voris. "I'm seasoned. We're on the offensive. We're rolling."

They'd come within reach of Japanese land-based bombers on November 16, but no enemy had been encountered. The Japanese fleet was occupied mostly with Allied war movements farther west and south, especially in the northern Solomons. Land-based enemy planes in the Marshalls and Marianas were the major worry. On the nineteenth, before dawn, with air attacks already begun by another task group against Tarawa, a hundred or so miles to the south, Admiral Radford's ships, including the smaller carriers *Belleau Wood* and *Monterey*, had commenced their own strikes.

Makin was a small, triangular-shaped coral atoll of tiny islets ringing a deepwater lagoon. Its total landmass was about five square miles. The atoll's center was Butaritari, an islet of white beaches, a small port, and heavy defenses. Voris had led his division on several raids against the island, including a tense first one. "I remember the strafing, right over [the army's] heads as they were coming ashore . . . We were trying to kill off anything in front of them because there was heavy ground fire from the beach into the landing boats . . . You could see the Japs. But once you open up with those six fifties [machine guns], boy, did they disappear . . . You could see our troops looking up at you, almost look them in the eyes as you came up over the top of them. They were ducking because we were dropping brass on them [the empty shell casings from their guns]." It was precision flying, similar to what he'd do in the Blues. Anything but steady-handed shooting and they would hit their own. The army, he said, placed large white markers of cloth, called panels, in the sand to show the Hellcat pilots where to aim.

Makin wasn't heavily garrisoned by the Japanese, and the landings had gone well. The army established a secure beachhead quickly and took the atoll in four days of essentially mop-up fighting. The human cost to the Allied side compared to other battles in the Pacific was light—some 60 killed and 150 wounded.

Tarawa was a different story. The atoll held the bulk of Japanese defenses in the Gilberts and included some six thousand dug in and well-armed defenders on its main island, Betio. Betio not only had an interlocking chain of cement and coral pillboxes and palm-trunk gun nests, but also a protective coral reef barrier that had not been scouted well and which kept the landing boats from reaching the beaches. The marines had had to disembark on the reef and wade through the chest- and neck-high water leading to the beach and thus had been easy targets. Once they'd reached the beach, many had lost their weapons in the struggle not to drown. They'd been pinned down in huge numbers. Casualties were horrendous. Eventually, over a thousand marines would die on Tarawa and over two thousand would be wounded. The preliminary bombardment by the Tarawa task force had not been as effective as at Makin. On the first night, marines pinned down on the beach had been subject to waves of near-suicide attacks and also strikes by Japanese night bombers.

The enemy had perfected night flying faster than America. They'd had years of fighting over China during the 1930s to do so. In the Gilberts, they were using swift, seven-seat, twin-engine Mitsubishi G4M1s, medium attack bombers which the Allies individually code-named "Betty." Bristling with gun turrets and carrying, among other ordnance, excellent naval torpedoes, the mostly dark green bombers, which were equipped with radar and had distinctive cigar-shaped fuselages, would wing down in groups from the Marshalls and Marianas and try to sneak toward their targets, low and fast, hugging the wave tops in an attempt to elude task force radar. None had reached the ships yet. But as the battle raged on Tarawa, they had gotten progressively closer and more numerous, hitting the marines and stalking the carriers.

Even before they'd started the assaults, Admiral Radford had guessed his ships would encounter the night raiders. They were the logical advantage the enemy could use. The task group's enormous firepower made day raids too costly. But at night the intruders were hard to see and aim at. The admiral had begun talking with his air group commander, O'Hare, about what could be done. Now, with the marines fighting for their lives and the numbers of night bomber "blips" increasing—some of the planes even getting close enough to be shot down—the situation had become intolerable. The packs of night-marauding Bettys had to be stopped. Voris was about to get what he likes to call an "opportunity."

The problem was in pinpointing the bandits. A daring plan was devised. It created the first night-fighter unit in the navy, dubbed "Black Panthers" by O'Hare, and later, "Bat teams" by the navy. Voris: "The skipper called me in and said we'd been volunteered by Butch and the admiral"—in other words, specially picked for the unit. Dean gave him an outline. Picket ships out ahead of the force would use their long-range radar to find the Bettys as they came down from the north. While they were still distant, two Panther teams would be launched in the darkness to attack them. Both teams would be made up of one Grumman TBF Avenger torpedo plane with a Hellcat hugging each wing. The Avengers had radar, not very powerful, but good enough for five- to ten-mile detection, depending on conditions. Once the ship had directed the teams to the area in which the bandits were entering, the slower, more poorly armed Avengers would try to pinpoint the enemy intruders and lead the faster, more lethal Hellcats to within striking distance. Then the fighters would use existing light, from the moon or exhaust flames, to home in. O'Hare and his wingman, Warren "Andy" Skon, a VF-2 lieutenant (j.g.), would pilot the Hellcats on one team; Dean and Voris would make up the other.

It was a simple enough plan, but none of them had ever practiced it, which, in hindsight, was ominous. After Dean explained it, he and Voris went up to the bridge to get a briefing from the admiral and CAG. "The admiral explained the importance of the operation and said we were going that night." Because none of them had ever landed on a carrier in darkness and because lighting the deck might attract any enemy submarines in the area, there was the problem of recovery. "If we didn't have enough gas to stay up until daybreak"—and that would depend on when they were launched and how much gas they used while in flight—"we weren't going to be able to recover aboard ship. He told us they'd vector us in front of the force and we'd bail out and the destroyers would pick us up." While the plan seemed "a little bit hairy" but "workable" to Voris, the last part gave him pause. "There were sharks out there, and I was skeptical that the destroyer could find us." But "I never thought about saying no. You go do it."

The "Tokyo Express," as the marauding Bettys were called by the task group, had established a recent pattern. They'd pass out ahead of 50.2 in the predawn hours heading south for Tarawa, which, with Makin now secure, was their last outpost in the Gilberts. Shortly after midnight on November 24, the day before Thanksgiving, *Enterprise's* intelligence center, according to O'Hare biographers Steve Ewing and John B. Lundstrom, alerted the admiral that the bombers were on their way. They'd taken off from Roi, a large Japanese air base on Kwajalein Atoll in the Marshalls. It was a cloudy, misty night with intermittent rain squalls, not ideal for the Panther operation. But the admiral, determined to act, ordered both teams launched, which, in this case—so the planes would get maximum boost in the dangerous launch conditions—meant catapulted, a method seldom used at that time.

The launches commenced around three a.m.

Voris was the last of the six planes to go. It was the first time he'd ever been catapulted, day or night. He termed it a "thrill . . . blacker than hell, like going into an ink bottle. That swoosh was something. When I went off the end, I'm wondering how do I keep from crashing into the water? You have no keys outside, just your gyro horizon [instrument] inside the cockpit. It's full power on. Keep the wings level. I worried about getting the landing gear up after I saw I was climbing."

Dean was just ahead of him. Each plane had a series of unique colored lights on it for individual identification. They could only be seen up close. "We were luckier than hell to even rendezvous," said Voris. Alvin Kernan, one of the TBF gunners on the teams and a key player in the subsequent drama, wrote in his autobiography, "It was a most confusing night." The ship's radar couldn't get them close to the Bettys, and the teams themselves never joined up in an effective manner. Joining was a tight maneuver and they had no experience doing it in the dark. The other TBF, piloted by Lieutenant Jon McInerny, a hero of the Battle of Midway, developed engine trouble and had to drop out of the hunt. Voris said they pretty well knew they'd lost the Bettys twenty minutes after launch. "I don't know if they turned around or what."

Ewing and Lundstrom write that the enemy formation was made up of three Bettys, only one of which bombed Tarawa. But all three kept more than a hundred miles away from the task group, which put them out of the Panthers' operating area. Voris: "All we did was stay at about 10,000 feet [orbiting] with the engines cut back and wait." But they did not get another vector. Their main concern then became conserving fuel. "I tell you, I could count the propeller blades going around waiting to get back aboard ship in daylight." Toward dawn they saw a huge flash in the sky. Kernan describes it as "like the sun rising." It was the escort carrier *Liscombe Bay* exploding after being torpedoed by a Japanese submarine. The torpedo hit the carrier's magazines, and the ruptured ship went down almost immediately, killing six hundred, a massive loss. The Panthers stayed aloft several more hours and then landed with the aid of daylight.

After this first grueling near-six-hour Panther flight, O'Hare decided to rotate the teams, using only one per night so the other would be fresh. The teams' pilots and crews also had to fly in the day. The battle on Tarawa subsequently turned in the marines' favor, and the Americans began securing the island. Thanksgiving Day was calm. O'Hare flew to the newly won Betio airstrip to see if it could be used as a possible night-landing runway in case, after the next launches, the Panthers were unable to recover on the ship. The atoll commanders would be less afraid of posting lights. But the field, battered by the recent battle, was still a day or two away from use. Morrissey writes that O'Hare returned saying the stench of rotting corpses on the newly conquered island wafted "several thousand yards" in all directions.

That night, more Bettys got within striking distance of the task group and dropped flares for torpedo runs. One was shot down, and the others roared around threateningly before retreating. But no Panthers were launched, either because the Tarawa field wasn't ready, the Bettys had come in too fast and surprised the task group, or *Enterprise* didn't want to give away its position by a launch. Maybe some or all of the above. At one point the carrier, playing cat and mouse with the nocturnal intruders, literally ducked beneath low-lying cloud cover in order not to be seen.

November 26's daylight hours were uneventful. But as dusk approached, the Bettys reappeared, and one launched a torpedo that barely missed *Belleau Wood* before that carrier's fighters shot it down. As more bandits appeared on radar, the Panther team of O'Hare, Skon, and the TBF, in which Kernan was navigator-bombardier, was launched. The TBF was piloted by Lieutenant Commander J. L. Phillips, the air group's Avenger squadron commander. O'Hare and Skon, contrary to the original plan, were immediately vectored to the bandits by the ship's fighter director, leaving the slow TBF to follow. It could not catch up. But it had the radar, and soon Phillips, without his fighters, found himself locked onto an unsuspecting formation of Bettys and coming up behind them. He called for the Hellcats, but they couldn't find him. He decided to attack on his own.

Firing the torpedo bomber's two wing-mounted machine guns, he surprised the marauders. In separate runs, he shot two down—one in a fiery mass that lit up the sky—and sent the others scurrying. Kernan, manning the Avenger's dorsal turret, fired so much, he wrote, that ignited gases from the .50-caliber muzzle momentarily blinded him. The gunner at the rear of the TBF was shot in the foot by one of the Betty's surprised gunners.

To the east of the Avenger, according to Ewing and Lundstrom, O'Hare and Skon had found their own Bettys. At least that's what they thought they had. The night was dark, and they shot only at "momentary fleeting shadows." Years later, said the authors, Skon told them O'Hare had indicated he had hit one of the phantom targets but there had been no splash or fire with which Skon could confirm.

Unable to find any more targets, and presumably having seen the fire from the Betty shot down by Phillips, O'Hare radioed that he wanted to rendezvous with the TBF. The planes were now about twenty-five miles from the carrier, and the ship's radar had both team elements on the scope. At O'Hare's request, Phillips fleetingly turned on his lights so the Hellcats could find them, and then the fighters, "all lighted up like

Christmas trees," according to Kernan, "slid suddenly in, coming down across our tail." Kernan now saw them for the first time. O'Hare, he wrote, had turned on a light inside his cockpit.

When they were close enough for him to identify O'Hare, Kernan said he suddenly saw an enemy bomber above and behind them. He doesn't know if the Betty was purposely coming in for an attack or was one that had scattered and now mistakenly thought it was rejoining its previous formation. But getting an okay to fire from Phillips, Kernan let go with a lengthy burst, emptying the machine gun's ammunition can. The approaching enemy disappeared, and he never saw it again. But almost simultaneously, O'Hare's plane, the cockpit lights now extinguished, slid gently away and down. Butch O'Hare was never heard from or seen again. Something white flared briefly below the TBF, and speculation later had it that it was either the splash of a plane or the opening of a parachute. Skon said he had seen tracers between him and O'Hare seconds before but could not tell where they came from, front or back. Were they the intruder's or Kernan's bullets? He did not see the enemy bomber or what happened to his leader to make him roll down in what he described as a fairly lazy descent. The injured gunner in the Avenger, with a view from its bottom window, said he saw the intruder.

Had the enemy bomber killed O'Hare with a stern attack? Had Kernan mistakenly hit the famous and popular CAG when he thought he was shooting at the enemy bomber? Was there, in fact, an enemy intruder at all behind the two Hellcats? Kernan writes: "Without doubt I had fired at the trailing Japanese plane that tried to join up on us, and he had fired at everything in his range, including O'Hare and us, but had I, blasting away, hit the group commander as well?" Ewing and Lundstrom conclude that it was probably an enemy who felled the popular leader. "Most likely [it was] a lucky shot from the forward observer crouched in the [Betty's] narrow glassed-in nose." But when what was left of the team landed on *Enterprise*, speculation centered on Kernan. "Right away," said Voris, "the talk aboard ship was that the turret gunner shot him down. It may or may not have happened that way, but that's what it looked like." The admiral immediately canceled the Panther operation. "We searched the next day but found nothing."

While confusion over exactly what happened lingered, the navy chose to keep the controversy quiet. As far as Admiral Radford was concerned, the Panthers, each night, had saved the task group from a possibly devastating attack, and all team members, including Kernan, who went on to become a distinguished scholar at Yale and Princeton universities, received awards. Voris, submitted by Dean for a Distinguished Flying Cross, got an Air Medal. His citation, signed by Pacific Fleet Commander Nimitz, reads: "For meritorious achievement . . . He, with unswerving devotion to duty and disregard for his own personal safety . . . operated as a night fighter. His cool and efficient performance . . . under extremely difficult conditions and his display of courage were in keeping with the highest traditions of the naval service."

Voris, although he wasn't present when the Bettys were encountered, had unhesitatingly put himself in harm's way. He had been a pioneer in US Navy night-flying combat, just as he would become a pioneer later with the Blue Angels. The navy had not attempted night-flying combat before. One can only imagine the feeling of utter helplessness, if not terror, albeit suppressed, each of those on the Bat teams experienced as they launched into pitch-black darkness with no visual references or prior experience, into what surely was going to be a deadly combat with no assurance they could return and land or would be picked up in an equally dark and unseen sea, detrimentally cold, should they go in the water. Such is the definition of bravery and courage. Dean, in submitting Voris for the medals, recognized the valor. He had done the same thing. If not for the luck of the rotation, either he or Voris, rather than O'Hare, might have died that fateful night.

★

As November ended, *Enterprise* left the Makin area and joined other ships in a newly reorganized task group. On December 4, after refueling and resupplying, the new force attacked Kwajalein atoll in the Marshalls, seat of Japanese military power in the area. Voris was one of the fighter leaders in the dawn attack. It caught the enemy by surprise, destroying many of his parked planes, moored ships, and landed buildings on and around the stronghold. Three Zeros—about all the enemy got into the sky—were also shot down. The raid, of course, alerted the Japanese to the new force's presence, and the US ships spent a tense night dodging Bettys hunting for a kill. But they emerged the next morning unscathed and headed back to Pearl Harbor.

Christmas 1943 was approaching. It had been two years since the devastating attack on the Hawaiian base and over two years since Voris had joined the navy to fly. The December 7 anniversary however, he recalls, was "just another day aboard the '*E.*'" A picture of the Rippers shot on a windy flight deck December 6 shows Voris standing tallest in the large group of aviators. He's near the middle, almost defiant, with his sleeves rolled up over the biceps, his .45 shoulder holster bulging, his stance more squared to the camera than the others. Its as if he's thinking, Bring it on. Any time, any place. Clearly, he's one of the squadron's stand-out leaders.

Having been picked by O'Hare and the admiral for the Bat missions had certainly anointed Voris a standout. Now the new CAG commander Roy Johnson, demanded that Voris fly with him whenever he [CAG] launched. "I guess he just felt my division was capable." Continuing as operations officer, he was now managing the daily combat flight schedule for the entire squadron, "a group of pilots each thinking he's the best in the world and maybe 20 percent of them scared to death." It was a constant juggling act. "I was probably the fifth down in seniority telling people senior to me who was going to fly combat air patrol, or go on a strike, or search, or sit standby." (A manned Hellcat was always ready to launch in case something went wrong with one scheduled.) "You always had the eager beavers. I was an eager beaver." And he had those who wouldn't or couldn't fly—the scared, the dangerous. "I was responsible for setting up the divisions. Who would lead them. Who the section leaders [the two planes making up the divisions] would be, the wingmen." Death, injury, fear, sickness, last-minute mission requirements, or other uncontrollable factors constantly disrupted the scheduling. "As you start to lose people, you try to rebalance. You try to keep each division relatively strong. But you can never get them all equal. You've got some leaders who are stronger than others. Wingmen who are different. When we had two or three losses, I might have to break up a division and spread things around."

When there were objections, he held his ground. "Go tell the skipper if you don't like it," he would say. To his knowledge, they never did, a sign that he was probably right most of the time. He had inexperienced replacements to deal with. "They'd come out on a jeep carrier and be shuttled over." He'd set them up, orient them, and hope for the best. And he had his own daily flying and missions to deal with. It was a heavy load, a leader's load. But he liked the responsibility. "I rode them hard. But I wasn't a screamer or nasty. I was firm. I ran a tight ship. If something had to be done, it got done. They called me Dean's indispensable man."

He was learning what it took.

Just before New Year's, the squadron, already at Barber's Point, was sent to NAS Hilo on the big island of Hawaii, the southernmost in the Hawaiian chain. The island was crawling with army, navy, and marine troops staging and training for future combat in the Pacific. The Rippers began doing the same. In their spare time, they played a lot of volleyball and badminton. Voris's competitive spirit and quick tongue, now bolstered with the confidence of a seasoned veteran, soon landed him in trouble.

His CO, Dean, liked sports and was as competitive as Voris. "I'm a great one to chide people, and I accept chiding back. [Dean would] miss a shot and I'd let him know. He always wanted to have a game, so we were out there quite a lot. When I got on the court, I forgot he was the commanding officer. In my mind, we didn't have rank on the courts. I could see his animosity building, and that made me pull his chain harder. If I'd been smart, I wouldn't have been out there with him. I'd have been at the O club or something." Dean finally got mad and dressed Butch down for a "caustic tongue," saying he had no respect for senior officers and later, as a result, gave him weak marks for loyalty and cooperation on his next officer fitness report, an important periodic navy record that would be used to determine his professional future. "He called me in and showed me the columns [on the fitness report]. I said, Well, all the others are at the top. I thought he was going to hit me."

But then, on February 27, the animosity dissipated. The skipper had a midair collision out over the ocean with Ensign J. M. Edwards of Norfolk, Virginia. The accident occurred during a training dogfight. Edwards was killed, and Dean bailed out with a broken rib. The first people Dean called to his bedside at the hospital were Voris and Tex Harris, who had become XO. "We patched it up there. He grabbed my hand and arm and I could tell our problem was over. From then on, we were very close."

SIX MONTHS LATER

CHAPTER 13

Butch had a nagging feeling, a premonition. It was gnawing at him. He wasn't going to return tomorrow.

His number was up.

He couldn't shake it.

He was going to die.

It was evening in the ready room's dim red light, illuminated in this way so the pilots launching that night could get used to the darkness in which they would be flying. He was posting, as he usually did, the next day's assignments on the squadron's blackboard, using chalk wetted in a glass of water to write the names so they'd shine and be easily seen in the crimson hue. The Rippers, along with other squadrons in the task force, were hitting the Japanese airfields on Guam in the Marianas the following afternoon. They'd be tasked with destroying the enemy's planes as a preliminary to the invasion that was scheduled to follow. D-day in Europe, June 6, 1944, had occurred only four days before. Fighting 2, leaving *Enterprise* early in the new year, was now part of Air Group 2; their original air group, on *Hornet,* (CV12) the new Essex-class "fast carrier" that had replaced the older namesake (CV8) Butch had watched sink at the Battle of Santa Cruz. He continued chalking in the names, setting up the sections and divisions, including his own, which would participate in the next day's raid.

But the feeling persisted.

"I can't explain it. It was in the pit of my stomach. An apprehension. We'd been through a lot of combat, so it wasn't the jitters. I'd never had this before and never would again. It was just a gut feeling that the next day wasn't going to be a good one."

For over two months, since they had boarded the new carrier and left Pearl Harbor in mid-March, the large task force, designated 58 and broken into four smaller groupings (58.1, 58.2, etc.) for separate missions, had ranged across the vast Central Pacific like a monster swarm of killer bees, attacking Japanese strongholds from Palau, nearest the Philippines, to New Guinea in the south, and Truk in the central Carolines. The task force had sixteen carriers of various sizes in the four subgroups. He had a large map covering one wall in his meager stateroom on which he was plotting the movement. Surprise and hit-and-run had been the tactics. The Japanese, with small exception, hadn't been able to keep up with them. The task force, commanded by Rear Admiral Marc Mitscher, had caused considerable destruction. It had been gratifying. Mitscher, an Oklahoma native, was one of the original naval aviation pioneers, a graduate of the first formal flight class at Pensacola in 1916. He'd commanded the previous *Hornet* (CV8) when Doolittle had lifted his Tokyo Raiders from it early in 1942 and, a few months later, at Midway. Like most of Nimitz's admirals, Mitscher was aggressive. Now they were starting a bold new leg that would swing them up north, toward Japan proper, beginning with the Marianas, which the Allies hoped to convert into bases from which landed bombers could, hopefully soon, begin assaulting the enemy at his heart—Tokyo and the home islands.

Butch had been in the thick of it.

At Palau, he'd helped strafe and sink a Japanese hospital ship, among others, leaving it to clog the harbor entrance. Intelligence had indicated that some of the enemy high command staff were trying to sneak away on it. That's all the justification for attacking the normally off-limits target they had needed. Approximately 150 Japanese planes had been destroyed at Palau and over 100,000 tons of enemy shipping sunk, according to historians. New Guinea, in Butch's recollection, had been relatively easy. "A few buildings, little opposition." Truk had been a surprise, in that VF-2 hadn't encountered the resistance the squadron had expected from such a major Japanese base, often compared to America's Pearl Harbor in size and importance. The Japanese, apparently sighting the task force prior to the attack, had moved much of their fleet out of the stronghold.

Through it all, he'd continued piling up the missions, bombing and strafing. He hadn't yet shot down another enemy plane. But his section leader, Mike Wolf, whose wife had just delivered a baby—making him the youngest father in the squadron—had. True, the fighting was getting more desperate, especially for the Japanese, who were now on the defensive. He'd watched squadron mates vomiting—"putting the bird," they called it—before launching, the fear for some was so intense. But it hadn't been that way for him. He had a coping mechanism. "Sure, your heart rate builds. It's like before a football game. But once you crank up the engine, you're a different person. Your bodily and mental processes go into, I don't know, very methodical condition." At least his did. "It's like you've got guns in your hands and you're pointing them and shooting them. But they're in the wings and you're pointing the airplane . . . All of us believe it's the other guy who is going to get killed. Otherwise you're scared, and you can't operate scared."

Even with the Japanese fleet largely absent—thus depleting the number of juicy targets—the three days of raids on Truk had been highly fruitful. Scores of Japanese planes and many ships in and around the harbor had been destroyed. However, rushing back after receiving an "Expedite Charlie"—code for return to the carrier quickly—his tailhook had missed the wires. He'd hit the crash barrier, upended, and had to endure taunts from Rippers whom he'd constantly lectured about proper recovery.

But that was only embarrassing, not frightening.

There was really no reason he could think of for the portent.

But he couldn't flush it. He kept it to himself.

After finishing the blackboard assignments, he'd gone to his stateroom and decided to pen a letter to his parents—a rare occurrence since he didn't write a lot. "I can't remember exactly what I said, but it was a little warmer than usual. Nothing about the premonition. I didn't want to worry them. It was just a little longer and maybe more thoughtful [than before] because I figured it might be my last."

The next morning, returning to the ready room, he'd placed the letter in the makeshift mailbox they had there to be taken from the ship and later delivered. He doesn't know what happened to it. It was a Sunday. Their launch time was one p.m. Normally they'd been striking at dawn but Admiral Mitscher, he said, thought that if they deviated they could catch the Japanese "in the O club drinking saki. We had that mentality because that's where *we* would be. But we figured wrong."

The two airfields they were going to hit on Guam were Agana and Orote, perhaps five miles apart and believed to be lined with aircraft. Dean led the raid: fifteen Hellcats, with Voris leading his two-section division. Other carriers were sending in fighters, too. But the Rippers would be first.

They launched about two hundred miles north of the island. The approach was without incident. They kept low over the water, which was their practice in order to avoid possible radar. The weather over the target, when they reached it, was clear, with low clouds, according to the after-action report, although they encountered intermittent squalls. The north side of the island had high ridges or mountains. They went up in order to clear them and then came back down on the airfields "guns blazing." There weren't as many planes on the ground as they expected. They only saw five twin-engine Nakajima "Gekko" night fighters, or "Irvings" as they were code-named by the Allies, some of which they left burning. But there were plenty of guns.

The antiaircraft fire was the heaviest the squadron had encountered. After one or two sweeps, the Hellcat of Lieutenant (j.g.) Howard Duff Jr., from Ridley Park, Pennsylvania, one of the most popular Rippers and a good pilot, was hit by ground fire. He radioed, "I'm going down five miles north of Orote," according to the after-action report. He was high over adjacent waters. Lieutenant (j.g.) Dan Carmichael Jr., saw Duff's smoking Hellcat make a good splash landing and Duff emerge from the cockpit into the water. It was probably at that time that the missing Japanese fighters from the base—approximately thirty of them—were first spotted diving down from above.

"The reason they weren't on the field was they were waiting for us," said Butch. Apparently, earlier contacts with the task force in which Japanese reconnaissance planes had been shot down had alerted the enemy. "They were coming down on our backs. I heard people saying, 'Look out. Look out. They're coming down.' It's an old trick [hiding in the sun]. You're looking for them when you come in, but you don't see them. You can't sit around wondering where they are. You've got to go ahead and do your strike."

Was his premonition coming to fruition?

"The thought never crossed my mind. Once we launched, I'd forgotten about it."

His coping mechanism had clicked in.

A huge melee erupted—planes fighting other planes throughout the visible sky.

The first thing Voris did was to pull up. "When you hear they're coming down, that's what you do." A stream of them were at his two o'clock (a position comparable to the numbers on the face of a watch). He estimates they had started down from as high as 30,000 feet.

One Zero, reddish brown, red "meatballs" on the wings, had targeted him. But with Butch rising, the attacker overshot.

"They get going very fast. You make such a move and they can't stop."

Voris thinks he was at about 800 to 1,000 feet altitude. He zipped in behind his flustered attacker, started drawing a bead.

The advantage had suddenly shifted.

The Zero pilot swung left, then right, losing energy, which slowed him down. He was trying to see his pursuer. But Voris was in his blind spot. It was almost a repeat of the time he himself had been trapped thusly near Guadalcanal. He moved closer. When he got approximately one thousand feet from his prey, he fired his guns. "Short bursts. Don't want to burn them out. You can't see him, but you can see the cockpit and the wings."

He hit the thrashing Zero near the wingroot, where the wing meets the fuselage and a vulnerable spot on the plane because of its proximity to fuel cells. Pieces started flying. Then the canopy came off. "Either I hit it or he was trying to bail out." They were above land. "He rolled over on his back and went in." Out of the corner of his eye, Voris saw a fiery explosion. "By that time, I was looking for somebody else."

All around him, individual air battles raged. Every conceivable maneuver he would later amplify, choreograph, and elongate for the benefit of Blue Angel air show spectators was happening for real all around him either to save lives or to take them—in the frantic melee.

He was in the midst of the ultimate air show.

But, of course, he wasn't thinking about that now.

Dean, according to the after-action report, had been "circling in search of Duff" when tracers started zipping by him. He and his wingman, Lieutenant (j.g.) Dave Parks of Houston, Texas, had immediately risen and "chandelled (turned on the rising fuselage's axis) to the right and left respectively" and met descending attackers.

Dean eventually shot down four enemy fighters; Parks, two or three (one was a probable).

The first "Zeke" Mike Wolf saw was streaking in at him head-on. He fired at it, causing it to veer, giving him a larger target for a second squeeze of shots. They penetrated the Zero's side. "It blew up," he says in the after-action report. Another Zeke challenged him. He got behind it, chased it, "firing several bursts and got it on the third or fourth burst. Fragments flew all over." A third enemy he attacked in a steep dive. When the pilot bailed out, Wolf was out of ammunition, so he intentionally flew through the man's parachute, severing him from it and killing him. "I was afraid the guy was going to land where Duff was," he explained over half a century later. "Maybe [the Japanese] who were getting in boats to pick up their own would come to rescue him and kill Duff."

Unlike in the European airwar, where downed Allied pilots and crew were generally treated decently by the Germans in prisoner-of-war camps, captured American flyers in the Pacific were warned that they stood a good chance of being tortured and beheaded. Wolf believes that at least one of those fates happened to Duff, who, after the air battle and his fleetingly observed moments in the water, was never seen again. "It's my understanding that the diary of the Japanese commander there [on Guam] says that they brought Duff into the town square and chopped off his head." While that couldn't be confirmed for this book, there are numerous accounts of beheadings of Americans, including pilots, by the Japanese in the Pacific. The most notable are of a crew of the Doolittle Raiders who crashed and were captured after their strike on Tokyo, and American naval flyers picked up in the water following the Battle of Midway. Some were on Guam.

Whatever happened to Duff, Voris wasn't long from his kill, perhaps thirty seconds, when he heard another warning over the radio about more Zeros coming down. He saw another of the attackers winging in at his side, roughly at his ten o'clock. "The guy, I don't think saw me, otherwise why would he be there?" He had a perfect shot, the enemy plane crossing in front of him. He fired. He saw flames erupt on the target and the yeoman keeping his log book penned in the kill, indicating he also believed Voris got two. But he was quickly distracted by other threats and did not see the plane go down. The kill was also not confirmed by any other squadron member, which, while the rule, was not surprising, given the chaotic nature of the fighting. Therefore it wasn't credited to him.

Eventually, the Rippers were credited with twenty-three enemy planes shot out of the skies over Guam that day. Several more kills by Ripper CAP over the carrier and a second sweep-strike to Guam later in the day brought the VF-2 total for June 11 to thirty-seven, approximately half of the total shoot-downs for the entire task force that day and easily a one-day navy record up to that time. Fighting 2 was earning a reputation. But few, if any, in the first Guam strike that day, including Voris, were aware of that fact as the remaining enemy planes fled and the squadron regrouped. They were concerned with Duff. But unable to spot him, they flew back to *Hornet*. Trapping on the deck, Wolf was puzzled at the pointings by deck personnel at his taxiing plane. He wondered if he had damage he didn't know about. When he got out, he saw the remains of the Japanese parachute he'd destroyed hanging from his tail. It had been flying like a flag as he'd made his curling approach to the deck.

"We had *Life* photographers on board, and it wasn't the kind of thing we wanted them to see," said Voris. Years later, he would be quoted in a book by James R. Whelan: "I remember reading paperback novels about World War I aviators, the Germans, the French, the Americans. How they would wave to each other when they ran out of ammunition, almost a salute, 'I'll come back and see you tomorrow.' It was an unspoken bond between people of this calling. That may not have been carried on in that same tradition in World War II because the character of the opponent was different. We got into shooting people out of their parachutes after they bailed out. It became bitter."

Voris would get an up-close, infantryman's look at the savagery of which he spoke several months later on a trip to just-secured Saipan, the next Mariana island north of Guam. In early July, after Saipan was officially declared conquered, he would fly there escorting a TBF torpedo bomber carrying top-secret photographs. With some time to kill because of unexpected repairs needed for the bomber, he'd gone to the end of the island with a friend from high school, an army pilot, where marines were still extracting recalcitrant Japanese soldiers from caves. During the trip, they found a little girl, "scared to death," hiding in a cliff dwelling. Her back had been split open with what they believed to be a Japanese bayonet. The wound was so deep that her ribs were visible. Driving her back in a jeep for medical care, they saw a dead marine flyer, USMC stenciled on his flight suit, hanging by a noose in a tree. His genitals and part of his face had been slashed and removed at least a week prior, they guessed. And since there was lots of blood around the wounds, they believed the mutilation had been done while the pilot was still alive.

"A dead body doesn't usually pump blood," said Voris, the former mortician. "We knew this kind of thing was happening, which was why people hesitated to bail out. You'd get shot out of your chute, or worse, so we did the same thing. No one talked about it. We had the *Life* photographers on board. You just did it [killed parachuting Japanese pilots]. Anybody that's an enemy in the air, you just went after them."

Prior to finding the little girl and the mutilated marine, they'd gotten as close as two hundred feet from the caves where the mopping-up was being done. The marines weren't taking many prisoners. "They were smoking them out with flamethrowers. You could see the Japs run out and just go up like you put a match to an ant." It was a hellish scene, he agreed. "But that's what war is."

On June 12, the day after the squadron's record-breaking score over Guam, the Rippers returned to the island and shot down eleven more Japanese fighters—but not without loss. The big guns there were probably better prepared for their aerial targets on the second day. Lieutenant (j.g.) D. "Demi" Lloyd, of Washington, D.C., was hit by antiaircraft fire and crashed. John Searcy, a short Texan who liked to wear flashy pistols, was also hit by the five-inch Japanese artillery but made a successful water landing and was rescued by a submarine stationed off the island specifically to help downed flyers.

Butch and Wolf were along on the morning raid. During it, the "lifeguard" submarine suddenly broadcast a call for help. It was under attack by a Japanese bomber. Voris peeled off to aid, Wolf following. The Hellcats, by this time, had an afterburner, probably one of the first to be put in navy fighters. It injected into the fuel a water-alcohol mix that made it more volatile and gave the fighter a burst of speed. The sub needed help immediately. Butch engaged the new afterburner, glad, among other things, to get a chance to increase his shootdown score. But the afterburner's switch wouldn't work. He watched with frustration as Wolf's afterburner kicked in and moved his section leader past him.

The bomber turned out to be one of the swift new Nakajima "Irvings." It ran from the sub at the first sight of Wolf, who began chasing it low over the water. "The gun on the tail [of the Irving] was more powerful than my .50 calibers, so I had to stay back. The plane was fast anyway." It looked like he might lose the Irving, so he started lifting his nose and "lofting" periodic shots in an arc to get more distance. "But when I raised my nose"—showing more of his fuselage—"I was a good target for the back gunner. We did a dance for a while. I wondered if I'd get him." Finally, one of the lofted shots penetrated the Irving and "it went right in the water." It was Wolf's fifth kill. He'd gotten his first when the squadron had been on *Enterprise*. Wolf was an ace.

On the following day, June 13, Ensign D. C. "Red" Brandt, a Ripper from Cincinnati, Ohio, was shot down by the big Japanese guns in a third day of sweeps over Guam. He was in the water and okay but too close to the shore for the submarine to surface and be safe from the shore batteries. So, in a novel approach, he grabbed hold of the sub's periscope and held on as it pulled him far enough out to safely surface and pick him up. The ride had its problems though. Protective grease on the periscope made it hard for Brandt to keep his grip and the sub had to start and stop many times. As a result, said Butch, the Rippers were the cause of a new navy pilot issue: a kind of lariat that they could affix to the greasy pole in order to hold on.

CHAPTER 14

Since failing to stop the American takeover of Guadalcanal, the Japanese fleet had retreated to safe waters to await an opportunity for a decisive battle. They hoped to spring a trap with which to defeat the American fleet. When the United States (Task Force 58, including the Rippers) went after the Marianas—Guam, Saipan, and Tinian, in particular—they decided they could no longer afford to wait. Seizure of the Central Pacific island chain threatened anew Japanese shipping to the East Indies and Southeast Asia and put the home islands within reach of Allied land-based, long-range heavy bombers. A plan to destroy Task Force 58 was instituted.

The plan, to be carried out by Vice Admiral Jisaburo Ozawa, commander of the fleet containing most of Japan's flattops, called for nine carriers with approximately 450 aircraft to strike the American task force in four waves from the southwest. The carriers would try to approach undetected and launch outside the range of the American planes. Helping the Japanese fleet would be land-based aircraft from the Marianas, fighters, and bombers flown in from Truk and Palau and other Japanese bases that would increase the number of attacking Japanese aircraft to some 650 planes in all. In addition, Ozawa's carrier planes were to fly on to Guam, refuel, and reattack the Allied task force on their return to the Japanese carriers, thereby further increasing the number of sorties against the enemy.

To meet the threat, Mitscher had approximately twice as many carriers (sixteen), nearly 900 aircraft, and, on the average, more experienced pilots. Many of the veteran Japanese aviators had been killed by this time. The Americans, for the first time in the war, had the larger and seemingly better trained force in a pending naval engagement with the Japanese. Mitscher also had the advantage of knowing the Japanese were coming. Code busters, coast watchers, and submarines were supplying him with crucial intelligence. Nevertheless, the Japanese, largely unaware of American advantages, were determined. A furious fight, which both sides wanted, was in the offing. Known as "The First Battle of the Philippine Sea," and including "The Great Marianas Turkey Shoot," as its start would be named, it would be the largest carrier clash in history. For Voris, who would be thrown in at a crucial time, it would be the beginning of the most intense period of combat he and the Rippers would experience.

★

Butch didn't know it at the time, but the June 11 raids on Guam in which he'd shot down one confirmed Zero and claimed another had helped Task Force 58 eliminate fully one-third of the land-based planes Ozawa was counting on to help him in the coming attack. Ironically, Ozawa himself didn't know about the disaster that had overtaken him. Because of strict rules prohibiting radio traffic about the planned attack, his commanders in the Marianas didn't message him.

On June 13, Ozawa's carriers, split into two elements, exited safe waters around Borneo and headed northeast toward the Philippines and the fateful clash. The following day, June 14, Mitscher, receiving reports about Ozawa's movements, sent *Hornet,* the carrier of his closest to the target, up north toward the Bonin Islands to strike Japanese airfields that he believed might supply the enemy with additional planes for the impending battle. The Bonins were approximately 540 miles from Japan proper, as close to the homeland as any American combatants had gotten, save those on the Doolittle Raid, in submarines, and unfortunate prisoners of war. Mitscher was right in his hunch. The Rippers found the enemy massing over airfields at Chichi Jima and at Iwo Jima south of Chichi. Multiple dogfights ensued. The Rippers shot down seventeen Zeros without a loss. Butch wasn't on the mission. In a gesture of fairness, he and Dean only sent pilots who, up to that time, had no kills. One of them, Lieutenant Lloyd "Barney" Barnard, who would later be among the first pilots tapped by Voris to help him start the Blue Angels, accounted for five of the shoot-downs, becoming an ace on the single mission. The seventeen gave the Rippers fifty-four shoot-downs in three days, which was among if not the best in the navy up to that time.

By the eighteenth, both fleets were searching for the other, each on high alert for the moment when the enemy was exactly pinpointed and planes could be launched. Despite the fact that Mitscher had excellent intelligence, Ozawa was constantly moving, and although the two fleets were closing on each other, the Japanese ships, now past the Philippines and in vast open waters, had not been seen for several days. Task Force 58, too, was elusive. While generally in an area off Saipan to defend that island's invasion, it was constantly moving. At one point during the eighteenth, aerial scouts for both forces sighted each other almost simultaneously. The American scout, a Hellcat, shot down his Japanese counterpart. Although neither task force had been sighted, both sides now knew the clash was imminent.

June 19, 1944, dawned clear with calm seas. Just before sunrise, Japanese scouts spotted the American task force. The scouts were shot down, but they got the coordinates out and the battle was on. Task Force 58 radars first began picking up sizable blips in the direction of Guam, the closest enemy position to the American carriers. Less than an hour later, according to Barrett Tillman in *Hellcat: The F6F in World War II,* pilots from VF-24 on *Belleau Wood* were launched and found numerous Zeros mustering above Guam's Orote airfield. Some sources say there were as many as fifty Zekes on the ground and in the air. The *Belleau Wood* Hellcats numbered only four. Radioing for help, according to Tillman, they jumped in and, despite being outnumbered, "claimed ten shot down for one F6F damaged."

One of the reasons the Hellcats did so well was their heavy armor and penetrating .50-caliber machine guns. Over and over in after-action reports, American pilots testified that they needed only a few hits on the Zeros and other Japanese planes to see them explode in flames or begin disintegrating in other ways while their Hellcats, with self-sealing gas tanks that the Japanese planes did not have, could absorb many hits from the smaller caliber Japanese guns and still, in many cases, continue flying and fighting.

Responding to the call for help over Orote, more Hellcats arrived and observed what can be called feverish launching by the Japanese, who, ac-

cording to an account in *World War II in the Air: The Pacific,* "were haul-
ing gassed-up, armed planes out of the tree-covered revetments and
pushing them off into the air with all the determination of bees swarm-
ing." The Hellcats eventually shot down thirty-five of the enemy planes
without, according to the account, stopping the determined launchings.

The Japanese were pulling out all the stops.

Ozawa's first launch from his carriers was at 7:30 a.m.—a swarm of
some sixty fighters and bombers. As he'd hoped, he was beyond the range
of the American planes. He could launch without fear of being attacked
by the task force—at least if he kept his distance. But his aerial swarm
was picked up by radars. The closest carriers were south of *Hornet,* and
they launched 74 Hellcats from eight different squadrons to meet the
bandits, according to Tillman in *Hellcat Aces of World War II.* Some forty
minutes behind was a second Ozawa launch of 109 planes, writes Tillman, who adds that 162 Hellcats were in turn sent up by Mitscher to
meet those. Never before had so many opposing planes been in the air at
one time aiming to do battle with each other. In effect now, there were
intermittent bunches of enemy airplanes heading for Task Force 58 both
from the south, where Ozawa was positioned, and from the north, from
Guam. Large dogfights erupted all along the linear stream as groups of
American defenders intercepted the attackers. It was into this maelstrom
at about 9:30 a.m. that Butch and a group of Rippers launched.

Some Rippers were already flying a scheduled combat air patrol over
Hornet and so were immediately involved. Tex Harris and Tex Vineyard
got a kill each. But Butch and the others, including Dean, weren't on
CAP and had been anxiously awaiting launch since predawn, some of
them sleeping in makeshift hammocks erected in the ready room. "We'd
been up since 3:00 a.m.," said Butch. "We were living in the ready room.
We knew they were coming." Early on, they must have gotten indications
of the battles that were starting, but they had to wait until the squadron
was called. That call appears to have come as the morning fighting at
Orote increased, because Guam was their stated destination when the
ready room's private intercom finally blared, "Pilots, man your planes."
Butch doesn't remember running out, but undoubtedly the room emptied
quickly. Who was flying and with whom had already been posted on the
blackboard and crucial details worked out. It was now just a matter of
getting on with it.

They launched in a group of what the records confusedly list alternately as eight or ten Hellcats beginning at approximately 9:30 a.m. Dean was in the lead; Voris headed the second division, which included Wolf's section. They were vectored to approximately 30,000 feet in order to be above any incoming enemies, Voris remembers, and they started having unexpected engine trouble. "The engines started backfiring and cutting out. We hadn't been up that high and didn't have the pressurization." In the thin air, sparks from the contact points in the magnetos were "arcing." Uncontained by the thicker air of the lower altitudes, the arcs were jumping around, not connecting in the cylinders to ignite the fuel where they should. The problem would later be fixed. But that was no help at the moment. The planes were sputtering, belching smoke, hesitating in the climb. Voris and undoubtedly others were beginning to worry when a "Hey, Rube" was suddenly broadcast from *Hornet*.

"Hey, Rube," like "Expedite Charlie," was code meant to get planes back to the carrier quick. Different commanders used different codes. According to Tillman in *Hellcat,* Mitscher, around ten a.m., saw so many Japanese planes on radar heading toward the task force that, in addition to launching more planes, he decided to recall fighters in the vicinity of Guam.

Almost as soon as Dean had turned his Hellcats around, they saw below them a large number of enemy bombers escorted by Zeros heading for the task force. "It was one of the few times we were above them," said Voris. "It looked like a huge flock of mallards. They had a lot of speed. Fortunately, we had altitude."

The bandits, according to the after-action report, were at roughly 10,000 feet, about sixty miles from the task force. Apparently they were already being attacked—perhaps by other returning fighters—because Dean is quoted as saying some of the enemy planes were "burning and crashing." He immediately attacked, leading the Ripper Hellcats in a peel-off stream downward. As they dived and picked up speed, their engines returned to normal.

According to Voris, who was right behind him, Dean got going so fast in the dive that he overshot. The Zero Dean was aiming at then got in Voris's sights and he squeezed his trigger. "Everything happened in a split second," recalls Butch. "I was behind [Dean]. Then I saw [the Zero's] cockpit. I was about one thousand feet above him. We were closing fast. He never changed course or tried to get away. I shot." Bullets tore into the

Elimination training gaggle. One screw-up and you're out.
(Courtesy Russ Reiserer)

The first picture the U.S. Navy took of Butch—right after elimination
training. They waited until he'd passed. *(Courtesy Butch Voris collection)*

Butch's first squadron, Fighting 10 (The Grim Reapers), on the flight deck of the USS *Enterprise*, 1942. "Reaper Leader" Jimmy Flatley is kneeling, fifth from the left. Butch is standing in the line behind Flatley, second from the left. *(Courtesy Butch Voris collection)*

Watching the air action over Guadalcanal. Butch, in a white T-shirt, leans on a jeep. Whitey Feightner kneels next to him. Two down is "Wick" Wickendoll, standing in cap and buttoned shirt. Tex Harris is on the end, shirt unbuttoned. *(Courtesy Butch Voris collection)*

Butch in the cockpit of his F4F "Wildcat." *(Courtesy Butch Voris collection)*

VF-2 "Rippers" on the *Enterprise* flight deck, December 1943. This picture was shot shortly after Butch O'Hare was killed. Butch Voris is standing eight heads from the left, sleeves rolled up, pistol bulging. Ripper skipper, Bill Dean, is in the middle standing, two down in the same line as Butch. A strong wind across the deck is evidenced by the blown-back pants on the officer at the end. *(Courtesy Butch Voris collection)*

Butch seconds after landing on the USS *Hornet* following a 1944 combat mission. *(Courtesy Butch Voris collection)*

Blue Angels First
Public Air Show

Craig Field Dedication
15 June 1946

LCDR R.M. "Butch" Voris, USN
First Flight Leader

Rare photograph of the Blue Angels at their first public show, June 15, 1946, at Craig Field, Jacksonville. Butch's Number 1 Hellcat taxis past the bleachers to park. The team wasn't yet named. Not until the planes were parked and silent did the team hear the applause and realize what a hit they were. *(Photo by Menard Norton, courtesy Butch Voris collection)*

One of the first photos of the team in the air. They are flying Hellcats. In the foreground is Butch in Number 1. "Wick" Wickendoll is in Number 2. Mel Cassidy is in Number 3. *(Courtesy Butch Voris collection)*

A precarious moment. In their first show at Pensacola, the dummy of a supposedly parachuting Japanese pilot accidentally got cut loose and landed dangerously close to an admiral who was watching. Butch, fearing the worst, is here trying to explain what happened. The admiral understood. "Just move it out a little further," he said. *(Courtesy Al Taddeo)*

Butch showing a map to the team. From left: Taddeo, Wickendoll, May.
(Courtesy Al Taddeo)

Butch had a big head after starting the Blues—literally. It was too big for the regular navy issue hardhat so, as skipper of the VF-113 "Stingers," he had to buy a football helmet and adapt it for carrier flying. Here he is briefing his pilots in it onboard the USS *Valley Forge*. He painted the helmet yellow, and some in the squadron called him "Old Yellow Hat." *(Courtesy Butch Voris collection)*

Butch, in the Number 1 F-9F Panther jet at the bottom, leads.
(Courtesy Butch Voris collection)

Butch and Thea Young were married in Santa Cruz in 1947, the first of fifty-six years together. Sadly, she passed away in late 2003. *(Courtesy Butch Voris collection)*

CAG Voris inspecting troops at Miramar.
(Courtesy Butch Voris collection)

Butch introducing the Lunar Excursion Module (LEM) as director of public relations for Grumman Corporation. *(Courtesy Grumman Historical Center)*

Declassified photo milliseconds after the midair collision above NAS Corpus Christi, Texas, July 7, 1952. Lieutenant (j.g.) Dwight E. Wood was killed, but Butch miraculously survived. The photo is a double exposure by David Eugene Gebhart, a sailor assigned to photograph the air show. Gebhart later testified that he had the camera trained on the jets when he heard a "bump. I shot the first picture. Then without changing the sheet of film, I shot the second." Butch's jet is the top one. It has extensive damage to the tail not clearly visible. Wood's Panther, with the nose sheared off, is at the bottom. A ruptured wingtip tank from Ray Hawkins's jet is shown streaming colored water, which the Blues carried for effect in the shows. A piece of debris near Voris's tail appears to be in the water but is actually airborne. It could be the nose of Wood's jet. *(Official U.S. Navy photo)*

Close-up of damage to the tail of Butch's jet suffered in the July 7, 1952 midair collision over NAS Corpus Christi. *(Official U.S. Navy photo)*

back of the Zero, behind the cockpit. "Pieces started coming off his airplane. He burned and exploded."

After the initial pass, a fur ball of dogfights erupted. Voris and Dean, who would be credited with two kills in the melee, got separated after diving through the bandits and zooming back up and around for another pass. "You do a 360-degree roll over the top," said Voris. "That's the way you look at them. I came back out of the roll and got another in my sights. I fired, saw pieces flying, but no burning."

Without it being independently observed, he was not credited with the second.

Other pilots, without emotion, testified to the fury of the fight—a swirling, wing-wrenching battle that, at its height, involved perhaps sixty to seventy airplanes.

Lieutenant (j.g.) David R. Park, apparently wingman to Dean, recounted: "I tally-ho'd and my earphones weren't working, so I didn't get any acknowledgment. The skipper [Dean] pulled away from me and went out of sight. I circled and saw a bogey below. I kept my altitude. The Zeke came up toward me; I did a wingover and came down on it from five o'clock. He jinked by, wobbling his wings. Then he did a split S. I hit his wingtips [presumably with gunfire]. Two-thirds of his starboard wing came off and he spun in."

Ensign LeRoy W. Robinson, flying wing to Butch, lost his leader on the first pass and joined up with Dean. "His [Dean's] flight [was] knocking down planes below me . . . I saw the captain [Dean] pull up into a [Zero]. At the same time, I got on one's tail and followed it down until it burned."

Dan Carmichael, who would get three confirmed kills in the battle, said he heard Dean "tally-ho" and then "saw a plane blow up at seven o'clock and another large group below me at eleven o'clock which I tally-ho'd." He and another Ripper "went down in a high side [attack] from five o'clock above. I shot down a Jill [a three-man Nakajima torpedo bomber] and saw it go in spinning and smoking as I pulled up to look at it. I dropped my left wing and saw a Jill alone below me. We went down and tallied in behind it. I could hardly gain on him. I rode him and he wobbled his wings violently from port to starboard. I was having a hard time getting to him. He finally burst into flames at 10,000 [feet]."

Mike Wolf estimated that there were as many as forty-five enemy planes in the groups they fought. He got one confirmed and one probable: "I made an overhead run on a Zeke from 20,000. I came in directly behind it." The Zero pulled out of a dive and tried to loop onto Wolf's tail. But Wolf pulled up and shot it as the plane went into the maneuver. "My pullout was violent and I blacked out, but I got him just as I did so."

Wolf went after several more. "All of the planes when engaged would try to turn, and if you stayed in the turn, they would dive and go into a loop. I would then stay in my dive and get considerable speed, pull out, circle, and climb back on the outside, coming in again from above."

While the Zeros engaged the Hellcats, and the Hellcats shot what bombers they could, the enemy bombers that survived, said Voris, continued on determinedly toward the American fleet. The Hellcats had to let them go, presuming that defenders down the line would stop them, as they themselves continued to attack the nimbler escorts.

When it was over, the Rippers, it was later confirmed, had destroyed twelve enemy planes with no losses of their own. Such tallying, however, was for later. Dean gathered what he could of his flock, got word to continue on toward Guam and set up a CAP there. Voris remembers regrouping and, once they arrived, starting a circular pattern to await more attackers.

Back at the task force, protection was holding nicely. Very few of the bombers that had escaped the Rippers with Dean and Voris had made it through to the ships. Other Hellcat CAP and surface guns spewing barrages mauled the already ravaged attackers. Only isolated intrusions broke the protective screen. Radar, pinpoint fighter direction, sturdier airplanes, and, on average, more experienced and determined pilots began carrying the day for the American fleet. Voris and section leader Wolf, who got separated at the end of the dogfight and had to battle his way home alone through two sandwiching Zeros trying to kill him, remember the rare display later by pilots landing and grinningly holding up fingers for the number of their shoot-downs.

By midday, the aerial kill tallies for the task force were rising into triple figures—with very few Hellcats shot down to offset them. Somewhere during the battle a pilot likened his mission to shooting nonflying turkeys and a name for the budding victory was born: "The Great Marianas Turkey Shoot." Wolf: "We got wrapped up in the scorekeeping, so to speak. It was like a high school football game, everybody cheering the other guy on." Voris plays down the excitement. "No clapping on the back or that sort of thing. As you land airplanes and they come into the ready room, they say, 'Hey, I got a couple. I got mine. But then the air intelligence people grab you and want to know what happened," an exercise he found superfluous because "they were only interested in numbers," not tactics or flying, and "I'm busy with flight ops, getting those ready who have to go out on the next combat hop."

As had become his habit, he was under control.

Earlier in the day, submarines, not restricted by the range problem, had reacquired the Japanese fleet and torpedoed two of Ozawa's most important carriers. At 8:10 a.m., the USS *Albacore* had struck *Taiho*, one of the latest and biggest Japanese flattops and Ozawa's flagship, with a lone torpedo. Several hours later, *Shokaku*, which had participated in the Pearl Harbor attack, the Battle of the Coral Sea, and the Guadalcanal fights, took a spread of torpedoes that, among other damage, ruptured her gas tanks. According to accounts, Japanese naval gas was dangerously unrefined, and rampaging fires fed by seeping gas fumes eventually caused both carriers to sink later in the day. Fighters and bombers still on board went with them. The loss further depleted the numbers of planes the Japanese could throw at the American fleet and caused immediate recovery problems for the returning and transiting enemy planes, which had counted on having the two ships' decks for landing.

Around one p.m., Ozawa's third wave, consisting of nearly fifty Zeros and Aichi D3A "Val" dive-bombers, neared Task Force 58. The Vals, with distinctive fixed-down landing struts, had been prominent in the Pearl Harbor attack. Among those vectored to intercept them were eight Ripper Hellcats, whose pilots, according to their after-action reports, claimed fourteen victories with only minor damage to one of their own. Andy Skon, who had been flying with Butch O'Hare the night O'Hare died, got two, as did Voris's former Reaper mate Bill Blair. The surviving Japanese planes did not enter the fleet screen and instead headed for Guam where they hoped to land, refuel, and return for another try.

Other engagements raged, including one in which Voris's Elimination Training buddy, Russ Reiserer, flying alone, encountered a large flock of enemy planes coming into Orote and downed five. And another in which Ripper ensign Wilber "Spider" Webb, also alone, radioed, "I have forty Japs surrounded" and shot down six. By day's end, the numbers were overwhelming. Some 350 Japanese planes (historians don't agree on the exact numbers) had been shot out of the air or destroyed on the enemy's fields and carriers. VF-2, it is believed, accounted for 47 of the kills. Admiral Mitscher cabled his troops, "The aviators and gunships of this task force have done a job today which will make their country proud."

But the battle wasn't over.

The next day—June 20—it would take a strange, harrowing turn.

CHAPTER 15

Task Force 58 had won a great air victory. But Mitscher and his boss, Admiral Raymond A. Spruance, head of the US Fifth Fleet, main architect of the Central Pacific thrust and a man described by a colleague, according to the *Simon and Schuster Encyclopedia of World War II*, as a "cold-blooded fighting fool," wanted more. Knowing the Japanese carrier fleet was crippled, they realized they had a chance to sink what was left of it before it escaped. Ozawa, shocked at his losses, was in full retreat westward, heading toward the Philippines, hoping to get refueled and rearmed with more planes to continue the fight. If the Americans could get close enough to strike, they could cut the heart out of the Japanese navy.

The chase was on.

First the Fifth Fleet had to find the retreating enemy. "We didn't know where they were," said Butch. "We didn't have any fresh intelligence." Their best guess, based on the just-concluded fight, was southwest, a huge swath of open ocean extending toward the South Pacific and the Philippines from below the Marianas. They headed that way, hoping to close the range, but couldn't start searching until morning because the task force's small number of night fighters was only trained for short-range interception.

The first launch came about an hour before dawn. Voris was part of it. "We had sectors. Three hundred miles out, 50 miles across, 300 miles back. It was a hell of a long way, I'll tell you. We used a dive-bomber with two fighters [in each sector]. The dive-bomber did the navigating. None of us had electronic navigation. We had to get low, use the natural surroundings, like reading the surface of the water . . . The whitecaps would tell you which way the wind was blowing and let you estimate its force. Then you crank that into your Ouija board–type plotting. After 650 miles, you hope your navigation is good and [when you return] the carrier will be where you think it is."

They didn't find anything. Voris and the first searchers returned exhausted. Pressure was building. If they lost the enemy, they'd blow a perfect chance. When would they get another? A group of searchers, leaving around 1:30 p.m., was told to go even farther than the previous scouts, stretching the range of their planes and extra gas tanks to the limit. The move paid off. "They adjusted the quadrants more to the east," said Voris, "and ran into a seaplane." Morrissey records that Ripper Lieutenant A. Van Haren Jr., of San Gabriel, California, shot it down. "That meant that the [Japanese] fleet was out there somewhere because they were too far from land for it to have come from a base."

Bolstered by the sighting, the search intensified. At around 3:30 p.m., according to most sources, scout planes and then even submarines finally found the retreating fleet. It was approximately two hundred miles to the west, practically the limit for the task force's planes when attacking and carrying a large, gas-guzzling bomb load, as opposed to extra tanks for the searches. In addition, it was already late in the afternoon. By the time any strikers returned from the distant strike, it would be dark. With the exception of the relatively few night fighters in Task Force 58, Mitscher's pilots weren't trained for night landings. He could lose many planes, wrote Theodore Taylor, a Mitscher biographer. But "every second of indecision . . . brought nightfall closer." The pilots, planners believed, needed at least some light for a successful attack. In his after-action report, Mitscher himself wrote that taking advantage of the momentary, late-afternoon opportunity "was going to cost us a great deal in planes and pilots." But the enemy fleet "could be destroyed once and for all."

He gave the order to sound the bullhorns.

Voris: "I was in my bunk in my stateroom sleeping when I guess it was emergency flight quarters that was broadcast. That gets your attention. It's loud, goes to every part of the ship." Still in the flight suit he'd worn on the morning's mission, he rushed to the ready room. "I looked at the ticker machine and it gave the latest sighted positions—bearing, distance, and so forth." The message, reprinted by Morrissey in *Odyssey,* says, in part:

> HAVE RECEIVED FOLLOWING CONTACT REPORT, ENEMY FLEET SIGHTED . . . THERE ARE 2 MAYBE 3 GROUPS OF ENEMY VESSELS . . . ONE GROUP IS NORTH OF THE POSITION GIVEN . . . THIRD GROUP IS ONE CV [CARRIER] AND MANY SHIPS. TWO LARGE CARRIERS AND TWO OR THREE LARGE CRUISERS AND TEN DESTROYERS IN NORTH GROUP X SOUTH GROUP LOOKS LIKE TWO SMALLER CARRIERS, TWO OILERS AND DD [DESTROYERS] . . . RETURNING TO BASE X.

Voris gathered the pilots he'd already chalked in for the mission, as did other division leaders, like Dean, whose "forebodings" about the coming action, wrote Morrissey, "were expressed in the somber act of checking his waterproof flashlight." They all raced to the flight deck. An ordnance decision had already been made to put a five-hundred-pound bomb on each of the Hellcats, which normally didn't carry them. "I'd been sleeping when they'd made that decision," said Voris, "so I didn't even know it until I got up on the flight deck and there they were. So, hey, I got a bomb. All right. That means I gotta drop it on something. But it's going to drag on the airplane so we're going to have less fuel reserve."

At approximately four p.m., according to VF-2's after-action report, barely a half hour after receiving the Japanese position, the hurried task force's carriers swung into the wind and prepared to launch. The first wave, according to Butch, consisted of 84 Hellcats, 14 of which were from the *Hornet,* 75 dive-bombers, each carrying a thousand-pound bomb, and 54 TBF Avengers laden with torpedoes, bombs of various sizes, and rockets—213 planes in all. (Some accounts give higher figures.) "Taxiing up to the takeoff position, Fly One's got an enlisted man with headphones and a blackboard beside him. He's the talker, and he's holding up a new enemy position. It's got bearing, course, and distance. Only the distance has changed. The new distance is a hundred miles farther. We're hot. We're wound up to go. That's one hundred miles more than we expected. Right then we knew we weren't going to get everybody back. The torpedo planes with the big torpedoes, they knew they couldn't make it. Couldn't possibly make it. Most of the fighters probably could.

We all knew the situation. But you don't say, 'Hey, I'm not going.' You're up there. You go."

The original transmissions from the searchers had been in error. As they rechecked their figures coming home, they relayed the longer distance.

Who knows what Mitscher would have done had he first known the true distance. He canceled a second strike planned for later.

But the first strike was on its way.

Voris: "We climbed to about 18,000 to 20,000 feet, using as little power as necessary." After rendezvous, the huge mass of warplanes— "clouds of iron" in today's vernacular—headed in streams directly into the setting sun, a blazing but darkening reminder of the immutable problem they all faced. Air Group 2, including the Rippers, was in the lead (perhaps because *Hornet* might have been the westernmost carrier in the task force). According to accounts, the flight, radiowise, was largely silent, devoid of the usual routine banter. "It was a tough situation," said Voris. However, as the flight continued, according to the VF-2 after-action report, pilots were periodically "heard to report over their interplane system (VHF) that half of their gas was gone. Fighters were more fortunate, having a greater reserve."

After nearly three hours of flight, the armada found its prey.

Voris: "I was off to the right of the skipper with my four-plane, and I remember him wagging his wings. About the same time I looked out in the distance and there maybe sixty miles ahead—you could see that far from up there—you could make out the wakes of the carrier task group. They'd gone to full speed because the water was churning. You couldn't see the ships because the sun was setting. They were turning into the wind, which meant they had some airplanes on board and were launching. They'd gotten us on radar, I guess. You could see the pure grinding whitewater and the long arcs of the whole force turning."

It was approximately 6:45 p.m., according to most accounts, perhaps twenty minutes of daylight left.

The approaching darkness would be the enemy's greatest shield.

The American flyers had to hurry.

Voris: "We kept going until we got to the point where we could see what type of ships there were." It was the task force all right—carriers, battleships, cruisers, and destroyers, some thirty ships in three distinct groupings. The planes readied for their attack. "The torpedo planes go down first because they have to make their runs low to the water. They get down to about 100 feet. The dive-bombers stay high and push over from about 10,000 [feet]. They want a steep angle. We go in ahead of them. Hopefully, if everything's perfect, the dive-bombers and torpedo planes arrive at the same time [forcing enemy gun decisions. Aim high or low?]. We're ahead of them suppressing antiaircraft fire and, in this case, dropping a bomb."

The Ripper Hellcats—first to reach the enemy, according to the after-action report—peeled off in trail, Dean in the lead. Below them, the enemy carriers, apparently having already launched some seventy planes—all the operational defenders Ozawa had left—were maneuvering desperately at high speed, trying to make themselves as hard to hit as possible. "We went in steep, building up speed." He said they took a sixty-degree angle. Almost immediately, they ran into "horrific" antiaircraft fire. "The whole force was shooting at us. I remember most the color of the smoke"— darkly beautiful lavenders, purples, pinks—a palette of death in the savage sunset. "They [the shells] were set for a certain altitude."

Despite the murderous barrage, said Voris, "you go on down until you can see the whites of their eyes. What you're trying to do is kill the gunners on the decks with your .50 calibers or make them take cover so that the bombers and torpedo planes can get in there effectively." Dean had picked out a large carrier, later identified as *Zuikaku,* monster sister ship to *Shokaku,* sunk the day before, and veteran of the Coral Sea and Guadalcanal battles. Its planes had damaged *Lexington* and *Yorktown.* They were diving toward its starboard side, just ahead of the middle island. "I can still see it now, turning hard to port," recalls Voris. The defensive circle it was steaming made any straight-on shot harder. "I'm in about a sixty-degree high dive. Lots of speed . . . You've got to be on a trajectory. You've figured the bombing angle, the lead . . ."

Guns blazing, shells exploding, he released at about two thousand feet. "Where the hell the bomb ever hits, you don't know. Bombs are going off everywhere, in the water, some on the flight deck. People are saying, 'That's my bomb!' 'No, it's mine.' [Dean claimed a direct hit, according to the after-action.] I don't know whether mine hit the ship or not. I had pretty good aspect. Now you've got to pull out. You're going like hell and [after leveling the plane and passing low over the carrier], you're on top of the water, jinking [moving the plane erratically so as not to be a predictable target]. You've got to get out of their screen"—the formation of ships' guns positioned to protect the carrier. "The battleships are firing at you. The cruisers are firing at you. Everybody's firing. It's a wonder you ever get through it. You just clench your asshole and ride. I don't think you breathe."

As he'd dived down from the high altitude, it had gotten "darker and darker. It was much lighter when you're above." By the time he'd dropped his bomb, the sun had gone below the horizon. It was twilight. "You cross the screen and you start up. It's getting black and dark in a hurry. You know it's a long way home." He looked for Dean. "We're high speed. I'm flying second division. One of my big jobs was to protect him. That's why I didn't shoot more down. I couldn't go out free-firing. I had to stick with him."

Zooming through approximately five thousand feet, he became aware of a Zero. "I caught him out of the corner of my eye. I'm climbing up and he flies right in front of me. I almost ran into him. I think he was lost. A lot of their best pilots were dead by then." At no more than five hundred feet away, he squeezed the trigger on his control stick and saw his bullets "peel back the side of the airplane," ripping a jagged line perhaps twenty feet along it. The cockpit shattered and pieces started flying. He could see the dark silhouette of an "individual. He probably was wishing he never joined the navy . . . He didn't burn but I knew he was dead."

It was the Rippers' only air-to-air kill in the attack.

He continued over the disintegrating Zero and joined the others. "We're only making one run. You don't turn back. We started home."

Behind him, other task force planes were just beginning their runs, or still approaching the dive or peel-off points—Hellcats, Avengers, and Dauntlesses from many different squadrons. They would score numerous hits, fight through Zeros trying to protect the enemy ships. Approximately half the estimated seventy Zeros defending the enemy fleet were shot down, while the United States, according to *Hellcat Aces,* lost six planes, including those felled by antiaircraft fire. Undoubtedly the lack of gas for maneuvering in dogfights, and the high resolve of the Americans to deliver bombs in spite of the defenses, figured into their losses. Wilbur Morrison, in *Pilots, Man Your Planes!* tells of a TBF pilot, Lieutenant George P. Brown, who purposely drew the fire of a line of ships, including a carrier and battleship, in order for other Avengers in his *Yorktown* squadron to approach less opposed and deliver their torpedoes.

Brown and his crew didn't make it.

Some forty minutes after the attack had begun, at approximately

7:20 p.m., the last task force plane lifted out of the enemy screen. Beneath it, the fleeing Japanese fleet was burning and in disarray but still steaming westward. The carrier *Hiyo,* a converted passenger liner with the capacity to carry fifty planes, was on fire. The crews who had benefited from Lieutenant Brown's heroic act, according to Morrissey, saw as they zoomed out, the medium-sized flattop "roll slowly over and sink." *Zuikaku* was damaged but survived for one more action. Ozawa's own log, according to sources, showed that out of the 430 planes he had begun the battle with the day before, only 35 remained. In addition, two oilers, the ships that furnished the enemy fuel and other vital supplies, had been sunk.

✭

Winging home, Voris and his division were in a loose stream with Dean at the lead. "It's getting blacker now. We have no radio navigation. It's all by the seat of the pants."

Others followed, some together, some alone.

Voris: "We started climbing. Didn't go very high, maybe 10,000 feet." The Hellcats had charts on sliding boards under the instrument panels. They had plotted their way in and hoped to retrace their steps. But even if that were possible in the obscuring and unfamiliar darkness, there was no guarantee the task force would be where they'd left it. It was moving. Hopefully it was coming toward them.

But they didn't know.

Many of the strike planes now had battle damage, making the return that much harder.

About a half hour into the return, said Voris, "Torpedo planes started calling out: 'Ditching . . . Out of gas.' It was just one after another. They'd usually try to land in the water before they ran out of gas so they'd have some control. They'd rather do that than try to dead-stick it at night."

No control into the water was near suicide.

The calls were calm and deliberate, he said.

Soon dive-bombers began going in. "I never heard a raised voice, and I listened to them all on the same frequency."

The returning stream's reckoning eventually proved sound. They finally got close enough to the task force—which *was* coming toward them—to be picked up by its radar and receive radio directional codes that allowed them to home in. "But the weather is worsening. It's dark and there's a sea haze," a misty, rising fog, "that reduces your visibility."

The sea itself was relatively calm, but scattered clouds further obscured vision. As the returning planes entered the airspace above the task force, they could only discern the white wakes of the force's ships, not the ships themselves.

How could they find the individual carriers, let alone their decks?

"Mitscher was facing the worst disaster in naval aviation history," wrote Taylor in his biography of the admiral, *The Magnificent Mitscher*. The lucky planes that had made it back were almost out of gas and no deck in sight. To make matters worse, lightning could be seen approaching in the distance, according to Taylor, disorienting some, who actually headed for it. Overhead, the admiral and all below could see the green and red approach lights of the returning planes as they moved erratically over the force, their pilots searching in confusion. He'd been getting periodic reports and knew the critical gas situation. As the picture worsened, writes Taylor, one of his aides finally blurted out: "'We gotta give these guys some light.'" Illuminating the ships would provide enemy submarines and airplanes a perfect target. Most sources say it was prohibited at the time. Mitscher, writes Taylor, moved out on the bridge, momentarily lit a cigarette, and then calmly delivered the now famous order: "Turn on the lights." Within seconds, the task force burst from the darkness. Carrier sides, at least parts of the sides, became illuminated with floodlights that were directed down them. Searchlights beamed into the sky. Cruisers fired star shells that momentarily lit large areas of the sea and fleet. "'To hell with the Japs around us,'" Taylor quotes a staff officer, "'Our pilots were not to be expendable.'"

It was a "gutsy," move, said Voris, who doesn't remember the searchlights in the air—only the lights showing ships. Maybe it took awhile for those to be turned on? At least the searchers now knew where to head. But the sudden illumination did little for pinpoint landings. The carrier decks themselves were not outlined or defined. Individual flattops were not distinguished from each other, or from other ships, for that matter. All ships showed various lights, some seeming like tiny pinpoints, others large searchlights raying up into the sky or down a part of a ship. The searchlights beaming downward usually were those of a carrier. But in the mounting confusion, not everyone was sure. Deciding on which ship to land on, and where precisely on that ship once it had been picked out, would prove to be a recurring problem in the recovery. To the returning pilots, Mitscher's order to illuminate was a blessing. Nonetheless, it preceded what would become a nightmare.

Voris: "We got closer and closer and lower and lower. We're going through clouds and then breaking out. And lo and behold, I see the lights of the task force down below. It's horizon to horizon. Now where the hell are you compared to your ship? And the force is still steaming toward us, not ready to land airplanes or anything." The carriers still had to turn into the wind. "The skipper went merrily into the clouds. I was far enough back and down that I eased over and went under the cloud. I always thought he was going to chew my ass for not following him, but my gas gauge was down close to zero."

Voris was one of the few who actually found his ship.

In the ensuing confusion, experienced even by Dean, Voris had made an educated guess—and had been right.

But he still had to land.

First he had to go low and find his approach into the wind.

"You're fifty to sixty feet off the water at night with no horizon . . . Nothing in the cockpit but the gyro to tell you if your wings are level. And you have your power indicators . . . You got one eye on that gas gauge. There's not much left, and you figure, how am I going to get down? It's a test."

He made his first pass. *Hornet* was still trying to align with the wind and hadn't done so yet. Consequently, Voris's approach—into the wind as it should have been—was thirty degrees off.

The problem wasn't his fault. But that was little consolation.

"They couldn't take me. I could see the big wave-off." The landing signal officer, in an innovation inspired by the crisis, used long lighted wands to direct him away. He zoomed over the turning carrier's stern and headed out downwind again to turn for a second run.

"It's night and dark as shit." He was exhausted, disheartened at the wave-off. His gas gauge was probably touching zero. He figured he had less than five gallons left—only a few more minutes of fuel. If he didn't recover on this next attempt, there wouldn't be another chance. He'd have to go into the sea. "My wheels were down, so I'm going on my back," an entry he most probably wouldn't survive.

He entered the turn to put him back into the wind. "I'm a little numb by this time. I guess I'm giving up mentally." Suddenly, a reflection outside the cockpit caught his eye. It was water on the sea shining in the relatively low-powered running light of his left wing. Somehow in the stress and dulled senses that the ordeal had produced, he'd gotten lax and descended until the wingtip on the inside of the turn was just feet from the water! It was a jarring realization. "I guess I'd gotten—well, you think you're not going to make it and you just kind of give up. Something was wrong in my thinking because you don't let that happen. I guess I didn't care whether I crashed or not."

In that millisecond of shocking realization, he made a crucial decision. "You've got to keep going or use the power you've still got to put it in the water." There was only time for one or the other. "I kept going."

Stiffened, he somehow reined in the adrenaline gushing through his body and lifted the Hellcat as precisely and steadily as he could. At that low altitude his altimeter wasn't registering. He had to dead-reckon it. He couldn't afford to wander the plane or expend more fuel than was precisely needed. He could run out of gas and drop into the water at any moment.

God was with him. Somehow he made it into a recovery pattern that was good enough to get a signal to land.

He dropped onto the deck, apparently the first in the entire strike force to land.

But the ship still wasn't in perfect alignment with the wind. It was perhaps ten degrees off. After touchdown, and because of the misalignment, instead of traveling straight up the shadowy deck, the trajectory angled Butch across it toward the carrier's hulking and fast-approaching middle island. Luckily, his tailhook engaged a wire in time to halt the speeding Hellcat just before it hit one of the island's reinforced turrets. "When I stopped, I'm right underneath both barrels of that big five-inch mount aft the stack. Had I missed the wire, I would have been killed hitting that massive gun mount."

Close behind him was Lieutenant (j.g.) Harry. R. "Stinky" Davis, from Oakland, California. Davis had been his wingman on the mission. "They pushed me back so I could turn and go up the deck, and here comes Stinky. I guess his hook didn't catch because he goes right into the barrier and upends. I saw him and jumped out and ran because you want to get out of the way of a runaway airplane."

Almost as soon as he got to a safe spot, a marine orderly came rushing up and said Rear Admiral Joseph "Jocko" Clark, head of *Hornet*'s task group, one of the four groups making up the force, wanted to see him immediately. Clark, half Cherokee Indian from Oklahoma and the first native American to graduate from the naval academy, was a World War I veteran and early naval aviator known for his aggressiveness, unorthodox dress, and salty language. He'd commanded a carrier in the invasion of Northwest Africa in 1942 and had used *Hornet,* which was commanded by Captain Miles Browning, as his flagship since the middle of March. Prior to that, he had served with Butch's former CO, Jimmy Flatley, on *Yorktown,* after Flatley had left the Reapers. "What a guy. What a fighter," said Butch.

He followed the marine up a ladder and was left with the admiral. "He always wore a gauze mask. Afraid of catching cold or something. He asked me—he knew me by my first name—he asked what had happened? He didn't have any intelligence so I told him everything I knew . . . We hit the carriers. Left two of them burning. He wanted to know how many [aviators] were in the water. I said, 'You've lost all your torpedo planes. [The survivors are] halfway back from the target area. Probably some of your dive-bombers will make it back, but they'll never land. Won't be any fuel. And you're going to lose some fighters.' He asked me how much fuel I had. I said less than five gallons. He was worried about the pilots. He was very humanitarian."

When Clark dismissed him, Butch made his way down to the Ripper ready room "to find out where our pilots were." The squadron's teletype was already clicking. "We were exchanging information . . . So-and-so landed on a carrier. So-and-so had a deck crash . . . So-and-so is injured . . . Things were getting panicky. No doubt about it."

Mike Wolf, who missed the mission because of mechanical problems in his just-launched airplane and thus was an observer as the strike force returned, remembers that the barriers used to stop careening airplanes "were gone very quickly. People were ignoring the landing signal officer and crashing . . . A friend of mine landed on another ship, chopping off the tail of his dive-bomber. It killed the rear-seat gunner . . . People lost the discipline . . . Guys obeyed the wave-off, crashed, and killed themselves. Others disobeyed, landed, and lived . . . It was unbelievable."

There were attempts to land on destroyers mistaken for carriers. "The sky flickered with flashlights as pilot after pilot bailed out," wrote Morrissey, and floated down into the cold water. Soon float lights blinked like fireflies as pilots and crewmen bobbed in the relatively calm waves trying to hail destroyers weaving dangerously among them hoping to make rescues. "Sadly," said Wolf, "it was the most exciting night of my life."

Ripper Jack Vaughan's after-action account was probably typical of what many went through:

"We didn't reach the fleet until ¾ of an hour after darkness had closed. There was no moon and no horizon . . . I was unable to distinguish our carrier. My flight became separated . . . My artificial horizon wasn't working . . . I finally found [*Hornet*] by means of the searchlight they sent up. There were 8 planes in the traffic circle when I entered it . . . I observed a deck crash, circled, saw another deck crash, circled four more times, and sought out another carrier. I observed a deck crash there, too, and I then went to a CVL [smaller aircraft carrier]."

He entered its traffic circle and was about to land when he realized his tailhook wouldn't go down. Everything he tried wouldn't lower it. Dangerously low on gas himself, he heard others in worse fuel states and decided to gain altitude and bail out. "But upon reaching four hundred feet, my engine began to [overheat and] detonate . . . I immediately turned into the wind and prepared for a water landing." By the time he hit the swells, his engine was on fire. Jumping out, he got tangled in the mix of parachute and raft anchor lines, exhausting himself to the point that he nearly drowned. In the tangle, his flashlight dropped into the sea. After about a half hour struggling in the water, a destroyer heard him blowing a standard-issue lifeguard whistle and picked him up.

All told, according to most sources, some 80 of the 200 or so planes that made it back to the task force were lost in the recovery, either by crashes or ditching. The Rippers were the hardest hit squadron, losing seven planes, although eventually recovering all their pilots. In a rare disregard of regulations, said Voris, *Hornet's* flight surgeon issued those in the ready rooms their choice of measured amounts of brandy, rye whiskey, or beer. "It's a night I'll remember unlike anything else," he said. "Men dying. Parachutes coming down. It's indelibly stuck in my mind. How the admiral felt. How we felt. Some of [the pilots] said they'd had enough. 'I don't want to fly anymore.' They felt different the next morning. But it was that tough a night."

★

The next morning, along the track back to the strike, task force planes located and rescued pilots and crew members who had spent the night in the cold water. "We covered a wide area and we began to find them," said

Butch. "In fact, I found the skipper of one of the bomber squadrons of another carrier. He and his backseat man in their rafts were tied together out in the middle of the ocean. They had red dye marker out so you could see them. They must have heard us, because there's only one shot with the dye."

The rescuers traveled in pairs. "Whoever had them eyeballed would never take their eyes off, just keep circling so he could transmit line of sight back to the carrier and they'd send out a seaplane from one of the cruisers that would land and pick them up. This went on all day."

The task force that morning also sent out a second strike to hit the Japanese, but they'd gotten away. The decision to help the pilots the night before had given the enemy the time they needed to escape. The task force had had to turn east—away from Ozawa's ships—because that was the direction the returning pilots had expected. Mitscher and his boss, Admiral Spruance, who supported the move, came under some criticism for the trade-off. But the two-day carrier battle of June 19 and 20, 1944, effectively destroyed the Japanese navy's ability to wage carrier warfare. While the Japanese still had six carriers, they were all in need of repair, and they no longer had enough airplanes or experienced pilots to pose a serious air threat to the Allied fleet.

For his participation in the battle, which was the largest carrier clash in history, Voris was awarded the Distinguished Flying Cross. Calling him a "daring and intrepid airman," the citation reads in part:

> For heroism and extraordinary achievement . . . on June 19 and 20, 1944 . . . Voris led his division . . . against overwhelming forces of hostile aircraft threatening our surface units and, despite intense anti-aircraft fire during a long range strike against major units of the Japanese Fleet the following day, executed damaging bombing and strafing runs against enemy warships . . .

Later, he was also awarded two Gold Stars as a result of the battle, one "in lieu of a second Distinguished Flying Cross" for the number of combat missions he'd flown up to that point and the other for the aerial kill he had made on the nineteenth.

Butch now had four confirmed kills and two unconfirmed. Although the Japanese carrier fleet was in retreat, the aerial fighting was far from over.

CHAPTER 16

With the Japanese navy retreating, air superiority was established over the Marianas. American ground soldiers could now finish their work at Saipan and Guam without fear of major enemy air or sea attacks.

The Japanese by this time, mid-1944, were on the defensive. Guadalcanal and the Solomons had been secured, giving the Allies a vital foothold for attack northward and the march to Tokyo. The seizure of the Admiralty Islands northwest of the Solomons, combined with victory in New Guinea, had effectively kicked the enemy out of the South Pacific. Their ring of empire was receding. Now in the Central Pacific, with the first Battle of the Philippine Sea, the Turkey Shoot, and the taking of the Marianas, the ring's eastern boundaries were receding. Clearly, the war situation had improved since Voris arrived in late 1942, over a year and a half earlier. The armada he was part of, Task Force 58, was threatening the approaches to Japan proper, the Northern Pacific, an area which was now Japan's most heavily fortified. To Task Force 58, the Bonin Islands, the eastern part of these approaches, were a threat. For instance, at Iwo Jima, where a major land battle would be fought, there were a considerable number of land-based enemy fighters and bombers.

While most of Task Force 58 went back to Eniwetok in the Marshalls to recharge and resupply, Admiral Clark, always aggressive, took a small group of carriers and ships, including *Hornet* and the Rippers, back north toward Tokyo to hit two Bonin islands, Chichi Jima and Haha Jima, each of which also had airstrips, planes, and other important targets. The Bonins are near an area of the Pacific where typhoons develop and, with the changing of the seasons, bad weather was beginning to appear—something that would factor into Butch's experience that summer.

On June 24, a large morning fighter sweep to Iwo Jima resulted in some sixty-five claimed shoot-downs by Hellcats of the task group at the cost of only six of their own. Fighting 2, according to Morrissey, claimed most of the wins. Voris had not gone on the early sweep. It hadn't been his turn. "Because I was scheduling, I had to be very careful not to take all the choice missions." Instead, he'd chalked himself in as an "alert" pilot to fly at a moment's notice should a replacement be needed. Stung but rousted by the morning raid, the Japanese decided to try and inflict some pain of their own and, at first, sent unprotected Iwo-based torpedo planes against the fleet. They were massacred by task group pilots, who included Russ Reiserer. Late that afternoon, as the day's second Hellcat sweep was back at Iwo dodging storms and shooting down another large number of enemy planes, the Japanese, according to the after-action report, sent a group of five torpedo bombers from Ito Jima, another of the Bonins, this time protected by twelve Zeros. The group was spotted incoming on the *Hornet* radar. Voris and his division, as well as another Reaper division, got the call.

Butch was to be the leader.

"My harness was inside my [administration] office next to the ready room. I ran in and grabbed it and forgot to duck going back out." With his headgear already on, he hit and damaged one of the protruding, ear-covering radio receivers. It wouldn't work unless he manually held a broken wire into the receiver. That left him only one hand with which to fly his Hellcat. They needed radio direction to get to the enemy. "So I turned [division command] over to Bill Blair, my second section lead and flew on him."

The incoming enemy planes were about a hundred miles out. The Hellcats knew the enemy flight's altitude and rose higher for an advantage. "We were at about 18 to 20,000 feet and they were below us at about 12 to 15 [thousand] feet." The weather was clear, according to the after-action. "We can see Haha Jima in the distance," he remembered, a long, narrow, high-cliffed island some twenty miles south of Chichi Jima.

The Zeros, flying protection above the torpedo planes, saw the Hellcats and surged up. "I rolled over and pulled down." In addition to being the more comfortable way to dive—because the G-forces would then press him into his seat rather than pull him up—rolling upside down onto his back gave him a better look through the top of the canopy as he came down.

Quickly, he and one of the Zeros, whose pilot had picked him out, were on a collision course, beak to beak, roaring at each other at a combined closure speed of perhaps 700 miles per hour. But being in a dive, Voris had the speed advantage.

Both started firing. "It's a game of chicken, really. Both of us shooting, neither hitting because we can't bring guns to bear [noses dead on] or we'll collide. I remember the muzzle flashes. You fire to scare. We passed at no more than ten feet apart"—cockpit to cockpit. "Any closer and we would have hit. I remember his face"—the only air opponent in the war whose distinguishing features he actually saw. "He had a round head, blackish helmet, jaw open, big white eyes. It was a flash. He had darker skin. You don't pay much attention to details except to say, 'Oh, shit, we almost hit!'"

The two fighters roared into each other's exhausts. "I don't know where he went, but the others [Zeros] are breaking up." He found himself momentarily looking down at the moving cockpit of another Zero trying to turn away. It was within his range. "You see the airplane and your mind quickly computes the lead angle." He squeezed the trigger. "Easy shot. He was turning up into me. Hit him right in front of the cockpit." Fire ignited. "He became a torch. That's the end of that thought."

He came out of the dive with considerable speed. "I pulled up, and my boys, they've got their own stuff going because you start picking individual targets." Glancing above, he saw a Zero barreling down on him. "I quick-rolled—hard right rudder, hard right turn." The Zero dived over him. Mistake. Still with good energy, he wrenched the Hellcat back into the descending Zero's wake and jumped on its tail. "He lost sight of me. The minute you do that, you're dead."

The Zero sped low, Butch following. In the after-action, he relates they neared the water. "He did a reversal trying to see me. You lose sight like he had, and you go crazy." It was a running tail chase—follow-the-leader at high speed, only in this case bullets or cannon to make the tag. The Zero pilot thrashed his plane from side to side trying to spoil his attacker's aim. But Voris was in his blind spot and kept firing. When he finally connected, the Zero burst into flames and crashed into the sea. "The fire started at the wing root and became a blaze."

Suddenly, as Voris searched for more, the targets were gone. "It's that quick. You start looking around for your boys . . . calling them, let's close it up, get together . . . We didn't have another target." They'd done their job. All the torpedo bombers were either shot down (as it was later claimed) or fleeing. "We started back for the ship."

The after-action report claims nine Zekes and five Kates (Nakajima B5N torpedo bombers) for the squadron. With the two new kills, both later confirmed, Butch now had shot down six enemy planes, all Zeros. Five was all it took. Landing back on the carrier, he was an ace. He doesn't recall any celebration other than maybe some more alcohol ration for arriving pilots in the ready room from the flight surgeon. "That was an intense time. There were a lot of aces being made," he said. In fact, according to *Odyssey*, VF-2 alone claimed 67 planes shot down that day and 177 since June 11 when Task Force 58 had started the Marianas campaign. To Morrissey, who was keeping count, the 187 total claimed shoot-downs since they'd started the cruise was "an all-time record for any navy or marine squadron." Maybe so, said Butch, but "we just didn't think about things like that then. Too much going on."

Also unthought-of was the effect the constant air fighting would have on his later start of the Blues. Dogfighting, as already alluded to, was the ultimate maneuver teacher—varied, incredibly tense, demanding perfection. Every air move imaginable was possible and probable during a desperate dogfight. It demanded precise execution and perfect form. Survival depended on it. In a real dogfight there was little or no room for error. The same would be true of flying with the Blue Angels. Luck did have its place in winning victories. But not over and over. Pilot error usually decided a contest. Experience was a great asset. Thus, in each dogfight he engaged and won, Voris, albeit unknowingly at this time, was polishing skills he enjoyed and had been perfecting since those earlier training times when he'd gone up alone and practiced them just to see what he and his airplane could do. Now he was literally flying at the edge of the envelope every day and succeeding at it, as becoming an ace proved. Such expertise would be required when he'd be called upon to start the Blue Angels.

★

After a short resupplying trip to Eniwetok in the Marshalls, the task group was back steaming toward the Bonins again. Iwo Jima was needed as an operating base for the new long-range Boeing B-29 "Superfortress" bombers that would eventually begin pummeling the Japanese home islands. Early in 1945, marines would fight a famous battle to conquer Iwo Jima, and Admiral Clark, as part of the pre-preinvasion softening, had made the destruction of the island group's remaining enemy planes a priority, so much so that eventually Dean, as well as others in *Hornet's* Air Group 2, including Butch, got tongue-in-cheek certificates in the "Jocko Jima Development Corp." which promised "choice locations" to all holders.

The first sweep was in the early morning of July 3. It was a large mission consisting of probably forty fighters from the carriers in the limited task group. Butch was leading two divisions and flying for the first time a new version of the Hellcat, the F6F-5, which had begun to appear as a replacement for the F6F-3 in April. Since the earlier model was essentially "right," according to its pilots, the newer version, which looked almost the same, was basically a strengthening and enhancing of the earlier's pluses. It had a sturdier, closer-fitting engine cowling, a strengthened airframe or body, and a little more speed and maneuverability. It also could now fire rockets and carry larger, heavier bombs. Nevertheless, it was a surprise to Butch when he saw on the ready-room teletype that all the Hellcats on the sweep, older and newer versions alike, were going to be carrying depth charges under their wings instead of their usual 500- and 1,000-pound bombs. "Depth charges carry the most explosive within a given weight of a bomb," he said. "They have thin shells. When you're exploding underwater to kill a submarine, you want a lot of concussion. Our intelligence showed that there were hundreds of airplanes at Iwo. It was a big staging area out of Japan. So if you dropped one of those [depth charges], the blast effect would blow wings off and tumble airplanes yards and yards." In other words, it would cause collateral damage that conventional bombs might not.

It was an innovative idea. But a nasty surprise awaited them at Iwo.

They were a couple of hundred miles south of the volcanic island when they took off, a long way from Iwo, said Butch, approximately an hour and a half flying time with rendezvous circling and other holdups figured in. When they arrived, just as they'd expected, there were lots of airplanes on the ground. "They were in revetted dirt mounds, three or four in each revetment. I figured you get the depth charge inside and you get all of them, so that's what we went for. But they [the Japanese] knew we were coming. There are all kinds of stories. Maybe one of their sub-marines spotted us or trailed us when we came out; maybe a fishing boat or a snooper [enemy plane] we never saw. But they were up in the sun waiting for us. Nobody saw them. We figured that there were so many on the ground that there couldn't be any more. But soon enough, about thirty to forty [Zeros] jumped us."

Most of the Hellcats had just finished their first pass over the enemy field. Explosions were going off everywhere beneath them. All were low, and some were starting up to go around for another run. "It was a good way to get us. They had the advantage . . . What a rhubarb. Everybody started shooting."

All the Hellcats now hoped they could get out and away in time to go back up and come back in a dive, which would give them advantage. "You never got into a turning dogfight with them because that's the same as saying go ahead and shoot me down. They're going to be inside of you in a turn and a half. They're so light wing-loaded that they can sit up there and float around and be on your tail. So you'd better hit him if you get the chance and hope he makes a mistake."

Guns blazing, Voris said he might have hit several attacking enemy planes but had no idea what happened to them as he gained altitude. He saw a Zero that seemed to be diving specifically on him. He turned hard left in an attempt to foil the descending attacker's aim. But instead of con-tinuing down or turning in the same direction so he'd still be a threat, the Zero pilot, still above, flipped over on his back, canopy now downward, and turned the opposite way. Then he seemed to just hover. "He had all this speed from diving down and he just sits up there upside down not do-ing anything." In effect, he was giving Voris his tail on an opposite-traveling parallel track above him. Voris turned back toward him and pulled his nose up for a shot. The distance between them now was just a little farther than the Hellcat's gun range, but closing quickly. Voris squeezed the trigger. A barrage of bullets stitched a trail of destruction in the hanging Zero.

The plane burst into flames.

"I didn't have to think of him again. I remember Mike Wolf, my sec-ond section leader, pulling up with me. He already had one, and we were going to go back down there and strafe, and here come some more."

Another group of Zeros was waiting behind the first.

The Hellcats were still trying to gain altitude.

"Mike and I both shot, and I don't know what happened [with those]."

A Zero cut across from his right and made a turn. "I don't think he saw me. Otherwise, why would he fly out in front of me? It was like candy from a baby. I chased him for a while, caught him on the inside. He just didn't know tactics . . . He should have been able to pull so I couldn't get a lead angle on him. But he didn't. Probably right out of flight school. I opened up . . . He caught fire."

Scanning the immediate skies, he didn't see the Zero crash. But it would later become his second confirmed kill of the day.

He now had eight confirmed and two probables.

"We pulled up, got the flight together, and just about that time I started having engine problems."

The new F6F-5 he was flying started backfiring and hesitating.

"You lose power . . . It scared me." The problem was later diagnosed as preservative grease globs getting in the carburetor and interfering with the fuel flow. But all Voris knew at the time was that he was still fairly low and in danger of going down. He also knew lifeguard submarines were on rescue duty just off the island. "What enters your mind is get the hell out over water so you don't have some Japanese sticking swords in your ears or some other torture."

He dropped his tailhook. "The sea was real glassy and you don't have good depth perception. If I'm ditching, I want to feel the surface before I go in. Otherwise, you might think you're at five feet when you're really at fifty."

Suddenly he heard a chilling call. "It was a massive dogfight, and someone"—he believes it was Lieutenant Robert R. Butler, from Oakland, California—"started screaming, 'Help me! Help me!' It went on for a while. His voice went pretty high. I remember that. I think he identified himself. He was a pretty calm, quiet guy otherwise. He'd shot down some planes. I guess a couple of Zeros were working him over, and he couldn't get out of the pocket."

Voris said he would have gone to the unlucky pilot's aid if he hadn't been in an emergency himself, "although I doubt if it would have done any good. He would have been dead by the time I got there."

Then he heard the chilling aspect. "This voice"—he doesn't know whose—"came on and said, 'Shut up and die like a man.' I remember that on the radio just like I'm talking to you, like I looked over my shoulder right now as if I could see him . . . That's kind of the attitude people had . . . Shut up. We got our own fight to deal with . . . There's always a lot of screaming and noise going on when you are in combat . . . Pretty hard words . . . Pretty chilling."

Voris said he got to about fifty feet from the water and the Hellcat stopped sputtering. "I circled the sub a few times and it didn't happen again." The raid was ending and planes were starting to stream back. "I decided to take my chances." The skies were now clear. The battle had taken only moments. The trip home was 225 miles, perhaps two hours. A time for contemplation? "There is a bonding among aviators you don't get in any other community," said Butch. "It's because of the closeness to death."

Back on the ship, Butler, who was credited with three enemy planes shot down in twenty-two missions, and another pilot, Ensign Roy J. O'Neal, a recent replacement from Springfield, Ohio, also credited with three shoot-downs, were declared missing—the only serious Ripper casualties from the fight. "Nice guys, but we lost them. It's the end of them. You get their things together and send them home."

★

The next day, July 4, 1944, was as memorable an Independence Day as Butch would have, but not in a way he liked.

Chichi Jima was the strike target. It had an important regional communications station that Allied planners wanted destroyed.* Dean and approximately twelve Hellcats, including those flown by Butch and his division, were sent to knock the station out, Dean leading the mission.

"We ran into bad weather," said Butch, "a tremendous storm. Must have been 60,000 feet high, much higher than we could ever fly our airplanes." It stretched darkly across the entire horizon, rain, winds, and lightning clearly visible. "You could see the viciousness of the swirling cumulus clouds inside."

They probed the massive front but found no openings. Flying into the storm would have been suicide, said Butch. Wind shear, pelting rain, the prospect of zero visibility were daunting. "You couldn't have kept formation. You would have lost control of your airplane. So Dean radioed back that we were unable to penetrate." An exasperated Admiral Clark took the radio and ordered him to go through. "You could hear the hackles go

---

*According to Washington's Naval Historical Center, which, in 1985, researched the Chichi situation because Lieutenant George H. W. Bush had been shot down near the island, it was concluded in a later raid that the enemy was intercepting US radio transmissions there and warning Japanese units of impending strikes.

up. All the pilots knew it would be suicide. I just couldn't sit by. Smart-ass that I am, I radioed, 'Eagle'—I think that was the admiral's call sign—'Eagle.' How's the weather where *you* are? You know, you're safe back there on the bridge and we're out here with the problem. Pretty sarcastic. Well, everything went silent." The admiral didn't respond to Voris's impudence but reiterated his order. Dean refused. "Wouldn't do it. He's the commander on the scene and he's got to use his judgment. He was right. I was right there with him."

They returned to the carrier. Voris hadn't identified himself when he'd made his transmission. "My mother didn't raise a stupid boy." But when they landed, the marine was there with an order for him to report to the bridge. Executive Officer Tex Harris, also on the mission and next in command when Dean refused—so also probably in trouble—had recognized Voris's voice. "He said, 'Jesus, Butch. You're going to cause us all kinds of problems.' I said, 'Well, to have somebody back there order us to do something way out there that would have killed us all, I just, well, it was uncontrollable. I had to retort.'"

He left to face the music. But Jocko wasn't mad at him. Nothing was said at all about the retort. Instead, the admiral had the task force weatherman on the bridge and said, "'We've got to get that power and communications center and I want you to go back and do it for me.' He knew me. He said, 'I think you can do it.' So here I am, the guy who has made it worse, and he's ordering me to take over the mission. He looked at the radar and could see some areas that might be less intense. He was smart that way. I remember the charts were laid out, and we went over them. He wanted that center [taken] down. What are you going to do? You salute and say, 'Yes, sir.' I hoped the skipper would understand."

He never found out whether the admiral knew who had made the wisecrack. It never came up again. But after leaving the bridge, he ran into Dean. "I didn't know what to say. I told him this was what the admiral wanted. I think he and the admiral talked later. I don't know what transpired, but Dean said to me, 'Sure, sure. I understand.' What else could he say? I think it hurt his career later." A refusal to obey orders could do that. Admiral Clark could influence the evaluation on Dean's fitness reports, as well as Harris's whom Clark probably expected to execute the order if Dean wouldn't. And fitness reports greatly influenced promotion and job assignment. "I talked to Tex [Harris] before he died [years after the war] and he said, 'You don't know what you did to us,

Butch.'" Voris never found out because Harris didn't explain any further. "But that's what he said. Anyway, I got sixteen fighters together, and I am now the lead dog."

They launched as soon as the return could be mounted. When they got to the storm, the situation had changed. They found some soft spots, "light areas where there was a difference in contrast. Not clear yet, but the rain and wind were lighter." He took the mission through. "It wasn't perfect, but it wasn't the threat it had been." When they got to Chichi Jima, they found an overcast of thick rain clouds down to two thousand feet. It prevented normal strafing. In order to see what they were doing, they had to stay below the clouds the entire time and couldn't zoom up after their runs, which was dangerous. They were constantly exposed to antiaircraft fire—the same that two months later, on September 2, would shoot down a TBF Avenger piloted by Ensign George H. W. Bush, the future forty-first president of the United States whose son, George W., would become president after him. But they got the job done. "We strafed it repeatedly. Then the bombers came in. I didn't lose any airplanes, and when I got back, I got called up to the bridge again and reported on what we'd done. The admiral wanted to hear all about it. I always felt bad for the skipper."

The fact that Clark picked Voris for the Chichi Jima mission is indicative of Voris's development as a leader, which was the other major aspect of why he would succeed when later asked to start the Blue Angels. Flying would be part of that coming success. But so would leadership abilities.

It wasn't the first time superiors had singled him out. O'Hare had done so for the Bat teams. Dean had done so by making the young flyer, then only a jaygee, a division leader and then his operations officer when higher ranking officers were usually picked for the job. The CAG, Roy Johnson, had tapped Butch as the fighter division leader above others he wanted flying with him. All had seen something in the tall, even-tempered aviator that made him stand out among other good men.

What was the reason? What had they seen? "I can't really tell you," says Butch today. "It's not one thing. It's day to day. You develop a reputation." His steady, unruffled personality undoubtedly was a part of it. His enthusiasm another. But ability to get things done because of skill and will appear to be key. "If I'm the admiral, I'm going to have a pretty good measure of the boys in my fighter squadron. I'd been the first back to Clark in the 'Mission Beyond Darkness' [as that night of chaos would become known]. I'd given him a pretty good debrief when he'd called me to the bridge. He knew me as an individual. Roy Johnson may have had something to do with it. I can't think of anything else. Every flight you get gives you more experience. I exercised authority over my division, always brought them back. I'd been on some of the most difficult missions. Every time you are put to a test and survive, you learn something more. I think it was just my nature. Take charge. Go do it. I'm a great believer in that. It's my basic instinct."

★

Despite the storm incident, Dean and Butch continued their close relationship. Almost every night during the cruise, said Voris, he and the CO would walk the deck together and discuss the next day's missions. Sometime during this period, as they were near the Bonins, Dean called him aside and told him a top-secret bombing mission to Tokyo was being planned. Only he and Dean would fly it. It would be the first since the Doolittle Raid. They were scheduled to sail the closest to Japan they'd been during the cruise, probably less than five hundred miles away, and presumably *Hornet,* the same carrier that in its earlier version had launched the Doolittle Raiders, would take them even closer. They didn't figure there would be enough fuel to make it back, so they'd have to ditch and be picked up by submarine, not an uplifting thought. But he was ready to do it. He was told never to discuss the mission with anyone else. But after several more mentionings by Dean, it was called off. "I didn't hear any more and thought it my business not to ask. It could have been Admiral Clark. He was always dreaming up ideas, and I was always getting tagged for them."

Also during their time near the Bonins, Voris was witness to a brutal shark attack, the only one he saw. He was one of several in the squadron qualified to take reconnaissance photographs with special cameras mounted in the Hellcat's belly. This particular mission was flown in support of a bomber strike on a Japanese merchant convoy heading back to Japan north of the Bonins. He was along to take damage assessment photographs. The ships were protected by destroyers with mounted antiaircraft guns. "Very dangerous." One of the torpedo planes, with a three-man crew, was shot down. "I knew the pilot. 'Pappy' or 'Pops.' A big guy like me. He was one of the older guys in Torpedo Squadron 2. I was low and they had just gotten in the water with their life vests on. Hadn't yet gotten in their raft. All I saw was white thrashing water. Then red. Then nobody around except the sharks. It was a terrible sight. There was nothing I could do."

He hadn't seen sharks since flying off Guadalcanal. "They were out there. We all knew it. You just can't see them in the deep water. Some battled them and knocked them away. Others got eaten. There was no sense worrying about it. You always knew they were there and hoped you didn't have to deal with them."

In the weeks ahead, in preparation for the July 21, 1944, landings on Guam, Butch flew strikes on the Orote and Agana airfields again. It was during this time that he visited Saipan and saw the horrors of war up close. His log shows strikes almost every day through July and the beginning of August. He was piling up the missions and would eventually finish with some fifty. Guam, the Bonins again, and the Caroline Islands, including Yap, were among the later targets.

After Truk had been neutralized, Yap had become the major Japanese naval base in the Central Pacific. The task force, now reassembled, was moving west toward the Philippines, ranging a vast stretch of ocean. On September 13, after raids on the Palau Islands and Cebu and Mindanao in the Southern Philippines, Butch participated in the first sweep over Luzon, the main Philippine Island, since the Japanese occupied the country in early 1942. "I remember seeing Clark Air Force Base coming in over the ridge from the east and knowing we had all kinds of prisoners down there and we had to go strafe and bomb. But we had intelligence on what buildings to hit."

For another week and a half, he flew strikes and combat air patrols in the Philippines. While ground fire was heavy, the Japanese were clearly on the defensive. They were evacuating the islands. Fleeing ships were prime targets. On September 24, Butch flew his last mission. His log says only "Cebu and Negros," both of them Philippine islands south of Luzon. "I was going home. I figured I'd done my job and would enjoy a little shore rotation." Two combat cruises were all a fighter pilot was allowed. "I'd be going to the training command . . . where my skills as a fighter pilot would be passed on to the new people coming through."

What had he learned?

"War really tells you about people. You see people cry . . . throw up on the side of their airplane before they get in. You see people quit right there on the flight deck and have to be taken below. It's really something that is hard to imagine. Everybody is made a little different. It separates the men from the boys, if you want to put it in those terms, although I felt sorry for them. I'd go in the john and you could hear them heaving in there. I guess it's just part of war.

"You learn about yourself. What kind of person you are. How much risk you can take. How you cope with risk. Risk is a big thing in the cockpit. It's there all the time. And when you stretch the envelope you are taking the risk right up against the point of no return. Hopefully just short of that. That's a big issue. They don't talk much about it, but that's like a self-evaluation. How far do you take it? What's your capability? Do you have what it takes? Not just courage but the capability to go with it? If you don't, it's a bust-your-ass situation. That's what you learn about yourself. If you go beyond your capability, that's false courage."

He'd bolstered his self-confidence "which is a major element in all this. I've been there. I can do it. You are not in an unknown. There's no upside down or right side up in a dogfight. Are you comfortable with that? You know what you can do. A lot of these crashes you see at [air] shows are people going beyond what they can do . . . I was now much more confident in my abilities, knew who I was as a fighter pilot and a leader. I'd been successful . . . I was a different person really . . . With all that fighting and so forth under the belt you were bound to change. Leadership was parallel. I was more mature as a pilot and a person. Aggressive, if you want a single word . . . Maybe initiative is a better word. I'd learned how to take more initiative because I had total confidence in myself. I didn't think about risk or busting my ass . . . Always knew the potential was there, but it was parked in the back of my brain somewhere. You know your machine. You know yourself. Nothing really is going to be a surprise."

Voris had won three Distinguished Flying Crosses, eleven Air Medals, one Purple Heart when he left Fighting 2, which was featured in the October 23, 1944, issue of *Life* magazine as "the hottest fighter squadron in the Pacific."

He was ripe for an opportunity.

PART THREE

FIRST BLUE

"Paramount in my mind was to beat anyone
else in the sky. I tell you my whole life at that
time hinged on that one thing. I guess it has
to if you're going to be the best."

—*Butch Voris*

CHAPTER 17

Navy Commander Leroy "Roy" Simpler had an idea. The former skipper of VF-5 on *Saratoga*, veteran of early air combat in the Pacific, including at Guadalcanal, helper in the design of advanced fighter planes later, was now part of the navy's Office of Information in Washington, working closely with the secretary of the navy. He knew well the problems his service was facing now that the war had ended. It was early 1946. The navy was downsizing drastically. Carrier aviation was losing planes and pilots, especially the good ones who had been naval aviation's backbone during the war but were now taking advantage of the peace dividend. They were leaving, pursuing dreams put on hold during the bitter fighting. Marriage, careers, raising families, schooling were taking priority. The newspapers, magazines, and newsreels were no longer chronicling the march of the fast carriers and their intrepid pilots across the Pacific. Simpler's job was publicity. The navy wasn't getting it like it used to. He'd heard his bosses, especially the CNO Admiral Nimitz, and Nimitz's boss, Secretary of the Navy James V. Forrestal, lament the fighting navy's dimming image. Recruiting was suffering. They needed public support so they could get money for navy programs.

A separate air force, to be created from the army, was being talked about—and getting all the ink.

What could be done?

It was a problem they worried about constantly.

Then he had his idea—or more accurately, the impulse to act on it. The idea of air demonstration teams had been around in various incarnations for decades. Air shows appear to have begun around 1910. By the 1920s and 1930s, spurred by the combat flying in World War I and a realization by military brass that air shows encouraged interest in the profession, the aviation branches of the services had spawned aerobatic or "flight demonstration" teams, as they called themselves. The teams became the highlights of the shows. The public loved the aviators and packed the rural fields and city airports where they performed. The army had Jimmy Doolittle and his "Three Musketeers," probably the first bona fide American precision flying team the services produced. They had humbled a hastily put-together navy team at the 1927 National Air Races at Spokane, Washington. One of the humbled flyers, D. W. "Tommy" Tomlinson, then created "the Three Seahawks," which performed admirably through 1928.

Others had followed.

But these service acrobatic teams had been largely unofficial weekend groups, practicing on their own, and often flying in conjunction with barnstormers and daredevil wingwalkers. They thrilled the crowds but seldom got the kind of service backing and support that allowed them to become permanent fixtures flying an officially sanctioned schedule of shows throughout the country. Perhaps because of the infancy of flight itself at the time and the lack of aviation's designation as a major American combat arm, the genre had not yet fixed itself in the minds of the generals and admirals as worthy of substantial commitment. Those military leaders were from the older, nonaviation generations. But World War II had changed that. The leadership was new. Planes and pilots were not only an important part of the military now, but aviation had emerged from the conflict as a dominant weapon and science with an attendant industry made up of giant corporations. It was taken very seriously. Aviation, with its carriers and long-range superbombers, had supplanted battleships as the most powerful component in any nation's naval arsenal. Now, thought Simpler, was the perfect time to start a new official navy demonstration team. It would keep the adventure, thrills, and accomplishment of naval aviation in the public eye and, as such, be an important tool in the battle for appropriations as well as for naval aviator recruitment. Recruitment was especially needed in the nation's coastless hinterlands—the great breadbasket of America stretching from the Mississippi River to the Rocky Mountains—where navy presence, like ships and air stations, was minimal.

Simpler took his idea to Admiral Nimitz, who liked it, as did Secretary Forrestal. On April 2, a message was sent from Nimitz to Rear Admiral Ralph Davison, head of the Naval Air Advanced Training Command "via" Vice Admiral Frank Wagner, head of Naval Air Training in Pensacola, Florida. "It is desired that a flight exhibition team be organized with the Naval Air Advanced Training Command," it said. "This team will be employed to represent the navy, as deemed appropriate and when directed, at suitable air shows and similar events."

Headquarters, said Butch, purposely chose the training command to keep the idea low-key and out of the public eye. In an era of mandatory cutbacks the admirals didn't want the effort, which could be construed by critics as unneeded, extravagant, or superfluous, to draw attention. The training command already had a good number and variety of planes and facilities appropriated. The assets could be used in the effort, and such events in the training command would not be as public as they were in, say, the fleet. The effort in the training command could be deemed experimental and disbanded quickly should something go wrong. The command also had a good supply of veteran combat pilots who were instructors, types the message said should make up the team.

Davison, in turn, gave the April 2 message to Commander Hugh Winters, a vaunted combat officer, who headed the Instructor's Advanced Training Unit, the cream of advanced training, the instructors who taught the instructors. Butch, by then, having left the war and been assigned new duties, was Winters's right-hand man, his chief flight officer.

★

Since leaving *Hornet* nearly a year and a half before, Voris had been adjusting. "Coming home was a return to normality—barbecues, parties, the things you don't do at sea and at war," Butch said. He'd returned via the West Coast. Mike Wolf, on his way elsewhere, recalls, "The last time I saw [Butch] was on one of those San Francisco streetcars. He was really hungover, hanging on for dear life . . . He'd really been on a tear." That encounter is dim in Butch's mind. But he remembers San Francisco vividly. "The first night back, 'Blood' [Lieutenant Landis E.] Doner and I are going to go out and have a big steak, a mile high. Oh, we were drooling. Hadn't had a real steak in I don't know how long. So we sat down and said we'll have the biggest cut you've got. Rare!" The waitress balked. "'Don't you know it's meatless Tuesday?' Meatless Tuesday?" It was a conservation measure instituted while they'd been at sea.

He'd gone home on leave to Santa Cruz and gas rationing, which turned out not to be much of a problem. "Our neighbors ran a trucking company, and they gave me all the gas I needed." His father already knew some of what he'd done. "The police chief had called him up one day and said, hey, do you know Roy's in *Life* magazine." Just about everyone had seen it. His father was proud. He was also noticeably less vigorous. "He'd had some heart attacks. He was not in the best of health. Mom was in good shape. I spent a lot of time with them. We didn't talk about the war so much. Just caught up with each other." There were write-ups about him in the local paper, which probably led to the following strange intrusion: The son of a woman he knew who ran his high school cafeteria had come to see him asking if he had any souvenirs from his war cruise, things like flight suits or guns. Butch said he didn't. The son wore the green uniform and cap of a Canadian military pilot and said he'd been flying two-engine Hudson bombers for them. He wanted to hang around and was persistent. "I knew his mother but it never sounded true. I didn't think he was a real pilot." Butch avoided him. Later, the man was arrested as an impostor. "He'd deserted from the army and I guess he wanted me to help with his cover. Those were the sad things, the disappointing things."

Perhaps the most important part of that immediate postwar leave had been meeting his future wife, Thea, although neither of them knew the long-term impact at the time. It was his first day home, and needing some greeting cards, he'd gone to a stationery store. Thea Young, several years his junior, and, as he describes her, "very pretty, the belle of [Santa Cruz High] in her grade," was there, too. She was also picking out cards. They recognized each other and struck up a conversation. "I knew who he was," said Thea. She'd seen him at school dances, older, seemingly aloof. Seeing him now in his uniform, tall and handsome, she was immediately attracted. He remembered her, too. "Real popular. Kind of unapproachable." That night he'd called her and asked her out. "I think we dated every night while I was home." While they had a great time, marriage wasn't on their minds. She was working for a stockbroker, traveling occasionally and enjoying it. He was looking forward to his next assignment, a job as an advanced flight instructor at NAS Daytona Beach, one of several training fields at the Florida sunspot famous for auto races on the uniquely packed Daytona sand. He remembered the detailer, a friend, who had made the assignment asking him, "'Are you married?' I told him no. He said I think you can best serve your country by going to Daytona near where there are 10,000 WACs [Women's Army Corps] in training." He'd be teaching newly winged carrier fighter pilots the art and science of modern aerial war fighting. He and Thea had agreed to keep in touch.

Although the women's training had closed down a week after he'd arrived, Daytona had been a dream assignment. "Never had a bad day there. It was flying, playing, swimming, living on the beach." The base was part of a training network opened by the navy at the site of the Daytona Beach airport in 1942 where newly winged pilots learned advanced tactics and gunnery. Butch, because of his experience, had been made chief fighter tactics instructor. Finding the course he inherited "a laughingstock," he had revamped it so it reflected current combat realities he'd seen in the war. "I was teaching mutual support, the weave, guns, and getting in the firing cone. Don't get slow and low. Offensive tactics. I enjoyed it." It was perhaps the beginning of a "show" mentality. He could show the young pilots how things really were supposed to be done. "I had models made [put on the end of sticks] so you could position airplanes and actually demonstrate the different situations. Then I'd go out and fly with the students."

As part of the revamp, he'd brought in some new, better-qualified instructors, combat veterans like himself. All students flew the Hellcat. Basic flight maneuvers had been part of the curriculum—loops, rolls, quick turns, inverted passes, reverses—moves he'd used during the war and would later use with the Blues. In what could be viewed as the beginning of his formal exhibition career, occasionally, at the request of his superiors, he had performed solo flight demonstrations. "Nothing like later. But I'd do a few loops, slow rolls, fly inverted. They knew I liked doing it and trusted me. I'd do it at the base open houses. Something for the visitors to see."

The end of the war in August 1945 had brought swift changes to the navy, changing his own situation as well. "They immediately started to reduce training." NAS Daytona had been given back to the city, and he had been sent up the coast north to NAS Jacksonville, where advanced training was headquartered. He had taken over flight operations under Winters, a CAG from the Pacific War and an ace like himself. "He was a very nice guy. We were teaching veteran pilots how to become instructors," although, as a leader, he'd mainly been involved with administration.

In early 1946, about the same time Simpler was coming up with his demonstration team idea, former British prime minister Winston Churchill had come to Florida after being defeated in his country's first postwar election. He had asked to see some naval and marine fighter pilots. Butch and a marine captain had been sent. "It was a real high point in my life." The Churchills were staying at the Palm Beach Bath and Tennis Club. "We met them after dinner. Just us, them, and the ocean. They were in one of those old-fashioned swings with chains and slats and a couple of cushions. It seemed quite private." Butch was in "awe. He wanted to hear about our experiences. We talked and he mostly listened. He'd ask questions and seemed to like our stories. He was particularly interested in carriers." They had refrained from asking him about himself. "We knew he wasn't well. The war was over and it had really hit him. It was just meeting this great guy."

Shortly after moving to Jacksonville, Butch had been promoted to lieutenant commander and accepted into the regular navy. "That was a big day. You go before the commanding officer and swear your allegiance and all that. I was excited about the flying. I liked the camaraderie. You have a closeness, a bonding between aviators that I don't think you find in other communities." It was the closeness to death that forged the bond. "Its the degree of hazard you face. You look at a fellow aviator, you see what he does and how he exposes himself to life and death, and that develops something inside of you, a sense of respect, camaraderie, whatever you want to call it." He liked the fact that promotion "wasn't gotten on the backs of others," but on "what you could or couldn't do." Sure, there were politics in the navy. "Who you know. Who you're related to. What school you went to." Especially the academy. But "as you continue, you develop your service reputation. You've earned it. It's nobody else's. And irrespective of what they put on paper, you are recognized for what you have become."

★

Butch was at his desk on the second floor of the instructors' advanced training hangar when he was summoned to Winters's office. "He said, 'Sit down,' and gave me the background. Washington was asking for comments on the advisability and feasibility of developing a flight demonstration team to demonstrate naval aviation and represent the navy at air shows and other functions as so ordered. I'm paraphrasing, but that's very close. [Winters] had been asked to prepare a draft answer, and so he called me. I'd done some air show work. Not a lot, but I had some knowledge."

Voris liked the proposal the minute he heard it. "Not for me [to become the leader]. I didn't even think about that. I just thought it was a good idea and hoped they'd approve it." Winters asked him to come up with a some suggestions as soon as he could. "I worked it out in the next day or so." The first problem was what airplane to use? He considered the sleek, gull-winged Vought F4U Corsair, which had followed the Hellcat in fighter development for the navy, and the twin-engine Grumman F7F Tigercat, the latest navy fighter, which had entered service at the tail end of the war. "I considered their characteristics as related to the types of maneuvers I thought we would be doing. Things like stability. The 'Hose Nose' [Corsair] was the nicest looking—the gull wing and all of that. But it had a deadly tendency. As you took it over the top slow and inverted, she'd snap-roll on you without warning." A snap roll was a quick rotation of the airplane on its longitudinal axis. The wings might go from level to straight up and down while it was traveling in a straight line. Or they might rotate a full 360 degrees. It could happen suddenly and be uncontrolled. "If you're close together," as he envisioned the planes flying, "it could wipe out the team." He was already thinking of the half-year season they'd be performing in, with its heart in the summer. "They'd be flying in some pretty turbulent weather in the middle of July." The risk of the sudden snap roll was too great. The Tigercat, he felt, was too big and not agile enough.

Not surprisingly he settled on the Hellcat. "I could have produced another kind of show with the other airplanes. You just had to work around the idiosyncrasies. But I already knew the Hellcat, knew what it could do. I'd flown it all through the war and trusted it. It was a totally honest aircraft," meaning it would do what the pilot thought and wanted. Lightened and partially fueled, he later wrote, "it was fairly sparky for its day." He actually took it out in the few days he had to get his answer together and tried some of what he had in mind. "I was just working out the parameters, seeing what speeds and altitudes would be needed." There were only so many maneuvers—loops, spirals, directional changers, climbs and dives, reversals, rolls, flying upside down. He'd done them all many times but never precisely and in such a confined arena as would be needed in a really good show. "What would be the altitudes in order to have a cushion [when he came down] so I wouldn't bust my ass?"

"I had to think about the wingmen. The leader couldn't be at full power because then he'd pull away from the others if there was any deviation. And with wind interference, stick correction, going from one maneuver to the other, there would be deviation. Speed was important. "You're always losing energy." Each maneuver would bleed speed, so in addition to writing down the safe altitudes, he penciled in the speeds each maneuver would need. "You run out of poop, you kill yourself." In the war and in training, he'd done the maneuvers at much higher altitude which gave ample time for recovery.

He determined they'd need good speed at the beginning in order to sustain energy as they climbed through the opening maneuvers. Climbing always depleted energy. They'd regain the energy as they came down and at various breaks in the show. There would be control problems. "In a roll, when your wings are pointed up and down [in relation to the ground], you don't have any real lift. That big nose [on the Hellcat] wants to go toward Mother Earth. So you are up on full rudder [to counter], and that's a real fine coordination of [applying] the rudder and then coming off the rudder. And then you are cross sticking [moving it to balance out what the rudder is doing]. It's a lot of coordination. You had to develop a feel for controlling the airplane."

He spent hours in the air going over each facet. "I had the time. I wasn't going to send a dumb answer back. It had to be an intelligent answer with the whys and hows. The selection wasn't going to be mine anyway. It was going to be made by the admirals and SecNav. I didn't have to have an exact show worked out, just something that was feasible. We had the pilots and ground crews available. The airplanes were available."

He wrote up his thoughts and gave the paper to Winters who sent it back up to Simpler in Washington. "I had a hunch they'd approve it because you could tell they wanted to approve it." But it took a little time. "They just wanted everybody's concurrence. It was a touchy subject. We're downsizing the navy, letting people go, closing air stations. The secretary was worried about Congress and all that, so Roy [Simpler] was spearheading. You could take a look at this thing and say how the hell can you be doing all the downsizing and then taking five or six good pilots and airplanes and dedicating them to stuntwork? So they passed it around to all the two-stars and three-stars under the premise that it would build esprit de corps and that bullshit. That wasn't the real reason. It was the advertised reason. And that was fine."

On April 24, according to Ron Williamson, Jacksonville Naval Air Station historian, a message from Admiral Nimitz directed the Advanced Training Command to organize "a flight exhibition team" with NAS Jacksonville as its base. Voris was to be the officer in charge. "Hugh came into my office and said, 'Looks like we got approval. How would you like to do it?'" The fact that the secretary of the navy and the CNO had picked him to create and run the team was inspiring. He was only twenty-seven-years-old. "You know, it was 'Yes, sir, yes, sir,' saluting with both hands and feet." But he knew the stakes. "My frame of mind was they didn't offer this to me to come in second to the army. I felt that if we weren't the best, it would be my naval career. Hugh and I talked a little about maneuvers, but then it was, hey, do whatever you feel is necessary and close the door behind you." He was on his own. "Nobody wanted to touch it. They were all scared." Not only were there the problems of keeping the effort quiet until the team had successfully hurdled the creation pitfalls, but the chances for accident were many, both in practice and at shows. "You could wipe out hundreds of people who are watching. But if you're going to be good, you're going to have to take acceptable risks." He resolved to forge a team second to none. "It was going to be the peak of competitiveness. You were representing the navy."

Years later, in describing his admiration for Butch, Mike Wolf said "the gutty thing about him was in breaking new ground. Nobody had done these things, nobody knew what those planes [the Hellcat and others Butch would fly in the coming air shows] could do in this new situation. In my opinion a better definition of a hero is someone who anticipates that he's going to kill himself doing something and goes ahead and does it anyway to accomplish the purpose." Voris, in accepting the challenge, was definitely stepping into the unknown. He'd flown the Hellcat and other planes in all kinds of maneuvers, at their top speeds and their slowest. He'd yanked and banked them and flipped them over upside down and plunged bulletlike in dives. He'd flown and maneuvered in sections and divisions and other needed combinations but never in the close-in proximity and exact precision that now would be required. "There wasn't going to be room for error," he said.

So be it.

This was an opportunity.

Right after meeting with Winters, he said he went back up in the Hellcat and continued working on parameters. He knew he didn't have much time. "We were under tremendous pressure from Washington. I was told they wanted it posthaste." He'd already begun considering his team. Three pilots would be the core. They'd be flying Hellcats in a V formation, the leader in front, two wingmen dropped close behind. He was to be allocated four airplanes plus a maintenance staff. He picked eleven of the command's best mechanics, who, at the time, weren't aware that they were doing anything other than new training duties. "We had no idea it was ever going to grow into anything like it did," said Robert Boudreaux, a tall, gangly aviation machinist's mate third class at the time. Neither did Voris. "I wasn't thinking much farther than the next flight." Beyond the core pilots, he'd need a spare or two to be in training as replacements.

All pilots would have to be personable. They'd be meeting with the public. Public relations was going to be a main purpose of the team. The directive had indicated team members should come from the command and be aviation cadets like himself, not academy graduates, who were considered already "captured" in terms of recruiting to aviation. They'd be trying to attract nonacademy men like themselves, the great rank and file of prospective naval aviators. He decided he only wanted bachelors like himself. "When you're married and you have kids, you've got more illness potential, more worry potential, keeping your wife happy. This was going to be new to all of us. We were going to be spending a lot of time together, traveling together, going out to dinner, staying in hotels. I wanted to establish a camaraderie, and I didn't think we could get that if they had families at home." He'd have some rules of conduct, he decided, governing drinking and partying. Not that they couldn't party, which they would, but flying was to take precedence, and they couldn't fly safely—especially the demanding flying they were going to do—if they'd been out all night. If something went wrong, "even if we'd been drinking ice water, they'd say we were drinking gin." Eventually, he would institute a ten p.m. curfew before show days. In all things, he'd be the example. He wouldn't ask them to do anything he wouldn't do himself.

Not everyone he interviewed was eager to join. "When they heard what was going to be required—the risks, the restrictions—some just walked away." First to accept, and happily so, was "Wick" Wickendoll, Butch's former Fighting 10 cruise roommate who had arrived at the command in February as a new instructor. "Good pilot. Steady. Bubbly," said

Butch. "He had the personality." Wickendoll welcomed the chance for challenging flying. The two were enthused to be reunited. Since leaving the Reapers several months after Butch, the twenty-eight-year-old Hutchinson, Kansas, native had served with another combat fighter squadron, VF-33, skippered by Butch's old instructor, Eddie Outlaw, and had won two Distinguished Flying Crosses and seven air medals. Piloting a Hellcat from the second *Langley*, a light carrier, he'd taken part in some of the same later battles Butch had, including the first Battle of the Philippine Sea and the Marianas Turkey Shoot, although they'd not had contact during that time. He'd flown missions against Truk, Iwo, Guam, Cebu, and Manila before coming home. Like Butch, the wide-grinning, almost boyish-looking Wickendoll was now a lieutenant commander.

Next to come aboard was Lieutenant Commander Lloyd G. "Barney" Barnard, an advanced instructor and combat ace from Donna, Texas. Barnard had served with Voris in Fighting 2. Like Butch, he had eight confirmed kills, five of them gotten on a single mission late in the cruise over Iwo Jima. "Our 'ace' of 'aces,'" Morrissey wrote in *Odyssey*—at least for that mission. He held a Navy Cross and two Air Medals. Wick was to fly right wing and be second in command; Barnard would fly left wing. As his first spare, he recruited a young lieutenant (j.g.), twenty-one-year-old Melvin W. Cassidy who had grown up in Cleveland, Ohio. Short, wiry, and sandy-haired, "Mel" or "Cass," as they called him, had gotten into the war at the end, flying VF-23 Hellcats from the *Langley* over Okinawa and Iwo, and in some of the first fighter sweeps over Japan proper. He'd earned a Silver Star, Distinguished Flying Cross, and seven Air Medals. He had started a "little stunt outfit down at NAS Opalocka [near Miami, Florida] and I heard about it. He was personable, so I interviewed him and talked to other people who knew him." The spare would train as a core member but do solos in shows until he was needed as a replacement. "He was a little sparky, an Irishman. Good pilot. So I brought him in on a conditional basis. They all came in on a conditional basis. Make it or you go."

More than anything else, Voris believed the team would sink or swim on teamwork. It's an "overworked word," he would write in 1979 in the foreword to *The Blue Angels: An Illustrated History*. But "absolute trust and confidence in those beside you" would be their "very lifeblood." Their safety would depend on it. Throughout their performance they would many times be just a hairsbreadth from disaster. "Close formation flying," he wrote, "demonstrated the ability to maintain the all-important leader-wingman mutual support" philosophy that had been so crucial in combat. The mainstay of the show he had in mind was something he said seldom, if ever, had been done before; at least he knew of no military teams that had ever done it. He called it "the blind roll." It was a roll of the airplane similar to the snap roll, but slower, precisely controlled, and entailed a full 360-degree revolution around the long axis of the plane as it traveled forward. The trick however was that all three planes would do the roll simultaneously while tight together in formation.

The close proximity of the rolling planes was the first danger. If they strayed from their individual lines of flight, even slightly, they'd probably collide. The fact that the two wingmen would at different times lose sight of the others during short portions of the roll was the other problem. "I wanted [the blind roll] in our routine because it was the hardest maneuver to do in close-in flying. Nobody else would be gutsy enough—or stupid enough, if you want to put it that way—to try it." The blind roll was the reason he'd chosen to go with a three-plane formation in the first place, instead of the more traditional four. "It would be too hard to do with four." It was dangerous enough with three.

"It would set us apart."

As he envisioned it, the blind roll would take maybe three or four seconds to complete. It was a smooth revolution of the airplane from upright to inverted to upright again—360 degrees—with no stopping between start and finish and while the three planes traveled on a straight flight path together. The three Hellcats, flying in a close V formation, would do the roll in unison. To the uninitiated the maneuver would look relatively easy. No jerking or sudden deviation. Just a straight revolution done together as in an aerial ballet. The problem was—and this is where it got the name blind—that as the planes rolled together, one or the other of the two wingmen would successively, because of the revolving of the cockpits, lose sight of the plane next to him. First one wingman, and then the other. He'd be "blind" for perhaps half the revolution—a very dangerous circumstance.

For instance, as the roll counterclockwise brought each plane's wings perpendicular to the ground, or vertical, the pilot flying the left wing would lose all sight of the two planes in the same position to his right. The other two could see the plane to their left and thus get that helpful sensory bearing. Then, as the roll continued and each plane brought the other wing toward the ground, the pilot on the right side would momentarily lose sight of the others. Not until the planes continued rolling back into level, right side up flight, and their cockpits thus moved to the upright position, would all pilots be able to see each other again.

Done solo, the maneuver wasn't so dangerous. But Butch's idea was that they would be doing it with mere feet separating the planes. Theoretically, a hiccup at that proximity could cause a midair collision. "It's a controlled roll. You had to maintain perfect and steady heading and altitude all the way through. The main problem was that big, heavy [Pratt and Whitney] 2800 engine in front. It wants to go down to Mother Earth, and it took absolute top full rudder [the pilot nearly standing on the pedals, manipulating them vigorously and precisely] to keep it from doing so. And you really had to hold that stick forward as you got upside down." In other words, the same push forward that would send the plane down when upright would send it up toward the sky when inverted, a juxtaposition that only the most experienced and skillful pilots could perform confidently. "And then the reverse of that coming around"—easing the stick back with exactitude to keep the plane from going down. "You can never do that perfectly. There's always some play." And many times, they would only be fifty to a hundred feet from the ground—no cushion at all should anything go wrong. "It required the ultimate rudder-stick interplay. You worked hard all the way through it."

With the initial team selected, Butch briefed each on the maneuvers he had in mind and then had them go out alone and start practicing. Essentially, these were the same basic combat maneuvers they'd all been flying in training and during the war—the loop, a circle up which brought the plane back down headed in the same direction it had been traveling, and the split S and Cuban eight, which were aerobatic ways of changing direction. The blind rolls as precision stunt and transitions. They would be using various combinations and variations of each as they flew through the show. "I wanted the show to be short, tight, and close to the crowd," said Butch. "It needed to be impactual [to the audience] on a gut level." It would take place in a chunk of sky roughly 7,000 feet wide and deep (the length of the runways) by 3,000 feet high, all of which would be in front of the spectator unless a vanishing exit was called for. The Hellcat's relatively short turning radius allowed for such a compact space.

Once both wingmen and Cassidy had gotten comfortable with what they would have to do, Butch went up with each and began coaching the maneuvers as two-man teams. To stay out of the limelight, they selected an outlying field, identified by Ron Williamson as what is now Herlong Field, a set of runways outside Jacksonville that Butch describes as being, in those days, "in the Everglades, so if something went wrong the alligators could eat the evidence." Starting comfortably high and many plane lengths apart, they gradually flew closer and lower. "Finally, you work them down to where if they bust a maneuver, they're dead." They wore parachutes, but to use them they needed altitude they usually didn't have. "It was always 'tighter, tighter, tighter.' I had to tug them a little bit to bring them in. It was high risk. Those propellers are twelve feet in diameter. You've got no room for slippage. You're flying a Cusinart. You have to be aware of that."

The blind rolls were the hardest to coax the pilots into doing. "When you lose sight, you've got to depend on things other than your eyes. You are out of sight for one to three seconds. You're doing it on guts and feel through your legs and arms. You can feel the pressure through the rudders and the stick. Through practice, you get to know the rate of roll and speed. You can be thrown off by the slightest variation."

Following their individual and two-man practice flights, they'd meet daily in Butch's second-story hangar mezzanine office and debrief and brainstorm. Feet up or sprawled out, taking turns at the blackboard or coffeepot, they eventually worked out a routine they figured would take about fifteen minutes. Some of it was based on what Butch had done previously in his solo shows at Daytona. Because the Hellcats were slow in getting started from the ground, which Voris thought would try the audience's patience, the team decided on a "high impact" opening from the air. From the right as the audience watched—and after coming down from high altitude in order to gain speed—they would roar in at a very low 50 feet, continue to the middle of the airspace and, right in front of the crowd, loop up to a height of 2,800 feet, teeter momentarily as they inverted and went over, then dive back down to 50 feet again. The dive would give them sufficient energy to roar onward on the right-to-left path out to the opposite edge of the audience where they would zoom up into a Cuban eight with the blind roll in order to change direction. Coming back down, they'd roar back across the field, left to right, 300 knots toward their entrance and zoom up into another Cuban eight with blind roll on the right side. The crowd, in effect, would see three swooping maneuvers going up and coming down with the blind roll featured on both ends. "We hoped it would be a crowd-pleaser."

Swooping around to the other side of the airspace, they would follow the opening with a blind roll, returning in front of the crowd in an arcing but straight flight path from left entry to right. The arc topped out at about 1,000 feet. Looping up and around, they would roar back from right to left and do a reverse echelon roll in which all three rolled together as a unit, not on their individual axes as in the blind, starting on one side of the flight path and ending up together in perfect unison and still in the V on the other side. The movement of the planes together around the single axis of the flight path would be a variation that everyone in the crowd could understand. Maneuver 4 would have them blind-rolling to the inverted (upside-down) position and holding it in a straight line as they roared left to right in front of the crowd at a mere hundred feet above the tarmac. They'd finish with some Cuban eights with blind rolls and echelon rolls of spacious half-loop direction reversals. The last of these would allow each plane to curl back toward the runway and land in one-two-three sequence, thus ending the show. "It was fast," said Butch. "In my mind, it was 'Get it up, get it on, get it down.'"

They hoped it would work.

Meanwhile, the Hellcats to be used by the team were selected and sent to the hangars to be modified and painted. The show planes would be slightly different from regular navy Hellcats. Grumman, maker of the fighter—perhaps among the first to sense the impact the team might have—now became involved and assisted in the modifications. "Basically, we had to strip them," said Butch. "We took out the guns, ammunition cans, and some armor. We're trying to lighten them in order to get a better power loading." They wanted to make them quicker and more nimble. All told, he estimates, they reduced the weight of each plane by approximately 1,500 pounds. That changed the center of gravity. "It's like balancing a pencil on a finger. Formerly, the center was between the wings and the cockpit. By removing what we did, the center, because of the heavy engine, went forward." To rebalance, they bolted the plane's tailhook in the retracted position and "sweated" (soldered) fifty pounds of sheet lead around it, in effect, encasing it in the fuselage. They wouldn't need the tailhook since the demonstrations were to be performed at landed bases and not on carriers. The internal center tank would hold plenty of fuel for the shows.

For color, they went with traditional navy blue and gold. But to be a little different, Voris picked a slightly lighter shade of dark blue than was normally used on navy planes in those days. The name of the paint was "insignia blue." That was just the name and had little to do with modern insignias since it was out-of-date and little used. He didn't want any fancy stripes or emblems on the planes. "The navy's very conservative," he said. But he had "US Navy" painted on the bottom of the wings and on the side of the fuselage behind the wings, as well as large numbers 1, 2, 3, and 4 on the tails to designate positions in the team. As flight leader, he flew number 1, and was commonly referred to as "the Boss" or just "Boss." A mystery is the fact that years later he found out that what he thought was gold paint on the Hellcats was actually very expensive gold leaf. "Talk about $8,000 toilet-seat scandals. I didn't know this until I got a call a few years ago [probably early 1990s] from the guy who had been my painter. He said, Captain, you must have had some pull to get that much gold leaf to lay on the airplanes. Somebody high up, I guess, was doing us a favor."

The lighter, reconfigured, and newly painted Hellcats were ready and delivered probably by May 9. May 10, goes the lore, is the date of the team's first official flight, meaning, apparently, in their new planes. While Voris can't be sure of the exact date, he does have an asterisk penciled in beside the tenth in his log. But other entries in his log on the days following, as well as written sources, including what Ron Williamson has, indicate that it wasn't until May 21 that the team began intensive training, meaning multiple training sessions daily. Why the gap, he doesn't remember, but the reason May 21 is cited, he says, is probably that by that day they had worked out the preliminary kinks, knew exactly what they wanted to do, and had begun practicing in earnest as a three-plane unit.

"We were under terrific pressure from Washington," Butch reiterated. "They were always asking, 'When are you going to be ready?' I figured it would take us about a month or so." Starting high and loose, he eventually brought the three Hellcats lower and tighter until "if we made a mistake, we'd die." His original idea had been to fly the show silent like the Marine Corps drill team performing on a pad. "They move without anybody calling out signals." But then the team was descending in a maneuver in one of the practices, and a team member forgot the sequence and began doing a different maneuver. "It was like a bombshell in the chicken coop. He had a mental lapse. We were down around hangar level. Could have been a disaster." Voris called a halt to the practice. "I said, okay, let's tuck it in, take it back home. You go down and talk it over. Anybody can have a temporary mental lapse." From then on he began calling the maneuvers over the plane radios. "I'd get a cadence in my voice to set the timing." It started as they hit the show line. "I'd say, 'Aaaaaand up we go' as I pull into the [four] G [upward turn]. I'm setting the rhythm. You don't have to talk all the way around the maneuver. It was just preparatory, getting the beat as we moved into it. Then setting it again. 'Now the loop.'" And so on.

They practiced above remote rural and forested areas with dirt roads that would give them a reference point, as well as the outlying Herlong and Brannon Fields. Brannon, another former World War II strip, had intersecting runways for visual reference. Pulling as many as six Gs in turns, flying inverted and at high speed, they didn't wear the bulky G-suits that are standard issue today. "We wore only the thinnest flight suits," said Voris, "so we could 'feel' the airplane. Nothing I know of takes such intense concentration as close-in demonstration flying, whether you're flying wing and holding your position on the leader or flying lead. If you look at the films of some of the guys [in later teams] you'll see them absolutely rigid with concentration. We'd have to be at least 2,000 feet up in the air and straight and level to jump out, and [once they got it perfected] we were seldom that high. That kind of flying doesn't accept a lot of mistakes. It accepts no mistakes."

In what appears to be the first public mention of the team, the *Jax Air News*, the area's navy publication, ran in its May 2, 1946, edition a back-page picture of some F4U gull-winged Corsairs flying in formation. The caption said that the as yet unnamed U.S. Navy Flight Exhibition Team had been "established last week in the Naval Air Advanced Training Command." Acknowledging that the team would be flying Hellcats rather than Corsairs, the paper promised that the "names of the team pilots" would "be announced next week." The lack of any substantial information—even the fact that the wrong planes, purposely or not, were shown—was indicative of the general secrecy in which the team was being created. The navy was still playing the project close to the vest. But in the advanced training hangar halls, everybody wanted to know when the new team would be ready. Sometime in the beginning of June, Voris felt they'd hit their stride. He informed Commander Dan "Dog" Smith, "I've got something to show you." While Winters was Voris's administrative boss, Smith, a seasoned fighter pilot who worked for Advanced Training Chief Davison as his fighter expert, was the person he reported to for "flying and performance" matters. Smith had been a fighter squadron skipper and air wing commander in the Pacific. He and Butch were personal friends who frequently double-dated together. If Smith liked the routine, they knew they'd get endorsed. "I said, here's what I propose. Let's go out to one of the outlying fields in alligator country, and we'll do a show for you. He said fine. I'll take a [Hellcat] out there, park at the end of the runway with the engine running [so the radio would work] and give you the cue when I'm ready."

Voris said he never doubted they'd do well. "We knew we had something really good." Smith flew out to the field and got ready. On cue, the team went into its first-ever performance for an audience—even if it was just one observer. If Smith gave his approval, he'd recommend the team to his boss, Admiral Davison. The team swooped in and looped into the big opening. "My idea was to take the most acceptable risk I could. I broke it down into two types of maneuvers. Those that were ultra high risk like the blind rolls, the inversions at one hundred feet. Those were meant to impress other aviators. The loops and V rolls were for the general audience to say ooooooo, look at that. To keep their attention. But the risk in those was reduced. You had to strike a balance. I knew if we didn't run into each other, we'd make a hell of an impression on Dog. He was a fighter pilot. He knew what we were doing."

Everything, felt Butch, went just as he'd wanted it, just as they'd practiced it. "It was probably the best show we ever flew. When it was over, I called him on the radio and said, 'That completes the demonstration.' He said, 'Roger, I'll see you back at the main field [NAS Jacksonville].' Nothing else. Not a thing about what he thought of what we'd done. So we went back and landed. We were about a hundred feet away and waiting when he parked. I jumped down and walked over to him. He was just coming out of his plane. He looked at me. 'You crazy sonofabitch. You're all going to kill yourselves. But you know what? I liked it. Hey, you guys are good. I'm going to talk to the admiral. I want him to see it.' He was enthused."

The next afternoon, June 7, they did the show for Davison and a small group of navy onlookers. Davison was the next in the chain of approvals. The airfield was closed late in the afternoon, and the team repeated what they'd done for Smith. At the end, Davison, too, was enthusiastic. "I can't remember the exact words he used, but he said he was going to recommend that Admiral Wagner [head of all navy training, headquartered in Pensacola] see us, and in the meantime we got clearance to perform in the Southeastern Air Exposition, which was going to be held at Craig Field near Jacksonville." It was only a week away. "I didn't know we were going to perform there. It would be our first public appearance."

In effect, the private show for Smith was the real "birth of the Blues," a phrase often used in recounting those days in print. Had Smith not approved, the team easily could have been disbanded. But now, given the green light by both the reigning fighter expert and by his boss, the top naval officer in the Jacksonville area, the show was up and running. It didn't have a name, and nobody foresaw the impact it eventually would have. "We weren't worried much about the next step," said Voris. They didn't even have a schedule, just a date a week or so hence that they were eager to keep. Voris had seized another opportunity. He credits teamwork and dedication. "Everyone felt the same as I did. If they didn't, there was going to be somebody else in their place."

CHAPTER 18

The news must have been a shock.

It was early Saturday, June 15, a week after the Davison show. Butch and the team were gathering in their NAS Jacksonville hangar for preliminaries before performing their first public demonstration. It was to take place at Craig Field, twenty miles away. The field, named after a Jacksonville native, navy commander James Edwin Craig, killed at Pearl Harbor, had been a military training auxiliary during the war but was now being given back to the city. Today's dedication event was being combined with the first annual Southeastern Air Show and Exposition and would feature flyovers and demonstrations by military and civilian teams and individuals. There had been advance stories in the papers heralding the event. Understandably, Butch and his group were keyed up and anxious, looking forward to their debut before a nonmilitary audience. It would be the next measuring stick.

Not every team member, it appears, was at the hangar. At least that's Butch's recollection. They were still gathering. The phone rang and Butch answered. "It was a member of Admiral Davison's staff. Can't remember his name. He was the multiengine [bomber] guy, just like Dan Smith was the single-engine [fighter] guy. He said, 'Butch, I saw Barnard out with some gal boozing it up at two o'clock in the morning. Did you know about that?' I said no. I had no idea. It was a complete surprise. He said, 'We can't tolerate that.' It was just that quick."

Barnard was number three, left wing on the demonstration unit, Voris's old squadron mate and crucial to the team, especially on this important day. "Carousing and drinking the night before a show wasn't going to work," Voris recalled. "It endangered everybody's life." It was also a breach of the trust and dedication they had all built up. Because the team was still forming, Voris hadn't yet instituted the ten p.m. curfew prior to shows. But "we all knew the seriousness. You just don't put people's lives in jeopardy like that. It was a good thing Cassidy was ready." Voris said he would have fired Barnard on the spot himself, but the caller, relieving him of that responsibility, said the staff would take care of it. Most probably Barnard (now deceased) wasn't at the hangar when the phone call came in because Voris can't remember seeing him that day—or ever again. Presumably, Davison's staff had already summoned the lieutenant commander and was just letting Butch know of the pending action. They didn't waste time. The Pacific ace was immediately dismissed from the team and reassigned to a job in the training command at NAS Corpus Christi.

"I must have said something to the others," said Voris, "but all I can remember is 'Cassidy, you're flying.' We were performing in a few hours. You can't dwell on it. You have to get on with things. Nothing, of course, went public." A story was concocted that since Barnard was senior to Voris in terms of time in grade, which was true, Butch being the boss might have caused leadership problems, and that was why Barnard was reassigned. The cover story was used both internally and with inquiries from the press. But the firing had occurred so suddenly that the publicity for the team's appearance later that day at the show still had Barnard's picture on it. Even today, references to Barnard being a member of the original team quote the seniority problem as the reason he left. Butch never corrected the accounts because he didn't want Barnard's family to suffer.

Putting the matter behind them, the team began the game day routine they would follow throughout the demonstration season: "Stand around. Drink coffee. Talk over the maneuvers. Watch the time. We were still at NAS Jacksonville and had to fly over to Craig. It's amazing. You congregate. You walk up and down the line. It's like a mental rehearsal. You get everybody's mind running on the show, and you try to keep it that way until you get into the airplane. It's talk, check your airplanes, do a lot of standing out on the concrete and under the wing trying to stay out of the sun. I tell you, when my mind went into show mode, everything else went away."

Concentration was key.

Barnard wasn't the only change to the team. The day before, on June 14, a new team member had reported. Lieutenant Alfred "Al" Taddeo had been serving with Cassidy at Opalocka in Miami. He'd volunteered for the team at the same time Cassidy had, but only Cassidy had been picked. Then, on the thirteenth, he'd received sudden orders to report immediately to Jacksonville. "Mel and I were pretty good buddies," recalled Taddeo, who was living in Southern California in 2003 after a successful naval and business career. "We both wanted the duty. When he got selected, I went about my business as an instructor until all of a sudden I got orders to Jacksonville." Voris hadn't passed him up earlier. It had just taken that long to get the twenty-seven-year-old fighter pilot requisitioned. Taddeo was a bit senior to Cassidy. "He had good references," said Butch.

Like the others before him, Taddeo, born in Portland, Oregon, was a combat veteran and a bachelor. Winged in 1942, he'd flown Wildcats off the light carrier *Nassau* in the Aleutians Campaign, and then Hellcats for Butch's first squadron, VF-10, in the Central Pacific. Like Butch, he'd been at the First Battle of the Philippine Sea. He told a story of a Japanese pilot who followed the returning American fighters home in the confusion of that night and tried to land on an American carrier when Mitscher turned on the lights. With three Japanese shoot-downs to his credit, he had several Distinguished Flying Crosses and a slew of Air Medals and battle stars. Most of all, he was a good pilot. The timing of his arrival was perfect, because with Barnard gone and Cassidy taking over as left wing, he would become the spare. "I knew something had happened to Barnard because there were rumors. They [the team] were very selective, and I was happy to be picked."

Also added to the team by this time was Lieutenant (j.g.) Gale Stouse, twenty-five, of Kokomo, Indiana, recruited specifically for a new crowd-pleaser idea of Voris's. The war was still fresh in the minds of the public, and Butch thought a simulated dogfight and shoot-down with a Japanese Zero would add drama. To that end, he had an old SNJ-6 two-seat, single-engine trainer like the one he'd flown in his early training put in the shop to be repainted bright yellow with large red "meatballs" on each side of the fuselage and the wings, and a blue zero on the tail. Pictures of it look surprisingly like the enemy aircraft. The refashioned trainer, later, according to accounts, nicknamed *Beetle Bomb* (Butch doesn't remember it being called thus when he was there), would have a rack on its belly that held smoke canisters that, when released, would simulate a burning aircraft. It also had a .30-caliber fake gun that fired loud blanks. At a certain part in the show, the three Hellcats would pursue and shoot down the Zeke in a demonstration of what had happened so many times in the Pacific.

Stouse, an aviation instrument instructor during the war, would fly the Zero through loops and dives, firing the blanks, as the Hellcats chased it. Then his plane captain, aviation machinist's mate Bob Boudreaux, one of the support crew riding in the backseat, would pop the smoke bombs as he tried to disappear behind an obstruction like a nearby building or clump of trees. When possible, a minor fireworkslike explosion would be set off at the site to simulate a crash. In addition, Boudreaux would be holding a sawdust-filled dummy with a parachute attached. After the smoke appeared and they headed for the fake crash, he'd release the dummy, dressed in Japanese flight suit and helmet, in a simulation of the enemy pilot bailing out. The dummy would float to the ground far enough from the crowd to be indistinguishable from the real thing.

At least that's the way Voris envisioned it.

According to Butch, the Zero wasn't yet ready for the Craig show. They hoped to integrate it soon.

As takeoff time approached, the first spectators of an estimated 35,000 who would attend the Craig show over Saturday and Sunday began to fill the bleachers. Air shows, promising speed, thrills, and danger, hadn't been seen in the area since before the war. Now, local newspapers had trumpeted, they were back! The excited crowd gathered and mingled on what looked like a "high school football field" or "the grounds of a county fair," wrote Bill Foley, a columnist for the *Florida Times-Union,* the large Jacksonville newspaper. He was there as a youngster and penned a column about it decades later. The onlookers were a "carnival-like crowd wandering about drinking soda pop and eating peanuts," wrote Foley. Rare photos of the event show young girls in crinolined dresses, military men in breezy summer uniforms, lots of parasols and white fedora hats to shade the sun. Also scheduled, according to a mimeographed sheet of the events kept by Taddeo, were air races, stunt flyers, old-time barnstormers, navy bombers, and Corsairs that put on simulated attack runs, a parachutist, "Sad Sack" the clown, and the first jet plane ever seen over Jacksonville, a sleek army air corps F-80 Shooting Star. Foley: "You could walk over and touch" the planes "when they landed" and the pilots "smiled and shook your hand before they flew and did wonderful things."

There was a friendly feeling to the event and awe and wonder in the mind of the young boy and future columnist. What worried Voris as he and the team took off and headed to Craig was the weather. They were scheduled to appear at the end of the show, late in the afternoon. As he recalled it, "The clouds build as the heat rises. We were airborne, in sight of the field, waiting to be called in, and I saw this layer of low-lying clouds moving in with the prevailing winds. They were at about 1,800 to 2,000 feet. Our vertical maneuvers [those going up, which were many] would take us right into them." They couldn't have that. They'd lose sight of each other. It would be too dangerous. "We'd have to do a 'modified,' or what we call a 'flat,' show—cut all the vertical stuff. It would be emasculating."

He didn't want to do it. He watched and hoped. "I could see the clouds coming in, passing over." Following the flyover of a PB4Y Privateer, the navy's single-tailed version of the army's B-24 Liberator, which did a wingover—a high-reaching turn that rolled it into the opposite direction—they were given the call. "Just as we started in, the clouds dissipated. Kind of a miracle really."

They wouldn't have to truncate their show.

"Now the moment of truth had arrived," he later wrote. "How would we be received and measured?"

The three glistening blue-and-gold Hellcats roared into the Craig Field airspace. "Aaaand up we go," Voris cadenced on the radio, beginning the rhythm. They zoomed skyward together into the first maneuver, the four-G high hanging loop. It materialized almost in the center of the crowd's view. In the stands, as the routine progressed, little Bill Foley saw "roaring, thrilling precision." The "three-ship formation . . . swooped the carnival crowd with the soda pop and cotton candy and left it open-mouthed . . . 10,000 oohed and aahed . . . Tightly, wing-to-wing the Hellcats flew, in rolls and loops and Cuban eights . . . I remember more the sounds and smells and shouts and thrills than the significance of it all . . . It marked the beginning of a tomorrow with limits as high and wide as the sky."

In the little boy's mind, a new age had dawned.

Out in the Hellcats, however, the heat was making it tough for the team. "God, it was rough," recalled Butch. "The rising air coming off the runway was causing such turbulence that you'd get a jolt every time you went through it. After every maneuver I had to recinch my seat belt or I would have hit the top of the canopy. It was jolt after jolt. The airplane would yaw [rotate sideways] and pitch, and you'd come clear out of your seat. You really had to fight to control it. I had a handkerchief around my neck because the sweat was running down my head. This is the way it is in the summer, and that's the heart of our season."

The show was twelve minutes long, described by Butch as "twelve intense, breath-holding minutes of grunt, pull, turn, and roll." Despite the bumps and jolts, he took the team as close to the ground as he could, fifty feet above the concrete in some instances, he estimates. "We had no limitations on our altitude, so I brought it right to the deck. We could see the expansion joints on the concrete. Might as well start down where they could see and get to know you." His radio was connected to the show's speaker system and the onlookers heard every cadenced call, every groan and grunt. They didn't yet have a narrator. That would come later.

While he felt good about how the team had performed, he didn't know how the crowd had reacted until the three chunky Hellcats came taxiing by the stands to park in front of the audience, a scene captured by rare photos taken by an onlooker, Menard Norton, using an old Brownie box camera. "You could see them all waving handkerchiefs and clapping their hands," said Butch, whose plane glistens darkly, engine running, in one of the photos. Norton sent them to Butch years later. When the engines were stilled and the pilots were exiting their cockpits, they finally could hear the approval. "It was a tremendous ovation. Real receptive." Commander Winters and other staff from Jacksonville were in the grandstand clapping along with the audience, and the team, all smiles and waves, walked over and shook hands with them. They repeated the show the following day, Sunday, and received a surprise—a three-foot-high shining bronze and wood trophy. It had engravings and an airplane on the top. "They called us to the grandstand. I didn't know they were going to do that. It was a big surprise. It was for the best performance at the air show."

After addressing the crowd in their flight suits—a *Florida Times-Union* picture the next day shows them sweaty and laughing on the podium—they probably went to the base officer's club for celebratory drinks and then definitely on to their favorite restaurant, Giupponi's Spaghetti House, in downtown Jacksonville, where Butch loved the sausages and the team debriefed the show between bites. "What could we do better here? How could we tighten up there? What did we do wrong?" The relaxed examination over dinner was the beginning of what would grow into a rigorous system of critical debriefing of pilots. It is integral to Blue Angels' success today.

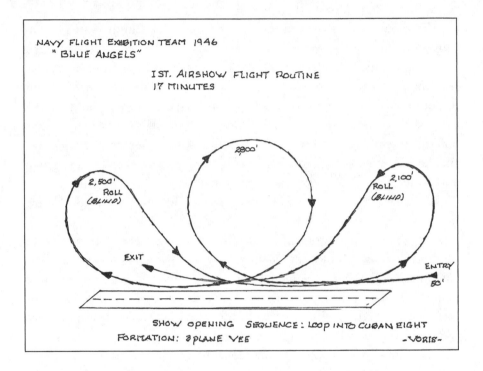

NAVY FLIGHT EXHIBITION TEAM 1946
"BLUE ANGELS"

1ST. AIRSHOW FLIGHT ROUTINE
17 MINUTES

2800'

2,500'
ROLL
(BLIND)

2,100'
ROLL
(BLIND)

EXIT

ENTRY
50'

SHOW OPENING SEQUENCE: LOOP INTO CUBAN EIGHT
FORMATION: 3 PLANE VEE   -VORIS-

★

Getting the green light from his superiors didn't mean everything would go smoothly for Butch. A day after winning the Southeastern Air Show trophy, he found himself leading the team's Hellcats to NAS Corpus Christi—future scene of the midair collision that he would miraculously survive—to perform for the chief of naval operations, Nimitz himself. While the team's schedule was only day to day at this stage, they'd been impressive enough already to be asked to fly at "Nimitz Day," June 18, at Corpus Christi in celebration of the admiral's visit to the south Texas base. Nimitz was from Texas. Butch had trained there and was looking forward to seeing it again and performing. But en route from Jacksonville and over the marshes of the Florida panhandle, his Hellcat engine began sputtering and losing power as his fuel pressure dropped. He was suddenly in danger of going down.

Pretty quickly, he guessed the problem: "I had water in my belly drop tank and it had burned up my fuel pump." Losing power, he was rapidly losing altitude. As in the carriers, it was common practice on air bases to pump water into storage tanks as fuel was pumped out in order to minimize the accumulation of explosive vapors. But the water, heavier than the fuel, would pool at the bottom of the tank. Occasionally, as gas dwindled in the tanks, water would be transferred with the aviation gas during refueling. The team's Hellcats had been serviced from a tanker truck prior to leaving, and Butch was not there at the time. Now he surmised that his plane had been last in line to receive the juice. Water in a tank had been pumped into the truck and then had transferred to his airplane. As the water had traveled to his engine, the fuel pump, normally lubricated by the petrol, had overheated and failed. The belly drop tank was an add-on. The Hellcats had three internal fuel tanks and an auxiliary fuel pump. Luckily, the internal fuel tank he quickly switched to was water free. The Hellcat sputtered a few seconds as its engine cleared and then started rising and flying normally again.

"Almost dumped my airplane in the swamps."

Because of the problem, they had to make an unscheduled stop at New Orleans Moisant International Airport. The belly tank was flushed out and refilled. They flew on to one of Corpus Christi's outlying fields. There they were met by Butch's former flight instructor, Eddie Outlaw, who, again, was stationed at Corpus. The two hadn't seen each other since the Pacific War when Outlaw had mistaken a navy TBF torpedo bomber for an enemy plane and "put something like fifty-seven holes in it." Outlaw, a fighter skipper at that time, had been ordered to *Hornet* to explain himself, and he and Butch had shared coffee in the wardroom. "He didn't tell me what happened, but I found out, shortly after that, he'd been summoned there to get his wrists slapped and explain how he could have made such a mistake."

The show the next day went off without a hitch. It was the first, according to Butch, in which the simulated attack on the Zero appeared. The dogfight was inserted near the end of the routine, following the low inverted pass, and added to the climax and stretched the performance to approximately seventeen minutes. Years later, Butch described it: "[Following the inverted pass] we take a little more room coming around. We enter full speed [diving toward the crowd] and here comes our Japanese Zero. He'd enter from behind the grandstand, out of their backs. And of course the announcer [subsequently added to the team] builds the scene. 'Here comes the enemy . . . ' So now we've got a rhubarb. We're head on with him and away we go. We'll pull up to seven Gs. It's a ballbuster because if you don't, you can't fly over the crowds. You grunt and pull. You're upside down and he's in the middle." The melee looped and zoomed. "He fires his guns. Pop, pop, pop, pop, pop. It's not like the Hellcat's six fifties but loud enough. After about three passes at each other, the smoke canisters are pulled. Now he's trailing smoke. He does a kind of wingover, rolls upside down and the plane captain ejects the dummy in the parachute. He flies off behind the grandstand as though he's crashed, and the fire trucks start wailing. The crowd is standing there thinking it's real and while that's going on we pull off full power again to get altitude and energy" for their landing maneuver.

As much as they could, they tried to incorporate real shoot-down maneuvers in attacking the Zero.

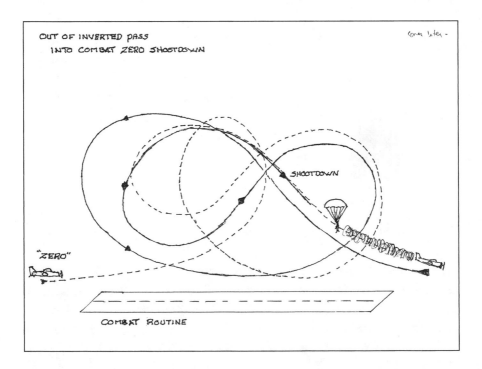

The show, conducted over the bay, was so well received that Voris was later sent a commendation letter, dated 24 June 1946, by his old battle commander from *Hornet,* Jocko Clark. Clark by then was chief of naval air basic training at Corpus Christi and had witnessed the show along with Nimitz. "The performance of yourself and pilots under your command," he wrote, "was outstanding. The skill and pilot technique displayed in performing precision acrobatic maneuvers in close order formation at terrific speed was breathtaking. . . . The demonstration of combat fighter tactics in shooting down the simulated 'Jap Zero' was cleverly conceived and exceptionally well executed. Your entire performance demonstrated naval piloting at its best."

Nimitz, too, was impressed. Butch says the CNO went away agreeing with an earlier, June 17, recommendation by Captain William E. "Bill" Gentner Jr., head of training at NAS Jacksonville, that the team should switch to the navy's newest and latest fighter plane, the Grumman F8F-1 Bearcat. Gentner's message to the CNO, kept by Taddeo, said in part:

TEAM IS AN OUTSTANDING CONTRIBUTION FOR PUBLIC INFORMA-
TION ON NAVAL AVIATION X ORIGINATOR FEELS THAT IN THE IN-
TEREST OF THE NAVY AND PUBLIC APPEAL THE SUBJECT TEAM
SHOULD BE EQUIPPED WITH F8F AIRCRAFT.

Designed specifically to replace the Hellcat, the Bearcat hadn't been ready for combat until after World War II ended. But it was the best operational fighter the navy had in early 1946.

The team would be flying it in a little over a month.

★

If there was a reason beyond duty, opportunity, and personal ambition for Voris to excel at leading the navy's newly formed demonstration team, it was to beat army—and any other pilots, or groups of pilots, he and the team might compete with. Like most good fighter pilots, beneath the appearance of even temper, he was extremely competitive. "That was my motivation from day one," he says about the Army-Navy rivalry. The army air corps, emerging triumphant out of World War II, didn't have an official flight demonstration team yet.

But it had some great pilots.

Voris would be competing against them soon enough.

Leaving Corpus Christi after the show, the team stopped for the night in New Orleans. This time the visit was just for fun. "We did that occasionally," Butch says with a smile. "We'd put in a full day's work. We deserved it." The next morning they flew on to Jacksonville, where, for about a week, they got back to business, honing the act through rigorous daily practice sessions and working Taddeo in as the spare at left wing. "You've got to do it [practice] almost every day or you lose your edge." Like professional athletes or actors rehearsing, they needed the constant tuning. "You could never be perfect, but that was always our goal." By now the word about them had begun to spread, and they'd started receiving requests for appearances. "We got our orders from the Jacksonville staff, at Dan Smith's level. The requests would come into Washington. [Washington would] make the decisions, tell my boss, and that's where we'd go. We never solicited shows ourselves."

Des Moines, Iowa, was next on the list. The Iowa State Fair, a major event in the nation's wheat and corn breadbasket, had been a casualty during World War II, having been called off so that the army air corps could use the fireproof buildings on the grounds as a supply depot. Now that the war was over, the fair was being revived as a part of Iowa's 1946 centennial celebration. The Hawkeye State, with its immense rolling prairies, was one hundred years old. Part of the festivities planned was a "patriotic dedication" featuring "demonstrations by the Army, Navy and Marine Corps." It was to this demonstration that the team was dispatched on June 30. And it was a good thing that they were scheduled to perform on the last day of the festivities, July 2. Although the fair was a multiday event, with many contests, shows, and exhibits, bad weather in the days preceding July 2, which was a Tuesday, caused cancellations and shifting of events, including bringing the horse show indoors and changing the time of the city's "victory parade" to accommodate "the Bob Hope show" at the fairgrounds—all this according to a newspaper clip in Butch's files.

"Navy Will 'Bag' Zero at Airport" is the headline on the story. Which paper it came from is not identified. Presumably it was the *Des Moines Register,* the city's major daily. The article was accompanied by a picture, possibly two [not clear from the article remnant], of the three show Hellcats in formation, obviously sent in advance, probably from Washington. Butch remembers the bad weather. "In those days, in the summertime, you had thunderstorms and tornadoes in that area [the Southwest up to the Midwest]. You had the cold air from the north meeting the warm, moist air from the Gulf. We flew some god-awful flights trying to get through it. If we couldn't get around it we'd go low and try to stay under." On this particular trip, he said, during the Jacksonville to Atlanta leg, they had to "break a few rules" and fly "three to four hundred feet off the ground or lower across Okeefenokee." The swamp would have been encountered just north of Jacksonville as they entered and began to fly over Georgia.

The trip took two days. The rain, wind, and lightning were so bad over the portions of Tennessee, Kentucky, and Illinois in their approach to Iowa that they'd had to spend the first night in Evansville, Indiana, instead of going on to St. Louis as they'd planned. "We had to secure the planes with stakes and tie-downs," recalled Butch. There was always the threat of tornadoes. But July 2 dawned beautifully and, arriving early at the municipal airport, where, according to the article Butch kept, the air show would begin at one p.m., they got their first real look at the competition. "That's where I met Dave Shilling," said Butch. Shilling, one of the army air corps' highest-scoring fighter pilots in the European war, had shot down twenty-two German planes flying a P-47 Thunderbolt, the barrel-nosed fighter Butch liked and had fought so much during training with VF-2. He was said to have been among the three most feared American fighter pilots by the Germans, along with Francis S. "Gabby" Gabreski, America's highest scoring World War II ace (thirty-one victories), and Hubert "Hub" Zemke (seventeen). Shilling, who would die in an auto accident in England in 1956, wasn't performing in the Des Moines show. Probably a colonel at the time, he'd brought a squadron of young army pilots who did some formation flying. Butch and Shilling watched them together from the ground at the show's beginning. "Just routine stuff. They rolled upside down and did some loops but nothing precision. They weren't a practiced team at all."

Butch met some of the army flyers and established a friendship with Shilling. "We were all aviators. There was a lot of common bonding." But he walked away confident that when the navy team took to the air, they'd prevail. "When you know you've got something that is better than anyone else, you can be pretty calm." Then the team was almost derailed by circumstance. Circling and waiting for their turn, the army kept parading plane after plane before the dazzled crowd. They included a B-29, a C-54 transport, and a C-47, according to *Des Moines Register* reporter Don Allen, whose article on the show Taddeo preserved. Eventually, wrote Allen, one of the Hellcats radioed the tower: "Tell the army if they don't hurry up . . . there won't be any navy show." The army finally concluded and the Hellcats got the go-ahead. While Allen's next day article began with, "The navy joined the army in an aerial blitz on municipal airport Tuesday afternoon," he devoted most of his coverage to the army. The army pilots themselves, however, after they landed, crowded Butch and his team and were abuzz with the close-in, slow, axis rolls. "They kept asking, 'How'd you do that? Where'd you learn that?' It wasn't much of a contest. We walked away with first place. It was hands down."

It wasn't going to be as easy next time—which was coming sooner than they knew. But in a fighter pilot sense, it would be more fun.

They stayed in Des Moines until July 4, when they headed to Kansas City, where they planned to stop for refueling and spend the night at the noted Muehlebach Hotel, the stately and venerable downtown landmark where then President Harry S. Truman would hold court when back in his home state of Missouri. July 4, 1946, was the first American Independence Day in five years that the nation had not been at war. Now was the aftermath of victory. Shows of U.S. military might were being held all over the country, including at Kansas City's Fairfax Municipal Airport. More than 12,000 people were there to see an array of army air corps fighters and bombers "give a review of the things learned in the war years," according to the *Kansas City Star*'s July 5 front page—only Voris didn't know anything about the show.

He wasn't aware he was flying into it.

Ten miles out, he radioed the tower for landing instructions and was advised that the field was closed. No one could land, except in an emergency. He was given the "notem" (advisory) number. "I don't know how I missed it," he said. "I'd read all the notems before we took off." He thought quickly. "I said, 'We're the Navy Flight Exhibition Team.' They said, 'Wait a minute.' Apparently they talked with the commanding general there who said they'd give us permission to land if we participated. I said, 'Affirmative.'"

As the team was parking and getting out of their Hellcats, a general came speeding up in his staff car. Cassidy had a Hawaiian shirt on under his flight suit, which didn't look too professional. "I told him to keep his suit zipped." The general stepped from his car surrounded by aides. "We shook hands. He says, 'Who are you? What do you do?' He was kind of gruff. I said, 'Normal fighter tactics.' He said, 'Well, you agreed to fly in our air show?' I said, 'Yes, sir, I'd be pleased to.' 'We'll put you on last—after our boys.'" He looked at his staff. "I could see he regarded us as idiots. It was a we'll-show-'em look."

According to the *Star* article, the army, in a static display on the ground, gave "Kansas City . . . it's first real close-up" of a P-80 jet, which then, after taking off, "passed by" with a "swoosh." Also flying were "a mighty B-29" with P-51 Mustangs off each wing; two "twin-boom, twin-engine" Black Widow fighters, "four or five" Mustangs "pulling up into almost vertical climbs" and then leveling off, and three B-26 "Marauder" bombers which "dashed across the field." This was the dawning of the jet age, and the P-80 was "impressive" to Butch, "fairly sleek. Lockheed had done a good job on it." And the piston-engined Mustang was a "beautiful machine. Good range. It had a tremendous history in Europe [during the war]." But he had no envy or yearning for the faster jets. "I was too concerned with our own flying and beating the competition." And what he saw of the army show above him wasn't worrisome. "They looked like a flock of geese going north and then south. It was all formation. They really didn't have anything that would make you think they were professional show people. We were chomping at the bit."

Finally, they were called to go up. Unfortunately, the runway the three took off from was too narrow for a formation takeoff. Cassidy, in the left wing position, started to swerve to the left which had a sizable gutter and could have led to a disaster. But he recovered, and, narrowly missing another obstacle—a large, arrow-shaped wind direction indicator in the field's center—taxied back, took off on his own, and joined the others in the air. The demonstration, without an announcer, went smoothly. As the *Star* reported it in their front-page article: "The show had a feature not on the program. Three Grumman planes of the navy landed at Fairfax . . . after a flight from Des Moines. The leader [mistakenly identified as] Lieut. Comdr. George W. O'Keefe, volunteered to take part in the program. The precision formation flying of the navy planes was as remarkable as their presence had been unexpected. . . ."

Despite the misnaming of the leader, the navy clearly had stolen the show. "We landed and the crowd gave us all the toots and whistles," said Butch. But as they exited their cockpits, the general came motoring up.

"He was madder than hell. 'You should have told me what you were!' He was beside himself. I played dumb. 'I'm sorry, sir, I tried to tell you.' He fumed. I can still see him stomping away and getting into his staff car, 'Yap, yap, yap, yap . . .' That was one of the good ones."

Later, after checking in to the Muehlebach, they went and found a party which really didn't end until the following morning when the girl sleeping in the bathtub hurriedly dressed and left for work. "When I look back I kind of shudder. We could have gotten some big complaints. But that [party] was private. As the schedule continued, we had a lot more of the public type social engagements. Everywhere we went we had to appear at a dinner and speak and do those kinds of things. That's why I always emphasized a single message: Go and have one drink, sip it while paying attention to your manners, and then get the hell out because if you drink more, it's going to turn into gin."

★

By this time, Butch's growing leadership abilities were making the team better. As officer in charge, he had approximately—depending on replacement status and such—eighteen men he was responsible for, thirteen in the maintenance crew and five or six pilots at any one time. And these weren't just any men. They were handpicked experts in their fields, whether pilot or mechanic. His tour as an instructor of instructors at the advanced training school had heightened his leadership skills. He never studied leadership or talked about it with others. It was inherent. "It's not something you think about. You just do it." But he had certain principles. "The best thing in leadership is to get everyone in support of your objectives. If you can do that, it's the maximum." And the way to do that, he believed, was "to have sound objectives that everyone understands." Perfection was one of those objectives. He knew they couldn't achieve perfection. "No one can." But by putting it up as the goal, he felt he'd get the highest possible performance from all. If they weren't shooting for the top, they'd never get near it. "I was demanding, but in a fair way. Still, you always have weak links and you have to understand those and play to them."

In the air, that translated into how he spaced the formation—"in training and in the shows, how close I could pull them in." Each pilot in the team was competitive and exceptional and considered the goal of perfect flying, perfect show as standard. But "some could handle more risk than others. Take Wickendoll. I could work him in just closer than hell [wings almost touching]. Never have to worry. Have total confidence in him. Others, not as close. But to keep symmetry in the flight—and you want symmetry in the show because it's part of looking good—I had to play to where everyone could fly and have Wick move out a bit. Then the symmetry was there. All my boys had different strengths and weaknesses and I had to understand those and almost always play to the weakest," because that was where everyone was strong.

On the ground, he showed his men, officers and noncoms alike, expertise, dedication, and respect—three more principals he believed in—and got mostly the same in return. "I never heard him raise his voice to anyone," recalls Bob Boudreaux, one of the original ground crew, who was the plane captain for Stouse's Zero. "Mr. Voris was, well, first of all, he was a gentleman, very calm in everything he did. And proficient. There are so many accolades I could pin on him I doubt you could put it all in one book. He was a great man, very cool in any situation, very skilled in his flying and in his leadership ability. There is nothing I could say bad about him."

Voris's calm, however, would be tested at Pensacola.

Arriving back in Jacksonville from Kansas City, the team still owed a show to Admiral Wagner, chief of all naval aviation training, headquartered at Pensacola. Their hastily enlarging schedule—and probably the admiral's schedule, too—had not allowed the two to get together earlier. So on July 10, in front of a rather small crowd—"2,300 openmouthed spectators," according to a newspaper clipping—the team roared in for a somewhat truncated show (the clipping, not identified as to specific newspaper, says it was only ten minutes long). Among the attendees with the admiral was tactics innovator Jimmy Thach, creator of the "Thach weave" which Butch and so many other naval aviators had used to defeat Zeros throughout the Pacific.

Thach was now a captain.

Since his weave was part of the dogfight simulation, Butch had extra reason to want the show to go well.

As Boudreaux recalls it, everything was progressing nicely until it came time to toss the dummy. So it could clear the plane before the parachute was deployed, the dummy had a lengthy static line attached to its rip cord. The cord released the parachute. The static line was coiled up in the backseat and fed out by young Boudreaux. Somehow, this time, the line got tangled and knotted. Thus shortened, it caught on the plane's tail. The parachute deployed from the flailing and hung-up dummy but not successfully. It was streaming behind like an elongated rag. "I grabbed the mike and told Lieutenant Stouse to kick hard left rudder," said Boudreaux. "That tipped the plane and released the dummy."

Trouble was, the dummy was now a missile sailing straight for the admiral and his high-ranking guests. "They'd put their chairs out on the [runway's] apron," recalled Butch, who, at the time, was watching with wide-eyed trepidation. "You had at least three admirals out there and half a dozen captains." The dummy and its malfunctioning parachute hit right in front of them. Not seen by Butch at the time, was the fact that one of the smoke bomb canisters, according to Boudreaux, had dislodged in the plane's tipping and also landed near the group.

That made two near misses.

Voris: "I thought, oh shit, that's the end of the team and my career. We're dangerous. I fully expected they'd call us out of the air right then."

But the call didn't come.

Butch continued as if nothing had happened. "We landed and, boy, I expected all hell to break lose. I approached the admiral. They're all around him. He's just sitting there looking down with his hands folded. There's a picture somewhere I have. I'm kneeling down on one knee in front of him because I'm tall and trying to talk to him. He's kind of shaking his head, and I'm expecting him to say, 'Well, we're not going to do this anymore.' I thought it was over. And he looks up. 'Butch. I have one suggestion.' 'What's that, admiral?' 'Move it out a little farther. But I like it.'"

As for Thach, he didn't seem to have a problem either. He commented on the rest of what he'd seen: "I don't think you [reporters] realize what was demonstrated here this morning," he's quoted in an article. "It was teamwork. One thing the navy teaches is teamwork, which is taught from the beginning of all training. Although speed is important, it is not everything in fighting. We had to have superior maneuvering ability to win the war."

Apparently, he felt the weave was correctly represented.

Butch subsequently moved the show farther out from the crowd—"An admiral's suggestion is an order," he said—and, at least regarding the dummy, there were no further incidents.

✫

Not too long after the team was created, those involved with it realized that if they were going to continue, they needed a catchier, less generic name than Navy Flight Exhibition Team. Voris and the others actually flying or maintaining the team had their hands full getting the show up and running and couldn't think of a name they felt was good enough. So by June 27, the issue had been handed to the base newspaper, the *Jax Air News,* which on that date ran a story asking readers to volunteer names for a ten-dollar prize, which, while not a lot, was probably in those days enough for dinner and a movie for two. "Can you think of a good name for the navy's new Flight Exhibition Team?" the paper asked on its front page. "It's fame will spread more quickly if known by a name with plenty of color and zip." The names should be "short and descriptive like the Cracker Jacks, the Flying Fools . . . or Helldivers," the navy's wartime dive-bomber. "The contest will continue until the judges decide upon a suitable entry."

By July 4, according to that day's *Air News* edition, entries had "poured in . . . breaking all previous records of past contests." Suggestions included, "'Jaxcats,' 'Jaxateers,' 'Com-Bats,' 'Death-Cheaters,' 'The Sea Eagles,' 'Goshawks,' 'Blue Bachelors,' 'Cloud Busters,' 'Cavaliers,' and 'Strat-O-Cats.'" But by the month's midpoint, and on the eve of the team leaving for its biggest show yet—the "World's Fair of Aviation," to be held the weekend of July 19–21 in Omaha, Nebraska—the navy flyers still hadn't seen a name they really liked. "We just weren't satisfied with what had been sent in," said Butch. The Omaha fair was another independent celebration heralding the return to air shows after the war. It was a big deal, especially for that part of the country, which was full of wide open spaces and few large cities. Dignitaries from Washington and foreign countries allied to the United States were to take part in opening ceremonies. Officials were expecting 50,000 to 100,000 people per day. The show was going to be the team's first real test before a large, discerning, aviation-savvy public. They weren't happy that they'd have to perform with a name "that had about as much impact as kissing your sister," said Butch.

Then, as Butch tells it, several nights before they were to leave for Omaha, they were all in his room after work in the bachelor officers'

quarters having some drinks and discussing the trip to New York City and
Grumman Corporation headquarters at Bethpage, Long Island, to pick
up the Bearcats into which they were going to transition. The trip was
coming quickly after Omaha. Grumman, makers of so many "cats" for
the navy already, knew a good thing when it had it, and the team was an-
ticipating being wined and dined. "We usually ended up at the Latin
Quarter," said Butch. "Wickendoll was thumbing through a recent issue
of the *New Yorker* magazine looking for things to do when he suddenly got
real enthusiastic and said, 'I've got it! I've got it!'" He showed them a page
he was looking at on which was an item about the Blue Angel, a famous
New York dinner-and-dance club, named for a 1930's Marlene Dietrich
movie, that Butch remembers occupied a good part of a block of Man-
hattan. "I think it had four orchestras going at once." They all instantly
liked the name. The "blue" was navy-appropriate and the combination
Blue Angels "had that little spark."

That settled, said Butch, they felt a lot better. They still had to figure
out how to bypass the contest and so decided to keep it quiet until they'd
returned from Omaha. The next day, however, Voris was called to the office of Captain Gentner, Dan Smith's boss, who had made the original
recommendation they get the Bearcat. Gentner was director of training
and chief of staff for Admiral Davison and therefore a man in the hierar-
chy above Butch of considerable clout. "We were friends. I'd been to his
house for dinner. He said, 'Sit down. How're you coming with the contest?" Butch didn't relate the latest. "'Well, we've got all kinds of suggestions. Just haven't seen anything that we really think is catchy.'" Gentner
said he'd been perusing the suggestion list. "Don't know how he got it,
but he did. He said there was a name he kind of liked—Navy Blue
Lancers." He asked Butch what he thought. Butch didn't think much of
it, but given Genter's position said it was "interesting." Good, said Gentner, "Why don't you take it. Go back and talk to the boys and let me
know what they say."

In Gentner's mind, it was a done deal.

Back with the team, Voris informed them, "We've got a problem." He
didn't remember Navy Blue Lancers on the list of submissions so they got
it out and checked. Sure enough, there it was. More important, the person who had submitted it they saw was Bill Gentner's son.

Now they knew they had a bigger problem.

★

Air shows are dangerously exciting, elemental events. Sun-drenched crowds gaze skyward in huge outdoor arenas and see breathtakingly thunderous and thrilling aerial exhibitions—always with the threat of violent, fiery crashes only a gasp away. The closeness to basics, including sudden death, is part of the draw, along with the skill and precision of the flying, the personalities of the flyers, known and unknown, the fun things like food and aviation items for sale, and the magnificent airplanes on display, mostly modern technological marvels but some old and venerable. There's something for just about anyone who is hardy, likes the outdoors or the power of machines, or is simply drawn by the romance and daring that is part of the aviator's trade.

Omaha was classic in many of those respects.

Set like Des Moines in the nation's great farm belt between the Mississippi River on the east and the Rocky Mountains to the West—only more centrally located as far as the nation went—Omaha's Offutt Field and the sprawling fairgrounds set up around it were as close to the middle of America in both place and culture as any city in the United States. Nebraskans were landlocked and mightily receptive to seeing displays of the aerial ingenuity, resourcefulness, and individual pilot achievement. Huge numbers of people had already purchased tickets.

Scheduled to be on hand for opening ceremonies Friday, July 19, according to Omaha's *Evening World-Herald,* were such military notables as Secretary of War Robert Patterson, army general Nathan Twining, leader of the famous bombing raid on the Ploesti (Romania) oil fields and future chief of staff of the coming United States Air Force; and army general Curtis E. LeMay, the B-29 commander who had led the devastating fire bombings of Japan and would later lead the air force's Strategic Air Command (SAC).

Slated to perform were P-80 "Shooting Star" jets, new marine F7F Grumman "Tigercats," the navy's first twin-engined piston (propeller) carrier fighter; Dave Shilling and his P-47 Thunderbolts, P-51 Mustangs, and the Bell P-59 "Airacomet," the forerunner to the P-80 developed in secrecy during the war. In addition to Butch and the team, the navy had its new PBM-5A "Mariner" jet-assisted amphibious plane, billed as "the world's largest." Two fleet pilots were demonstrating the new Bearcat to which Butch and the team would soon transition. Although produced too late for the war, the compact single-engine fighter had been designed by Grumman as a specific answer to the Zero's nimble maneuverability at low altitude. It was smaller and lighter than the Hellcat but had even greater climbing power. The navy wanted to show it off. Gliders and skydivers were scheduled. Representatives from Britain, the Netherlands, Sweden, China, and the Dominican Republic were to be on hand, and displayed outside the entrance to the huge exhibition hall was to be an actual captured German V-2 rocket used to menace England at the end of the war.

Butch's old *Hornet* boss, Jocko Clark, was going to be there Saturday.

It was a big occasion.

Butch and the team arrived on Thursday after a two-day flight via Memphis and Kansas City. They checked into a hotel for the flyers who were taking part in the fair. It was the day before they were to give their first performance, so they were mindful of preflying conduct but went down to the hotel lounge that night to make a courtesy appearance, drinking lightly, if at all. Taddeo saw a friend from postwar Florida, an instructor he'd served with at one of the bases there. Lieutenant Jack Baldwin had been born in Omaha, according to the local newspapers, so it was kind of a homecoming for him. He was one of the two fleet pilots demonstrating the new Bearcat. It was a hot machine, he was saying while drinking, said Taddeo, and boasting that he was going to do a slow roll when he took off the next day. "We all do it," said Taddeo about such bar talk. The slow roll he had in mind was the same Butch and the team did in unison—the dangerous roll around the plane's long axis. Done without other planes close by, it wouldn't be so dangerous, except that, on takeoff, the Bearcat would be very low to the runway, and that left no room for recovery in case something went wrong. The two renewed acquaintances, and then Butch and the team exited for their rooms, leaving the others presumably to continue at the bar.

The next morning out on the field as they prepared for the show, Taddeo said he saw Baldwin. "I looked at him and said, 'Hey, Jack, had a pretty rough night, huh?' He says, 'Yeah, too much to drink.' I said, don't screw around. Don't try to do the slow roll. It was the thing to do in those days. He says, 'Yeah, I'm just gonna make a high-speed climb up.'" The navy part of the show was beginning. The two Bearcat pilots were to give their exhibition following the Hellcats. Voris, Wickendoll, and Cassidy, airborne, were roaring in toward the field to start as the two Bearcats were taking off for their show. As the Bearcats lifted, Baldwin—contrary to what he'd told Taddeo—started to roll. "He was only forty or so feet off the runway [press accounts say a little higher] when he went upside down and lost it," said Voris. Without the roll completed, he crashed into the pavement. All three of the Hellcat pilots were watching as it happened in front of them. "There was a tremendous explosion," said Butch. "He was full of fuel." A large picture on the front page of Saturday's *Morning World-Herald* showed an enormous fireball mushrooming upward. It resembled a mini atomic bomb blast. "I saw him take off and knew right away," said Taddeo, watching from the ground. "He started the slow roll and never finished it."

The Hellcats pulled up and went into a fuel-saving holding pattern as fire trucks and an ambulance raced to the runway's middle. The firetrucks began extinguishing the towering flames. "He was gone in an instant," said Butch. "What a way to start the navy hour." Taddeo recalls it as "putting a damper on things for a while." But his three teammates circled for about ten minutes as announcers "repeatedly told spectators to stay where they were," according to a *World-Herald* story by Lawrence Youngman. "The plane was demolished and parts of it were strewn over 150 yards." After the runway was cleared, the Hellcats came in so low that one *World Herald* picture of them shows two streaking just above a parked fighter on the side of the runway. "They just don't stop shows because you get killed," said Butch. "They just pick up whatever's left. It's a cruel game." They were going low for impact, hoping to impress the crowd. Reporter Youngman wrote: "True to navy tradition, which requires that other fliers carry on after a crash [probably not true], the team put on a magnificent exhibition. Several times their close-formation maneuvers brought them over the still-smoking wreckage of the crashed plane."

Making matters worse was the fact that Baldwin's father, an Omaha attorney and former public defender, was among the estimated 25,000 who witnessed the crash.

Saturday, according to Youngman, the navy issued a statement: "The maneuver in which Lieutenant Baldwin was killed was not cleared with the Navy officer controlling the Navy's part of the show. The Navy regrets the loss of this pilot, who had a very fine record throughout his service. However, it is emphasized that the records of our pilots throughout the war are to a large measure the result of their individual daring and skill.

As long as you have airplanes and young men, mistakes will be made. No set of rules will ever completely control such accidents."

By the next day, crowds had swelled to 50,000, and by Sunday, the final day of the fair, to as many as 120,000, according to estimates. "You could see them all over the grounds and on the distant hills," said Butch. "They were coming from everywhere." The team was a big success. Friday evening, they were guests of the Knights of Ak-Sar-Ben, one of the big sponsors of the fair, at a "cocktail party and buffet supper" on the roof garden of Omaha's Blackstone Hotel, one of its oldest and finest. They were made honorary members of the Aeronautic Club of Omaha, and on Sunday night they were special guests at a barbecue given by the Storz's family in the Trophy Room of the Storz Brewing Company, one of the Midwest's largest beer makers. They'd arrived, they felt. But they still didn't have a recognized name that they liked.

Voris decided he was going to fix that.

Sometime during the three-day event—he's not sure exactly when—he was talking to a reporter in one of the press tents. "I think he was a member of the national aviation press. They used to show up at the shows. I told him our little problem about the Lancers and how we liked the Blue Angels. He said maybe I can help you." There wasn't much more to it and he forgot about it. When they arrived back in Jacksonville, he was surprised to be summoned almost immediately to Captain Gentner's office. "What's this about the Blue Angels?" Gentner asked. Butch didn't know what he was talking about until Gentner showed him a military dispatch referring to the team by the name they liked. The dispatch was congratulatory and referred to the "Blue Angels." Butch surmised it had come from a story written by the reporter he'd met. Thinking quickly, he told Gentner that he couldn't explain it except that some of the reporters at Omaha had felt the team was so good that they'd said "we looked like Blue Angels up there."

Gentner eyed him and knew what was up.

"Get out of here," he told the poker-faced leader.

Although it would take another month for the name to catch on—and they would be called "Lancers" in at least one later press story—the issue was settled as far as the team was concerned.

"From then on we were the Blue Angels."

CHAPTER 19

Sometime around mid-July, possibly earlier, the team acquired
two new members. First was Lieutenant James W. "Barney" Barnitz of
Indianapolis, a dive-bombing instructor at Jacksonville and a friend of
Taddeo, who recommended him. "He had the gift of gab, was well met,
and had a good voice," said Butch. They took him on as the team's announcer and advance public relations man. He would also fly the two-
seat SNJ "Zero" to and from shows but not *in* the shows. The team's
ground support crews traveled in a two-engined transport.

As a new pilot, Voris brought in Lieutenant (j.g.) Ross F. "Robby"
Robinson, a young ace from the war who had served with him in Fighting
Two and would start off as a spare. Robinson had recently been assigned
to Jacksonville as an instructor. Like Wickendoll, Butch had a special relationship with the twenty-four-year-old Robinson, whom *Life* magazine,
in the 1944 article, had christened "the handsomest man" in the Rippers.
Robinson was an orphan and had been close to Butch during their shared
cruise. Butch had an almost big-brother feeling for him. "It was because
of what he was, the type of person he was. In the air, he was aggressive.
He was a very good pilot. And on the ground he had a great personality,
got along with everyone. He was a good-looking young man and had the
qualities I kind of liked in a person."

The relationship, unfortunately, would end in tragedy.

Thus bolstered, the team returned from Omaha where Barnitz had been the announcer, and, on August 8, following a small exhibition less than a week earlier at Mayport Field, Florida, near Jacksonville, went to Bethpage, New York, to pick up their newly stripped down and painted F8F Bearcats. "Oh, boy, what a piece of metal that was," remembers Butch. The new Grumman cat was like a race car in comparison to the larger Hellcat, it's predecessor. It had a similar look, but a taller tail fin to help maneuverability, a less blunt, sleeker, more tapered nose, and a little bubble canopy giving greater outside vision. Symbolic of its increased horsepower was a huge, twelve-foot-diameter, four-blade propeller, as opposed to the Hellcat's three-blade. "I was often lifting straight up halfway down the airfield. It would just start climbing and for years held the time-to-climb record up to ten thousand feet."

The team was given four of the new planes. Robinson was the only Blue who had flown it before. But their modified models weren't ready when they arrived. They were still in the Grumman hangars being worked on. For the next few days, team members took regular, unmodified Bearcats destined for the fleet up in the air at the company's field in familiarization rides. "I could hardly fit in the damn thing, it was so small," said Butch. Because of his size, he had to forego any kind of comfortable seat cushion and sit on what was nearly the bare pan at the bottom of the cockpit, his legs jutting straight out forward. A small life-raft pack with a hard carbon dioxide bottle for inflation nudged under his right rear buttock. There was nowhere else to put it. It would be the same in the modified planes. "It would get terribly painful on long trips. My head rubbed the top of the canopy. It was like strapping into a capsule." But the compactness meant a feeling of greater control. The stick jutted up close between his legs. He could therefore rest his arms comfortably on his thighs while moving it. The instrument panel was hardly a foot from his face, which was much closer than in the Hellcat. "It made you feel like you were part of the airplane, which is better than flopping around in a bigger cockpit."

For the Blues, he said, "it was the absolutely perfect airplane. Everybody loved it."

The Bearcats the team would take back to Jacksonville and use in shows were still being modified. So Butch took up an unmodified model to see what it could do. This wasn't going to be a routine familiarization ride. "I wanted to push the envelope. How fast would it go. How would it react. If you don't know where it breaks [its limits], you won't be able to get the most out of it."

Hesitancy was always a fighter pilot's enemy.

Putting it into a high-speed dive, he got going so fast—"right up to the Mach barrier"—that the sliding canopy, reacting to increasing air pressure, "got sucked inside the rails." It wouldn't slide. He was locked in. "That was a scary feeling."

When he landed, ground crews had to pry him out with crowbars.

It was the first time in all the new fighter's development that the canopy had broken in this way. Later models were modified so the same buckling wouldn't occur again.

About a week before the team's arrival at Bethpage and while they waited and flew the regular models, the Bearcats to be modified and given to the team to take back to Jacksonville, according to the August 14, 1946, edition of the Grumman *Plane News,* had been brought to the company's hangars and stripped of about "one-tenth of their weight [normally near 12,950 pounds] in a series of engineering and mechanical operations which removed the water tank, armor plating, armament [four guns] . . . even their paint." They'd been hued a lighter blue than the Hellcats but had the same navy's gold lettering.

Finally, on August 14, the modified showplanes were ready. The team was anxious to get back to Jacksonville and start practicing. They needed to get comfortable in their new steeds. They had a show to do in two weeks at Denver, Colorado, and then the vaunted Cleveland Air Races, an aeronautical event "as big . . . then as the Superbowl is today," wrote the authors of *Blue Angels: Fifty Years of Precision Flight.* Cleveland would be their biggest test yet. But before they left, they gave a final show in the old Hellcats for Grumman officials and workers. It was well received and perhaps a bit nostalgic. The venerable fighters had seen their best days, and with the coming of jets to the carriers, they were destined for aircraft boneyards. Following the show, as part of a ceremony, Voris formally returned the original Blue Angel Hellcats to Grumman. They included his own number 1, Bureau of Aeronautics number 80097, which forever would be the team's first airplane.

The newly modified Bearcats they were taking home, however, hadn't even been flight-tested. After the ceremony, Voris insisted on the team's taking the newly renovated planes up and circling the field a few times "to make sure they weren't throwing oil and that nothing else was wrong." They all flew beautifully. Since the planes had been stripped and now weighed less than originally designed, he was concerned that their centers of gravity had shifted, as had happened when the modified Hellcats were lightened for the team. But he was assured by project engineer Jim Zuzi that the center of gravity was within specified limits and that sheet lead, the usual remedy, was not needed.

With tanks full, the team left for Norfolk, Virginia, first stop on their way home. Voris remembers feeling like he was driving a new car with its alluring fresh smells and fun discoveries. He saw the compact, surging new fighter with its 2400-horsepower engine as an opportunity to make the team even better. "I was delighted."

Norfolk, a giant fleet anchorage with surrounding airfields, was a planned fuel stop. They approached over Chesapeake Bay, Butch leading. He got permission from the tower to land and had entered the pattern with the others preparing to do the same in trail when he noticed something wrong. "I'd only made one landing in the airplane [a regular, fleet-ready, unmodified model], and it had handled nicely. Now it was different." As he'd dropped the wheels and slowed the Bearcat in his approach to the field, the stick had started pulling forward. "It wanted to nose over. I realized I had a problem." The first thing that flashed in his mind was the parting conversation he'd had with Jim Zuzi and the fact that "my center of gravity was so far out that I'm not going to be able to fly this thing."

They had left Bethpage without drop tanks, meaning the only fuel they had was in a single large tank in the fuselage below the cockpit. The full tank and the forward thrust of takeoff and subsequent forward flight had checked the pilot's sense of any irregularity in their plane's center of gravity. But as they traveled south, the steady consumption of fuel had begun to shift the plane's center to the heavier front, where the engine was located. Butch and the others hadn't been aware of the shift, subtle under the circumstances, because they'd automatically been compensating, as pilots do in flight, with various constant hand and foot controls like "trimming," the raising and lowering of small "tabs" on each of the plane's two rear stabilizers to fine-tune airflow over the tail. The compensating had masked what was occurring. Not until he'd dropped the wheels and reduced power for landing, thus slowing the plane and lessening its forward thrust and lift, had Butch found himself fighting to hold the Bearcat up and steady.

He trimmed as much as he could and got the stick "back to the metal"—as far back as it would go—but the plane still wanted to nose over. "That's the end of my control. There is no more. I couldn't keep it level. I called the tower and said I'm pulling out of the pattern. Within seconds, Wick, right behind me, says he's got the same problem. Then numbers 3 and 4 chimed in. I said, 'Everybody clean up and pull up.'" Landing like that, they all would have crashed. "We pulled our wheels in and got out of there and just about that time the tower frantically calls me, 'Navy One!' or whatever it was, 'Grumman aircraft engineering advises aircraft unsafe for flight! You're grounded!'" Even though he was in the midst of a dire emergency, he had to laugh. "Now they tell me."

After the team had departed Bethpage, Zuzi and his project people, disturbed by Voris's concern, had gone back to their figures for one final check and discovered they had made a mistake. The lightened Bearcats *did* need some compensating weight. It just so happened that they'd made their discovery right when the suddenly dangerous airplanes were trying to land. Knowing the flight plan, they'd phoned their representatives at Norfolk.

"On the ground, they're hysterical," said Butch, "and all I can see is the end of my new Bearcats because at that moment I didn't know exactly what was wrong. They said, 'What are you going to do?' I said, 'I'm trying to determine that.'" The Bearcats didn't have ejection seats. If they couldn't land, they'd have to go out high over the water, climb out of the cockpits and jump. "But I didn't want to lose these brand-new airplanes all painted so nicely and such. They were beautiful. You always fight never to lose an airplane."

Now all his airplane and flying knowledge would become crucial.

Pretty quickly, as the team and he circled, he figured out what was wrong and what he had to do. In a test, he put his wheels down and found that if he kept his power (speed) up and the stick back toward him almost as far as it would go, he had some control and could keep the nose up. Nose down and he'd dig a hole. Normally, the Bearcat landed at about 85 knots, which was now not an option. He would have to go faster to keep control. But at approximately 130 knots, which was terrifically fast for the plane at touchdown, he figured he might be able to keep the heavy nose level. "So I told the others, 'Okay, here's what I'm going to do and here's how I'm going to do it. If I kill myself, go out over the bay and you know what to do."

It was a do-or-die situation. They all knew it. With the others hovering and watching, he went around for his final approach. By this time, the tower had fire trucks and ambulances out on the runways. Grumman representatives were in the tower. With the stick almost all the way back in his lap, he began powering his way down. "Normally, you'd cut power, but I had power on until I actually touched the runway." Once down, he had to start lightly tapping the brakes. "Hit them hard and you'll get a wheel lock. The friction will burn right through the tread, and they'll blow."

Blown tires would probably kill him, too. But he speeded onto the runway and slowed the plane perfectly and eventually came to a stop. "It didn't run off the end of the runway. That could have been a problem, too." Thus demonstrated, the other pilots, who were watching and listening, went through the same dangerous procedure. "We got them all down. We taxied up to the line and, God, all the Grumman representatives and navy representatives came running up. We had a big conference." He wasn't mad. "I never got mad. Grumman had just made a mistake. It happens. If it wasn't for their continued support before and after, I don't think we would have ever made a show on time. But they were embarrassed."

Now they needed to fix the planes so they could get home, but the facility at Norfolk didn't have what was needed to perform the soldering job. Because of the time they were losing, they didn't want to wait for special help to arrive. They had what they needed at Jacksonville. Working it out on paper, it was determined that if they kept the tanks half full or more, they could fly without danger. "It was only after a half tank or more of the fuel was expended that the center of gravity shift really began to show," said Butch. So they decided to make a nonscheduled refueling stop at Charleston, South Carolina, en route to Jacksonville, in essence "hoping" their way home.

The plan worked and that night they were back at base. The Bearcats were immediately put into the hangar, and the soldering was begun. Fifty pounds of lead were sweated around the tailhooks, just as on the Hellcats.

☆

The next morning, the planes were fixed, and the team was up early to begin rigorous two-a-day practices for the Denver show, slated to begin the weekend of August 22, which was less than a week away if travel time was figured in. They had to get sharp in the new airplanes and get sharp fast. The normal flying they'd done in the Bearcat at Grumman and in the flight home had been good for orientation. Now they had to develop precision and symmetry with the close-in maneuvering needed in a good show. Because of the time constraints, it would require extra work and concentration. "It was a Grumman," said Voris. "We were all familiar with Grummans," which had similar cockpit setups, controls, and handling characteristics. "But we were rushed."

Since the Bearcat had such eye-popping performance, he decided to add a new wrinkle to the show. One of the pilots, either Taddeo or Robinson, would demonstrate the new fighter's exceptional maneuverability and quick climbing speed. He'd do so in a solo show prior to the regular routine. The hot Bearcat allowed them to go somewhat higher and faster. Other than that, their show in the new airplane would remain the same.

Early on in these first Bearcat practices, the young team almost became history again. They were practicing the scary inverted pass. In the show they did it streaking low in front of the audience. It was a fast pass at perhaps 300 miles per hour requiring an approximate thousand-plus yard upside-down line of flight at about fifty feet above the runway—a thrill to chill even the most avid roller coaster rider. The inverted portion usually took about three seconds and required super concentration. "Let your stick slip," said Butch, "and you're into the ground and a fireball immediately."

To the uninitiated, the inversion was a fleeting period of fear-inducing contradiction. The pilots were upside down which was disorienting enough. Controls were seemingly reversed. To go up or down, they moved the stick opposite to what they would when right side up. For instance, forward stick, which when the plane was upright would send it down, would move it up when they were inverted, and vice versa. Key to holding the aircraft steady and on a straight flight path during the inversion was the pilot's upside-down vision of the ground whizzing by in relation to what he could see of his aircraft. Butch would fix in his perception an angle between the rushing ground and the tip of the nose of the plane. As long as the angle remained constant in his vision, he knew he was on a path that would keep the plane the same distance from the ground from the beginning of the inversion to the end.

In other words, he wouldn't hit the ground.

This was the way they'd done it with the blunt-nosed Hellcat, the way it was inculcated in them.

But the nose of the smaller Bearcat was tapered, which demanded a slightly different and larger nose-to-ground angle than the one they'd been used to in the Hellcat. The taper, in effect, rounding back upward to the propeller, caused the perceiver to dip the plane ever so slightly in order to get the tip of the nose in sight. He could then fix the angle. Without realizing it, Voris made the subtle dip thinking everything was still the same as it had been in the Hellcat. When he did—when all of them did—the three Bearcats irretrievably but instantly began heading imperceptibly downward. In the tense microseconds of the inversion, and because of the speeds they were traveling, they were rapidly losing altitude and weren't aware of it until Butch suddenly saw the runway growing larger.

"Great Scott," he remembers, "I could count the expansion joints going past. We probably couldn't have been more than twenty feet off the ground."

And descending!

He ordered, "Roll!"

The three scattered like flushed quarry. By that time they were already over the St. John's River at the end of the practice runway. Taddeo remembers glancing back and seeing "three prop washes churning the water."

"That's the closest I ever came to killing the whole team," said Butch.

They still didn't know what had caused the error.

Landing, they went back to the office and debriefed. "I took out the [stick] models and held them over the briefing table and put in what would be the normal angle of level flight inverted. Whoops! There it was. The tapered nose." They hadn't figured it in. "You live and learn."

★

On August 21, the team departed for Denver via Montgomery, Little Rock, and Hutchinson, Kansas, where they spent the night. Voris felt confident they were ready for their first show in the Bearcat. Hutchinson was Wickendoll's hometown, and the team had dinner at Wick's parent's house. During their short stay, the team did a pared-down, impromptu show for the Wickendoll family and friends, recalls Taddeo. Neither he nor Butch remembers the particulars, but the team probably took the opportunity to practice.

Next morning the team left Hutchinson early. Wickendoll had some mechanical problems and had to delay departure for several hours in order to wait for parts. Butch and the others went on ahead. The boss was itching to get to Denver, not only because he was anxious for the team's first test in their new fighters, but because Thea Young was coming to Denver to be with him and see the shows.

Since their first date more than a year and a half earlier, the two had exchanged letters and seen each other at Christmas and possibly during other leaves. Their relationship had grown. Since Denver was relatively close to Santa Cruz—the closest Butch had been able to get to Thea while working from the East Coast—he'd sent her a ticket on a United Airlines DC-3 and arranged to have a woman naval officer, Lieutenant Commander Frances Biadez, from the navy information office in Washington, to be her host. "When you are a member of the team, you don't have much time to be with family or sweethearts." He was grateful for Biadez's help but wanted to be in Denver to meet Thea when she arrived.

He made it. She did, too—barely. He remembers that one of the first things she said when he greeted her was that the flight had been pretty rough through the often windy Rocky Mountain canyons. In those days, passenger planes like the DC-3 weren't pressurized and consequently had to fly through the lower altitude mountain passes to reach Denver from the west. The high peaks would have required more oxygen for passengers and crew, which the airliner didn't have. Regardless of the trip, she had a wonderful four days and found the air shows at both Stapleton Airfield and nearby Lowry Air Force Base thrilling. Butch didn't get to see her much during the day. "They keep the crowds far from the planes," she said. But at night they went to nice restaurants and elegant private parties, like that given by the Stapletons, whose name the Denver airfield bore, in the Silver Glade Ballroom of the city's downtown Cosmopolitan Hotel. The banquet honored pilots and the military.

By the Denver show, the team's new name and reputation was finally preceding it, a fact they learned by accident in the lounge of one of the hotels the first night they were there. Voris: "We were all sitting there at a table and there's this guy up at the bar surrounded by four or five beauties and he's telling them all about the Blue Angels and how he's a Blue. Cassidy, the little Irishman, wants to go up there and haul him out. I said no. Let's listen for a while. He's flying his arms and telling them this and that. I finally said to Cassidy, okay, now's the time. He got up there and I'll tell you, did that guy ever leave the premises in a hurry." It turned out the faker was a pilot from Jacksonville and knew all about the team. The Blues without dates, said Butch, "of course, ended up with his ladies."

Some 50,000 spectators watched the Sunday show at Stapleton, according to a story by *Rocky Mountain News* writer Al Nakkula preserved in Taddeo's scrapbook. Heavy rain threatened to stop the proceedings but then let up. Army Shooting Stars made mock attacks on B-29s. Aerobatic champion Jess Bristow twisted his red biplane "in a series of chilling smoke-trail maneuvers," and navy lieutenant commander Robert Clarke put his service's first prop-jet aircraft, the Ryan FR-1 "'Fireball' through all its paces, sweeping past the field at 425 miles an hour." Butch didn't think much of the Fireball, designed as a carrier interceptor, but the navy was trying to promote it. "Nobody liked it. It couldn't do anything. With the jet engine burning, it would run out of gas too soon." Then came the Bearcats. "By the time the navy's portion of the show was in progress," wrote Nakkula, "skies had cleared and the famed Blue Angels again hurled their F8Fs through a spine-tingling demonstration of formerly secret air combat tactics."

Nakkula's was a positive review, as were others. But probably the most memorable part of the multiday show to the team leader—besides Thea being there—remains meeting and becoming lifelong friends with some of the other up-and-coming military demonstration stars on the circuit, in particular exhibition marvel-in-the-making R. A. "Bob" Hoover and dashing squadron leader Robin Olds. Hoover was a tall, gangly army air corps lieutenant and self-taught stunt pilot who had flown Spitfires in Europe and Africa. Shot down after fifty-nine missions and captured, he had repeatedly escaped Nazi prison camps. The last time he'd escaped, he'd stolen a German fighter and flown it to Holland. Legendary pilots like generals Chuck "Right Stuff" Yeager and Jimmy "Thirty-Seconds-over-Tokyo" Doolittle would later call him the best they'd ever seen.

At this time in his career, 1946, Hoover was still forging his reputation and flying a Lockeed P-38 "Lightning," dubbed "The Fork-Tailed Devil" by German pilots who had faced its speed, maneuverability, and blazing guns. Hoover's job at the time was test pilot for the army. On weekends, at the request of his superiors, he would do spins and other routines in the twin-engine fighter. The maneuvers were often as dangerous as Butch's slow rolls or low-altitude inverted flight. But like Butch and the team, Hoover knew what he was doing, having practiced them over and over, and thus was well qualified and had earned the respect of professionals as well as awed and oooing spectators. Butch remembers Hoover's dead-stick landings with both engines shut off out of a loop. He still had enough control after landing to roll the plane slowly toward the audience and "bow" as it came to a stop. "They'd never allow it today, but that was his signature."

Robin Olds was a John Wayne-ish contemporary. His father had been an aide to air tactics maverick General William Mitchell in the 1920s and 1930s and had become a general himself by the time he died of a heart attack during World War II. Robin, six-foot-two, ruggedly handsome and outspoken, had followed in his father's wake, flying P-38s and P-51s in Europe, shooting down thirteen German planes and becoming an ace two times over. During the Vietnam War, he would become a mustachioed legend flying an F-4 Phantom jet and downing four more enemy fighters, coming home to head the air force academy. But in 1946, he was demonstrating the P-80 Shooting Star. He and Butch met at a hotel in Denver. "He had a reputation," said Voris. "We were in one of the lounges. We introduced ourselves to each other, sat down, and had a couple of pops." Talking about their lives, Olds showed him a shining wristwatch he'd received from Ella Raines, the Hollywood movie star to whom he was engaged. "They'd exchanged gifts. That's where I got to know him."

A third contemporary Butch was impressed with at Denver was Bob Clarke, the Ryan Fireball driver. The prop jet resembled a conventional fighter with a propeller on its nose. But in its fuselage it had a jet that boosted its speed and capability. It had been hurried into production as a weapon to be used against Japanese suicide planes in the Pacific and was the navy's first jet aircraft. Clarke, a native of Pittsburgh and a Pacific combat veteran, was a test pilot at the Naval Air Test Center, Patuxent River, Maryland. Wickendoll was locked into another assignment after his Blues tour, so Butch was looking for a replacement to follow himself as leader. "Bob was a nice-looking guy, would do well with the public and that sort of thing. And, of course, he was a great aviator." As a lieutenant commander, he had the rank. And he'd flown the Bearcat at Patuxent. "I talked to him about relieving me, and he said, sure, he'd like that." It was a step in perpetuating the Blues. Clarke would join the team in December as a prospective officer in charge.

The Denver air show was four days long. When it ended, Thea returned to Santa Cruz, thinking Butch would be leaving shortly. The team had planned to make a leisurely trip to the important Cleveland National Air Races to take part in them over the Labor Day weekend. Cleveland was a once-a-year gathering of the best flyers and aerial acts and displays in the country. Pilots would compete, show their stuff and planes, and establish a national pecking order, titles and prizes, often substantial, included. It was aviation's World Series, an event that could really put the Blues on the map. They were excited. But as they prepared to leave, a low ceiling of heavy, obscuring weather moved into Denver. The Bearcats weren't equipped well for instrument flying. They couldn't get out. Butch's log shows him not flying for three days. He says if he had known what was going to happen, he would have asked Thea to stay longer.

Finally, on the twenty-ninth, the weather lifted enough for them to fly under it. Once east of Denver, conditions got better. But the delay cost the team. Flying via Omaha and Chicago for night and gas stops, they arrived too late on the first day of the four-day event to make their scheduled Friday 1:15 p.m. appearance. An army P-51 group was put in their place. "We got there like two p.m.," said Taddeo. The Blues parked their planes and went out on the tarmac to watch the army show. "So we're looking up, and all of a sudden you hear their announcer saying, 'For the first time, you're going to see four airplanes in maneuvers that have never been done before.' They did everything we did except the slow rolls." After the army flyers had landed, said Taddeo, the team went over to find out "why they'd copied our routine. We really went at them verbally, and they said, 'Wait. Wait. Here's what happened. Our commanding general said you guys have been taking second place [to the navy] in every show for the last three weeks. You'd better get competitive.' They'd stolen our show."

Butch doesn't remember it that way. The only rivalry he recalls was the unspoken competition smilingly present at all the air shows. "We watched them do their show and I felt real comfortable with what we had and what I saw in a relative sense. There are only so many maneuvers any team can do, and they weren't doing our good stuff." The talk with them afterward, he said, "was just good fellowship. I usually told everybody, hey, that's good flying. Enjoyed watching it. I didn't confront. That's not my nature. My nature is to smile and say we're going to go get them. All I cared about then was beating everyone else in the sky, which I was confident we would do."

Perhaps the two memories just reflect the differences in perception— one the leader's; the other, the newest member's. Whatever the details, team members were raring to show their stuff. They got their chance the next afternoon, Saturday. The races were the first since 1939, the war having curtailed them. Events included combat demonstrations by the sleek, silver Shooting Stars, B-29, and A-26 attack bombers. Dave Shilling was there, as was Robin Olds, according to newspaper accounts. The heralded events were the actual air races over courses hundreds of miles long, usually flown in short laps. Active military pilots like the Blues couldn't enter the races, which featured esteemed civilian stunt and speed pilots Tony LeVier, Mike Murphy, "Bevo" Howard, and Sammy Mason, among others. But the military, which had fostered great changes in aviation during the war, did most of the crowd-pleasing demonstration flying. Fleet Admiral William Halsey arrived Saturday. Bell Aircraft Corporation chief test pilot Jack "Buff" Woolams had crashed and died in Lake Ontario en route to compete. Jimmy Doolittle was there. It was a pressure-packed opportunity for the Blues as they mounted their Bearcats and prepared to take off. Butch relished the opportunity.

Then he suddenly got stomach cramps.

"I'd had a fish dinner the night before and must have picked up food poisoning," he remembers. "My stomach started churning, but I couldn't leave the airplane." They took off and started their routine. "It hurt. I was doubled over in the cockpit, but I could still fly." They had a "sleeve" for urination in the plane but nothing for defecation. "I just had to hold it. I wasn't sick to my stomach or vomiting, thank goodness. It was strictly the rear. It was the severest pain you could imagine." The G-forces quadrupled it. "I just held it through the turns. I don't know how. You grunt and keep flying. It almost killed me."

Somehow, he got through the seventeen-minute ordeal. Lives depended on it. He, Wick, and Cassidy, flew a perfect show, often bringing it down to no more than a hundred feet above the runway, thrilling the crowd, which had never seen such a tight, low, and intricate formation display. The September 11 Grumman *Plane News* later reported that Bearcats and other company planes that followed them at Cleveland "more than matched anything the Army had to show and held the attention of the huge throng for almost an hour." Regarding the lone Bearcat demonstration put on by the Blues, the newspaper quoted a company official at Cleveland as saying, "'I don't think a person breathed as the plane shot upward, spiraling, as it disappeared into the blue." Finally, it quoted Butch as "declar[ing] openly that he could have easily won the Thompson Trophy race, the greatest closed course race in the world, if he had been allowed to enter it in a Bearcat."

CHAPTER 20

The weather over NAS Jacksonville wasn't very good that Sunday, September 29, 1946. It was described in the official report to the navy's judge advocate general as "only fair." There was a ceiling of clouds mixed with emissions from a nearby paper pulp mill that produced a brown haze starting at approximately two thousand feet. The haze greatly reduced visibility, remembers Butch. But such a condition was not a reason to call off the show. It was early afternoon, just past one p.m., when they had gotten airborne. The team—Butch, Wickendoll, and Taddeo—were warming up in the distance and waiting to come in over the field and do their show for an estimated 4,000 to 6,000 spectators, mostly military with civilian residents who lived near the base. It was Open House Day at the air station, hosted by Jacksonville's naval air reserve training unit, which had recently moved there from nearby Cecil Field. The team's appearance, its first at home in the Bearcat, was to be the highlight of the day's activities.

The Blues—still just called "the demonstration team" in the base newspaper—had performed two shows since Cleveland, both memorable for different reasons. Parkersburg, West Virginia, right after Cleveland, had taught them to watch their Bearcats more closely during static displays, something they'd not thought of doing before. They'd gone there for dedication of the mountain community's new $4 million airport, constructed by leveling the top of an Appalachian hill and heralded as a huge boon to the coal mining area's economy. Parkersburg was the hometown of a Pentagon rear admiral, Felix Budwell Stump, who would later be promoted to vice admiral, and thus the team had been dispatched there. It was scorching hot and the governors of West Virginia and Ohio were in attendance and made speeches, as were a host of barefoot mountain residents—"hillbillies" to outsiders—who kept spilling over onto the runway in curious mobs, blocking the Blues' takeoffs. Earlier, one of them had tried to carve his initials on a Bearcat's fuselage. Voris: "We're up there with all the moonshiners, big overalls, jugs over their shoulders. You read about such things, but it was really like that. All of a sudden I hear, 'Skipper! Skipper!' I turned and here's one of these guys with a pocketknife scratching away. Can you imagine? I told him as diplomatically as possible he couldn't do that. I guess he didn't know any better. We'd never thought of keeping the crowds away." From then on, they erected rope security fences around the planes.

The following week, an appearance at NAS Ottumwa, a training base in Iowa, had been a success as well—at least until the performance was over. The base's commanding officer had invited the team to a cocktail party and dinner at the city country club their last night. At the CO's request, Butch had driven to and from the dinner with the captain and his wife. Returning at about eleven o'clock, he said, "there was a circular driveway leading up to the BOQ." As the car approached, it's headlights swept across the building's porch to reveal a pair of nylon-clad legs with high heels separated and "jutting to the moon." Obviously, a couple was celebrating. "When the lights hit them, [the pair] suddenly scrambled. It was Billy May [a new, young lieutenant (j.g.) pilot from Wheaton, Maryland, who had just joined the team] and a girl he'd met at the country club. I gulped but didn't say anything, and the captain and his wife [both in the front seat] didn't say anything either. But when I got out and thanked them, he said, 'I'd like to see you in my office tomorrow morning before you leave.'" Butch had to talk his way out of that one with both the captain the next morning and his own superiors at Jacksonville when he got home. "You had to watch Billy. In the air, he was a good pilot, but on the ground, you never knew what he'd do next."

But none of this was on the team members' minds as they prepared to swoop in.

They were concentrating on what they were about to do and waiting for Robby Robinson to finish a solo demonstration in the Bearcat, his first flight in a Bearcat as part of an actual show.

Robinson, according to the official records, had just "crossed the field at a very low altitude and climbed up at a very fast rate of speed" to an estimated 5,500 feet. There, he'd inverted to come back down in the first leg of a Cuban eight, a relatively easy maneuver which, when diagrammed, looks like the figure eight lying on its side. The pilot goes from one circle of the two-circle figure to the next. Diving down in a 45-degree angle, Robinson was supposed to do no more than a roll and a half, testified Butch, which would bring him right side up at the bottom and give him plenty of time and distance (from the tarmac) to continue on to the second circle of the eight. But for unknown reasons he decided to do extra rolls—one or two more, depending on various witnesses' accounts. And before the final roll, as he came roaring down, he hesitated. Just a microsecond. That's all it took. He was going nearly six hundred miles per hour, and the hesitation rocketed him much lower than he should have been. Butch believes lack of visibility as he passed through the brown haze was the culprit. "He misjudged where he was."

The extra roll or rolls didn't leave him enough space to pull out.

Still, with luck, he might have made it. All witnesses agreed that in the middle of the final roll he seemed to realize he was too low and made a sudden, wrenching attempt to pull the Bearcat upward. According to the reports, the force of his attempt was more than nine Gs, a tremendous amount. Investigators believe this because the Bearcat's wingtips were designed to sheer off at exactly 9.7 Gs at sea level—at least that was the official statement of witness Jim Barnitz, who was announcing the show when the accident silenced him in midsentence. The intention of Grumman designers regarding the wingtips was to help pilots in high-G dogfights or other extreme stresses to the airplane's structure. The tips, rather than the wings, were to take the stress. But it was always envisioned that this would occur at higher altitudes, where the resulting short-winged plane would at least be able to provide the pilot some alternative ways of surviving, like rising to an altitude where he could use his parachute. The immediate problem for Robinson was that only the left wingtip came off. Left was the direction he was pulling, and thus the region of greatest stress. The dip threw the Bearcat out of balanced, level flight, and the shortened wing grazed the tarmac. The plane's momentum was already thrusting it downward at tremendous speed. Full of fuel—in a nonlevel attitude somewhere between cartwheeling and pancaking—it smashed into the mat, the hard surface area bordering the runway, and exploded in a violent orange fireball.

Robinson died instantly from massive injuries. The impact was so violent that his decapitated and limbless torso, still strapped into a deploying parachute, was hurled horizontally some fifty feet through the exploding fireball. Horrified spectators, no more than a football field or two away from the crash, judging from photos of the scene, covered their eyes and were speechless, according to newspaper accounts. It was a horrific scene. Butch, Wickendoll, and Taddeo, still in the air and waiting, were too distant to see it. "I got a call, a recall, from the tower," said Voris. "They said Robinson had crashed fatally."

The words were a shock. Throughout the war he'd been able to check his emotions. But Robby was special. "All I remember is I landed and I broke down a bit and stayed right in the cockpit, didn't get out of my airplane for a few moments. Finally pulled myself together. I don't remember much beyond that." He called off the show. "Hell, I wasn't going to fly. It was the only time we ever canceled." He gave strict orders that photographs showing Robinson's remains flying through the air be locked up at the base and not released. "I could see them being put in *Life* magazine. I wasn't going to let that happen. We'd fought together in World War II," he said about the twenty-four-year-old former Ripper and ace who'd made it back to *Hornet*, like himself, with a gas gauge registering zero when Admiral Mitscher turned on the lights. "I'm emotional deep down. I just don't show it . . . I brought him to the team . . . He was young. Always smiling . . . What can you do? He just hesitated. It only takes a second."

The others took it hard, too. "We were devastated," said Taddeo. "We were all very close, and our feelings [toward one another] were very strong." Unconfirmed reports persist that Robinson had a girlfriend or fiancée in the base control tower to watch his first show and that she became hysterical after the crash. Butch as well as others have heard the rumor. "I was [later] told she had been invited to the tower, but it was without my knowledge." As an orphan, Robinson's next of kin, according to the *Jacksonville Journal,* were an aunt and uncle in his native Minnesota, although he did have some brothers and at least one sister, according to Nettie C. Brown, publisher of the *El Centro* (California) newspaper, who wrote a series of articles on the Blues. Machinist's mate Bob Boudreaux was airborne in the backseat of the SNJ out over the St.

John's River when he and his pilot, probably Billy May, got the word. "It was very sad. Robinson was a great pilot. It was my understanding he shot down five Zeros in the first two hours of combat. One thing I remember. They called us to come in, and we taxied up to the ramp and there were these two middle-aged women. They came running up to me and had their handkerchiefs in their hands, and they said will you take these and go dip it into his blood. I said hell no, you get out of here and don't think about something like that. They must have been sniffing something . . . or been in some cult."

It was a black day, perhaps the blackest for Voris in his flying career. He'd been through greater carnage and loss. But this wasn't war. It was peacetime. He'd recruited Robinson himself. The death was the first in a list that would eventually total twenty-three Blue Angel pilots killed in show or training accidents through October 28, 1999, according to a CNN news story on that date. They all knew the risks. Still it was a shock, a setback. "But you shake it off when you go back to work the next day," said Butch. "You control it." He put the team's remaining Bearcats into the hangar to have the wingtips strengthened. It was a simple matter of replacing rivets that had been removed to allow the tips to fail. "If you're going to have a failure at that low altitude, might as well have it in the middle of the wing." Alerted to the danger, the navy tried placing small explosive "ropes" at the wingtips to separate them simultaneously. But that didn't work either. Eventually all navy Bearcats were reriveted. Years later, Billy May told Nettie Brown that during a practice of the Cuban eight he and Robinson had conducted alone, they'd come up with an extra roll in the dive. "I told him the maneuver was spectacular, but . . . it didn't have much of a margin for error."

Had Robby tried it because of that practice?

Butch would never know.

★

Butch's log is unclear about how long it took before the team was back in the air practicing. Partially erased entries indicate it could have been nearly a week. The logs, kept by aides, sometimes had errors. Butch recalls that it took at least several days. In any case, by October 12, Butch, Wick, and Al Taddeo had made the long trek to the Southwest via Mississippi, Texas, Arizona, and Riverside, California, and after basing at NAS Alameda, roared in at approximately five thousand feet

above San Francisco Bay, heading for a crowd of 100,000-plus spectators at Oakland (California) Municipal Airport. The occasion was the
first Oakland Air Show since before the war and they, in an afternoon
slot, were sharing top billing with the Ryan Fireball at the mostly navy
show.

Butch's mother and father had made the trip up from nearby Santa
Cruz, bringing Thea. The three were probably awaiting the team's arrival
with the expectant crowd. Butch and Thea's romance had been growing,
and although she would only be there for the day's activities because he
had official duties that evening connected to the show, he was looking forward to the short time they'd have together. The tragedy of Robby Robinson's death was now locked away in some coping recess of his mind, and
his concentration was lasered onto the task at hand: swoop in with a tight,
terse, five-hundred-mile per hour entrance and move smoothly into the
first loop.

Wickendoll and Taddeo were concentrating on Butch's wings.

Suddenly, Butch remembered, "I see this United Airlines DC-3 coming right at us. It shocked me."

The airspace above air shows is always restricted. Bulletins are sent
out in advance so pilots nearing the area will be aware of the hazard.
Butch didn't know it at the time but said he found out later that the twin-
engine cargo plane he was about to collide with was carrying a full load of
orchids from Hawaii. Its pilots, he said, were trying to see the goings-on
below and not looking forward, in the direction of the oncoming
Bearcats. "I could see the copilot's eyes as I flashed over the top. Wick
and Al, I think, went under."

It was a hairfine miss that almost certainly would have been catastrophic. "Would have been quite a flower show," said Butch. "Gives you
an extra heartbeat, but it's history once you've made it. I just pulled them
together and we came back around."

The team continued unfazed, garnering the usual accolades from the
press. Later that night, at an evening party in their honor, Butch was told
by a United vice president that the pilot of the flower-bearing DC-3 had
been suspended. "I never heard anything more about it."

The team left Alameda the next morning to fly in an air show at Santa
Maria, California, several hundred miles south. Butch remembers "the
Truculent Turtle," the navy's long-distance submarine hunter, being
there. The sleek, dark blue, twin-engine "Neptune" had just set a world

record for nonstop flight—11,236 miles from Perth, Australia, to Columbus, Ohio, in 55 hours and 16 minutes without refueling. The plane was a flying gas tank. It's crew had been taken to the White House and personally honored by President Truman who could now truthfully say that the growing threat of Soviet submarines off the American coasts would be monitored by vigilant crews flying the aircraft.

But what Butch remembers most about Santa Maria is a fistfight between star Lockheed test pilots Tony LeVier and Herman R. "Fish" Salmon, both of whom had been flying on the show circuit that year. LeVier, fresh from a dazzling appearance at the Cleveland races, was in a speedy little show plane with Salmon in his backseat. In a scary exhibition, he turned the plane upside down and flew it no more than ten feet above the runway. "I don't think Fish knew he was going to do it. It was awfully dangerous," said Butch. "Maybe he was trying to scare him. They were both great friends." When the two landed, said Butch, Salmon jumped out and started throwing punches at LeVier. "I was right there. They broke it up before anybody got hurt." Later, Butch, LaVier, Salmon, Bob Hoover, and other flyers had a dinner together, lasting well into the evening.

The show—minus the lone Bearcat demonstration, which Butch had decided to eliminate following Robinson's death—had gone great.

After Santa Maria, the team went back to NAS Alameda in order to have periodic maintenance performed on the Bearcats, mandatory after every increment of so many flying hours. The team's own mechanics did the maintenance. Back up in the air the following day, October 16, on the first leg of their trip back home, they were cruising down the California coast at about ten thousand feet in sunny skies above scenic Monterey. Suddenly, Billy May radioed he was losing oil pressure in the spare Bearcat he was ferrying.

Butch was flying ahead of him.

"I immediately turned around and joined up with him. The whole bottom of his airplane was slick with oil."

Butch didn't know exactly what was going on. Busted oil lines? Leaky containers? Whatever it was, it was an in-flight emergency. When the aircraft lost all its oil—which it obviously was about to—its engine would stop. It would fall like a rock.

May had to get down fast.

Butch, who knew the area, which was just below Santa Cruz, told

May to turn back north and fly to Watsonville, where there was a field on which he could land. It was about twenty miles away, a relatively short distance at their speed and altitude. "I told him, 'Don't pull your power back because the engine will freeze.'"

Butch was worried. May didn't have a lot of flying time and very little in the Bearcat. He was going to have to land at high speed and with systems failing. Further, because of their approach, he was going to have to make a right-hand turn onto the Watsonville field. Navy pilots weren't used to such turns. Most of their turns, as when landing on a carrier, were left turns.

With Butch on his wing advising, May made it to Watsonville, but his engine quit just before touchdown. The Bearcat, wheels down, banged on the runway. And May hadn't made the turn correctly. Instead of completing it and hitting the runway straight on, he was angled across it, about twenty degrees, which was, in effect, crossing it.

The Bearcat careened across the strip at approximately one hundred knots and roared through the adjacent grass and into a large drainage ditch that paralleled the runway some sixty to seventy yards away. Hitting the ditch at such speed tore off the landing gear and pitched the plane into the air. It came down on its right wing, spinning and tearing the wing out of the fuselage, rupturing the fuel cell under the pilot. The cell was relatively full, and fuel and fumes spewed out everywhere.

May, bruised but not seriously hurt, jumped out of the cockpit and started running.

"He's the luckiest man alive," said Butch, who was right above him when the accident happened. "It's a miracle it didn't torch." As it was, the airplane would never fly again. He thinks the fact that the engine had quit and cooled somewhat meant the sources of ignition were minimized.

The field's fire department was already on the way.

"I did a one-eighty [turn], came in and landed, and ran over to him. Other than being real excited, he was okay. The plane should have gone up like an atom bomb."

Once the excitement died down, they began salvaging what they could from the destroyed plane with the help of the fire department and other Watsonville workers. It was eventually determined that a Blue Angel procedure was the culprit. The Blue maintenance crews worked in teams servicing the Bearcats. One team would drain the plane's oil. Another would refill it. A third would come in and safety-wire the containers so vibration in flight wouldn't loosen the sealed engine caps. One of the teams missed the plug on the oil reservoir of Mays's Bearcat. Vibration on their homeward flight popped it lose. Butch wasn't mad. "Our maintenance crews were the best. It was just an oversight." But he changed the procedure. They dropped the assembly-line approach and started making one man responsible for multiple jobs.

Since Watsonville was near Santa Cruz, Butch called his father and asked him to come pick him up. The accident gave him a chance to see Thea again. His dad made the twenty-minute drive, and he and Thea had dinner together that night. The Watsonville fire department, volunteering to help, put up the maintenance crews on fire department cots, while Wickendoll, Taddeo, Barnitz, and May either stayed with them or found other accommodations. By the next morning, leaving the remains of the wreckage, they were all on their way to Long Beach, California, near Los Angeles, which was their original first stop on the long trip home.

★

Through October and November, the team flew shows in Miami; Marietta, Georgia; and Cape Canaveral, scene of the later 1960s moon shots by astronauts who would become America's most famous pilots. But before the "Right Stuff" astronauts, the Blues were getting the publicity. All the services' fighter pilots knew they were doing the most cutting-edge flying. "We were having a magnificent year," said Butch. "We were the stars of the air show circuit."

On December 4, the team went to Whiting Field near Pensacola, a busy training facility for young naval aviators and a growing hub of navy and marine air traffic. Attending the air show was Butch's old Reaper squadron mate, Dusty Rhodes. They hadn't seen each other since just before the Battle of Santa Cruz, when Rhodes had been shot down and picked up by a Japanese destroyer. They had a catch-up meeting over cups of coffee. After three years in Japanese prison camps, Rhodes was going through flight refresher courses at Whiting. Following his near drowning and capture by the enemy, he'd been shackled, starved, threatened with death, and beaten so severely with Japanese kendo clubs that he'd passed out. His legs had swelled "to the size of my trunk," he said in 2002. "It took a long time for them to get back to normal size." He'd endured many other hardships and indignities, including Allied bombing while he'd been captive in Japan.

Rhodes was very impressed with the show he saw and told Butch he'd love to be doing that kind of flying. While not really aware yet of the place the Blue Angels would eventually have in aerial history, Butch was beginning to feel he had a personal stake in the team. He'd designed it and made it work. His superiors still pretty much left him alone to make all the decisions. In a way, it was his. While he'd already picked his successor—Bob Clarke—he also had begun to think about who would succeed Clarke, who hadn't yet arrived in Jacksonville. Rhodes, a lieutenant commander, was the right rank, and a good pilot. But he was married. "It was just after I got back to the States," Rhodes explained, "and we didn't know each other, so [the marriage] didn't last." But the split hadn't occurred at the time of Butch and Dusty's reunion.

Once he'd finished refresher courses, Rhodes had been assigned to Patuxent River, the navy's Maryland flight testing center near Washington, D.C., and the Chesapeake Bay. No longer married, he wrote Butch a letter reiterating his admiration for the team. Meanwhile, Bob Clarke had reported to the Blues in the later part of December and begun his training under Butch's tutelage. The time was coming when Butch's tour would be up and Clarke would take over. One day, unannounced, Butch and Clarke flew into Patuxent in their clearly distinguishable Blue Angel Bearcats. "I like to surprise people," said Butch about the unscheduled visit. "Dusty was the assistant [operations] officer there and really had no function. He'd gone through hell in the war. Here was a chance to pull him back out." Rhodes remembers seeing the two Bearcats landing and taxiing up. "Boy, I was excited, because I kind of thought it might have something to do with the letter I'd written. I said 'Hi,' and Butch popped the question. He said, are you still interested in being on the team? I said I sure as heck was."

While Rhodes wouldn't report to Jacksonville until nearly midway through the following year, he would eventually become the Blue's third leader (1948–1949), following Clarke (1947–1948), who would be its second. Voris was already forming the line of succession as he and the team moved toward the second Blue Angels season, which would begin in early 1947.

★

Not quite a week after seeing Rhodes at Whiting, Butch had an emergency while making a fuel stop at Biloxi, Mississippi. The team was en route to El Paso, Texas, to fly in the International Aviation Celebration to be held there on the American-Mexican border. Touching down for a landing, his left wheel strut buckled. The sudden collapse dropped the wing, and it dug into the runway, sending the Bearcat out of control and into the dirt and grass. "Very dangerous," said Butch, who fought it all the way. The plane could have flipped, caught on fire, possibly exploded. But it didn't, and nothing was hurt except his pride and the Bearcat's four-bladed propeller and left wingtip. A consolation—if one could call it that—was that the Biloxi base was run by the army air corps. Unlike navy bases, aviators didn't have to be in proper uniform to go into the mess. They could get snacks in their flight suits. "We got a sandwich and didn't have to change," said Butch. The team's mechanics, always in trail, were later able to fix the fighter. Butch used the spare in the four-day air show.

El Paso was the last show date for the team before they took Christmas leave. Butch's brother Dick was getting married on December 21, and Butch was looking forward to going home and being at the wedding with Thea. He'd probably by that time been given word about his next assignment, line instruction at the naval school in Rhode Island, because during the wedding activities, he and Thea decided to get married. "I didn't propose. We just agreed on it." While there are several pictures of Butch posing with models and beauty queens on or near his airplanes, he said he was ready to commit. "What am I? Twenty-eight? Any more bachelor life would have killed me. I'd come to terms with that. I was going to get married for the long term. In those days, people stayed married." Although he still had approximately five more months of flying with the Blues, he knew that he had to move on if he was going to advance in his naval career. There were requirements he had to fulfill. The stable year of schooling in Rhode Island, he felt, would be a good time to start a new life. He wouldn't be flying much or traveling during it. "I was ready to settle down. I remember talking to Thea's father because that seemed the right thing to do. He seemed happy enough."

The marriage date was set for the following June. Butch returned to Jacksonville in early January 1947 for a succession of shows in the winter and spring, most of them in southern and southwestern states because of the better weather conditions. At Tampa's annual Gasparilla Day, February 10, the Bearcats came in so low over the water in mock attack of a supposed pirate sloop that its costumed crew members dived in panic from the rigging. The situation was reversed, however, at Annapolis, on April 23, when the team did a show for the academy's midshipmen. At the very crest of the first loop, Butch, inverted and poised to bring the team down in their scripted element, came face to face with a light plane rushing toward him. "That was a thriller. I'm upside down and slow. There's not a thing I can do. In that attitude, you're locked." The off-limits intruder, a single-engine Cessna type, was powering forward head-on at exactly the same altitude as Voris. "Of course the others didn't see it because they're locked on me. I pulled it underneath as tight as I could. Either I'm luckier than hell or the Lord was watching over us because I don't think he missed us by more than fifty feet." The close call could have been the end of the Blues. "Killing a hundred naval academy midshipmen isn't going to go over too well." They were in a tight area over the students because of the restricted physical characteristics of the bay at Annapolis. A midair very well could have wreaked havoc. The near miss scared them all momentarily but then they went on to do an acclaimed show. Butch doesn't know what happened to the intrusive pilot. "He probably went somewhere, landed, threw up and hid. Never heard another word."

Other shows that winter were at Dallas, Corpus Christi, Orlando, Charleston, and Jacksonville at least three times. "They used us," he said of the home base. "It was good practice." As spring advanced, Taddeo left the team in late March or early April to join an East Coast fleet fighter squadron, something he was looking forward to doing. Lieutenant Chuck A. Knight of Crestline, Ohio, the newest Blue, had already come aboard and was training, thus keeping the pilot contingent at replenishing levels. The evolving team performed again at the Grumman factory at Bethpage on May 26 and at Philadelphia, May 28. Butch didn't fly at Philadelphia. It was his last show with the founding group, and he did the announcing. Bob Clarke, who would officially take over on May 30, flew Bearcat Number 1. "It was the first time I'd seen it," said the leader. "Pretty exciting. It's a wonder we didn't kill ourselves." Back at Jacksonville, the team had a good-bye party and gave him a large silver serving tray with all their names engraved on it. "And then they were off to the next show."

Butch wasn't sad. "We'd bested our competition, started something that looked like it would continue, although I didn't really know how long." He'd established a policy of striving for excellence and recruited Clarke and Rhodes to continue that direction.

It was up to them now.

He was looking forward to his marriage.

CHAPTER 21

Any delusions Lieutenant Commander Voris might have developed about his importance for founding the Blue Angels would have been dispelled when he detached from NAS Jacksonville. He had to wait around like any ordinary sailor until midnight, when the detachment day started, even though he was about to get married. "You're in the military and it goes in the log. What if I left early and had a big accident outside the gate? If I falsify the time, they can court-martial me."

Finally getting in his new Buick Super just after midnight, he drove to Chicago and arrived in time to catch a matinee performance of the popular harmonizing quartet, the Ink Spots, whose wartime songs "If I Didn't Care" and "Java Jive" had been big record and radio hits. He was also able to store the car, reserve a honeymoon room at the Palmer House, one of the city's finest hotels, and still catch a four p.m. plane to San Francisco, where his brother met him to take him to Santa Cruz. Earlier, he'd bought a ring. The wedding took place on June 25, 1947. He and Thea spent the first night in San Jose and the next in San Francisco, where, walking together along the famous Fisherman's Wharf, a passing seagull dropped a present on Butch's new fedora. It had missed his new suit. "We dressed in those days, not like today, when you'd go down there in cutoffs."

Not one to fret, he tossed the fedora.

The next day they were en route to Chicago on the California Zepher, a speedy luxury train with a sightseeing dome car. At the Palmer House, the management, in a surprise gesture, gave them the bridal suite, complete with waiting fruit and flowers. Although he was a returning veteran, he wasn't sure why he was held in high regard in those days. Maybe they'd heard of the Blue Angels and his connection to the team. He hadn't told them.

Retrieving his Buick from storage, Thea and he motored up through Canada and back down to Niagara Falls. "Traditional honeymoon trip," he volunteers. They spent a fun month traveling the Northeast and then in mid-July arrived at Newport, Rhode Island, and General Line school where Butch as a student would get his introduction into being an officer fighting from surface ships. "No aviation. You already know that. This is gunnery, gunnery, gunnery"—with a lot of navigation, ship driving, and traditional navy information thrown in. If he did well, he'd get an executive officer's slot, or "number 2," in a fighter squadron preparatory to becoming its skipper. That's what he wanted. "I'd started thinking about that during the war. I looked at my first skipper, Jimmy Flatley. He was a god. That was it. That's what I was shooting for. You're always pointing toward being selected for command."

The year in Newport was a happy one. They lived in navy married quarters called "the Anchorage." It was a "four-plex" with two units upstairs and two downstairs. "The walls were so thin you could hear through them. Flush the toilet and everybody on both floors knew. But we were all the same type of people." Eddie Outlaw, who had just completed War College, was moving out when Butch and Thea arrived. They bought his furniture for a little under $300. "You're a schoolboy. We didn't have any kids. We did a lot of traveling on weekends. Went up to Boston to the theater. Newport is a prime location, lots of places to go and see. Good seafood."

While he couldn't keep his piloting skills honed as he had at Jacksonville—too much studying to do amidst the traveling—he got away enough to fly at least four hours a month so he could continue receiving his flight pay. He did so out of NAS Quonset Point, where his old Rippers had finished stateside training during the war. "I'd go get an officer up in Maine or practice instrument flying." His class picture shows thirty-one student officers in khaki long sleeves and ties. He did well at the courses except for celestial navigation. "Where am I going to use that in a fighter? I guess I just didn't put my heart into it." But he graduated with overall good marks and received his certificate of completion, dated 29 May

1948. To his chagrin, however, he was ordered to an East Coast attack squadron, a dive-bomber squadron. "They wanted some fighter experience." He and Thea had hoped to go back to the West Coast. "We were Californians. But those were the orders." He was resigned to it. Then a chance discussion with a navy decision maker changed things. The decision maker told him, "You don't want that." Butch took his advice and appealed. Decision makers in the navy above the bureaucrats agreed. In early August, following a four-week course in "airborne electronics and submarine warfare"—a requirement for fleet fighter squadron piloting at that time—he reported for duty as executive officer of Fighting Squadron 113 based at San Diego's NAS North Island.

Not only was he back in fighters on the West Coast, but he was being screened for command, exactly where he wanted to be.

★

The skipper of VF-113, which flew Bearcats, was World War II veteran Lieutenant Commander Robert S. "Bob" Merritt, a large man like Butch with the call sign Moose. "He was a fighter pilot and a good one," said Voris. "Well liked by the men, very even tempered, affable. We became like brothers."

VF-113 was a brand-new squadron, having been formed from several others. It had a lot of young aviators, among them a sizable contingent of rare "Flying Midshipmen," pilots graduated from flight school but not yet commissioned. The short-lived program had been instituted right after the war as a way of quickly replenishing the navy's exiting pilot corps. The midshipmen, so called because they were likened to Annapolis students who hadn't yet graduated, had agreed to wait several years before being commissioned and thus forego for a while an officer's pay, a concession that would help the postwar, money-strapped service. In exchange, the navy agreed to pay for two years of their college educations. As a result, VF-113 had a small core of seasoned veterans such as Butch at the top and a lot of green aviators with little experience.

The lack of experience probably worked in the squadron's favor. Merritt, his XO Voris, and the few other veterans running the unit were held in high esteem if not awe by most of the younger pilots, who, for the most part, welcomed the battle-tested flyers and the expertise they offered. "I think we got a real good start with those people," said Lyle Olson, one of the squadron's midshipmen, in an interview in 2003, when he was living in Burnsville, Minnesota. "It was an advantage being trained by World War II fighter pilots, the way they treated us, the way we flew. You had to be completely relaxed. It didn't make a difference if you were going straight up, upside down, sideways, or whatever. They don't make fighter pilots like that anymore. Back then it was close-in fighting." Chase-tail dogfighting. "Very abrupt. You just reacted." A pilot expected to see the enemy plane he would try and shoot, not like today when he mostly fights or bombs a blip on a screen that represents a target miles away. "It was a lot of fun. I think I got a lot of advantage from being in that squadron."

But there were problems. With the tight military budgets of peacetime, money was scarce and reluctantly advanced. When Butch first arrived, the "Stingers," as VF-113 would be nicknamed, were short of allotted money for practice fuel. The fuel money was called "Bravo" funds. "We were in tough straits. One of those months we were down to four hours [flying time] per pilot." His job as executive officer was to facilitate the skipper's programs and wishes, do all the leadership grunt work so the CO would be free to concentrate on the most important matters. If he did well, he'd become commanding officer when Merritt left. "We still had to fly competitive exercises, bombing and rocket shooting, that sort of thing. We had to go to great lengths to do it. We hid fuel in drop tanks and [storage] racks. Did everything we could think of to have enough to practice with. It was very difficult."

But the cold war, although only in the political background for Voris at this time, was building. The Berlin Airlift, the first serious postwar confrontation with the Soviet Union, had begun the previous spring, and Mao Tse-tung's peasant army was on the verge of turning mainland China into Asia's first communist nation. Navy leaders had to take notice. The squadron's fuel shortage soon eased, and in December 1948 Butch transitioned to jets. "They were sending all COs and XOs." Merritt had just finished the course. Now it was Butch's turn.

While the navy had developed a number of jet fighters, including the Ryan Fireball and North American FJ "Fury," similar to the air force's F-86 Sabre jet, the service had lagged behind the air force. The problem had been carrier suitability. Early jets weren't quick to spool up power, and therefore launching was a problem. They also guzzled fuel at low altitude, where the air was thicker. That meant pilots couldn't circle around and wait as they could in prop planes when there were landing delays. Jets took a lot more mental activity than props, said Butch. "You had to stay ahead of it. Fuel consumption was critical."

Complicating things was the fact that the carriers were still straight-decked instead of angled, as they would become in later years. With angled decks, as are now on modern carriers, the pilot can keep his power up when landing and just lift off if things go wrong. But with straight decks, because planes were parked in direct line ahead of the landing area, the pilot had to cut power and hit the barrier if he missed the wire. If that happened with a jet, the jets coming in behind were in trouble. They didn't have the fuel to go around and wait until the deck was cleared. "We had to learn how long the missions would be [in order to gauge for fuel] and to operate with 'ready decks,'" an extra carrier nearby to take planes if their own carrier deck was fouled.

The jet's fuel systems themselves were more complicated. In prop planes the pilot basically controlled the fuel with his hand on the throttle. It was relatively simple. In jet planes, which needed more precision in fuel mixture, moving the throttle only sent a message to the jet's fuel control, which then automatically injected an exact mixture, or ratio, of gas and air into the engine. Altitude, air pressure, and density were factors that had to be taken into account for the mixture to be right. Hence the automatic injection. Wrong mixtures would cause flameout and other problems. So there was a lag, minute as it might be, from message to actuation, and that was not good in tight situations demanding quick reactions.

Positives, however, were faster speeds, higher altitude ceilings, and smoother, quieter rides. The speeds approached the sound barrier, in excess of 600 knots or more in good conditions. Normal operating altitudes were in the 35,000 feet to 40,000 feet range, much higher than in prop planes. And in the thinner air, jets thrived, using much less fuel than at lower altitudes.

Butch was to make his jet transition in a Lockheed P-80, the plane he'd encountered so many times on the circuit with the Blues and one of the first jets the navy had acquired. They'd bought it from the army air force and renamed it the "TO-1." There was a special squadron of them, VF-52, at North Island specifically for the transitions. He was excited. "It was like going from a Ford to a Corvette." A photograph shows him flight-suited and smiling, helmet in hand, about to board the sleek silver bird for his first orientation. "You had to anticipate more. Full throttle didn't bring the power up fast. I remember seeing the end of runway coming up." He wondered if he'd be able to lift off. "But then I was up and made a left turn and it was quiet . . . and smooth . . . I'm watching the engine . . . Hey, this is pretty neat." He took it up to 30,000 feet. "You climb to altitude four times faster than in a prop airplane . . . Did some rolls and maneuvers and got acquainted . . . All you had to do was get one taste and you were hooked."

After about an hour, he went down to land.

That's when his problems started.

Coming in on approach, he found himself unable to see out of the usually clear bubble canopy. The problem was the cockpit's pressurized atmosphere and his unfamiliarity with it. Enjoying the air-conditioning it provided—another plus of the jet age—he'd neglected to switch it lower as he came back down. The lower altitude was more humid, and moisture quickly fogged the Plexiglas. "It started blowing out ice and fog and water. I couldn't see a thing. I had to tell them I was going around again." His unfamiliarity with the jet made the situation worse, but he finally switched on maximum heat as one might do in the same situation in a car and the fogging cleared. He made a safe, albeit sweaty, landing.

His next problem, however, was a by-the-book emergency.

"An instructor nearly killed us."

The transition took an entire month, designed to give each student thirty hours of flying time at completion. On this particular December day, an instructor had taken four of the students up to approximately 15,000 feet for a gunnery lesson. The jets were in a line, one after the other, all zooming skyward. Butch was number four in the line, tail-end Charlie. "We're out tail chasing and mentally I'm computing we're too high and too slow to do this. You lose performance when you get up into the thin air. We pick up speed and we're supposed to continue climbing and pull into a loop." The instructor was leading. "He gets up around 18,000 and runs out of speed. He starts sliding tailpipe backward." The others, trying to avoid him, start "kicking" out of the line, splaying to the sides like peels on a banana.

Butch, as he'd expected, was experiencing the same loss of airspeed as the instructor. Caught at the end and basically at the mercy of the others—because he didn't want to run into any of the frantic peelers—he was backing straight down. "You can't do anything about it. You no longer have control." As the others peeled, his TO-1 flopped on its back and inverted into a nose-high flat spin.

The plane wasn't flying anymore.

He was upside down, revolving, and falling like a rock.

There was little he could do about it.

"Inverted is a bad thing. I remember all the crap floating up in the cockpit." Point Loma, a San Diego peninsula opposite North Island, kept swinging in and out of his G-distorted vision. His altimeter was unwinding as if he were in a steep dive. "I've got to punch out," he remembers thinking.

But he was doggedly working the controls, especially the rudder with his feet, rocking the out-of-control jet—until finally "it flipped over and went into a normal spin."

At least he was upright. "I felt I could pull it out if I had enough altitude left."

He was at approximately 10,000 feet. He decided he did.

He pushed the stick forward, trying to gain airspeed and engage surfaces. When—and if—it did, he might stop the spin and start flying again. "I'm trying to get airspeed up, pressure over the surfaces." He finally started flying and had to continue diving even lower in order to fly out of the fall.

He was running out of sky.

He finally pulled out and started back up. He estimates he did so only one or two thousand feet from the ground.

If he hadn't, there wouldn't have been enough time or distance left for him to have escaped by parachute, given the high speed at which he was diving.

Back on the ground, all four of the students were livid and verbally tore into the instructor. None of the others had gone into a spin. But each knew he could have.

It was another air lesson learned.

★

At Jacksonville with the Blues, Voris's job had been to build a team that could fly better than any other. Now, at North Island, he was second in command in forging a squadron into an aerial war fighting team. The squadron's mission was to be ready to fight. And fight well. The intricacies of precision flying, while important, were not now paramount. Dogfighting, aerial shooting, bomb and rocket delivery were the tasks to master.

Just as he had in World War II, he was back to leading four-plane divisions, the traditional battle formation.

"Butch didn't talk much about the Blue Angels," said Ken Burrows, one of the young Stingers then who flew on Butch's wing. "But you could tell he'd been with them. He was a hell of an aviator, very smooth. But very safe. He'd never horse around like some of the other [veterans] would." Burrows kind of resented it. "I wanted to do Blue Angel stuff. I don't want to say they were reckless, but some of the other divisions in the squadron, let's just say they did more hairier things than we did. That's a criticism from the standpoint of a guy who didn't know a damn thing at the time."

Still, Voris taught precision. E. J. Klapka, a nugget ensign when he joined the squadron, remembers the thrill of being number four, the position he flew, in Voris's division. "When we took off [from North Island], we wouldn't go one by one on the runway. We used the mat so we could all take off together. We'd get airborne and turn left and go down the channel past the Point [Loma]. Number four would slide into the tail of the diamond. That's what the Blues were using. We'd fly around in a diamond all the time." In fact, several months after Butch left Jacksonville, Bob Clarke had been directed to get rid of the high-risk slow roll and add another Bearcat to the basic three-plane performing unit so it would be more like a two-section combat division. "[The three plane] had served its purpose," said Butch. "They were on to new things."

The Stingers made frequent trips to the bombing and gunnery ranges at El Centro, the isolated training base near Mexico in the southeastern California desert. Burrows remembers Voris disciplining a younger pilot there. The pilot, against all teachings, had done a sloppy job of preflight before taking off on a training mission. For one thing, he hadn't checked his fuel state. Just as the mission was progressing, his low-fuel light came on. He radioed he was returning to El Centro. "The Bearcat ran out of gas as he touched down on the runway." Afterward, Butch took the errant pilot aside, who later, Burrows said, told him what had happened. "Butch said, 'Lou, that was a pretty stupid thing you did today.' Lou said, 'Yes, sir. It certainly was.' He says, 'You're going to have to be punished for this.'" Lou was defensive. "Punished? I didn't damage the airplane?" The pilot could see his career going in the toilet. "Butch said, 'You're the squadron duty officer, permanent for thirty days.' That was his punishment. Answer the phone and do routine paper work. Never went into his record. Says something about the type of leader Butch was."

Merritt encouraged squadron social functions. Burrows remembers a grunion beach party. Grunion are small fish that spawn on beaches in the summer months. Massing in waves, usually at night, they come to shore flopping silvery in the moonlight. "We'd run out with pails and grab them before they retreated," said Burrows. "One time I ran out of pails and yelled, 'Goddammit, Butch, bring me another." In the heat of the scooping, he'd forgotten he was only a nugget and Butch was a lieutenant commander as well as his XO. "Butch came running with the pail. Didn't say a word about it." Butch recalls, "When you're at play, you're at play. We had a lot of parties and beer busts and the youngsters would take great delight in mobbing me and throwing me in the ocean. That was always a must."

★

One night following one of the Stinger squadron parties, Butch woke up around three a.m. with a terrible stomachache. "I was doubled up. It hurt bad." Thea wanted to call the doctor but he told her no. He'd recently been on a fishing trip to Mexico with Merritt and a few in the squadron and wondered if he wasn't just getting a delayed reaction from bad food. "It'll go away," he told her. But it didn't. He went to work the next morning but eventually had to rush to the hospital to undergo surgery for acute appendicitis. Recuperating, he had chance encounters with two marines, both of which left lasting impressions, one amusing, the other darkly pertinent to his chosen profession.

Both marines had rooms near him. One was the famous lieutenant general Holland "Howlin' Mad" Smith, who had commanded troops through some of the worst ground fighting in the Pacific, including on Saipan, where Butch had flown and toured, and Iwo Jima, above which Lieutenant Robert Butler had been killed. Smith was in the hospital for a routine checkup and was known for his cigar smoking, feistiness, and ferocious temper. But contrary to expectations, said Butch, "He was a wonderful guy." They talked. "Actually, he did most of the talking. He's three stars. I'm a lieutenant commander. I was more of a listener."

And the famous general brought his needlepoint.

Needlepoint! "Who would have thought? I guess it was his hobby. Tremendous."

More sobering was the other marine—a fighter pilot who'd crashed and burned in a Corsair. "I'll never forget the screaming." Almost all the skin had been burned off the pilot's body. "I think he was a lieutenant colonel. They'd take him in and lay him down in a tub and soak off the packs they had on him and he'd just scream. The packs were his skin and it was just raw meat underneath . . . You're living with fire in an airplane. You know it's there but you don't like to think about it. I mean in the Wildcat, in the deck of the cockpit . . . it had two floorboards where your feet went and then the rudder. And right below is this big bladder full of fuel . . . You just hope you're never in that situation."

★

In early June 1949, Voris assumed command of the Stingers. Merritt, moving on, wrote in Butch's fitness report: "Lieutenant Commander Voris . . . has performed his duties as executive officer in an outstanding manner, combining all of his leadership and organization talents to promote a very effective, high caliber executive policy."

Butch was now a senior aviator with over two thousand hours of flight behind him, most of it in combat or demonstration flying. The step to commanding officer of a fighter squadron was a milestone, the bump every good fighter pilot hoped for. Butch was no different. Fighter squadrons are the tip of the navy spear; their skippers the chosen men the navy counts on to lead its pilots into battle and prevail regardless of the obstacles. Getting the squadron was a culmination of all he'd accomplished and learned since he'd become president of Lancers really, way back in junior college. For it was there that he first began using his skills as a leader, understanding that organization, discipline, fairness, and initiative were keys to success. Now he was a lot more mature, had strong experience in fighting and flying, and a "bag of tricks," as aviators call their special flying skills, arguably as good as—thanks to the Blue Angels—anyone flying. At least, he probably thought so. He'd had fine mentors in men like Jimmy Flatley and Butch O'Hare, both recognized heroes, when heroism counted most in the service—at war. And with his straightforward, calm, uncomplicated approach, stressing teamwork and proven by-the-book fighting and flying methods and procedures, he moved relatively effortlessly into a higher echelon of navy leadership.

"I ran a tight ship." he reiterates about that important step up. "You demand performance." If he hadn't already, he went up and fought each pilot in simulated dogfights—a practice he'd continue in later commands—"so they'd know what I had and I knew what they had." He emphasized fighting skills like target and bombing practice. "The squadron and its commander are measured by their shooting exercises. That's what goes down on the record. My job was to have the squadron perform as competitively as possible."

To help do that, he set himself up as the standard, the one to beat. "That's how you motivate them." Most of the times he won the dogfight or shot the best score. Even then he challenged himself as well. Bob "Sport" Horton, one of the squadron's young midshipmen, said Butch "would come back from a gunnery hop and claim he didn't hit the banner [when in fact] he'd shot hell out it." Horton felt Butch was too demanding and that his self-deprecation at his own minor flaws was just a way to call attention to himself. Butch scoffs. "You complain when you get a gun jam and lose even five rounds. I was quick to jump on things that were less than perfect." Most others in the squadron interviewed said they appreciated Butch's demanding style. "He was fair and treated you well," said Klapka. "We had a great squadron because of the standards."

Still, even the best intentions can go awry.

One day around midafternoon several months after he'd assumed command, Butch was in his hangar office starting to fill out paperwork. He and other pilots had been out on a shooting exercise and had just returned. A plane would tow a target and they'd take turns attacking and firing at it, tallying the scores after the towplane landed. They'd parked their Bearcats at the tie-down near the hangar and dispersed, waiting for the tallies. Suddenly, he heard a loud rat-a-tat-tat. The sound was unmistakable. The squadron had recently transitioned to Bearcat-2s, updated versions of the fighter. They were armed with a 20-mm cannon in each wing, and he recognized the popping immediately.

He ran outside with others to see what had happened. It didn't take long to deduce the obvious. After any exercise using live ammunition, the pilots landed, taxied over to a "clearing" area facing the sea where a squadron ordnanceman—the plane's engines still running—removed any unspent rounds. "They'd open up the panels and take out the leftover belts." Then the pilots would taxi over to the hangar and park in a line facing the city. Something had obviously gone wrong. Somehow, approximately sixteen rounds hadn't been removed and had been accidentally triggered.

Butch could see his career crumbling.

A few people were already on the Bearcat when he got there on the run. He ordered them off and impounded it. "Put jacks under the wings so nothing can move, not even an eighth of an inch." He knew there was going to be a major investigation. "Here comes the command duty officer in his jeep with the red lights going. He's saying, 'What happened? What happened?' I said, 'Looks like an automatic firing. Nobody knows yet why.'" They both knew the possibilities. "We were scared to death that we had probably killed some people. Shot up a school maybe."

Ballistics experts arrived with maps and plotting tools. They got right to work. The planes were parked on the far west side of the island, facing east. With noses elevated thirty degrees in the parking stance, the rounds would have arced several miles toward the mainland, curving up over the width of the island and the narrow channel, called North San Diego Bay, on which its east side fronted and into downtown or higher ground beyond. "I remember leaning over the charts they were using. They had parallels and were figuring the winds and such." When they finally arrived at an answer, he was somewhat relieved. "They said it went into the San Diego Zoo [just north of the downtown area]. Right around the bear cages. How they knew that, I don't know." Captain Bill Gentner, the same fellow who had wanted to name the Blue Angels "Lancers," was now on the admiral's staff at North Island. When he arrived, said Butch, "we all put our heads together, and the decision was made not to volunteer anything. We were going to wait and see what happened."

An hour went by. Then another. "We began to think maybe we'd lucked out." He spent the night at the base. Still nothing happened. "We began to assume that we hadn't killed or hurt anybody. We would have heard about it." Well into the following day, there were still no inquiries. "No press. No nothing. It was just plain lucky." In the meantime, Butch determined the ordnanceman responsible. Incredibly, he had missed the large rounds and then a later handler, not knowing they were still in the chambers, had accidentally triggered the guns. Butch decided to court-martial the sailor. The lapse was that serious. He thought that would be a good lesson and end the matter.

Not so lucky.

A week or two later, he was at the base's quarterly safety meeting. COs, XOs, ordnance and safety officers from every squadron on the base were in attendance. The hall was packed. Gentner was chairing. After preliminaries about current safety concerns, the captain suddenly—at least that's the way Butch remembers it—said, "Today we have a special treat. Butch Voris, commanding officer of VF-113, will come forward and tell us all how he was able to fire sixteen rounds into the bear cages at the San Diego Zoo and do so without hitting a single soul."

Not even, apparently, a bear.

Was Gentner still mindful of the Blue Angel naming shenanigans?

"At the time, I was still waiting for the ax to fall. I said, oh, shit, and went forward." But nothing else happened. He told the story and explained it was human error and what he'd done to correct it. "I made a kind of lesson out of it: make sure your people are schooled in the procedure and when they do it their minds aren't elsewhere." The subsequent investigation, he said, found him blameless and apparently put a lid on the events, which could have been extremely embarrassing and damaging to the navy. "We were all sworn to secrecy." Lyle Olson, squadron legal officer at the time and thus prosecutor in the summary court martial, said he lost the case against the ordnanceman because he couldn't prove the rounds went into the city. Unlike Butch, he didn't have access to the ballistics data—never even knew they existed. In hindsight, he supposes the navy kept them from him. He was just an ensign. "They would prefer to have the prosecutor lose the case and have the rounds go into the bay."

★

In November 1949, the Stingers took part in what ships' histories and other sources indicate was the largest US naval war games exercise in peacetime up to that time. Operation Miki was a multiweek joint maneuver involving between fifty and ninety ships, depending on accounts, amphibious landings, and army and air force units. It was a simulated retaking of the Hawaiian Islands, concentrating on Pearl Harbor and Oahu. Enemy troops supposedly had invaded and occupied the territory, just as was feared at the beginning of World War II. Butch doesn't say much about the exercise because "it was just the kind of thing we did in the absence of war." It's dim in his mind. But it is noteworthy as a glimpse of the kind of fighter squadron he forged.

By this time, Butch was firmly entrenched as the Stinger skipper. "I could drink more martinis than the others . . . No, actually this is where you're building your service reputation, what kind of commanding officer you are . . . Part of that is your color on the ground, how you act in the role." He still had an acid tongue. Burroughs remembers Butch razzing him for being the squadron's shortest flyer. "I'd [retort] that his head was so slick [Butch's hair was now thinning on top] that he used a washcloth for a comb." He was an early riser, usually the first in the squadron office. "I do my best thinking then. My mind is as clear as a bell." On his desk, he kept a toy clenched fist, the middle finger of which he could extend if he'd had a bad day. He'd always had self-confidence and admits to a skipper swagger. "I don't know why. It's just part of the fighter pilot role. We think we're a little bit better than everyone else [on the base], and we make sure everyone else knows it." But he was still a "good guy," approachable and unpretentious. Sometime in this period, he'd begun smoking cigars, especially Manila Blunts and the longer, smoother Tabacalera, his favorite. "We called them a 'one-movie cigar.' It would last the whole picture . . . I chewed on them as much as I smoked them."

Operation Miki launched in late October or early November. The Stingers were part of Air Group Eleven flying from *Valley Forge,* a nearly 900-foot-long, straight-deck, Essex-class carrier. Shortly before the squadron left for the exercise, Butch was shocked to be informed he wouldn't be allowed to participate. The early Bearcats had a bubble canopy with no overturn structure. Large pilots, the doctors determined, weren't protected well from injury. Their heads and trunks protruded in the bubble. The Bearcat had a tendency to flip if it went into the barricades. Recently, there had been some ugly accidents involving crushings and decapitations. The navy was still in the process of switching from cloth to hard hats. The choice of hat was optional for most aviators, but Butch, given his size, had no choice; the flight surgeons said he couldn't fly in the Bearcat without the hard hat. And the largest one they had was too small for him. "Don't laugh. It was a catastrophe. I'm the skipper and I can't go with my squadron?"

He wasn't going to be denied. At a local sporting goods store, he bought a hardshell Wilson football helmet for $21. With a domed cranium, it was certainly big enough. He had his shop mechanics adapt it with earphones and a microphone for communications and paint it bright yellow—a decision that earned him the nickname "Old Yellow Hat" behind his back. "You want it to be easily identifiable in case you go down," he said. The doctors accepted it.

He was back at the helm.

Operation Miki commenced with round-the-clock launches. On one, Butch again almost lost his life. "I was being deck-launched and was back in the pack. Deck launch is not on a catapult like they do today. We were just taking off one after the other down the straight deck at ten-second intervals. We're real close. We always cleared to the right or left [when lifting off] so the prop wash"—a dangerous windy wake—"would clear the deck." A young pilot from another squadron was just ahead of him. "He cleared left and then came right back across in front of the deck." Butch was just becoming airborne. "The Bearcat has twelve-foot-long propellers, and that blast was like a horizontal cyclone. Tremendous." It flipped his fighter upside down, and Butch started plunging toward the sea. He had about sixty feet to fall, which was only seconds away. "Here I am wheels almost pointing toward heaven, looking at the water. I chopped the throttle [brought it to idle]"—something that had become second nature to him in numerous tight situations with the Blues. "That took off all my torque [part of the force that helped flip him]. The plane snapped right side up again." In the interim, he estimates, he'd fallen thirty to forty feet. If he had not righted the diving Bearcat, the probability was that if he somehow had survived the impact on the water, which was not likely, he would have been run over and killed by the huge bow of the carrier. It was steaming powerfully into the wind and could not have stopped in time.

Once Butch recovered, however, he dismissed the incident—at least he didn't go after the offending pilot as others might have. "I think the ship talked to him." The rest of the operation, at least for the Stingers, went much as Butch had hoped. There were a few tense moments, for instance, when Sport Horton took three or four passes to finally land. "I got a bug up my butt," said Horton. But those things happen. As Miki was winding down, a Hollywood movie company came and filmed a big-budget drama later released as *Task Force.* The highly acclaimed movie, about the birth of carrier aviation, starred Gary Cooper and Wayne Morris, a young actor who had been an actual Hellcat ace during the war. One scene was shot in the Stinger ready room. Butch wasn't there, but Ken Burroughs remembers, "We [Stinger pilots] were backdrop. We're all in the squadron room with the bright lights and it's hot as hell. Everybody's sweating and wishing they'd get the damn thing over with. The door opens and Wayne walks in." The Stinger operations officer at the time, Charlie Sanders, a later skipper of the Stingers, had served with Morris in the Pacific. Burrows: "Wayne walked over to Charlie and stuck out his hand. 'Charlie, how the hell are you?' Charlie just glared at him.

'You son of a bitch. I was hoping I'd never see you again.' Well, things got real cool fast. We found out later [that Charlie regarded Morris] as a real hot dog. [Charlie said Morris would] break formation and go chase Zeros. He resented him."

Morris, according to Barrett Tillman's *Hellcat Aces of World War II*, died of a heart attack at the age of forty-five. This happened while he was visiting his old CAG, Captain David McCampbell, the top Hellcat ace of the war (thirty-four kills). Consequently, Morris's side of the story can't be told. Sanders, if he's still alive, couldn't be located. Butch remembers having dinner in the wardroom with some of the actors. "Gary Cooper had a beautiful wife. We sat at opposite ends of the table, so we didn't speak much." When he returned to San Diego, Butch received a commendation from *Valley Forge*'s commanding officer, Captain H. B. Temple. Citing exceptional aircraft maintenance by the Stingers, the letter, dated 21 November 1949, said, "VF Squadron 113 maintained one hundred percent aircraft availability during all phases of Operation 'MIKI' . . . This outstanding performance reflects great credit on the Squadron under your command . . ." Butch had accomplished his mission. "We were ready."

CHAPTER 22

Although Butch had built the Stingers into a combat-ready squadron, he wouldn't take them into combat. His tour as skipper ended, and he rotated out of that slot before VF-113 transitioned to Corsairs and went to Korea when war broke out in June 1950. If he wanted promotion, which of course he did, it was time for him to do shore duty. "Today, they keep you on flying status a long time. Back then, we rotated shore to sea, sea to shore." He was assigned to the Bureau of Aeronautics in Washington, D.C., hub of the nation's military and political power, where he'd get his introduction to the major administrative workings of the navy and begin a behind-the-scenes involvement in naval aircraft development to which he would return in successively higher positions periodically in the years ahead. But he hadn't thought much about that deepening bureaucratic involvement yet. In pilot parlance, he would be flying a desk, not often relished by fighter pilots. And when he first reported in March 1950, he was intrigued to be at the seat of power but didn't think he was technically qualified. "I thought, what the hell? I'm not an engineer. Why in heck am I going to the bureau?"

He was assigned to the Pratt and Whitney (P&W) desk of the In-Service Engines section in the bureau's Power Plant Division, one of hundreds of desks in many sections of the giant bureaucracy's multiple divisions. Those sections included maintenance, supply, experimental, and so on. The Bureau of Aeronautics dealt with all phases of naval aviation procurement, including selecting the planes to be contracted for and, once built, keeping them flying with the best possible engines and systems, which were constantly being corrected, strengthened, and updated. Butch would be the naval officer in charge of all changes and updates to engines on current fleet airplanes being built by Pratt and Whitney, one of the largest suppliers to the navy of aircraft engines, or "power plants," as they were called. For instance, the Grumman-built F9F Panther, the navy's main carrier fighter plane by that time, had a P&W J42 jet engine in it. It was one of the navy's first jet engines, and Butch would be in charge of approving or rejecting all changes or upgrades to it. Since the Panther was the main navy fighter, this meant he was being put in an important position.

But with his own questions about his qualification still bothering him, one of the first things he did after arriving at the bureau was to pay traditional respects to Admiral Alfred M. Pride, a naval aviation pioneer and the three-star who headed the bureau, and to ask him, "Why me?" Pride had been the first non–college graduate in the navy to make flag rank. In that sense, he was like Butch, who only had two years of civilian college. "He told me, 'You know we have to have people here like you who fly these machines, not just people who design them and fix them. I need people with operational experience so they'll know what works and what doesn't.' " It made sense. Butch left the meeting determined to give it his best. He'd always been good at mechanics. As a kid, he'd loved building wooden race cars. It was one of his hobbies. He loved to tinker. With the Blue Angels he'd been involved with much of the maintenance and repair. At the section, he was given a desk and telephone. "It wasn't much, but that was a critical period because we were changing from piston engines to jets. I spent a lot of time at the [P&W] factory [in Connecticut]. I was learning on the job."

One of the first problems confronting him involved the J42 engine. Panther pilots were experiencing the same sudden loss of power in flight that he had experienced in the Hellcat when he'd almost crashed in the Florida Panhandle, and for much the same reason. Water was getting into the fuel. Jet fuel, more viscous and more lubricating than gasoline, hadn't yet been developed. The jets were still flying on the basic aviation fuel, which was kept in big tanks on the carriers. The tanks contained water in their bottoms to displace volatile fumes, and when even tiny amounts of water got into the more sophisticated J42 fuel pumps, it would interfere, causing a flame-out. In the jet engine, fuel acted as a lubricant as well as a propellant. It lubricated the fuel pump pistons that injected the gasoline. But if there was water in the fuel, it would cause the pistons to seize and the fuel pump to stop and flame out.

It was a deadly problem, especially on launch or landing of the Panthers. P&W engineers worked hard to correct it and had to get Butch's approval at each new step. In addition to phone approvals, he'd take trips to P&W headquarters in East Hartford, Connecticut. "I'd take the night train, get a sleeper, and P&W people would pick me up the next morning. I could work for the day." As solutions to the fuel-water problem, they tried putting grooves in the piston sides so the water would be collected and not stop the pistons. It didn't work. "We tried gold plating the pistons. Platinum. Nothing stopped it." They finally started adding oil to the gasoline as a temporary fix. It lubricated the fuel better and helped the pistons move in spite of any water. "That was a big task on board ship. Finally we got JP fuel [jet fuel], which was a heavier lubricant fuel." The problem ceased. Since the country was at war, the solution helped national security, and Butch, as a player in reaching the solution, had a definite hand in saving pilot lives.

A peripheral project Butch helped on gives a glimpse of him at the bureau. John O. Emmerson, at the time a young engineer working for the navy on the first helicopter to mesh separate propellers—a radical idea in those days—needed some engine turbines from a discarded helicopter in the bureau's inventory. If he didn't get them, his project might be canceled. He was directed to Butch. Writing in an article he proposed to Smithsonian's *Air and Space* magazine in 2001, Emmerson, now owner of his own company, recalls, "My impression was that Butch . . . was BIG; but now I'm not sure if it was his physique or his enthusiasm . . . It's a long, long stretch between . . . leading a slow roll in tight formation [as a Blue Angel] and the mental perambulations of swapping engines in a . . . helicopter; but Butch bridged the gap with ease. 'We must do this,'" Emmerson quotes him as saying after Emmerson laid out the facts. How could he help? When told, "Butch did a high-speed 180 [degree pivot in his] chair," made a phone call, and, a minute later, swiveled back "with a wide grin. 'We will have two turbines on your dock within thirty days of contract signature.'"

And they did.

Of greater impact, Butch remembers the drama of seeing the first captured enemy MiG-15 jet fighter engine brought to Pratt and Whitney. The Korean War, which started when North Korea suddenly attacked South Korea at four a.m. on June 25, 1950, had taken a lot of people by surprise. At the war's beginning, the Soviet-built MiG-15, flown by the North Korean Air Force—with the aid of Russian and Chinese pilots— seemed a better jet fighter than any in the United States or South Korean inventory. Most of that had to do with aircraft design, specifically the MiG-15's sweptback wings, and some with preparation for the war. But the MiG-15 and the Panther used basically the same engine, an upgrade of a British-built Rolls Royce turbojet called a J48 by the United States and a VK-1 by the Russians. The Russians had gotten the base engine from the British in 1947 when relations between East and West had been better. The big question for Butch and others when the engine arrived amidst great secrecy was how the Russians had overcome certain problems that had been plaguing the American engines. It was the first enemy fighter the United States had procured in the new war.

Naturally there was great excitement. "I was there when they took it out of the crate." Exactly where it had come from is unclear. But the consensus of some of those who were there and were contacted recently is that it came from a plane shot down and recovered in either a Korean bay or river. "The engineers began to disassemble it, and the ooohs and aaahs started. 'Look what they did here. Look at this.' I'd been there long enough by that time to know what they were excited about."

What was chiefly drawing everyone's interest, including Butch's, was what the Russians had done to stop the engine's turbine blades from cracking, a problem the Pratt and Whitney engineers were still struggling with.

A jet engine is a huge processor of air. The air is ingested, compressed, mixed with fuel, and heated to make a gas that turns the turbine blades at terrific speeds in order to shoot the mixture rearward and create thrust. In the intense heat of that process, the American J48 turbine blades were expanding and hitting the metal shroud that encased them and being ground off at the tips. To remedy the problem, P&W had been chamfering the blades, "taking the mass out of the tip so it became narrower at the end and wouldn't have a tendency to [expand] as much." But the resultant smaller blades meant the engine was operating at only about 95 percent efficiency. American pilots weren't getting the power they should.

The Russians, in contrast, had developed, through metallurgy, a stronger metal for the blades, and that in turn allowed them to put small air passages in them. These created an internal air cooling of each blade, which could be likened to the cooling method of a car radiator. Air coming from outside through the ducts was used in the cooling. The blades thus didn't heat up and expand as much. There were other subtle improvements that helped in the process. But that was the main one. "This was a critical part of the engine. There are many blades and they turn at tremendous speed—11,000 r.p.m. [revolutions per minute] . . . It was marvelous. We'd had this problem we hadn't been able to fix, and all of a sudden we get enough clues to make changes." The American engineers had no compunction about copying the Russian design. "We needed to improve. Our planes would fly better."

★

One Friday in early October 1951, Butch was at his desk in the bureau and got a call, as he remembers it, late in the afternoon from Commander Bill Pitman, a fighter expert, in the CNO's office in the Pentagon. "He said the secretary of the navy wants the Blue Angels back in the air as quick as possible. Could I write up what would be needed?"

When the Korean War had started, the navy, because of post–World War II reductions, was short of fighter pilots and fighter squadrons. The Blue Angels, at that time under Lieutenant Commander Johnny Magda, who had succeeded Dusty Rhodes, volunteered for combat service and became the nucleus of a new fighter squadron, the VF-191 "Satan's Kittens." One source, *Blue Angels: Fifty Years of Precision Flight,* says it was decided that sending the Blues to combat "would make good public relations." Most others indicate it was because the navy lacked pilots. Whatever the reason, on March 8, 1951, Magda, commander of the Kittens, had been shot down by antiaircraft fire while strafing a Korean bridge, becoming the first Blue Angel to die in combat. Now, apparently, says Butch, the navy, with the war continuing and still short of pilots, wanted to quickly revive the best pilot-magnet they had. The war was proving lengthy. Since Magda was no longer available, they'd turned to him. "They wanted to get back in the limelight . . . I was close and handy."

He told Pitman he'd get right on it. That weekend "I sat down at home with my Remington typewriter and typed out what they'd need." Thea saw what he was doing and asked, "'You won't be going back, will you?' I said, 'Of course not. I've already done my tour.'"

The plan didn't take long to formulate. He knew how to do it from his previous experience. He recommended getting some of the core pilots from the Blues' last tour. The team would fly the new F9F-5 Panthers, the latest and newer version of the same jet they had been flying before they left for Korea. It was a little longer, had the new Pratt and Whitney J48 turbojet engine, the development of which he'd overseen while at the bureau. "It had more power, which would be appreciated." Control would be one of the big differences since he'd left the Blues. "In a prop plane you've got the big engine up front. You roll and it continually wants to pull you toward Mother Earth. The only way to keep the nose up is through coordinated rudder use with the stick. With the jet, the foot peddles for the rudder are mostly just a place to put your feet. It's essentially a stick airplane." And there wouldn't be the constant fighting with the torque as the engine tried to turn the plane opposite to the direction of the propeller.

A Grumman "Ironworks" product, the Panther was sturdy and, for crowd appeal, sleek, and its air-conditioning and ability to fly high and thus longer without refueling meant easier, more comfortable transit from show to show—something the pilots would gratefully appreciate. "The minute you took your hand off the stick in the Bearcat, it would roll left or right and start heading for the ground. You had to pay attention all the time while flying cross-country."

The routine would remain basically the same except that the team would now be flying the four-plane diamond formation, and their rolls would be in formation around a single axis—the crowd pleaser—not the dangerous slow rolls performed together around each individual plane axis. "Basically, they'd be going faster and [flying during a show in a larger space of air] because it takes more time to turn in a jet. But the maneuvers would be the same." The close management of fuel required in normal jet flight at low altitude wouldn't be a problem because they wouldn't be up long enough to empty a tank. Maintenance would be simpler in some ways because jet engines had fewer moving parts. The lack of torque would also mean a more stable ride, which was better for close-in precision flying. He recommended they fill the longer turning times with more individual performances. The simulated Zero was out because "Japan was now an ally."

Monday morning a messenger came and picked up the recommendation.

That afternoon he got a call from Pitman.

"'We like it,' " Butch recalls Pitman saying, " 'but you haven't recommended a leader.' I told him I didn't think it was my place to do so. That's your call. He said, 'Well, we want *you* to do it.' I said, 'Oh, my God, I've already had my tour.'" Butch was flattered but Thea hadn't seemed to like the idea, and he wanted her to have input. "We talked a bit about it, and they suggested a cocktail party at Pitman's house." It would be an easy and less threatening way to present the proposition. He'd hold off discussing it with her until then. "It was their idea. I said, okay, we'll see how it goes." He and Thea hadn't even talked about his next assignment. This one would be more dangerous than most and require him to be away a lot.

The cocktail party, remembers Butch, was a small gathering of three or four couples. It was hot and the group was out on Pitman's screened porch. Captain William Floyd "Bush" Bringle, a distinguished aviator who would become a prominent admiral in the Vietnam War era, broke the ice. "We've got drinks and he's saying, 'Hey, we appreciate all the work you did [on the reorganization plan], but now we've got a real problem. We've got to find a leader who can do this and do it the way it has to be done.' He looks at me and I know Thea's listening. He says, 'Hey, Butch. Why don't you do it?'" Butch feigned reluctance. "Oh, I've already had my time. You should get one of the other guys." Thea, however, didn't seem concerned at all. "What's the matter?" he said she asked. "You scared?" An affronted Butch shot a hand out to Bringle. "I'll do it. Nobody calls me scared."

★

Butch was given ten days to settle affairs and report to NAS Corpus Christi, where the team had moved its headquarters after he'd left Jacksonville. As the new officer in charge, he was given office space in Hangar 42 along the seaplane ramp and quickly got to work gathering the new team and readying the Panthers. As before, the jets had to be stripped of excess weight and repainted. The first two pilots selected were former standout Blues, Ray Hawkins and Pat Murphy.

Lieutenant Commander Hawkins was a near triple ace from World War II who had flown with the Blues from 1948 until they'd gone to Korea. There he'd flown approximately forty combat missions. He had three Navy Crosses and later would be inducted into the Texas Aviation Hall of Fame. Not only did he have fourteen confirmed kills from World War II but launching from the *Cabot* near Truk Island on April 30, 1944, he'd gotten what was probably the quickest kill ever by a navy pilot. According to Acepilots.com, he was barely seconds off the *Cabot*'s deck when he saw an attacking Japanese torpedo bomber and gunned it down. The tall, slim, twenty-nine-year-old Texan was happy to return to the Blues, and the navy, pulling out all stops to accommodate Butch, got him there in record time.

Lieutenant Murphy, described in the press as a "quiet, rugged-looking Irishman," had served with the Blues through much of 1950 and then, like Hawkins, had gone to Korea to help make up the core of Satan's Kittens. While there, the Brookfield, Illinois, native had been involved in a dramatic incident. According to *Pistons to Jets,* an official navy publication, he'd been wingman to Ensign Floryan Soberski when Soberski's Panther canopy had been hit by enemy artillery during a bombing mission off Wonson Harbor. The canopy had exploded, and fragments had nearly blinded Soberski. He could only see slightly from the right eye. Flying alongside him and using their radio communication, Murphy had guided his squadron mate back to the carrier *Princeton* and helped him land.

Others initially recruited were mostly from the training command: Lieutenant (j.g.) Dwight E. "Bud" Wood Jr., a balding, twenty-six-year-old pilot from Columbus, Ohio—soon to die in the horrific midair at Corpus Christi—was known to Hawkins and Murphy from their combat in Korea. He would fly the slot, the anchoring fourth and rear position in the diamond. Lieutenant Wallace "Buddy" Rich, coincidentally from Butch's hometown of Santa Cruz, had also flown in Korea. Lieutenant Tom R. Jones, of Savannah, Georgia, a Navy Cross winner who had piloted Corsairs during World War II, was recruited as a spare and would fly solo Panther performances in between the team's maneuvers. Butch figured they'd need more solos because the team's exits and entrances now would take longer. Finally, Lieutenant Bob Belt, a nonflyer who had served with Satan's Kittens in Korea, was brought in to head maintenance. A picture with story in the *Corpus Christi Times* edition of November 7, 1951, shows Belt, Voris, Hawkins, and Murphy viewing a wall map of the local area while the headline proclaims: "Blue Angels Will Be Ready to Take to Air Next Week."

The declaration was premature. Practice, according to Butch's log, wasn't started until December 12, and mechanical problems soon surfaced. Fire lights in the cockpits glowed when they shouldn't. Worse, the high-speed, low-altitude maneuvering inherent in the Blues' performances— and, in this case, their initial practices—started causing protective engine intake screens to collapse. The air at the low altitudes they were flying was thicker and more punishing. Broken screen pieces were being dangerously ingested. The screens needed strengthening. After being painted and modified for show work, the recently delivered Panthers had to be sent back to Grumman a second time for more extensive work. This was in January 1952. With no jets to fly, Butch decided to put the team's pilots, including himself, through instrument refresher courses, a process that eventually would be required anyway. It would take several months.

Meanwhile, a political problem arose. Chance Vought, the Texas-based airplane manufacturing company that had produced the vaunted World War II gull-winged Corsair, had built a new fighter for the navy, the F7U "Cutlass," a twin-engine jet with swept-back wings and no tail. "It wasn't a good plane for our type shows," said Butch. "It was still being perfected." But Chance Vought had clout in Washington and wanted it publicized. Butch was directed to put the Cutlass in his performances. "That was the farthest thing from my mind. But Texas politicians won out. You know how the game works." Two of the "bat-winged" jets were painted with Blue Angel colors and markings and sent to Corpus Christi in January along with Lieutenant Commander Whitey Feightner, Butch's old Fighting 10 squadron mate. Feightner by then was the Cutlass's chief test pilot at Patuxent River. Basically of the same mind as Butch about the Cutlass, Feightner was there on orders, too. Once at Corpus Christi, he enlisted Lieutenant Harding C. "Mac" Macknight, a former Blue Angel in the training command, to fly the other Cutlass. "Thank goodness Whitey came with the plane," said Butch. "I made him my so-called exec and told him the program was all his. You run it."

It was decided that the Cutlasses would perform solo between the team's diamond maneuvers. As the Panther team was still going through instrument refresher, Feightner, who would later become an admiral, gave several Blue Angel demonstrations alone, and later with the Panther team, proving, at least in Butch's eyes, the Cutlass's unworthiness. Butch: "Our engines were still being repaired, so I'm in ground control at the edge of the field. We call Whitey in to start his demonstration. He came in fast and beautiful-looking and started a maximum right roll. Well, the plane started to look like a chaff dispenser"—chaff normally being little bits of metal released to confuse enemy homing missiles. "The landing gear doors peeled off. Part of a vertical fin peeled off. Feightner himself says in *Blue Angels: Fifty Years of Precision Flight* that "big pieces of the doors went through the crowd . . . Fortunately, nobody was hurt."

In another demonstration, Feightner's controls gave out, and he was lucky to survive a near crash, as was Macknight when the Cutlass he was flying caught fire outside Chicago en route to Corpus Christi. The Cutlass had one of the first hydraulic control systems in a navy aircraft, and after Macknight landed and spewed hydraulic fluid all over a runway, maintenance chief Belt, according to Feightner in the above source, "just gave up on the airplane. He could not maintain them anymore." By that time, said Feightner, he was wanted back at Patuxent River to test the new, improved version of the Cutlass, the F7U-3. He was one of the few in the navy who could fly the plane.

He left the Blues—as did the Cutlasses.

That was in late summer 1952, probably August. Earlier, in April, the renovated Panthers were back from Grumman, the refresher courses were completed, and practices began again on April 16. Because of the initial problems and loss of time, the team basically had to start over. As they had in 1946, the pilots began by reviewing their routines alone, then grouped in pairs and threes, and finally in the four-plane diamond, descending progressively lower until Butch felt they were ready for the dangerous near-to-the-deck flying. "It wasn't harder than before. Just different." The higher speeds and greater altitudes were an adjustment. But the major difference between before, when he had started the Blues, and now, as he was resurrecting them, was the diamond formation and the fact that the configuration of the jets allowed for the planes to get even closer together during the maneuvers, which was something he felt was important for audience impact. "You make your mark by flying closer than anyone else."

It was dangerous, but they didn't have the huge propellers—the "Cusinarts," as he came to call the props on the Hellcat and Bearcat—to watch out for, nor the difficult blind roll which they'd featured back in '46. On the other hand, the diamond presented its own special new danger. "It wasn't a true diamond. We compressed it at the top and the bottom." The number four Panther, the "tail-end Charlie," was so tightly tucked up under and behind the leader's tail that even a slight unintended movement of the stick could cause the two to collide. Rear-flying number four had to contend with the leader's potentially deadly jet wash and rely on the leader's—Butch's—steady, unerring hand. "If you slid back even three or four feet and then had any major vertical [up and down] displacement [as, in fact, would happen in the terrible midair to come], you are going to hit the rear Panther." Even five pounds of unintended pressure on the stick, a small amount, could cause disaster. But as he coaxed them, Butch strove for perfection. "That's my basic character. I had to keep calling, 'Let's move it in closer. Let's come in a little closer.' Second place wasn't good enough in my mind."

An innovation in the new show was the team's use of food dye in water to produce colorful red, white, and blue streamers from the Panther's torpedo-like wing tanks. It meant extra work for maintenance. Crews had to disengage fuel lines, empty the tanks, fill them with the colored water, and then reestablish them as fuel tanks when the show was over. They got in trouble at first because the streamer residue fell on local backyard laundry lines, prompting complaints from housewives. As a result, they moved practices out over unpopulated areas, which also lessened noise complaints.

Butch's own adjustment from prop to jet was made easier by the fact that before leaving Washington the previous fall, he'd gone to Patuxent River and flown a Panther to familiarize himself. "You have to work at it," he said. "But it eventually all comes back." For the first time, he said, he began to realize the impact the Blues had made since he last had them. "Washington was very responsive. We were getting everything we wanted." Lieutenant Commander Frank Graham, another World War II and Korean War veteran, was brought in as an announcer, advance man, and public information officer. He was "a very smooth show caller," Butch wrote Grumman representative Dave Scheuer years later in response to a query. Finally, after all the delays and a nearly two-practice-a-day schedule for a month and a half, the reorganized Blue Angels were ready for their inaugural show.

It was on June 16 at Corpus Christi and held specifically for the news media. Representatives from print, film, and the new medium of television gathered at the water. "In a dazzling preview for the press here yesterday," wrote John W. Johnson of the *Corpus Christi Caller-Times,* "the Blue Angels brought the jet age down to a grass roots level. This brilliant band of Navy pilots . . . gave a near-matchless exhibition of military aviation at its precision best . . . Flying gleaming blue 600-mile-an-hour Panther jets in breathtakingly tight formation they ran through a repertoire of stunts that kept the small audience on edge for the full thirty-minute show . . . Newsreel, press and television cameramen recorded every maneuver [as] the team looped . . . rolled and whipped through half Cuban eights—all in perfect diamond formation. Then shifting into a step-down echelon . . . they executed cross-overs . . . on their backs . . . Hugging tight . . . the rolling Panthers looked like some fantastic cluster of blue grapes, suspended in the sky . . . The maneuvers, spectacular enough in themselves, became things of real beauty when the planes, jettisoning colored water . . . streamed long vapor trails behind . . ."

Despite windy conditions that Johnson said "bounced" the Panthers "like Ping-Pong balls," the debut was quite literally a roaring success. The *Caller-Times* ran a picture of Admiral A. K. Morehouse, chief of advanced training, congratulating Voris, who was still in his hard hat and flight suit, a spiffy new dark garment with a Blue Angel patch embroidered on the breast. A United Press story, appearing in Tennessee's *Memphis Press-Scimitar,* in whose city the Blues were next scheduled to appear, noted that the "crack" team hoped "to resell America's youth on aviation with displays of spectacular aerobatics." In the *Caller-Times* Johnson quoted Butch as saying, "With the advent of jets, military aviation lost touch with the people on the ground. Because they operate at altitudes of 40,000 feet and higher, they lost all chance of an audience. The people . . . have no way of knowing what's going on anymore. It's the intention of the Blue Angels to bring jets down to a level where they can really be seen."

The next day, the team was on its way to NAS Memphis, where writer George Sisler of the *Commercial Appeal* described its dramatic June 19 entrance to a three-day show: "Four specks appear on the horizon . . . Soundlessly they loom larger . . . as they wing ever nearer spectators massed on the ground . . . Then whoosh—they streak overhead with the sound of a giant blowtorch and melt swiftly into the distance." And so it went. The returning team was welcomed with awe and excitement.

But even as Butch was occupied with getting the team up and running again, there was something else important happening in his life. He and Thea were trying to make a family. "We wanted to have children, not a lot of them, because in my line of work there are odds that I might not come home one day." But their efforts had been fruitless. Early in a first pregnancy, Thea had a miscarriage. A little over seven months into a second pregnancy, a baby girl was born prematurely and lived only a few days. In one of the few times Thea could remember, she saw Butch cry. "He's a private person. He keeps it inside," she said.

By now they'd begun to think about adoption. Thea's mother worked for a doctor in Santa Cruz. Several months before the first show, her mother had called with some news. The doctor she worked for had a family that was expecting a baby and couldn't afford it. Once it was born, they were going to put it up for adoption. The family was Catholic and had physical characteristics similar to Butch and Thea's, aspects they both felt were important. While Butch and Thea weren't Catholic, they were Christian. The doctor vouched for the family. Would they be interested?

Working through the doctor, whom Butch knew as the team physician when he'd played football in high school, they had satisfied state adoption requirements and contracted with the family to take the baby. "We never met them," said Butch. "They had something like four or five other children and just couldn't take care of another." The contract stipulated that the Vorises would pay all costs of the hospital delivery and subsequent adoption process. The baby was born on May 23, 1952, a day in which the Korean War still raged, the Dodgers beat the Phillies 5–1, and a tornado hit upstate Texas. It was a girl. They eventually christened her Jill, a name they liked after a search.

Thea, who was handling most of the arrangements, didn't leave Corpus Christi to pick up the baby until about a week after the birth. She would have to stay there throughout June and early July in order to satisfy various adoption requirements and get things ready to bring Jill home to Corpus Christi. Butch, leading the Blues through the first shows, was looking forward to their return. He, at last, was going to be a father, a new milestone in his life. That was his personal situation when the devastating midair collision that opened this book occurred on July 7 at Corpus Christi.

CHAPTER 23

Prior to the midair, the team had returned from Memphis and scheduled performances in Chicago, Pensacola, Los Angeles, and Seattle. The ten a.m. July 7 show at Corpus Christi was regarded largely as a practice, as it was, as they say, in house, specifically for naval midshipmen visiting the air station for aviation orientation and not part of the official public show schedule. Not that it was any less demanding or conducted under less rigid safety rules. In fact, because of high winds that frequently occurred at the Gulf-side base, the show had been called off twice. July 7 was the final day that it could be held. The midshipmen had to leave.

Contrary to what was planned, however, what the prospective naval aviators had witnessed was naval aviation in the extreme. Speed, precision, danger, sudden calamity, and death, courage and miraculous survival, were all aspects of the profession a naval aviator, especially a fighter pilot, could expect to encounter. And the midshipmen that morning saw some of each and more—from the thrilling high-speed diamond pass to the sudden and unexpected collision to Butch's heartstopping plunge toward what seemed an almost certain crash. That they also had to witness Bud Wood's emergency ejection and death as he hit water almost as hard as stone because of his speed, was, to say the least, regrettable. But included, too, was Butch's miraculous, treetop ride to save himself and his plane, his gutsy and, as it turned out, wise decision to stay with the crippled jet, and, finally, his near suicidal but successful high-speed landing that few at the show thought possible.

Miraculously, again, he'd pulled it off.

There was a lesson there about taking chances, going for the gold, and simply hanging in when all hope seems gone and all you can do is go with your gut or die.

Not until the careening, crippled jet had come to a halt had Butch allowed himself to go into momentary shock. "I tried to get up, but my legs wouldn't support me. I more or less collapsed." Ambulance crews wanted to take him to the hospital but he shook it off. Basically, although cut and bruised and with a sore neck from being hurled to the top of the cockpit, he was unhurt. Just shook. He was concerned about his men and, more important, Bud Wood's wife, Patricia Jean, who he knew had been in the special viewing section up front and had witnessed close hand her husband's ejection and violent demise.

Admiral Morehouse had sent a plane to the outlying Kingsville field to bring Voris back to where the wives were being gathered in the admiral's quarters. "I went up there and, you know, what can you say? She [Wood's wife] was crying, of course. I put my arm around her and tried to . . . What can you do? You can't do anything . . . There's always wondering, well, why did it happen? The air turbulence? Should we have been a little farther apart? But we were right in the process of getting them farther apart when we collided . . . We were all trying to console each other. It was a tough day."

An admiral's aide contacted Thea in Santa Cruz. She'd already been told about the accident by her mother. Local police had heard about it while she had been out and called the house. "She asked if I was all right, and I said yeah, well, sore neck and so forth. She said what are you going to do? I said get some new airplanes and re-form. We really didn't talk about it that much. I never liked to bring the office home." Years later she recalled that Butch always told her not to worry. He said he was too good to get hurt. "So I didn't."

Late that night, alone with his thoughts, he wondered if he could have done something differently, maybe have prevented the accident. But after three days of testimony from participants and witnesses, and months of investigation, the board of inquiry concluded in a report dated February 26, 1953, that the accident was unavoidable and "not caused in any manner by the intent, fault, negligence, or inefficiency of any person or persons in the naval service or connected therewith." Unable to make a definitive determination, it speculated that the wind shears from the hangars were the probable cause.

Butch had long before put the accident behind him. "You can't see a wind shear," he said. "We're always trying to attain perfection, but there are unknowns and we're human." The important thing was to get back in the air as soon as possible. They had demolished one Panther and nearly another. Two more needed extensive repairs. It was two weeks, July 21, before replacement airplanes arrived and they were back in the air practicing. "The planes had to be modified, painted, and all that. Then we went right back into it. It's like getting back on a horse after getting thrown. You're a little skittish but you get right back on. I remember when we did our first flight. I said we're going to go out and put a little altitude between ourselves and the ground and work our way down to the deck. That's what we did."

By the end of July, the team was back on its show schedule. Even before that, Thea had brought little Jill back to Texas. San Antonio, about a hundred miles away, was the closest airport she could fly into from California. Butch met them at the airport. "I made an ice chest with formula and put it in the Buick with baby blankets and all that," said Butch. It was a memorable occasion in an otherwise hazy, hectic period. "She [Jill] was just like our own." It wasn't long before they found out the baby was severely allergic. "She'd get asthma and couldn't breathe. We had to put her on all kinds of things." One was goat's milk. "She couldn't handle cow's milk. We bought cases of goat's milk." Doctors couldn't determine the cause. In time, Butch would volunteer as an injection guinea pig to try and find a cure. They couldn't have carpets in the house. He'd have to rise for work an hour early in order to wet-mop floors. Thea had even more to do. One time Jill was having so much trouble breathing, the doctor, reached by phone, told Butch to rush her to an emergency room. Running red lights, he was stopped by a cop who pulled a gun on him. "I told him I had a critically ill child. He looked in the back, saw her eyes rolling backward, and escorted me."

But that and the guinea pig testing would come later, in 1953.

In late July and early August 1952 the team was off to the West Coast for shows at NAS Los Alamitos and Marine Air Station El Toro, both in Southern California. The Los Alamitos show, near Los Angeles, was given in conjunction with the National Model Airplane Championship meet. Proof that the team was back in top form came from no less a judge than secretary of the navy Dan Kimball who was in the audience. After the show, Kimbell sent an August 4 message to key commands, including Corpus Christi. It said, "The magnificent demonstration of precision flying executed by the Blue Angels . . . was the outstanding event of the program. Thousands of spectators were thrilled by a display of airmanship that convincingly demonstrated the navy's continued preeminence in this field."

On August 9, the team opened the famous Seattle, Washington, Gold Cup Races by winging in low over Lake Washington east of Puget Sound and the city. The races, part of the area's annual Seafair activities, featured speed competition by some of the world's fastest yachts, motorboats, and hydroplanes. Although the cold war was still just a newspaper term to Butch at the time, he got a rude introduction when, after the show and flying back down the West Coast, bad weather diverted the team to March Air Force Base inland, near Riverside, California. March was an important Strategic Air Command hub. It was under the overall command of General Curtis E. LeMay, head of America's largest nuclear bomber fleet, the prime deterrent, it was believed at that time, to Russian aggression. LeMay, a cigar-chomping commander who would serve as air force chief of staff from 1961 to 1965, was very serious about the security at his bases. "We landed and I was getting out. All of I sudden I see this jeep with two airmen and cops with submachine guns. I'm standing in the cockpit just about to go over the side and one of them points his gun at me and says, 'Sit down.' I'd never seen anything like this." He obeyed. "They said, 'Throw your identification card over the side.'" He took out his wallet and hurled it to the tarmac. "I started to get out again and they waved the gun at me."

He sat back down.

The jeep went down the line doing the same to each member of the team. An air force F-80 landed and pulled up next to them. "He was from TAC [the Tactical Air Command] and apologized to us. He didn't go for it either. But, anyway, the guards went up and down the line collecting the ID cards and didn't give them back. Then they brought a truck out with the windows covered in black so you couldn't see out." The captive pilots were delivered to the operations office, which had opaqued windows. "The duty officer there was given our cards and asked, 'What's going on?' I said, 'You tell me.'" The Blues had to stay in operations until the weather broke and then were put back into the blacked-out van and taken to their planes. "They never left us alone. They escorted our planes to the end of the runways when we took off. I was glad to get out of there."

In Detroit, on August 30, the danger inherent in their job was underlined again when air force major Donald E. Adams, a Korean War ace, and his rear-seater were killed in a spectacular crash of their twin-engine F-89 "Scorpion" jet. Lifting off after the Blues had performed, the air force interceptor, turning with considerable Gs, lost a wing at about four hundred feet and then literally began disintegrating. Adams fought heroically to fly the crazily swirling remains over a huge crowd. If he'd ejected, speculation had it, hundreds might have died. According to an article by Dick Peer on the *MiG Maulers* Web site, spectators saw the pilot "spurning possible survival [by ejecting], fighting at the controls in an attempt to get the plane past the crowded section of the field."

The Blues, said Butch, were back at their hotel when they heard about the accident. "Detroit had some of the worst industrial smog there was. Worse than Los Angeles. In the air, you could see maybe a mile. Making turns, you lost sight of the field. We'd had to turn strictly by the numbers. [Adams] had trouble aligning himself with the runway because of the smog, so he pulled into this maneuver and his right wing snapped off at the root. It was right in front of the crowd. He rolled over the grandstand upside down. We were on our way back to the hotel when it happened."

The show, as usual, went on. The Blues met, and were favorably impressed by, the air force's "Skyblazers," the four-man demonstration team that preceded the "Thunderbirds," the surviving air force team that was still a year away from being formed. The Skyblazers, organized by a group of air force pilots stationed in Europe in 1949, flew Republic single-seat F-84 "Thunderjets" and were making among their first appearances in the United States after demonstrations overseas. Both teams got great press in Detroit, which was holding its annual three-day International Aviation Exposition over the Labor Day weekend. In an unbylined story headlined, "Navy's Jet Angels Leave Earthlubbers Gasping," the *Detroit Free Press* called the navy flyers "swashbuckling young men . . . that had even veteran airmen gaping." Curt Haseltine, the *Free Press* aviation writer, wrote, they "fly as though the wings of their jets were welded together."

All wasn't accolade for Butch in his second tour as Boss. He'd refused an admiral's request for him to ferry the admiral's dog back from New York and incurred the officer's wrath. The dog was big and Butch could see it "getting panicky in the cramped cockpit." In another instance, the team, wanting to land quickly at Corpus, had come in too low and gotten close to an influential lawyer's house on the beach. The noise of the jets had upset an intimate moment the attorney and his wife were having, and the result was some minor injury to her. The attorney had gotten furious and threatened the base with a lawsuit, but Butch's profuse apologies and invitations to the man to visit the team turned him into a fan.

A problem that could have adversely affected his pilots' careers—but showed how Butch protected his men—occurred when, under a newly instituted policy, the captain of the base directed that Butch rate his pilots on their fitness reports by the bell curve method. Using a bell curve would mean that some would have to be ranked lower in performance than others and one as unsatisfactory. Butch refused. "I got a nasty note from the captain. It had one word, 'Comply.'" Butch went over the captain's head to Admiral Morehouse. "The next morning I got a funny call from the captain's secretary. Could I possibly find time to see him? I went up there and he's got tears in his eyes and he's wringing his hands. The admiral took him aside and skinned him alive. 'What do you expect Voris to do? Have an unsatisfactory man on the flight team? They're all hand-selected.' Shows the lack of mentality sometimes. If I rated someone down, I'd be awfully stupid to have him on the team. My butt is out there with them . . . I never hesitated when I thought I was right . . . for my pilots or my enlisted. I'd go as far as I had to."

In the next few months, the team would perform at Pensacola; Olathe, Kansas; Denver; Lincoln, Nebraska; Birmingham, Alabama; Dallas, and Jacksonville. At Pensacola, the show was performed for a carrier in the Gulf of Mexico. The navy had invited industrial leaders to the ship to show them the latest in naval technology. Butch didn't like performing at sea. "I was more comfortable over runways. You just don't have the depth perception over water."

At Olathe, a newspaper picture caption proclaimed, "The Blue Angels, under the leadership of Lieut. Comdr. R. M. Voris, Santa Cruz, Calif., is considered the best flying team in the nation." It was an indication that Butch had done what he had been sent to Corpus Christi to do—get the team up and running and in the limelight again. As his tour ended, "I'm thinking I'd better do something else in the navy if I'm ever going to get promoted on up." He figured that meant returning to Washington. But then he got a call that Admiral Robert Hickey, commander of Task Force 77 off Korea, wanted him. "That took care of that decision." After an absence of eight years, he was bound for war again.

CHAPTER 24

The Korean War, two-and-a-half years old when he arrived in late January 1953, was a frustration for Butch. "It was 90 percent political. We had so many restraints. We couldn't go to the heart of the threat"—attack China or the Soviet Union, instigators and clandestine participants in the war. "The politicians were afraid. How are you going to win? I suppose somebody had to stop them, but we were seldom on the offense, always trying to defend what we had. After World War II, it didn't seem like a real war. It seemed kind of Mickey Mouse. I'd served at the right time when there were no restraints. In Korea, we'd go after hordes of Chinese. There was no way to measure effectiveness. Killed so many coolies? Knocked out so many rickshaws? It was an embarrassment. We weren't prepared for that kind of war."

While it was a brutal and, in many ways, heroically fought war, that, in essence, was his view from the carrier.

Butch wasn't a flyer in the Korean War. He was a staff officer for Admiral Hickey, who, when Butch arrived, ran Task Force 77 from the bridge of *Kearsarge,* one of three carriers, including *Oriskany* and *Philippine Sea,* plowing the icy waters off North Korea.

His first night on *Kearsarge,* nicknamed "Mighty Kay," had been more hazardous than most of his subsequent duty. Catching a cramped transport flight to Hawaii, Midway Island, and then Japan, he'd been ferried to the flattop in the Sea of Japan in a modified TBF bomber that served as the ship's COD (carrier onboard delivery) plane. The trip out must have been nostalgic, given that Butch had fought so hard over the Pacific during World War II. Landing, he'd reported to Hickey and been assigned the high bunk in a two-man stateroom and given the four a.m. watch for the following morning. So keyed up to get a good start had he been that when the wake-up call came, he'd tumbled six feet to the floor, bashing his ribs on a desk. "It was sticking out and I caught it on my side. Didn't break anything, but, boy, it winded me. Almost knocked me out." He'd recovered and stood the watch, which became a regular duty for him.

Kearsarge was a straight-decked, refurbished Essex-class carrier of some 30,000 tons. From time to time the task force staff would move to other ships as carriers went back to port or otherwise left the line. As part of the staff, Butch was given the recently vacated job of operations analyst. "I didn't know an analyst from a bowel movement. I said, what am I supposed to do? They said don't worry, we've just got to fill the billet. That doesn't mean you're going to have to do that job. I said okay, fine with me if you say so."

As it turned out, he quickly mastered his duties, which included being staff tactical officer and some other roles. He settled into a routine. Basically, his job was planning air operations—which planes from what carriers would go where and when. The task force was mainly conducting bombing and strafing missions. Shortly after he arrived, the task force began heavy attacks on the eastern industrial port of Wonsan, south of Hungnam in North Korea. His planning job was a return to the kind of duty he did on a smaller scale as operations officer while flying with Fighting 2 in 1943 and 1944. By this time he had nearly 2,500 hours, mostly in fighters, and drew on his experience to assign missions to squadrons and plane types depending on their fuel, ordnance, availability, and other factors. "As far as the pilots were concerned, it wasn't the type of war they liked . . . You're interdicting railroad lines, truck convoys, bridges"—flying low, subject to tracking fire that could always get lucky, not often pitting skills against enemy flyers which most navy fighter pilots would have preferred. While the air force, flying up to the Chinese border and MiG Alley on the other side of the Korean peninsula engaged in frequent dogfighting, the carriers in the Sea of Japan seldom saw MiGs. The North Koreans didn't have much of an air force, said Butch. It was mainly Chinese and Russian pilots in North Korean and Chinese MiGs who were fighting the air war. His days got very repetitive.

"We'd spend three days on line and one day off." The day off was for meeting the "resupply train"—"oilers, ammo ships, supply ships"—and replenishing. We'd make rendezvous by radar in the early hours of the morning, come up behind them, and take fuel, ammunition, ice cream, mail, all those things . . . If you're taking flak like the pilots were, [the missions] might be exciting. But for those of us not flying, it was mostly routine after routine." His involvement with planning nuclear strikes made the duty "a little more exciting. All the carriers had nuclear weapons . . . These were tactical [atomic bombs] not the big, 'Fat Boy' types [like those on heavy bombers]. They were long and could be carried on our tactical airplanes [fighters]." They were kept in security areas heavily guarded by marines "and never spoken of or talked about. Security was real high." The staff knew there was little chance they would use the nukes. Not only was there a political aversion to it, but "we didn't have the hard targets. It wasn't an appropriate weapon."

Periodically, they would break from the line and go back to port at historic places like Sasebo, Japan. Sasebo, in centuries past, had been a little fishing village on the western side of the southern Japanese island of Kyushu. It was right across from Korea. In 1904, the Imperial Japanese Navy had sailed from there to their dramatic sea victory over the Russians, and it had grown after World War II to become the main launching point for US forces fighting in and around Korea. He held no animosity toward his former enemies. "It was a little strange in the beginning, but I liked the Japanese way of life, the food, the hot baths. They have a beautiful culture. We spent a lot of time sightseeing and buying stuff and sending it home. Raw silk. Mikimoto pearls . . . brocaded skirts and jackets for the wives . . . We'd go to the pearl farm and up to Tokyo . . . Their children were so well behaved . . . You'd see the little girls in their blue sailor suits holding hands and getting on the train for school. Well-mannered, beautiful little kids . . . I remember the 'honey pots' by the homes. You'd smell them as you went by. They'd use them for fertilizer for their vegetable gardens . . . I saw as much of Japan as I possibly could."

Sometime in March, according to his log, the routine was broken when Butch was asked by Admiral Hickey to go on a secret, undocumented mission. This wasn't a normal, regular-duty mission. It was an under-the-table, only-between-Butch-and-the-admiral mission. The admiral, as far as Butch knows, had conjured it up. It wasn't even directed against the enemy per se. It was an offer of air support from the navy to the army and was designed to circumvent the ruling air force, which the admiral apparently felt was badly performing a mission that the navy could do better.

Throughout the war, there had been friction between naval aviation and air force as the two services conducted operations that sometimes conflicted. Since the air force pretty much ran the air war, the navy, in such disputes, had to acquiesce. One issue involved close air support (CAS) for ground troops. Infantry soldiers sometimes needed planes to bomb and strafe the enemy. Some units didn't have artillery or got in trouble and needed help. CAS was so important to the marines that it was the main mission of marine air. The navy also had a strong tradition of close air support stemming from World War II, and practiced it. Butch had conducted many close air support missions. The air force had no such tradition, didn't practice CAS as much as the other two services, and seldom gave it high priority when asked to provide it. But since the air force ran air operations, the army had to depend on the air force when it needed CAS. "Their idea was to drop it from five thousand feet and leave," said Butch. "That's nearly a mile. You can't see anything from there. It was a laughingstock. We go down to a hundred feet. You can look over the side and see the eyes of your own troops. We knew what we were doing."

Once in a while, the navy, which got its daily tasking from the air force, would get a block of free time to do with as it wished, usually a week or so. When one of these free weeks loomed, Admiral Hickey, Butch speculated, apparently saw a chance "to get a lick in . . . I'm sure he had the blessings of his superiors; otherwise I don't think he would have done it." He remembers the admiral calling him in and saying. "If you get caught, Butch, we'll deny the whole thing." Exposure of the ploy could have repercussions, possibly hurt his career. Some on the admiral's staff warned him. "I was sticking my neck way out." But he was happy to accept. Not only was the secret mission to offer the army unauthorized help a welcome diversion for him, but "it was an opportunity to pull something off. I always liked those kinds of things."

With instructions to keep the mission secret from everyone except those who needed to know, Butch took the COD in mid-March to Seoul and the war-running Joint Operations Center (JOC), where the services each had an office. Playing "dumb" for a while and attending briefings as if that were his purpose, he finally went to the Eighth Army headquarters and asked to see the commanding general. He thinks it was General Maxwell Taylor he was ushered in to see. Taylor, an airborne hero of D-day who later became an advisor to President John F. Kennedy, was Eighth Army commander at that time. "They couldn't figure out why a lieutenant commander had any important business for the general, but when I told them I had a special message from the commander of Task Force 77, they took me in. He [the general] was very personable. 'Sit down, have a cup of coffee.'" The others left, and the general closed the door. "I explained who I was and why I was there. I said, 'You can understand why we're approaching you quietly with this offer.' He had a twinkle in his eye right away. We shook hands and I went back to the navy office in the JOC where I could get a coded message back to the admiral that we had reached an agreement."

According to his log, he left Seoul in the COD on March 21, accompanied, he said, by several of the general's key staff members, including two colonels. By that time, *Kearsarge* had departed for San Diego and the task force staff had moved to another ship. Once on board, they worked out all the details. Exactly where the close air support went is buried in the records of that conflict. But it was flown fairly soon after, said Butch. This was at a time that the war was moving toward an uneasy truce to be signed that summer, and both sides were beginning to jockey for final position. Some of the worst fighting occurred in the next few months, including several of the seesaw battles for the infamous Pork Chop Hill and those for Old Baldy, a hill near Pork Chop. "We were at their disposal for one solid week. It was a successful endeavor. Once the air force got wind of it, it was too late. I'm sure we had our excuses all laid out. It was a real coup for us. There was nothing they could do about it."

Butch continued on line with the staff until late spring when his team was given a break and he went home to Santa Cruz for what he thought would be a lengthy stay. In an unexpected but joyful development, Thea had become pregnant just before he'd left for Korea, and he now thought he could spend some long overdue time with her and baby Jill. But only a few days after he arrived, he received a call from the chief of staff to return posthaste. The war, in its final throes, demanded their presence again. They were leaving for Japan immediately. When Butch returned to the Sea of Japan, the navy and marines together launched some of the highest combined total sorties of the war—910 on June 15 alone, which was the record for a single day. Undoubtedly, he was involved in the planning and dispatching. There was furious fighting by both sides right up until the signing of the armistice on July 27, 1953. Then, with the absence of war, things really got routine. "Combat air patrols, photographic intelligence over China, things like that. Not very exciting, except you are up round the clock, still standing watches, monitoring whatever is the potential hot spot." There were personal low points, as when he got an emergency message from the Red Cross. "It said that my daughter Jill was critically ill. Life expectancy uncertain." It was another attack of acute asthma. "They didn't have the medications in those days. Boy that's rough when you're nine thousand miles away and there's no way to get home." Luckily, she pulled through. Randie, his natural and second daughter, was born shortly after he left during the truncated leave. He wanted to be there but wouldn't return home for a full nine months. Thea wasn't happy about his absence. "It was tough on the family, but that was my life."

★

In early 1954, Butch, still on staff, was promoted to full commander. The hike in rank and pay was welcome. He would need it with the larger family. It also signaled that his tour was coming to an end. Because of the rotation, he figured he was destined for another less-than-exciting desk job. Even if he could swing more sea duty, he wasn't senior enough to get the next plum in an aviator's career, CAG, command of a carrier air group. "Flying seemed out of the question." So he was surprised when the group commander asked him to succeed Bob Elder, a noted contemporary slightly senior to him who at that time skippered the VF-191 Satan's Kittens, the squadron that had been started by the Blue Angels several years before. "I said I've already had a squadron and the Blue Angels twice, so I don't think there's much chance of BuPers [the Navy Bureau of Personnel, which assigns selections] approving this. The superior said, "Let me take care of that."

Getting a squadron after having already commanded one was highly unusual. VF-191, however, was a highly unusual squadron, one of the best at that time and most important in terms of personnel and aircraft in the fleet. It had the new F9F-6 "Cougar," the navy's first high-speed swept-back wing fighter. It could go supersonic. It was also one of the first with a control system run by hydraulics, making stick and rudder movements easier and faster. It had been developed to counter the

MiG-15, and though the Korean War was now over, the navy wanted to be sure that its introduction into the fleet was completed in the best possible way. Elder had started the introduction. But he had to leave early. There were still bugs to work out, unforeseen problems possibly to deal with. Naval officials wanted a standout pilot to take over. "Butch was available and capable," remembered Elder years later.

The new Cougar was a streamlined derivative of the Panther, which, of course, Butch was now a master of. It looked similar to the Panther except for the swept-back wings and the fact that it had no wingtip tanks. It had a more powerful engine, a new radar fire-control system that could tell the pilot his distance from the target, ground or aerial, and a high-sitting tail, a rare innovation called a flying tail, designed to swivel in its entirety for better control at high speeds.

A week after the discussion about succeeding Elder, Butch received orders to NAS Moffett Field to assume command of VF-191 when Elder departed. Moffett, where the squadron was based, wasn't far from Santa Cruz. Butch would soon be back in the cockpit and near where his and Thea's families were. "I was tickled pink. Now the fun starts again."

CHAPTER 25

It was a clear day like most at Fallon Air Field, Nevada, gateway to the navy's remote desert weapons ranges. Good conditions to fly in, except that it was windy, with sudden gusts. Butch and his four Cougars had been out at the Black Rock gunnery range shooting up a towed target and were returning in anticipation of a few good hours at the Fallon O club bar, a righteous place of sweaty flight suits, loud music, and hands flying. "Have a few pops and argue about who is best and that sort of thing."

The postflight ritual.

Almost as good as sex.

As they approached the field at about four hundred miles per hour, he—their skipper—wanted them to look sharp. "Show off. It's the nature of the fighter pilot."

They were in a right echelon formation. It swung them out in a line abreast, swept back like the Cougar's thin wings. Butch, "Tiger 1," was in the lead. They were cocky and had good reason. The Cougar was the navy's best—the new generation of weapons platform in 1954, sleek and capable of supersonic speed, albeit, admittedly, only in a dive. Even the word supersonic was new and prestigious. And supposedly their fighter was a match for the MiG-15, the nimble Soviet-produced swept-wing jet fighter that had proven so dangerous at the beginning of the Korean War.

They—the three Satan's Kittens and their CO leader—were among the first in the fleet to fly the Cougar.

But it was still a tricky machine.

"In all honesty," said Butch, "it was rushed out too quick." He'd already lost two pilots to its mechanical failures. And he would lose three more. "Trying to track down mothers and fathers, next of kin. That was hard. Like the young ensign of Mexican descent whose father was a foreman for the Southern Pacific Railroad. The "flying tail," one of the Cougar's touted innovations, "went away on him. He dived straight in. Couldn't pull out." Butch had to go through the railroad's field offices to locate the father and then the telephone hookup had been bad. "He didn't speak good English, and I didn't speak good Spanish. I had to explain to him that his boy had just been killed. I hated those calls. You at least wanted it to be person to person."

They had just shot the hell out of the towed sleeve on the range. It had been a successful training exercise—even if he had called the CAG a "seagull," as in "Seagull 1, this is Tiger 1," when they'd reached the range. "When are you guys going to be through?" It had been a typical Voris jibe at a superior. "You know what a seagull is: a gray dirty bird, good for nothing, that flies around and shits over everything."

He still had to answer for that.

But so what. It was all in fun.

The four swept-wing fighters were distinctly Satan's Kittens: navy blue with bright white numerals and signature white bands circling each nose cone, wingtip, and high tail fin. As an added touch, little red diamonds were painted in the bands and chained through them—a bit flamboyant for Butch's taste, but he had inherited the jets. And who knows, someone watching them then could rightfully dub the Cougars "streaks of freedom," which was an honest observation. They were there to protect.

The four roared low above the runway's length. There were no speed restrictions at Fallon in 1954. At the runway's end, they'd make their sudden breaks, each in succession banking smartly, left wings dipping, plane forms curling smoothly all the way back around to the front of the runway, descending as they curled. Then they'd straighten out, bring their wings level, and drop seemingly effortlessly to the tarmac, a picture of military precision. In fact, it would take considerable stick and rudder control to make it look effortless in the twenty-five-mile-an-hour gusts that were frequently occurring.

Reaching the runway's end, its markings tiny below him, Butch gave the customary finger tap to his helmet, signaling his intention to break. He slammed the stick hard to the left. He expected his left wing to drop precipitously and the plane thus to bank, wing down, hard in that direction. But that's not what happened. Nothing happened. The Cougar just kept jetting straight ahead, beyond the runway beneath him and out towards the wilds—as if he'd never moved the stick!

He jammed it left again.

Same result.

Roaring on forward, he realized he'd lost lateral control. It was almost like driving a car without the steering wheel.

Now one of the reasons he'd been specially picked to skipper the squadron would come into play.

His wingman, flying up alongside, radioed: "Your airplane's wet." It didn't take long for Butch to realize what had happened. The Cougar was controlled by hydraulics, a system using a viscous fluid to replace the old cable and pulleys. Pressure from the compressed thick fluid powered the control panels and other vital functions. Hydraulics were easier to manipulate and gave the pilot quicker, more nuanced control. But a break in the system meant loss of pressure, sometimes sudden, sometimes gradual. What his wingman was reporting was dark red hydraulic fluid streaming from the Cougar's nose, running back under its belly. The jet's hydraulically charged guns were housed in the nose, and it was there, after much firing on the range, that the leak, he realized, must have occurred. Loss of pressure had not been instantaneous. But when he'd slammed the stick hard for the break, that particular part had ruptured.

"Here I am going straight ahead with nothing in my stick." Backup for failed hydraulics in the Cougar was a small air bottle with thirty-two "cycles," or bursts, of pressurized air. Each burst powered one stick movement—and one only. In other words, he had only thirty-two stick movements, extreme or slight, with which to get down. "It wouldn't have been so bad if it hadn't been such a rough day," he said. "The winds were blowing in from the desert" and constantly jostling the jet. The plane, not dynamically stable as some are, always wanted to roll. Somehow he had to curl full circle and descend for landing—maneuvers involving much movement of the wings—while simultaneously fighting the gusts and tendency to roll. Each stick-moving cycle raised small "flaperettes," control surfaces on larger "flaperons," which were like ailerons on the wings. The raised flaperettes, because they were smaller, weren't as effective as the flaperons at catching outside air pressure and pushing the wing down. But they were all he had, and they would help keep the wings reasonably level, which was crucial at landing. A roll would quickly use up all the cycles, if not be uncontrollable. He had to avoid the roll. The only other means of steering he had were the feet-controlled rudder pedals. They caused yaw, a generally side-to-side movement, depending on which rudder he hit, which he could use to steer the plane left or right. Yaw was an uncomfortable, almost uncontrollable skid, like a vehicle sliding on an icy road. Now it would become the centerpiece of what he would have to use to try and get down.

Feet moving vigorously but purposefully, he started a wide arcing turn, the other Cougars making room for him by spreading high and above. All they could do was watch and advise. Going wide, he wouldn't have to curl so precisely. "It was touch and go," he said. Sudden bursts of wind tossed the plane and he kept correcting. "The main thing I did was keep an eye on those cycles." The gauge, a clocklike instrument with notches from 32 to 0 and a descending needle, was on his right panel. "Each time I moved the stick, it dropped another notch." He had to be careful and extremely judicious. He was down to about "fifteen cycles when I start the final turn." Was it enough? That was reduced to "five or six" as he straightened out and dropped for the landing. "There's a crosswind . . . It's ultra gusty . . . throwing the airplane around . . . I've got to make correction . . . It's pretty basic. Lose control and I crash."

Run out of cycles and he also crashes.

But he was lucky, or, in his own mind, so good, that he was able to pull it off. He made it down and "then no problem." In reality, his vast experience, cool head, and preparation had made the difference. He'd made it his business to master the plane he was flying. He'd known exactly what to do at every step—and he had done it. From there, it was "taxi up to the line and all this fluid is running out." He unstrapped and jumped to the tarmac. By the time he'd made his report, the emergency was largely forgotten—a few tense moments that would make good conversation at the O club that night. "Those on the ground didn't even know it was happening."

An earlier Cougar failure had concerned him much more.

Perhaps ironically, it had come right after one of his most pleasant navy assignments. Producers of the 1954 Miss Universe contest had asked the navy to supply a distinguished officer to award Miss Conge-niality, one of the preliminary crowns, her trophy. The contest was being held in Long Beach, California, down the coast from NAS Moffett, where VF-191 was based. Headquarters, probably mindful of Butch's public relations prowess, had asked him to do it. The pageant was being held on a Sunday in the Long Beach civic auditorium above the old horseshoe pier under which he'd paddled many times as a kid.

"Tough duty," he recalls. "Somebody had to do it."

From Moffet, he'd flown his Cougar down to North Island. A driver in a yellow pageant convertible with a banner on the side had picked him up in his dress whites and chauffeured him to Long Beach. Navy photos show him smiling handsomely on stage as he hands the gleaming trophy to Effie Androulaki, Miss Greece, while a crowd of beauties, some in one-piece bathing suits, others in formal gowns, smile and clap behind them. Available publicity about the event on the Internet says it was on national television. "The whole thing was great." They had driven him back to North Island and he'd taken off early that evening for Moffett in a thick fog.

"There probably was a hundred- or two-hundred-foot ceiling." Above that was dense fog. "You could barely see the lower terrain of Point Loma [the peninsula across from North Island]. I knew I had to make a quick turn seaward because Point Loma was right ahead." Just as he did and was continuing to climb, he got a warning light from the Cougar's engine compartment. The compartment was behind the cockpit and housed the jet's powerful J48 engine, the same engine, although enhanced, he'd worked with while at the Pratt and Whitney desk at the Bureau of Aero-nautics.

He knew it well.

A fire in the engine was a precursor to an explosion.

"That's a hell of a time to get [such a warning]. I'm only at two or three hundred feet and deep in the soup." He called departure control and said, "I have an emergency situation." They wanted to know his inten-tions. He said, "Stand by." He wasn't sure what he wanted to do. He had to get to at least two thousand feet to eject because it would take that much altitude to separate from the ejection seat and deploy his parachute, and the fog, he felt, prevented him from turning back and trying to land on the obscured field. "My first thought was to get to two thousand. I could have called for them to vector me back around for a landing, but then I'd be blind."

He opted to continue climbing.

His main worry while climbing was the large amount of jet fuel being sprayed into the engine. "The J48 had a high-pressure fuel system. I was at full power for takeoff spraying about 1800 psi, which is real high." If he did have a fire back there, an explosion could come any second.

He eased back on the throttle and the fire warning light went out.

He throttled up and it came back on.

He quickly pulled it back.

"Finally I popped up over the top of the overcast, I guess at about eighteen hundred to two-thousand feet. Could have ejected then, but got brave." Mindful of the Cougar's many teething problems, "I figured, well, this is just a warning system short circuit or something like that." They'd been having problems in most of their systems. He didn't want to lose a jet when it was probably just a faulty light. "So I notified departure that I was proceeding to Moffett."

He crossed his fingers.

With the throttle at less than full power, the warning light did not come on again. Weather conditions at Moffett when he reached it were good, and he landed without incident. "They just had a Sunday watch crew on. I wrote up my remarks and went on home." The next morning when he arrived at work, his engineering officer, chief, and several mechanics were waiting for him at the door. In one of their hands, wrapped in a dirty rag, was the fuel filter from his engine. "It was a double canister thing, maybe a foot long, with two barrels each about four inches in diameter." He invited them in. "What'ya got?" They showed him a large crack in one of the barrels. "Every time I went to full power it was spraying fuel back into the hot section of the engine and burning and flashing on it. It just as well could have fractured all the way open on my takeoff, which would have caused a massive explosion and the end of me at that low altitude . . . Everybody was shaking hands and saying we're pretty lucky that I got back down . . . I was shaking hands, too, but I'll never forget it . . . That was about as close as I ever want to come."

✦

Despite the cease-fire signed between North Korea and South Korea, the cold war continued in the Pacific. North Korea was hostile and belligerent. Its ally, the People's Republic of China, resented the 1949 establishment of an opposition Nationalist Chinese government on the island of Formosa, also known as Taiwan. They continually threatened invasion. The Soviet Union, behind an Iron Curtain of secrecy and oppression, attacked Western reconnaissance flights, even innocent commercial flights. In late July and August 1953 alone, the Russians and North Koreans, in separate incidents, shot down three Allied planes. In the first half of 1954, at least three more similar incidents occurred. In addition to American victims, one MiG was shot down.

It was during this time of heightened international tension that Butch assumed command of VF-191. Satan's Kittens had just returned from flying with Task Force 77 in the Sea of Japan when he arrived at NAS Moffett in June 1954. The squadron was scheduled to return to that volatile area on the carrier *Oriskany* at the beginning of 1955. In the interim, Butch's job was to get the squadron's pilots and planes ready for possible combat and at the same time work out the kinks in the Cougar. This interim period was called "workup" and involved extensive training, like the two-week weapons deployment at Fallon where he'd nearly crashed. Butch "was the smoothest flight leader I've ever encountered," said Paul Gillcrist, who would go from a nugget pilot in those days flying under Butch's tutelage to one of the navy's storied rear admirals. Gillcrist's autobiography, *Feet Wet,* contains some of what happened during Butch's reign. The "ultimate" in their combat training, writes Gillcrist, were the "division tactics fights" against "dissimilar" but capable air force jets from nearby bases. "In the violent arena of the dogfight you learned to exploit your strengths against the opponent's weakness."

Butch, Gillcrist said in a 2003 telephone interview, was a master at aerial fighting. "He was tough . . . his eyesight was unbelievable . . . It's not that his vision was any better than ours but he knew where to look. He knew what size speck they [the oncoming enemy aircraft] ought to be and where to find them relative to the horizon," a skill Butch said he was born with and perfected through experience and concentration, including squinting his eyes. Most of the time the Kittens fought gleaming silver F-86 Sabre jets, icons to the air force as much for their distinctive color as their prowess. "They were a little bit better than ours in terms of thrust-to-weight ratio. In other words, they could climb a little faster. We'd show up randomly in the arena looking for each other . . . Butch would spot them from a sun glint off the canopy [or a glimpse of wing or fuselage]. Everybody else would still be looking. He did that just about every time. Then he'd position us in a way so we'd have the advantage," usually using background or the sun to "bounce" them from the rear.

While Butch, who was also tasked with devising combat tactics for the Cougar as part of readying his squadron, liked to stay in a relatively tight "fingertip four" formation—four planes close together for support like nails on a hand. Gillcrist said the practice dogfights usually degenerated into one-versus-one or two-versus-one contests. During one melee, he said, Butch was fighting the skipper from the Sabre squadron and holding nothing back. "The guy knew he had been had . . . Butch had no compunction at all about nine-G turns in the fight, and the F-86 was only a six- or seven-G airplane . . . [the Sabre skipper] was pulling so hard that he cracked a wing spar and called off the entire division. He didn't want to break any more Sabres." At the postfight brief, he was "sort of apologetic. He asked Butch what he thought they could do to get better. Butch said well, you might think of some other paint job than silver."

Butch, at this time thirty-six-years-old and with nearly fifteen years as a naval aviator, was probably regarded with considerable awe by most of his pilots. Few squadron skippers had his combination of résumé, flight skills, and imposing physicality. Gillcrist, every bit as large as Butch, remembers fearing his relatively short career was over when Butch "called me in and gave me that icy blue-eyed stare." The young pilot had done some unauthorized acrobatics at a weekend air show and then landed his Cougar on a runway that was dangerously short. Either act could have ended in disaster. "But [Butch] was a pretty good guy and judge of character and figured he had me fairly cowed and I was never going to do anything like that again in my whole life. Promise, skipper. So he let me off. I always felt that the real reason he let me off was that I got away with a landing that no pilot in his right mind would ever try again."

Despite, as in any navy squadron, having subordinate officers for all the main jobs, Butch "ran everything," said Gillcrist. Not that he was meddling or micromanaging. "He just knew what was going on, and he was very hands on. They assigned us three or four extra pilots at the beginning, and the understanding [used by Butch] was that two or three would be left behind [when they went on cruise]. Believe me, nobody in a fighter squadron ever wants to be left behind. That was a harsh way to treat kids, but it made for a lively competition. I made a vow that I was not going to be the one left standing on the pier. So we all worked very hard at doing a good job and being as good as we could be in our collateral duties [like legal officer, public information officer, etc]. But mostly in flying."

Training out of Moffett continued through mid-January 1955. Then the squadron flew out to *Oriskany,* a straight-deck attack carrier, for three weeks of precruise exercises that included carrier landing qualifications. "If you can't land on the boat," said Butch, "the rest is down the toilet." The unique problem for VF-191 was that the Cougar was a new airplane, and few in the squadron had ever landed it on a carrier. With its new devices and unpredictable problems, the prospect of qualifying probably caused more than the normal amount of trepidation among the squadron's aviators, three of whom were air force exchange pilots with little or no carrier experience. Butch led the landings, qualifying first. Only one aviator didn't qualify. He was one of the air force exchange pilots. "He was a top fighter pilot in the air, but that boat scared him to death. They'd start to wave him off way out in the pattern." He feared slowing to the required speed. "I'll tell you, that really separated the men from the boys."

By early February, the squadron was readying to leave for Pearl Harbor. Tensions had heightened between Red China and the Chinese Nationalists. The United States was sending the *Oriskany* as a show of force. On February 11, the *Oakland Tribune* ran a near full page of pictures and stories under the banner: "Exclusive Photos of Alameda Flattop on Secret Exercise." Their reporter, Ralph Craib, was aboard *Oriskany.* He wrote: "The assignment to help guard Formosa is less than three weeks off . . . Old professionals like Commander Roy M. (Butch) Voris, skipper of Fighter Squadron 191 and formerly leader of the Navy's stunting Blue Angels . . . make this point: They've spent their entire Navy flying career in war or near war. There is no use trying to get ulcers over this one, they say, when it could be worse." Skipper of *Oriskany* was Captain Leroy Simpler, the man who Butch says first came up with the idea of starting the Blue Angels. Simpler told Craib, "We'll just be doing our job, and I feel that we know how to do that very well."

Undoubtedly Simpler was right. But the Kittens were flying the still-new Cougar. On the way out, Butch lost another of the air force pilots, this time violently. Captain Booth Holker had shot down two MiG-15s in the Korean War. He was number five in the launch sequence as the squadron, coming into Pearl Harbor, lifted off in the predawn darkness in order to arrive at Barber's Point around sunup. "I was the first one launched," said Butch. "I'd just cleaned up [retracted his wheels and was out of the launch pattern] and was climbing. We were all going to rendezvous up ahead. All of a sudden I hear, 'Chicken in the water! Chicken in the water!' Fighters were chickens then. Booth had just made his clearing turn off the deck and had a flameout." He'd gone in the water to the side and in front of the carrier. Unable to stop, the ship had plowed him under. "He was never recovered. His father was a significant man in the State Department in Turkey so we had all kinds of problems explaining this and that. We never really knew exactly what had happened."

Once on station in the Sea of Japan, the squadron became part of a round-the-clock CAP for hostile aircraft. Four carriers, operating together, composed Task Force 77. They steamed in an enormous box formation. Gillcrist writes: "To be overhead . . . at 20,000 feet and see four carriers . . . all turning into the wind together is spectacular." Flying as one of the two wingmen in Butch's division, he describes the sudden "flashing by" in their airspace of an unidentified aircraft, presumed to be a MiG, and Butch's exasperation at the carrier's inability to warn them. "How in Christ's name am I supposed to shoot down MiGs," he quotes Voris as saying, "if I don't even know they're up here." The Cougar had no search radar, only a small set that helped aim its guns. They lost the bogies.

But the worst enemy inevitably was the bad weather at that time of year. It was often cold and stormy when they launched. Shrouding sea fogs were frequent. "Right down essentially to the water," said Butch. "You couldn't fly in it, couldn't land in it." Gillcrist writes about one patrol that almost became their last. They were flying CAP at 45,000 feet just thirty miles off North Korea. Below them was a huge storm, and the carriers, approximately one hundred miles away, were hidden somewhere beneath it. As they ended the CAP and started back, they were worried they wouldn't be able to find *Oriskany*—or any of the carriers for that matter. Descending through the angry monster, Gillcrist writes, Voris's lead was "smooth, but we were getting tossed about pretty badly." The storm "was so black and dense" that the division "snuggled into a very tight diamond just to keep each other in sight . . . I had never been in a blacker cloud in my life."

Lower and lower they dropped, with no break in the tempest. Rain blasted their Cougars. "We were in serious trouble," writes Gillcrist. Butch says they were in communication with the ship, but rendezvous without the ability to see the carrier was in serious doubt. Even if they found it, how would they manage to land? Visibility was almost zero. At about 250 feet, they emerged beneath the storm's swirling skirts "only to be greeted," writes Gillcrist, "by the sight of black raging seas, angry whitecaps, and torrential rains." Catching a sudden, fleeting glimpse of the carrier's superstructure about a half mile away, the young wingman was astonished to see Butch's plane vanish as quick as the superstructure—and he did so without radioing a word. "Either he just didn't give a damn about us, or he had tremendous confidence in our ability to follow . . ."

Butch: "We had to act fast . . . We were running out of fuel and had to get down right away . . . I just flipped over the top . . . You either do something, or you know you're through." Gillcrist: "Aviation experts will, I am sure, take issue with me, saying that the lead airplane cannot break out of a diamond formation without colliding with his left wingman, but the skipper did it." He did it by somehow hurling the plane up and then over—a doctoral-level stick-and-rudder maneuver that only an expert could effect. The three others then, not so dangerously close, followed in his wake and miraculously—their jets "tossed" like corks "in a wild sea," writes Gillcrist—found the carrier and landed in minimum visibility. "I'm sure Butch Voris felt that necessity was the mother of invention," concluded Gillcrist. But "how the four of us managed to get aboard . . . is simply beyond comprehension."

International tensions subsided. *Oriskany,* during that 1955–1956 winter-spring cruise, ranged from Japan to the Philippines to Hong Kong. At one point, the Cougars flew cover for a mock marine invasion of Iwo Jima. The jet's sonic booms made the leathernecks scatter thinking old World War II mines were exploding. At Clark Air Force Base, Butch got to fly the new air force supersonic fighter, the F-100 "Super Sabre." In 1953, it had set a world level-flight speed record of 755 miles an hour. "It was bigger and heavier than I'd been used to and handled a little differently than our navy machines." The controls were more spread out, and "the stick was farther forward and much higher than in a Grumman. I never felt that comfortable with it."

But he judged it "a good machine."

On board, Butch became embroiled in a squadron rivalry. Such competitions are staples of any carrier cruise. Each squadron wants to be known as the best, and individual rankings from the skipper on down are at stake. But this one, between the Kittens and the VF-193 "Ghost Riders," flying older F2H3 "Banshee" night fighters, spiraled. It had started back at Moffett when Alan Shepard, later lionized as one of "the Right Stuff" pilots in the Tom Wolfe book of the same name, had tried to transfer from Banshee squadron to the Kittens. "He'd been a test pilot and all that, and he wanted to fly the new Cougar." But Ghost Rider skipper, Commander Maurice "Mickey" Weisner, a short, pugnacious aviator, senior to Butch, who would later rise to four-star admiral, wouldn't have it. He accused Butch of trying to steal Shepard. "I said wait a minute, Mickey. He came to me . . . I think he wants to be a daytime fighter pilot instead of all-weather [night]. That got [Mickey] upset."

The feud continued on board the *Oriskany* over everything from who would get the best ready room to accusations by Weisner that Butch was unsafe in the air—the result of Butch diving his division through a more orderly VF-193 grouping when the ship radioed an "Expedite Charlie," which meant land quickly. On one liberty, said Butch, Weisner had "a few more drinks than he needed" and came at him swinging. "I'd just grab him on the top of the head and push it down and tell his boys to take care of him." Reached in Pensacola, Weisner, retired, questioned Butch's version of events. "Sounds like you've got something overblown. There might have been a case where one of his airplanes cut inside our formation or something . . . but there was nothing between me and Butch concerning it . . . That's not my memory anyway."

Butch sticks by his recollection.

Whatever the details, Butch's cruise ended with *Oriskany* captain Simpler singling him out with two letters of commendation for helping the carrier and its Air Group 19, first, pass its readiness test successfully, and then, after the cruise, win "the COMAIRPAC [Pacific Fleet's] Battle Efficiency Pennant and 'E' for fiscal year 1955." Butch's "initiative and high devotion to duties" were cited, as was his squadron's efficiency in flying and completing missions.

But any satisfaction Butch took from that success was tempered when the ship was returning to Japan and he received a Red Cross emergency notification that his father had died. "Bob [his brother] didn't tell me until after the funeral was over because he didn't want me to try to get back." The cause of death was a postoperative thrombosis following a hernia operation. "My mother had been expecting it because Dad's health was going down." There wasn't much Butch could do except grieve alone as *Oriskany* left Sasebo and headed for home.

CHAPTER 26

Butch, due for another shore rotation when he returned from the Pacific, spent the next two years in Washington in the Deputy Chief of Naval Operations Aviation Training Division, "Op-56," as the Pentagon office was euphemistically called. Basically, he helped shape policy about how the navy trained its aviators in the use of the new weapons and armaments that were evolving in the jet age. Guided missiles, specifically the heat-seeking "Sidewinder" and radar-directed "Sparrow," were coming into use. Tactical nuclear weapons were being written into battle scenarios. Planners envisioned air conflicts where the fighters and bombers kept their distances and shot missiles and dropped or "lofted" atomic bombs instead of getting in close and dogfighting and delivering solely conventional ordnance. "The emphasis was to do away with guns," said Butch, a gunfighter by tradition who had his doubts about the policy. Regular bombs and rockets continued as part of the aerial arsenal but pilots had to learn standoff and high-altitude delivery of the nuclear weapons. Otherwise, too close to the explosion, they'd be killed, too. "We provided guidelines to the fleet about the new training. What percentage of it should be put into what weapons and so forth." The "how" was essentially done at the fleet level.

Eventually, the deemphasis of guns would prove to be shortsighted. The Vietnam War would show that close-in dogfighting was not dead as the war planners believed. Guided missiles had specific envelopes out of which they would not work. Too far from an enemy aircraft or too close to it and the missiles, heat or radar, wouldn't track. But navy pilots in Vietnam, forced to visually identify what they were shooting at before firing a missile, increasingly found themselves in close-in, out-of-missile-envelope dogfights with no guns with which to protect themselves. To correct the problem, the famous "Top Gun" Navy Fighter Weapons School would be created in 1969. Fighter pilots and crew would have to be retaught dogfighting. But that was more than a decade in the future. Butch, now largely bound to a desk and nonflying duties, found his work in Op-56 "not a fun job except for the weapons meets," yearly gatherings of the navy's best fighter pilots and squadrons in which competitions for commendations and bragging rights were held. Butch's office was in charge of the meets, held annually at the Yuma (Arizona) Marine Air Corps Station, a desert base near the Mexican border. "You had air-to-air [dogfighting], air-to-ground [bombing], rockets, and strafing." Air admirals liked to attend. "It was a tremendous week of camaraderie."

But most of the time, he was bound to the Pentagon desk. One day an officer friend from the Pacific Fleet stopped by en route to the Bureau of Personnel. They had become close on *Oriskany*, and they socialized over cups of coffee. The friend had a notebook with him. He put it on Butch's desk, opened to a specific page. Butch: "He says, 'I've got to go to the john. Don't let anybody take this. It's confidential.' Well, naturally, I took a look, and here I am penciled in for commander of Air Group 5," the same he'd served with off Korea. The friend returned and put the notebook back in his briefcase. "Nothing more. It's supposed to be super secret until it becomes official because there are still a lot of considerations and hurdles before you're approved." The friend left. It was an exciting possibility—CAG—the promotion for which he'd been hoping. "About a month later I got orders for the air group."

★

Before Top Gun, there was FAGU, the Fleet Air Gunnery Unit, a 1950s training school where select navy and marine fighter pilots were sent to improve their skills. Pronounced "Fay-Goo," it was a graduate-level course in gunnery, bombing, and dogfighting. It was headquartered at hot and dusty El Centro. And it was where Butch, the new CAG, was ordered before taking command of Air Group 5. "All prospective CAGs and COs had to go." His twenty-one-member class was 8–57, the eighth that year. "I took the nuclear delivery course. You either enrolled in bombing or air-to-air. I already knew air-to-air and felt that if I was going to command an air wing, I'd better learn the other."

Ironically, in a reversal of roles, Paul Gillcrist, Butch's former division rookie in 191, turned out to be his FAGU instructor. Interestingly, Voris had sent Gillcrist to FAGU before Gillcrist's squadron tour was up because he felt the young pilot was instructor material. But he hadn't explained that to Gillcrist who, still inexperienced and unknowing about FAGU, had gone away perturbed thinking his skipper had deprived him of prime fleet duty. Then later, as Gillcrist explains in *Feet Wet*, the young pilot realized "how lucky I was." FAGU, like Top Gun after it, was status and fun city, a prime and prestigious assignment for any navy fighter pilot who loved to fly in the 1950s. Butch was "irrepressible, of course," Gillcrist recalls, "and it was hard for a former wingman"—even if he was a vaunted FAGU instructor—"to be standing up there in front of his ex-leader telling him how to shoot or fire rockets or go drop bombs. But Butch made it easy. He couldn't have been more interested."

Voris: "First they put you through ground school. You learn nuclear and how the heavier bombs affect the plane's aerodynamics." The class used F9F Panthers, Butch's Blue Angels jet. "Six bombs in a rack." They learned different deliveries, depending on terrain and other conditions. For the "loft maneuver," they'd come in low, maybe a hundred feet off the ground until they were over the target. Then it was "straight up to four thousand feet and over [on your back] in the direction you came. Just as you're curling back, the bomb is released and continues up [with momentum] maybe another two thousand feet until it flips and comes back down on the target. By that time, you've rolled upright and hopefully are far enough away not to be hurt." The "pitch maneuver" was used if there were mountains or hills in the area and the pilot couldn't fly low. "You pitch it out before you get there. If you have the right speed and angle, it'll go forward and hit the target." For both maneuvers, "you had to make corrections for the wind. I enjoyed it. It was acrobatic flying. I liked learning new things."

CAG was—and probably still is—just about as good an assignment as it gets for a seasoned fighter pilot looking to move up. The air group commander is in charge of an entire carrier complement of combat squadrons: fighters, bombers, support planes—most everything seen on a carrier's deck. Air Group 5 had just returned from the Pacific when Butch took over. He got it right as workup was beginning. By then he'd gotten tired of going to the barbershop and cutting the remaining hair he had left on top and started clipping himself bald. With a cigar clenched between his teeth, blue eyes blazing, and his considerable size, he could strike a formidable pose. But the tag that endured with his men was "Mr. Clean," a reference to the slick-headed, ear-ringed and muscled Procter and Gamble cleaning stud that debuted as an animated character the year he took over, 1958. Photos indeed show him with a marked resemblance to the smiling housewife helper. Gag cartoons from magazines were passed to him, like one showing the bald symbol in bed smiling coyly at a pretty lady hugging covers and exclaiming, "Before you, I always felt dirty." True to the hulky mascot's benevolent nature, Voris as a CAG was more instructor than lord.

"Everybody admired and respected Butch so much because he'd been the first Blue Angel," said George Whisler, skipper of the VF-142 "Fighting Falcons," a squadron of new Chance Vought F-8 "Crusaders" at the time. The Crusader, a droopy-winged, supersonic jet fighter would become known as the "last of the gunfighters" not only because it was the final US fighter designed with guns as primary weapon in that budding missile age but also because of its stellar performances helping shoot down MiGs at the beginning of the Vietnam War. VF-142 was attached to Air Group 5 while it worked out some early mechanical kinks that prevented it from going on cruise. "He was the greatest guy, down-to-earth," remembered Whisler. "We both bought houses on September Street in Clairemont Mesa, were neighbors for nearly a year . . . He led by example. He was such a good fighter pilot and an ace. Everybody wanted to be like him but you couldn't quite achieve that because he was a cut above everyone."

The air group was based at NAS Miramar on the outskirts of San Diego. In years hence, Miramar would become known as Fightertown, home of the navy's West Coast fighter fleet. Butch had a kid-in-a-candy-store situation. As commander, he could fly just about any of the planes in the air group whenever he wanted—provided they were available. Not that he'd commandeer them. He didn't. But that was his privilege. During his approximate year-long tenure, several of his squadrons transitioned from one jet to another, so, in addition to the Crusaders, he had a variety to chose from. These included the FJ-4 "Fury," the navy's version of the air force F-86 Sabre jet; the F9F Panther, which he'd flown with the

Blues; the FJ-4B, the bomber version of the Fury; and the F3H "Demon," a short-lived fleet fighter that, in his particular wing, he was forced to ground. "It was a cute little thing," he said of the McDonnell Douglas product that pilots described as looking like a "'pregnant guppy.' We lost the first few of them within sight of the airfield. The afterburner fuel pump casing exploded and they flamed right off the runway."

He also had a squadron equipped with the McDonnell Douglas F4D "Skyray," nicknamed the "Ensign Killer" by wary young pilots, and another squadron flying the new F-11F "Tiger," a slim, agile jet fighter that would gain fame later through use by the Blue Angels in the late 1950s and all through the 1960s. Butch preferred the swept-wing Tiger and made one of them his own special jet by having the traditional zeros— "double nuts"—painted on its nose. "When I took over, I went out and fought every pilot in the air group. You can do a little instructing that way. We called it 'tail chasing.' Get in the stream and away we go . . . I'd get them upside down and at the top of the loop and change lead. 'Okay, you take it. Get us down . . . It got us acquainted and they enjoyed taking on the old man. It caused a lot of talk around each squadron. 'Hey, he turned it over to me at the top of the loop.' They'd get excited about it."

That's what he wanted. His main job, regardless of obstacles, was to make sure the group would be able to go to war from a carrier when workup was completed—or, if need be, before completion. To that end, he accompanied his pilots to ranges and on weapons deployments all over California, including El Centro and China Lake, where the navy had a nuclear testing facility. Problems with the group's airplanes and a restricted budget didn't make the job any easier, as attested by Captain Robert E. C. "Bob" Jones, Butch's boss in fleet headquarters at North Island. "During the period . . . CDR VORIS has been faced with many logistical problems," Jones wrote in Butch's fitness report for the last quarter of 1958. "Two of his assigned squadrons have changed aircraft type and his air group has been forced to train with a minimum of operating . . . funds. In spite of these handicaps . . . VORIS has demonstrated ingenuity and effectiveness in maximum utilization of the resources available to him."

Commanding the navy jets defending Southern California in a large, mock joint navy–air force exercise labeled "Blue Bolt," Butch received a letter of commendation from Jones. "The skill exhibited by those aircraft squadrons attached to Carrier Air Group FIVE in detecting, reporting sightings, and attacking BLUE forces not only played a major role in the success of this exercise, but is indicative of the high state of training of Commander Carrier Air Group FIVE . . . As you are undoubtedly aware, the purpose of this exercise was to test our capability, provide additional training, and prepare us for war . . . I am pleased to state that you and those units under your operational control are ready NOW."

But, thankfully—because, deep down, few soldiers, including Butch, ever want the killing—he didn't have to go to war. In fact, the group never deployed on a carrier. His tenure with it was up before that occurred. "Luck of the draw," he said of not going out and proving he'd done the job. And what sticks in his mind mostly about the stint are two aspects worthy of note: an essentially comical incident at El Centro that could have earned him a court martial; and second, the fact that he was one of the founders of Tailhook, the organization of carrier pilots that got in so much trouble after the 1991 Gulf War because of its rowdy parties. The radical feminists and political correctness proctors missed out on the glorious opportunities in Butch's day.

First, El Centro: Butch had brought the air group for a month's worth of competitive weapons training. It had been a tough thirty days. The base hadn't supported them well, and they'd had to do triple what they normally would to get the job done. But they'd done it and were going back to Miramar in the morning. "Now it was let-off-steam time." The squadrons were all at the officers club. "They're out at the pool swimming and roughhousing. The booze was flowing, of course, and pretty soon they're throwing each other in the water, some with their clothes on. I haven't been out there yet. I'm in the bar and don't have a clue what's going on. I guess I should have, but I didn't."

Unknown to him, the commander of the base, a navy captain, was hosting his daughter's engagement party at the pool. "They're all dressed up and having cocktails all around and my guys are really getting rough." Training competition between all the group's squadrons had been fierce. "It's summertime and warm and, naturally, the two fighter squadrons are at each other's throats." All of a sudden water comes splashing into the bar. "I hear 'CAG! CAG! Help me!' I turn around and here's one of my smaller pilots handcuffed and in the hands of a large marine MP [military police] major. He's got [the pilot] by the scruff of the neck and the back of his wet shorts. He brought him up to me. 'This your man?' I said, 'Of course, yes. First of all, put him down. Get your hands off him. Now tell me what the problem is.'" About that time, the captain of the base came angrily in. "I thought, oh, shit, we're in trouble now." Butch was just a commander. The captain was furious. "He tells me about the engagement party and says, 'Get your people out of here right now or I'll call the rest of the marine guard.'"

Apologizing, Butch did as he was ordered. He herded the rowdy pilots back to the lobby of the BOQ. But lined up against the walls, still dripping water, the pilots, facing each other, continued to want to fight. Butch had had enough. "I said, 'Okay, if anybody wants to fight, you're gonna have to fight me first. I'm gonna walk down this line. Step out and I'll take you on. Any one of you. No rank. No consequences. Just step out here and we'll settle it. Just me and you.' Well, they started to sober up and realize what they'd done."

The captain had told Butch to report to his office the next morning at seven a.m., which he did. The secretary was noticeably cold. "Didn't offer me a cup of coffee or anything. So I go in. I knew it was going to be tough, but I had a strategy. You stand at attention, say good morning. He started out, 'Do you realize how out of control your organization is?' I tried to explain how they'd been under a month of high intensity work and how competitive it had been. He didn't want to hear it. He says, 'I'm going to report you to your commanding officer, all your superiors.'" That did it. "I said, 'You know, I'm going to have to talk to my superiors about *you*. This is the worst run air station I've ever been on. It's absolutely nonsupportive. I've had to take my own supply people, have them do your jobs. That's what I'm going to report.' I didn't use any swear words, just told him what I thought. I apologized again, but I said, 'I think you're absolutely unable to do the job you're supposed to be doing for us. We did it in spite of you.' All of a sudden the atmosphere changes and he asks me to sit down and would I like a cup of coffee?"

The captain never reported the incident, although Butch did, thinking it might be wise. But he got nothing but laughs from his superiors, which is why he knows the captain never did. "Bob Jones said good for you, Butch. Maybe we'll get better support there in the future."

It could have gone the other way.

Tailhook: The organization had its genesis in 1956, according to the Web site of the association that bears its name. The first gathering was at Rosarito Beach in Baja California, Mexico. It was a limited affair organized by a small group that included Bob Elder, the respected test and fighter pilot whom Butch had succeeded as skipper of VF-191. It was called a "reunion" then, and the idea, said Butch, was for carrier pilots, who uniquely among aviators go through the stresses and strains of operating off seaborne flight decks, "to get together, close the door, tell lies, and be entertained."

Butch missed the first reunion. It was at the Rosarita Beach Hotel, a forty-five-minute drive from San Diego. "I was in Washington, so I couldn't attend. I was at the second [held in 1957]. It was good camaraderie and fun." The Rosarita had a big wall around it with iron gates. "It was low-slung, nice. Not a motel. We could get everybody inside, lock the gate, take car keys [away], and do what we wanted." They imported strippers from Hollywood. The hotel had a big bar and restaurant. "We had a deal with the Mexican police that they would make sure everybody stayed inside. There were no presentations like there are now. No promotion. It was just all fun."

When time for the third reunion rolled around in 1958, Elder was leaving San Diego for a new assignment and asked Butch, then CAG 5, to chair. By this time, he said, some of the big aircraft companies, seeing a chance to ingratiate themselves, stepped in and picked up the bill. They were always there to help aviators, even to the point of stuffing a wad of cash into military pockets without saying a word when, in the company's opinion, it would be appreciated. It was good business. The plan was to go back to the Rosarita. He and Thea even went down and made some preliminary plans. But then they heard about a young fighter pilot who had been arrested in Mexico and was being kept there in a jail. They decided to have it at the Bahia Hotel on San Diego's Mission Bay. "It was new at the time and had no gates. We still collected the car keys." A nicely printed invitation booklet that Butch preserved has on its front an artist's drawing of an LSO, flags extended for landing, a fighter winging in under his direction. Inside are listed as cosponsors Grumman, Douglas, Chance Vought, North American, and McDonnell, and a mostly tongue-in-cheek "program," masking the real goings-on, with items like, "Third Floor—Song fest" and "Final floor show—Irish tenor."

Everything was going fine, said Butch, until around midnight, when one of the dancers, now without a stitch on, got too close to the cheering flyers, some of whom had put their drinks on the edge of the stage. An enthusiastic pilot grabbed for her leg. "She lost her balance and came down on her bare butt on top of a martini glass. The stem broke and gashed her in the right cheek. She wasn't bleeding that much because there was enough of a fat pad. But we threw a kimono on her, took her to our medical officer's cabin, Dick Phillips, who gave her a pain shot and sewed her up. We got a drink for her and went back out. She seemed fine. I got up on the stage and addressed everybody about being officers and gentlemen, and she watched the rest of the show with us." Later, her husband came by to pick her up. "We bought him a drink and sat with him awhile and apologized. I thought it was over."

Early the next week, Butch and the grabbing pilot were served with civil lawsuits. "Oh, boy. We don't have any insurance and we don't have an attorney. What we do have is [Vice] Admiral Alfred M. Pride, probably the most straitlaced flag officer in the US Navy. He's Commander, Air Force, Pacific Fleet, and oh, gee, there goes my career again." But he knew he had some influential friends. He called North American Aviation in Los Angeles. "I said we got a problem." The next day, after work, he was meeting with two North American lawyers in Ceiling Zero, a little bar in the BOQ at North Island. "So we're sitting at this cocktail table saying what are we going to do? And in comes Dick Phillips, the medical officer. He's also a photography buff. He says I got some pictures from the other evening and opens up his briefcase." What the pictures indicated was that the dancers were egging the pilots on. "The lawyers said, hey, I think we may have a case of provocation."

After seeing the photos, the plaintiff's attorney dropped the suit. But that wasn't the end of it. It turned out the dancer's husband was a member of the San Diego Police Vice Squad, and he was looking for revenge. The following year, 1959, Butch was on ComAirPac staff (Commander, Air Force Pacific), which was still in the area, and had to cochair the reunion again. "It was my job to find a new chairman, but everyone was scared to death." He got a cochair but ended up having to do almost all the work himself.

Again they were on Mission Beach but at a different hotel. He thinks it was called the Outrigger. It was a big place with an upper-floor curtained stage with adjoining dressing rooms where they held the performances. "We had the same type of entertainment from Hollywood. It wasn't gated, so I had people stationed outside." Suddenly, a lookout came running in saying the police had arrived. "He'd gotten a look at

them, and they were members of the vice squad." Butch pulled the curtain and sent the girls to the dressing rooms where Hawaiian muumuus
were waiting. By the time the plainclothes squad reached the room, the
girls were back out on the stage, discreetly attired, doing Hawaiian
dances and chants. The plainclothes cops "watched awhile, finally shook
their heads, and left. Once they'd gone, we were out of the Hawaiian
mode and back to our old stuff."

★

Butch's time as CAG was the last good flying he did. In late 1958, he got
a call from Bob Elder, whom he seemed to be following in jobs. Elder, a
bit senior to him, was leaving the Pacific Fleet staff position he had at
North Island as head of Air Group Training and Readiness and wanted to
know if Butch would succeed him. "He said he'd talked it over with the
others, and they all wanted me. It's a prime position, probably best on the
staff." Butch, who hadn't thought much about where he'd go next because his normal time for leaving was still awhile off, accepted. "I'd still
be in the air group stream, only a step higher."

Fleet CAGs would report to him.

But the new job was a milestone. In effect, he would be moving from
the operational side of naval aviation—the flying, fighting, tactical side—
to the administrative, back-home-making-policy-decisions side. From
now on, he'd be sitting in senior management chairs, assessing the larger
picture, helping figure out what the future flying navy was going to look
like, need, and do, while simultaneously helping administer its daily
needs. The days of hard, innovative flying, turning and burning, meeting
the enemy in combat, forging new aerial tactics and his own flying reputation were, in the main, over. But that was the price of moving up to be
considered for eventual command of a carrier and hopefully make admiral, a track he certainly was on and wanted.

"You have your regrets, like not being able to be a Blue Angel again,"
to fly and fight in the charged environment. "But you've got the younger
boys coming on. You've had your turn. It's somebody else's now . . . I
looked at it as a positive. I'd been fortunate. You either go up or out.
There's no alternative . . . I've seen people that never get over the fact that
they still aren't flying. You've got to get over it. Think ahead. Sure you
miss it, but you can't stew. Maybe you stew because you want somebody
else to think you're a hot person, piss and vinegar and ready to go, that

kind of horse crap. But when it comes time to go, you let go. What's the option? You're going anyway. Sure, you can still pop around the sky getting lobster and oysters, maybe even fly a hop with your pilots. But the real flying days are over. I saw it as an opportunity. Make the best of it."

And he would.

CHAPTER 27

On December 21, 1958, after Butch had assumed his new job as training officer on the Pacific Fleet air force staff, an article about him appeared on the front page of the *Clairemont Sentinel,* his local Southern California newspaper. Written by Bette Piper, it stated "Since their first flight demonstration on June 15, 1946, the Blue Angels have thrilled an estimated 35 million people with the most exact low-level formation flying ever performed." While Butch is still unsure exactly when he grasped the Blue Angel's impact, that figure twelve and a half years after the fact is testament that it was, by then, substantial. Thirty-five million having seen the navy's flying ambassadors is certainly proof that his early effort, dangerous, unprecedented, and fledgling as it was in the beginning, was a huge professional success. The article was accompanied on the front page by an above-the-fold picture of the current Blue Angel jets in flight—four gleaming new F11F-1 supersonic Tigers.

The team had come a long way.

Butch's picture, too, shows the journey.

No longer the quiet young leader, he has the mature look of a seasoned administrative officer. Gone is the cloth helmet he wore through the formidable years. Instead, he sports a fashionable jet-age hard hat, probably the one he used as a CAG. A big painted arrow on top points forward at its peak. "It used to be a breeze in the old days," Piper quotes him as saying. "Now, in jets, from the moment you are rolling down the runway, you are constantly aware of your responsibilities. The complex control panel is lit up. You are too busy to think about anything personal."

But, in fact, for the first time in a while, his new navy job was in the same town as his old, meaning his personal family life would have more continuity than before. Instead of him shipping or flying out again, he and Thea and the girls were, for the first time in his career, living in the same house longer than a year or two. Although Thea always chided him because, she said, his career had left her to raise the children alone in the early years, he was now able to spend more time with all of them. "We moved a lot," remembers his younger daughter Randie, now married to a naval academy graduate. "I'm a neatness freak today, I think, because my life was so chaotic when I was small . . . We were always moving . . . I think it was myself or my sister, he'd come home from being overseas or wherever he was and we thought he was the mailman because of his uniform."

Her father was complex, said Randie. "If he'd had boys, I think he would have been like, who was that? The Great Santini." He had a "tough edge, right out front. It was his way or the highway. He was very opinionated, very strict . . . It was tough for him, I think, living with three emotional women . . . I remember he built us wooden race cars. Mine was green. My sister's was red. We were the envy of every boy on the block . . . That was his way of showing affection . . . He had a hard time expressing his feelings, but when he did, it was overwhelming . . . I remember when I got pneumonia in the eighth grade, he was really concerned and brought me this big candy bar . . . When I split my knee, he was so kind . . . There's a big warm spot in there he tries to hide. I think that's partly his upbringing and partly just the way they were in those days. It was different."

It was also probably his constant striving for achievement in the dangerous and demanding world he worked in.

Such intensity was hard to switch off at night.

Butch's primary job as fleet training officer was to decide who got what from the always tight and limited fleet aviation budget. "We called it 'Bravo' money." A squadron would get more or less depending on what stage in training they were in. Those closest to deployment would get the most. "You'd get anxious COs coming in and pleading their case." These were the leaders of the most important elements of the fleet, the fighter and attack squadrons. If the squadrons weren't ready, the navy wasn't ready. "It was a crucial job. I enjoyed it. It taught me the other side of being ready."

He quickly became proficient. Although he'd only been on the job for two months, his boss, Admiral Pride, wrote in his first fitness report, "CDR VORIS has been able to step into his duties . . . with an amazing alacrity and effectiveness . . . He has mastered the intricacies of the budgetary problem and . . . is fully capable of providing the leadership necessary to guide the very fluid and difficult air group readiness problem."

Once familiarized with the way things were being done, he took a bold step and proposed changing the way squadrons were based in the entire Pacific Fleet. The system he was working under had squadrons housed according to air group. Fighters, bombers, and other aircraft in a given air group were kept together on the same base—as they were at Miramar when he had Air Group 5. This called for duplicate support functions and facilities at each base—maintenance, armaments, parts, and so on. Butch proposed to eliminate the duplication by basing aircraft together by type. Air groups weren't the tight, esprit de corps units that squadrons were, so basing their elements at different places wouldn't upset morale, he argued. Thus, for example, NAS Miramar would become "Fightertown," and NAS Lemore in Central California would house bombers. A third base would take heavy attack planes and so on.

It was a radical change, but it would save "millions and millions," Butch argued. Understandably, it was met with resistance when first proposed. An influential admiral high up in the navy chain of command in Washington said, "Butch, you're crazy. What do you want to do that for?" But as Butch laid out his stats, he said, "Look, I'll talk to some people, see what they think." In the meantime, Butch had got the backing of the new three-star who had taken over the Pacific Fleet air force, Vice Admiral C. E. "Swede" Ekstrom, "a big guy, bigger than me." Ekstrom went to see the CNO himself about the idea, and it was implemented. The change would stand for decades.

Butch established new training and testing methods to certify that the squadrons under the new basing scheme were ready for combat. When the training command, headquartered at Pensacola, requested that the fleet's preparatory Replacement Air Group (RAG)—which was now housed at Miramar with fighters under his new plan—be relocated to its Florida fields, Ekstrom picked Butch to lead the fight against the move. The RAG was the last stop for new fighter pilots before they were sent to fleet squadrons. It was there they were trained and oriented to replace veteran fighter pilots leaving for new assignments or those who were injured or killed. Butch and fleet leaders believed such training belonged near where the spirit and application of fleet doctrine was strongest. "The training command was a different mentality. One was shore duty; the other, the real navy. You're pointing toward deployment in the RAG, getting closer to the big game. You see it in the O clubs or wherever there is a gathering of these [fleet] pilots. You want the new ones exposed to that when they are about to join the fleet."

The proposed move to Pensacola seemed favored in Washington. The Pacific Fleet had its work cut out for it. A major meeting about the move was scheduled at the Florida base. In addition to preparing arguments, Ekstrom picked Butch to voice them. "It was a training issue, so it fell to me. They really threw me into the breach." Two- and three-star admirals were in the audience. The proposed move was a crucial issue. The training command made its presentation first. Butch then took over and briefed for several hours. The new basing plan, which had just been implemented, was part of his argument. Take the RAG from the fighter base and you distance the new pilots from the fleet, he stressed. At Pensacola, RAG instructors would not be recently returned fleet pilots, as they were at Miramar; they would be pilots just graduated from the training command, which was not the same. The navy would lose time and money moving the RAG and still end up with a lesser product. "I remember my immediate boss, Tex Harris [whom he'd served with in Fighting 10], was in the front row, and he signaled for me to tone it down. I was getting a little forceful and maybe too loud. But I really believed in what I was saying, and I knew in about ten minutes that I had them. You could tell it on their faces. There really were no counterarguments, so it was kind of nice to be in that situation. But if I'd failed, I'd never be given a chance to do anything like that again."

He prevailed. The RAG stayed at Miramar and became famous not only for being part of Fightertown, but for delivering successful pilots to the fleet during and after the Vietnam War.

Toward the end of 1960, Butch was promoted to captain, a cut, he said, made only by 17 percent of those who were eligible. Life was good. He was on the fast track, a recognized senior naval officer with a reputation for courage, excellence, and innovation. Personnel detailers penciled him in to attend the Armed Forces Industrial College, a Washington,

D.C., school that taught senior officers how to liaison with private industry. It didn't excite him, but he was resigned to go. Then Admiral Ekstrom called him in and said it wasn't the best career move. The navy's front-runners usually attend the War College in Newport, Rhode Island. Butch asked how he could go. The admiral said he'd take care of it.

Not long after, he received orders to Rhode Island. It was another cut. "Not everybody is selected for these schools," he said.

He and Thea and the girls would be moving again.

He didn't know it then, but it would be nearly his last move in the navy.

☆

The US Naval War College, established in 1884, was housed in a former Rhode Island asylum for the poor that had been built in 1820. A booklet on it kept by Butch shows a formidable fortresslike structure of large stones, watchtowers, and ancient cannon on the stately grounds. Going to Rhode Island was a respite for Butch and the family. They rented the upstairs of a former carriage house of a rural mansion surrounded by wooded grounds with a pond. "Weekends in the library, lunches with [Henry] Kissinger [then a Harvard defense expert], the CIA director, CNO, that level. It was scholarly stuff, grooming you for higher command. The big thing was getting your study habits reestablished. You have to change your mentality. It's not the fleet. You're studying the strategic political aspects of the world, bringing you up to where you better be cognizant that there's more to it than using a gun."

The nearly yearlong course included many presentations. Butch was made chairman of his class's "Industrial Commission," a study group that worked on military-commercial relations. To graduate, which he did, he had to write a research paper. His was entitled, "Force: The Foremost and Final Factor of Power," about which one of the two reviewers, only identified by number, wrote: "This is an excellent paper. It is indicative of considerable research on the part of the author and an example of the high-quality work expected of War College students. All the attributes of a scholarly effort are present. The reader's interest is captured at the outset . . . Facts and arguments . . . are pertinent . . . and a logical buildup of facts results in a basis for suitable, feasible, and acceptable solutions . . . If any criticism is to be offered, it is a feeling that the author decided before he wrote the paper that force is the foremost and final element of national power, after which he set out to prove this point . . ."

The other reviewer liked it, too. Not a bad academic performance for a student with only two years of college and attendance at a few navy schools. His instructor, J. H. Raymer, suggested that Butch "consider reworking" the paper for submission to *Naval Institute Proceedings,* the navy's scholarly journal. "You express yourself well," he commented on the review. But "the last thing I wanted to do," said Butch, "was think about publishing it. I wanted to get away from it." Like most aviators, he loathed writing and paperwork. Receiving his diploma in late June of 1962, he was itching to get back to the action navy. He was informed that he was going to be sent to Pensacola as commanding officer of the Naval Pre-Flight School, the first stop for all prospective aviators. "I said, 'No, no, I don't want to go there." It was a big command with stately quarters, and a car, a driver, but he regarded it as basically being sent out to pasture.

Then he got a call from his old buddy, Eddie Outlaw, who was by then on staff of the Deputy Chief of Operations for Air Warfare (DCNO-Air) in Washington, reporting directly to the CNO. "What's this I hear about you going down to sit on your ass in Florida," Outlaw began. Butch said, "Well, I'm penciled in." Outlaw said, "Let me put someone on the phone." Vice Admiral Robert B. Pirie, the DCNO (Air) himself, came on the line. Butch knew him from previous assignments where they'd become friends. "He's a great big guy, about six-foot-four. He says, 'You big bastard'—that's the way he talks; you know that if he doesn't call you that, he doesn't like you—'you big bastard, you're not going to go down there and waste away. You're coming to work for me. I want you down here [in Washington, D.C.] within a couple of days. Just pack your bags and get on down here right now.' "

It was a great job, as good as Butch could have hoped for, right in the heart of the action.

And the action in Washington was heightening.

CHAPTER 28

The year 1962 brought a new atmosphere to Washington. John F. Kennedy, young for the country's chief executive, had been elected president the previous November. He succeeded a much older Dwight D. Eisenhower, a two-term president, World War II leader, and symbol of an older generation. Kennedy was the embodiment of a new kind of American leader, stylish, quick-witted, adept on television, bringing with him modern, postwar ideas and methods to deal with America's challenges, including security. In this vein, Kennedy recruited Robert S. McNamara, president of Ford Motor Company, to become his secretary of defense. Although McNamara had served in the army air corps during World War II, the auto executive was chiefly a Harvard-educated practitioner of consolidation, cost cutting, and efficient management methods like systems analysis and planning-programming-budgeting systems, concepts and terms largely foreign to a US military establishment that tended to use tradition, need, threat evaluation, and the latest technology to shape its product.

Almost immediately upon taking office, McNamara ordered a review of important weapons programs at the Pentagon with a view toward forging a leaner, more cost-effective, more modern—as he defined it—fighting force. To help him, the new secretary recruited a staff of civilian stars from business and academia, professors and executives as cost conscious and determined as he to change things. Some had been "whiz kids" with him at Ford. None had any operational background in the military or combat experience, a fact which mattered little to them or to McNamara, who, according to David Halberstam, in *The Best and the Brightest,* an acclaimed book about the Kennedy-Johnson years, was a professionally cold, driven man who loved power and whose power was derived from his almost encyclopedic command of pertinent facts—such as he was gathering at the Pentagon.

It was into this tension-filled atmosphere between the administration and the navy that Butch arrived back in Washington in mid-July 1962 to take up duties at DCNO (Air). He was quickly put to work. "I was involved in a lot of things. I was writing speeches for Admiral Pirie. My regular job was policy, defending the carriers whenever there was an attack on them by the air force." One of the first directives McNamara issued after assuming office was that the three services get together and develop a combination bomber and close-air-support plane that would be flown by all three. The idea was repugnant to each. Each had different requirements; each needed, in essence, a different aircraft. The army cared mostly about close-air support. Carriers demanded economy of size and weight. The air force wanted a larger plane that could carry more armament. Butch helped argue the navy's case. "I always left late and would go in on weekends." Eventually, the joint work would produce the A-7 "Corsair," a single-seat attack jet, which both the navy and air force would use for decades, through the First Gulf War.

But Butch was only involved in preliminary work on the Corsair. He hadn't been in his air warfare post long when he got a firsthand dose of the new attitude at Defense. "They wanted to reduce spending, but they didn't know how. [The military] wasn't their game. I had to go up with [Vice] Admiral [William A.] Schoech [who replaced Admiral Pirie] to see Charlie Hitch." Charles Hitch was a Rhodes scholar and Rand Corporation executive who later became the president of the University of California at Berkeley. "He was the chief money man for McNamara [an assistant secretary of defense and comptroller and also one of the Whiz Kids]. He would embarrass the admiral, just chomp away at him. 'Why haven't you done this? Have you analyzed that? What's the cost trade-off on this?' Those are questions you ask an operations analyst, not a three-star admiral. He's a policy man. I'd be there and answer some, but he [Hitch] wanted the admiral to answer it. Schoech hated him."

Approximately six months after he had arrived, the proverbial dung hit the fan. The secretary, said Voris, directed the admirals to justify why the carrier force should not be cut. "I think we were at sixteen and he wanted to bump us down to twelve. He was bent on reducing the carrier task force numbers. It would have been disastrous." As it was, said Butch, at any one time, four of the carriers were always in repair or overhaul, two were needed for training. That would leave the navy with only six. "A major overhaul takes two years. No repair is in today and out tomorrow. We couldn't cover every ocean with six. They'd be out all the time. There'd be no time for R&R [rest and recuperation]. You need more than one carrier in each ocean . . . They [the Whiz Kids] wanted savings and didn't care how they got it."

By this time, Admiral Schoech, pronounced "Shay," had replaced Admiral Pirie as DCNO (Air). Schoech was a World War II veteran, a decorated aviator, former commanding officer of the carrier *Ticonderoga* and, just prior to coming to the Pentagon, commander of the US Seventh Fleet, operating in the Pacific. Schoech was directed by the CNO to head the study that would answer McNamara. It was called the "CNO Sea-Based Air Strike Forces Study Group." The future of naval aviation depended on its findings. Butch, as number four on Schoech's staff, was appointed to the study group and would act as chief liaison to Admiral Schoech, who would be chairman, as the thirteen-man panel built its case.

Among those also on the study group were Rear Admiral Turner Caldwell, a hero of the air battles around Guadalcanal and a former holder of the world's speed record in a jet, and Captain Evan Peter Aurand, a noted carrier pilot who had served as President Eisenhower's naval aide in the previous administration. "It was probably the biggest study naval aviation ever did up to that time," said Butch. "Peter Aurand was my immediate boss [in DCNO (Air)]. He was one of the early jet jocks in the navy. Wonderful guy. I worked with him in putting the study group together—the people from the other bureaus, experts on specific aspects of what we needed. I was designated the study administrator. I'd brief the admiral on where we were and then tell the compilers what he was thinking."

The group took approximately three quarters of a year to do its work. McNamara never consulted with them, said Voris. He assigned one of his Whiz Kids, Alain Enthoven, to be his liaison. Enthoven, like Hitch, had been a Rand Corporation economist, when tapped by McNamara. "He never talked to us. He wasn't smart enough to talk our game. He didn't know anything about it, and we never asked him a question. All he did—he had a sore back—is walk around in the study room, stretch his trunk and look out the window. He was just kind of making sure there was progress. We didn't care. He was in Indian Country when he was with us. He couldn't compete on our level. He could only think in terms of cost effectiveness."

What it all came down to, said Butch, was what was the cheapest, quickest, most efficient way to respond to trouble spots anywhere in the world? Was it with the carriers? And, if so, how many were needed? Or could the air force take care of most of the problem? What were the comparative costs? McNamara, he said, thought there were places the carriers couldn't reach. "We had to figure how much of the world's surface we could cover. It was a massive undertaking. We had to study the entire world." Danger from the shore and vast land masses with difficult-to-reach targets had to be considered. "But we found out that it got pretty close to 90 percent that we could cover, and the carriers were totally self-sufficient, thoroughly supplied and equipped. We had nuclear if we needed it." The air force couldn't cover nearly as much in as short a time, he said. They had to obtain basing rights from foreign countries, which were not always available. And it takes time and money to move them, whereas we're already there or near there."

When it came time to present their case, the entire group gathered early in McNamara's conference room, a large place with a long table, seating perhaps fifteen on each side. It adjoined McNamara's personal office. The meeting was scheduled for nine a.m. "There's a door with a clock over it that goes into his personal office. I'd never met him or been directly exposed to him. I'd heard the tales about how the biggest thing to him was that he opened the door at exactly when the second hand hit the number. So we're all there watching the second hand and we looked at the door knob and saw it twitch. He's behind it waiting for that second hand to get right straight up and then he opened it. He didn't say a damn word. He didn't say, Good morning gentlemen. Thank you for coming. He went to the head of the table, peeked off to the side where the briefing charts were, and sat down. Didn't have a notepad. Just sat there, nodded, and said 'Begin.'"

Aurand's briefing was perhaps two hours long, said Butch. "He knew his stuff. He went through all the assumptions we made and the premises and all the other things you have to put in. Finally he said, 'And that concludes our presentation.' McNamara didn't say a word. He just stood up and walked back through his door. Not a single word." But the study reaped success. "It apparently convinced him not to cut." Although they never got a written or verbal reaction, the carriers were left at their current number and two more were allowed to be ordered. "We called our office 'Carrier Sales' because that's what we did."

As a result of the work he did with the group, Butch got a special commendation from the CNO via Admiral Schoech. Dated July 1, 1963, it called the group's work a "vital study . . . that will play a decisive role in determining the navy of the future." It says in part, "Your extensive research and analysis led to conclusions and recommendations which clearly demonstrate keen judgment, imagination, and foresight . . . You were selected to be a member of this Study Group on the basis of past performance and your potential to contribute to this major undertaking. Your performance has supported this selection . . ." On his fitness reports, he was recommended for command of a "deep draft," a ship's captaincy preliminary to getting and commanding a carrier, which, in turn, was part of the track to becoming an admiral, the track he wanted and was on.

Then the roof fell in. "We captains [rank] in Washington were invited over to the Bureau of Personnel to meet with the detail officer and see if we were on the deep draft list." Butch was confident. He'd been informed he was number three among candidates, certainly high enough to be given a ship. Mickey Weisner, his rival from *Oriskany* days, was the detail officer, which probably should have put him on the alert, although Weisner, then a captain, too, was simply the administrator, not involved in the selection. The meeting was private, each captain brought in for a personal conference with Weisner. "I went over and sat down. I remember he pulled the list out of the left-hand bottom drawer and started going over it. He took some time and then looked at me. He said, 'Butch, I'm sorry. You're not on it.' I said well, I guess that's it. It probably gave him a lot of satisfaction. We shook hands and I left."

Butch said he knew "before I walked out the door" that he was going to retire. "It's sudden death. You're not on the fast track anymore." Disappointed, puzzled as to why he'd missed the cut, he went home that night and typed out his letter requesting retirement. "As far as I was concerned it was the end of the track I'd be satisfied with in the navy, so it was time to go." He didn't want to go sideways, pushed out to pasture somewhere.

It was up or out. In that sense, the decision was easy for him. "Never had any second thoughts. Neither did Thea. I went home and we sat on a couple of barstools in a little bar off the kitchen and talked it over. She said, 'Let's go,' and that was the way it was."

He turned in his request the next day. It would take effect at the end of the month—nearly twenty-three years after he'd first joined the navy. "I had no regrets." But he was still puzzled. That afternoon Bush Bringle, who had asked him nearly ten years earlier to lead the Blues for a second time, stopped him in a Pentagon hallway "and took me aside. He'd been on the board that had made the selections. He said, 'Boy, I regret that action because you're so qualified and it's so wrong.'" He told Butch what had happened. The board was dominated by "black shoes," nonflying ship's officers—aviators wore brown shoes—who had lately become disenchanted with aviators, who had recently had a spate of accidents while captaining ships. For instance, Bob Elder, whom Butch was perpetually following in assignment and rank, had been blamed when his harbor pilot had run the ship he was captaining aground in a fog in San Francisco Bay. As a result of that accident and others, the black shoes had decided to change policy. Where before, ship handling duty had not been a prerequisite for getting a deep draft, the black shoes, just prior to Butch's consideration, had made it mandatory.

"Roll of the dice," said Butch. Still, he'd been cognizant that such ship's duty would help his career and in fact had queried detailers back when he'd left the Blue Angels before he'd accepted the staff job on Carrier Division Five. "I asked, now is this [the staff job] going to get me full qualification for deep draft, and they said, 'Oh, absolutely. That's the policy.' Well, the policy changed. That cost me. In retrospect, I should have gone to a job on a carrier. I needed actual ship handling. What I got was task force handling." Admiral Schoech was distressed enough about Butch's leaving that he wrote in Butch's final fitness report, dated 1 April 63 to 31 July 63: "Captain Voris is one of the outstanding officers of this year's group [of eligible captains]. I have never had a contemporary of his working with me that I would prefer to him. With his ability, personality, and dedication, he is equal to any task. His retirement is a great loss to the navy."

Within a month, however, Butch would be on a new career path, unknowingly heading toward aiding the navy in a crucial way he couldn't have if he had remained in uniform.

CHAPTER 29

Word of Butch's impending retirement spread quickly. Within days of turning in his retirement letter he had employment offers from Northrop, General Dynamics, and Grumman, whose planes he'd flown throughout his career, especially as a Blue Angel. "I knew I was going with Grumman. I knew people there." They flew him up to Bethpage, where he met with the chairman of the board and the senior vice president of business development, Lew Evans, an acquaintance who had extended the feeler and with whom, in the future, he would build a bond and work closely. His salary was upped substantially from what he would have made in the navy, and they wanted him to head the budding F-111 program into which Grumman was now launching.

By this time, the second half of 1963—marked so precipitously by the assassination of President Kennedy and the beginnings of the Vietnam War—McNamara's vision of a common fighter for all the services had split into two basic airplanes: the A-7 Corsair for the close-air support role, and the TFX (Tactical Fighter Experimental), or F-111, as it would be called by the services, for the multiservice fighter-bomber. The idea was still repugnant to the military but they were trumped by McNamara and his Whiz Kids and were trying to comply. Two versions of the F-111, slightly different, were slated. The F-111A would be the air force version, with speed, range and payload the priorities. The F-111B would be the navy version, designed to operate from aircraft carriers. The basic plane, however, would remain substantially the same.

In a controversial decision—the first of many regarding the twin-engine, variable sweep-wing jet—General Dynamics had been awarded the contract by McNamara to build both versions of the F-111 despite the services' unanimous recommendation that Boeing, whose proposal they preferred, be given the job. In what many saw as a political move—because then vice president Lyndon Johnson was from Texas, home base of General Dynamics—General Dynamics had been forced on the navy and air force. General Dynamics, in turn, had farmed out the aft section of the plane in both versions to Grumman because, among other reasons, Grumman had such a long-standing good relationship with the navy. It was this newly subcontracted work that Grumman wanted Butch, who had, they knew, a sterling reputation in the sea service, to oversee. "I was to get to know things and then take over."

While his family was happy with the prospect of staying longer than a few years in the nice home they bought near the water on Long Island, Butch said he soon became aware of the sometimes unpleasant—at least to him—differences between his former career and the new one on which he was embarking. "It was surprising. I was used to the nice straightforward way we did things in the navy. You fight against standards and levels of performance, not say bad things about people . . . no back-stabbing or fake praise. At least I never saw it . . . Somebody said something to you, you could take it at face value . . . You got promoted for punching the right boxes and keeping a good record." Not in the aeronautics industry. "It was dog eat dog. Keep your back to the wall." There were factions. "You were either on one side or the other. It gets vicious."

He took it in stride, attaching his loyalty to Evans, whom he found smart, aggressive, and personable, and learned quickly on the job. When he came on too fast, up-front and strong, as he had as a fighter commander, Evans had counseled him to "slow down" and back off; be more subtle, otherwise he'd make hurtful enemies who would resent his military approach and try to stymie his career.

In time, he would make the adjustment.

Originally, the plan had been for him to stay away from Washington and the Pentagon, at least for six months or so. The contract Grumman had with General Dynamics specifically forbade any direct contact between Grumman and the navy regarding the F-111. Grumman was always supposed to go through General Dynamics. But after about three months of orientation, the chairman and Evans called Butch in and changed the plans. "They felt I knew what I was facing [regarding the contractual rules], and they wanted me to go ahead and start showing myself as a way of alerting the navy that I was there if they needed me." The company wanted the lines of communication open. It was one of the reasons they had hired him. "They said just watch your step. We know you've got a lot of good friends down there, and we know you know how to handle it."

Soon Butch was back in the halls of the Pentagon and the Naval Air Systems Command, this time as a civilian, talking with old friends and making new acquaintances. Primarily, he was just renewing ties, having a cup of coffee with a former pilot buddy or introducing his new position over a hasty cafeteria lunch to decision makers working on the F-111B while being mindful of what he could and couldn't say. As long as money or the specifics of the contract, including airplane details, were not discussed, he was okay. Meanwhile, the preliminary design people at Grumman were receiving early data from General Dynamics on the F-111 being planned at the Fort Worth, Texas headquarters. This included data on the front of the fuselage, cockpit, wings, fuel tanks, and engines—the areas on which General Dynamics would be concentrating. Grumman needed the data in order to build the aft sections they were responsible for, including the rear fuselage, landing gear, which had to be fortified in the B model for the violent carrier landings, and tail section. Chief among those receiving the data was Grumman's head of preliminary design, Mike Pelehach, an aeronautical engineer of stellar reputation who, in 1980, would become president of Grumman.

Pelehach, who died of a stroke in 2002, was a soft-spoken 1941 graduate of the Academy of Aeronautics in Flushing, New York. Launching his career as an engineer for the Martin Company, later to merge with Lockheed, and then for Chance Vought, makers of the famed World War II Corsair, Pelehach knew what he was talking about, and he didn't like what some of the figures he was getting were suggesting. In order for the airplane to operate safely and well on a carrier, it had to be relatively light and perform to certain standards, all of which the navy had specified in its contract with General Dynamics. While General Dynamics said it was keeping to the specifications, careful examination of the figures by Pelehach indicated to the engineer, according to Butch, that the F-111B being planned and beginning construction in Texas was going to be heavier than what General Dynamics was reporting to the navy.

And there were other discrepancies.

"Because they knew I was from the navy, our preliminary design people, particularly Mike Pelehach, whom I worked closely with and had a great rapport with, began telling me on the hush-hush that it looks like we've got some problems . . . Because of the different requirements of each service, things were having to be added, like more stuff for heavier landing gear for the navy and more fuel capacity for the air force." Eventually, Butch has told audiences he's spoken before, the plane seemed to be growing almost a thousand pounds a week from what was originally proposed. Adjustments being called for primarily by the air force were conflicting with navy specifications and causing the weight growth. To illustrate the growth, Butch told the audience, "You can think of a cartoon of an F-111B landing on an angled deck and pulling the whole flight deck off with the wire at the end of its hook."

The plane, as it came to be nicknamed, was becoming a pig.

But the situation wasn't dire yet—at least those alerted at Grumman weren't yet aware of it being that bad. They were just getting indications. So, without letting General Dynamics officials know—because he didn't think he'd get any good official answers—Butch and some others quietly contacted friends they had at the Fort Worth company and asked what was going on. What they found out, in essence, was "that General Dynamics was distorting the numbers when they gave them to the navy . . . They knew [the true, larger figures] would be a problem, so they were [making the plane appear lighter] and projecting better performance in the air with the hope of correcting the problem later . . . Can you imagine that?" Later, addressing the TFX problem in her 1993 biography of McNamara, *Promise and Power,* Washington-based defense and science journalist Deborah Shapely wrote, "McNamara's stubborness was creating a fatal pattern." His insistence on the plane's acceptance by the services put "subordinates under tremendous pressure to distort reports and even lie . . . Honesty had gone with the wind."

While Shapley was speaking mainly about the Department of the Defense, Butch was alarmed that the dishonesty had now spread to the contractors. Restrictions or not, he decided to take what he'd learned to the navy, in effect, become a whistle-blower. He couldn't let the navy be deceived. He met with a navy friend high up in the program who doesn't want to be named (but has been interviewed for this book) and who brought in the navy's air weapons expert, civilian George A. Spangenberg, director, at the time, of the Evaluation Division of the Naval Air Systems Command, the specific navy department overseeing the F-111B development. Spangenberg, who died in an auto accident in 2000, was, like most of his colleagues, a critic of the TFX program. He "fought against the 'compromises' that . . . were making the navy plane unsuitable for use," according to his biography on the Web site established under his name by his daughter and carrying his oral history and papers. "He was Mr. Performance," said Butch, who, with the friend, went over the ominous data with Spangenberg. "Mike [Pelehach] would make notes. I'd put them in my pocket and go on down [to the Pentagon] and discuss it with them. We kept things pretty quiet."

Because of their sensitive nature, there is little written confirmation of these initial or subsequent meetings. But in an internal navy memo of Spangenberg's, titled "Lessons from the F-111 Program" and dated March 13, 1967, Spangenberg writes it was "early 1964 when the weight problems first came to light." This is precisely the time frame—late 1963, early 1964—Butch says he was having the private meetings.

In the meantime, Grumman executives were in a quandary. Butch had informed his immediate boss, Lew Evans, now a close personal friend, about everything he was doing. Evans, with trepidation, was backing him. "The company's reputation was on the line. Nobody wanted to be a part of any deception. We'd been sterling with the navy for decades. You lose that trust and confidence and you lose 90 percent of your bidding power." But there was concern about losing the money the contract represented. Two factions formed. "Understandably, some feared losing the business. Some said don't rock the boat. We need this airplane."

Butch's faction won out.

Top executives, including Evans, told him to keep working with the navy, but to be careful. "I remember Lew telling me, 'Butch, you are on your own. If you get hung out to dry, we are just going to have to deny everything.' "

Butch, as he had during the Korean War, accepted the risk.

The small, private note-checking meetings continued. Soon his friend suggested they go see the admiral, who happened to be Bill Schoech, Butch's former boss at DCNO (Air), who had commended Butch for the work he had done on the carrier study. Schoech had recently taken over as Commander, Naval Material Command, under which the friend worked. When Schoech, who knew Butch was headed for Grumman, had said good-bye to him less than a year before, the admiral, Butch said, had oddly remarked, "I think you'll be able to do the navy more good where you're going." Butch hadn't understood the remark and had forgotten it. But now he recalled it and wondered if Schoech had foreseen the serious events that were unfolding.

They purposely made the meeting after-hours, in the evening, so they wouldn't be seen. Butch, his friend, and Admiral Schoech, according to Butch, met in Admiral Schoech's office, doors locked. Butch's friend said he had so many meetings, he doesn't remember it, but he doesn't contradict Butch. Butch had in a briefcase all the contrary data he and Pelehach and the others at Grumman had amassed. "He [the admiral] had to trust me explicitly in order to agree to see me. We had a very good relationship. I guess I spent an hour with him. I had all the papers out in front of me. He didn't say much. Just listened. Then I got up and I was going to put the papers back in my briefcase. He put his hands on top of them. He didn't say can I have them or anything like that. Just put his hands on them. I took the signal. He thanked me for coming in, and I left with an empty briefcase. That's when I knew we'd moved the alarm to a higher level."

In several weeks—Butch is uncertain of the interval, but remembers it was fairly soon—a second clandestine meeting was organized. This one was for the purpose of getting the individual technical experts from Grumman and the navy together so they could go over the data together and make concrete determinations. The meeting was purposely set up for a late Saturday afternoon at the Bureau of Aeronautics because the building was normally empty and secured at that time. Butch brought Pelehach and other aeronautical engineers down from Bethpage by commercial plane, approximately six in all. Spangenberg brought his staff, who were there in Washington. The admiral, who died in 1982, and Butch's friend were not present.

Butch: "It was a real cloak-and-dagger situation. They arranged to leave the back door open, which was normally locked on a weekend . . . I think we worked for about three hours, guards outside the conference doors . . . We laid everything out for George [Spangenberg] and his staff. They massaged the numbers we had and were in full agreement with us.

This was a very sensitive thing with McNamara. Just slightly before, Admiral George Anderson, the past CNO, had told the secretary that the F-111B was a plane we were never going to be able to use. He was retired and sent to Portugal as the ambassador, and we never heard his name again. Things were very political."

But there were no repercussions. The meeting went undiscovered. The navy, which may have had indications elsewhere that something was wrong, did not immediately act on what they knew or ever tell how they knew it. Rather, they sent a fact-finding team to General Dynamics, where all phases of the plane were being collated to see what was actually transpiring. "I remember we got our heads together and said let's send our people down to Fort Worth and see what they got," said Joe Rees, the naval officer who took over management of the F-111B program for the navy shortly after it began. "They came back and said yes, the airplane is considerably overweight from what we had. It was a shocker."

Spangenberg, in his Web site–posted oral history (Tape 12, Side B, about ¼ down) is more specific: "We sent our senior weight engineers, Keith Dentel and Ray Hook, down to Fort Worth . . . It turned out that the contractor, General Dynamics, had really been keeping two sets of books. He [General Dynamics] reported a weight increase to us of 2,000 pounds . . . when it was actually 5,000 pounds. They had not reported 3,000 pounds on the basis that there would be a weight-reduction program that would get rid of it. Well, with any kind of weight increase of that magnitude, of course we were in deep trouble."

Admiral Schoech was the highest-ranking naval officer with direct responsibility for the F-111B program. With the reports turned in by the weight engineers, he convened a special meeting of entities connected with the program—contractors, admirals, and air force generals, project directors and their staffs. Spangenberg: "I remember Admiral Schoech called a conference and we all met in the boardroom with lots of people from General Dynamics and from the air force. Admiral Schoech pointed out that life couldn't go on that way, that this was a joint program and we could not tolerate those kind of weight increases." In view of the evidence he possessed, the admiral was being charitable. He proposed a moratorium on F-111 development until General Dynamics corrected the problems.

But the weight increases continued.

Spangenberg: "The air force couldn't really back off. The airplane as it turned out was short-legged anyway [didn't have the range they wanted]. They had no choice but to put in more fuel." Backed by McNamara's dogged insistence on its completion, the F-111 continued to grow. Problems with engine thrust were found. The navy, stonewalled and disregarded, decided to wait until actual flight tests of the first experimental B models were made to confirm what they suspected, that the plane would never be suitable for carriers. Early tests confirmed their worst fears. Not only was the plane many tons overweight, but the chief Grumman test pilot, Ralph "Dixie" Donnell, died in the testing.

Seeing the handwriting on the wall—that the plane would never fly from navy decks and therefore Grumman had to come up with a justification for all the time, money, and effort that had been expended or probably see the company go bankrupt—Mike Pelehach hatched a plan whereby key elements of the F-111, already paid for and developed, could be incorporated into a new navy fighter. This new fighter, which would become the vaunted F-14 "Tomcat," could use much of the technology and aeronautics of the F-111, especially the new and revolutionary swing wing. It could, at last, be specifically designed in the way the navy wanted—a fast, long-range interceptor, light enough to be easily launched and recovered by the carriers, but maneuverable in air-to-air fighting and equipped with long-range radar and multiple missiles. Its main purpose would be carrier defense. Most important, because it would utilize much of what had been developed under his F-111 program, McNamara might be prone to accepting it as an alternative. He could claim the F-111 as an important step in the envisioned new plane's evolution.

It would enable the embattled secretary to save face.

Early on, since the controversial decision to award General Dynamics the F-111 contract over Boeing, McNamara had come under increasing political fire, most powerfully by a House subcommittee chaired by Democratic senator John L. McClellan of Arkansas, who became embroiled in a personal battle with the secretary. McNamara had appeared before McClellan's subcommittee and defiantly defended his decisions on the airplane. He and McClellan had become strident enemies. And when the first operational tests of the actual F-111B had produced not only failures, but the deaths of test pilots, McClellan and his subcommittee's opposition to McNamara's methods and choices and Whiz Kids had gained significant press backing.

McNamara began feeling the heat.

Grumman saw a chance to salvage something for both itself and the navy.

"To cover our backsides," Butch has written, "Mike Pelehach . . . commenced looking at how Grumman [could] pull this debacle out of the fire . . . I spent many a Sunday afternoon at Mike's home as he worked over his drawing board and as we traded ideas on what to do [regarding designing another airplane]. The governing concept was to use as much F-111B technology as could be incorporated in a new fighter. This was essential if any new proposal was to eventually [get] McNamara's blessing or get him somewhat off the hook for his looming failure."

Early on, Grumman gave Pelehach company money to develop his ideas on the newly envisioned swing-wing fighter, which was not yet named. Butch's help was just as a knowledgeable carrier pilot whom Pelehach could bounce ideas off of and who would council him on the best way to implement those ideas. "He was the genius," said Butch. "I was the schemer, the facilitator of how we're going to move this in, get it done." The swing wings were the big innovation, the first in a carrier plane. They would enable the new fighter to travel at supersonic speeds when swept back, as would be needed in pursuit or to exit quickly. Extended, they would increase maneuverability and handling at slower speeds, which was important during carrier launch or recovery or close-in dogfighting. The TF-30 engines were still troublesome but the best available at the time. And the plane would house a new, long-range radar and fire-control system that would enable it to target and shoot multiple long-range missiles, a capability the navy felt was essential to combat future threats to carriers.

After the death of the test pilot Donnell, Butch has told audiences, "the navy said we've got to make a formal approach to the secretary of defense and lay it all out." George Spangenberg, now thoroughly briefed and in agreement with the new replacement plane Grumman was working on, took it first to Paul Nitze, secretary of the navy at the time, "who was scared to death of McNamara," said Butch, and McNamara "didn't want to buy it." But at a later date, Spangenberg took it directly to McNamara himself, who was by then—1966 or 1967—turning weary of the assaults on him for not only the F-111, but his conduct of the Vietnam War. "That broke the camel's back. McNamara decided we had better go ahead and save what we can out of the navy version of the TFX know-how, and we got a go-ahead for a preliminary study on what became the F-14 . . . It had a Phoenix missile system, and it could acquire targets in excess of one hundred miles away and fire at them shortly thereafter."

The twin-engine Tomcat, with its two-man crew of pilot and radar intercept officer (RIO), or backseater, as the RIO is often called, became, arguably, one of the greatest fighter-bombers ever produced, certainly one of the greatest carrier jets. Its swing wings gave it small-fighter maneuverability. It could fly in excess of 1,500 miles per hour at high altitude and track and fire missiles simultaneously at multiple enemy airplanes long before such planes could threaten the fleet. Its titanium sturdiness and multiple-systems versatility has enabled its use as a devastating and pinpoint bomber and wily reconnaissance aircraft. Although it became operational too late to be involved in the Vietnam War and suffered through some early engine problems, it was deadly in clashes with Libya in the 1980s, was decisive over Kosovo in 1999, was instrumental above Afghanistan and Iraq in 2001 and 2002, and has protected the fleet for more than thirty years, which is a long time for any fighter.

Butch never flew the Tomcat, although he was present at many of its early flights, including the crashes. "I'm from a different era. I was never one for a two-man airplane." But its sophisticated systems "were too much for one man to handle." Friends who flew it "loved it. I imagine I would have, too. Until it came along, we didn't have the ability to fire at long range. That was a big step forward." However, despite its maneuverability and handling characteristics, he doesn't believe it would have made a good Blue Angel plane and, to his knowledge, was never envisioned as such. "Too big, too costly. Too hard to maintain. They used the F-4 [Phantom, a heavy Vietnam War–era fighter] for a while but then went in the opposite direction, to the A-4 [a smaller aircraft]. It [the Tomcat] just wasn't the type for close-in tight-formation aerobatics."

As a result of what he did, General Dynamics, which eventually heard about his clandestine activities, tried to bring a conflict-of-interest suit against Butch. But the navy wouldn't go along with it, and Butch never heard anything more about it. "I don't know what they could have done to me, give me a letter of admonishment for my file or a cease and desist order? Maybe I could have been fined." But the basic work had been done by the time he learned of the attempt. And along with the basing plan he had created while on the Pacific Fleet air staff, keeping the RAG with fleet pilots rather than allowing it to go to the training command, and helping save the carriers from McNamara's intended cuts, raising the F-14 from the F-111B's ashes ranked as one of the most satisfying accomplishments of his life. "When you're satisfied, you're happy. It was great fun. I had a great feeling we were pulling one off, which we were. We were doing something to improve things, to make things better."

AFTERMATH

"I wish I could go up and do it again.
I wouldn't change a thing."
—*Butch Voris*

CHAPTER 30

Butch stayed with Grumman for ten more years. As the F-111B died and the company began to concentrate on developing the F-14 in earnest, Butch was promoted to director of public relations, where his emphasis would shift to Grumman's growing space projects, particularly the coming Apollo moonshots, among the most ambitious and adventuresome scientific-technical ventures in the history of man. Grumman won the competition to build the lunar module (LM) or "lander," known at first as the "LEM" (Lunar Excursion Module), the historic smaller space vehicle that would detach from the orbiting main spacecraft and land the first astronauts on the moon. The company wanted a strong and credible face on its public profile, and Butch, with his low-key, confident, and knowledgeable manner was their choice. He had the background, the stature. All the "Right Stuff" astronauts knew him or of him. He had been one of their mentors, so much so that once, at a casual Cape Canaveral lunch, astronaut Charles "Pete" Conrad had surprised him by remarking to another's question, "Hell, Butch is a living legend. We all know what he did." Butch: "See, I hadn't known Pete before. I hadn't really thought about the influence the Blue Angels had on them."

But the Angels then also had the right stuff—and still do—select, highly revered aviators who could take it right up to the edge of the envelope and yet somehow, in spite of the knowledge of where they were and the awful consequences of any sudden wrong move, be good enough, artful, brave, and crafty enough, to tease the demon but not suffer its deadly sting. And do it over and over. Conrad, who would be the third man to walk on the moon and who died in a 1999 motorcycle accident, had been a navy test pilot and knew Voris by reputation. "I knew most of the navy pilots personally," said Butch. These included Alan Shepard, who had tried to get into his squadron when he'd had the Satan's Kittens; Jim Lovell, commander of Apollo 13, which would give NASA and the world a huge scare when trouble developed during its 1970 moon shot; Dick Gordon, Gemini and Apollo astronaut; and John Glenn, a marine, one of the first Americans in space, and later a US senator from Ohio.

The lunar module, with the exception of the F-14, "was the most complicated project ever undertaken by Grumman," according to Terry Treadwell, author of *Ironworks,* a history of Grumman published in 2000. Some 2,400 Grumman engineers and over one hundred subcontractors were involved in the LM's design and construction. When, in early 1967, a routine exercise on the launchpad at Cape Canaveral ended in the appalling incineration in the main module of astronauts Gus Grissom, Ed White, and Roger Chaffee, work on the lunar module—although not involved in the fire—had to be reexamined. A too-high concentration of volatile oxygen environment, along with faulty wiring and the rush to put men on the moon, were found to be the probable causes of the flash fire. In addition, the module doors had been locked and were found to have been too heavy and complicated to open quickly in an emergency. The burning astronauts, a subsequent investigation showed, had tried and failed.

"The modules had an almost 100 percent oxygen environment," said Butch. "All you had to do was have a little glow and you'd get a massive fire and explosion." There had been a short circuit under one of the seats in the command module. "That's all it took. And, of course, the pressure from the fire had expanded the hatch and they couldn't open the door . . . redesign issues set the program back almost an entire year." During that time, Butch was the Grumman public spokesman—not on the hot seat, because it hadn't been Grumman's design that had failed—but nonetheless on the defensive because of Grumman's integral Apollo involvement. "We had some real issues and were delaying the whole schedule."

Behind the scenes, NASA got mad at Grumman. And because Butch was looked at as the liaison with the company, he was called down to Washington and "scolded. Not me personally, but the [Grumman] board and leadership. They said we were holding things up, not delivering as we should. Grumman had a reputation of being—I'll use one of NASA's descriptions—'out of the loop.'" The company had been doing business in Washington so long, said Butch, that it had a haughty, elitist attitude, even toward its own employer. It felt it knew better. "We had board members [who had] been around since airplanes were made of cloth. The company had a case of the know-it-all. Everybody else was stupid."

Lew Evans and he were part of a new company faction that agreed with much of the NASA assessment of Grumman but had no power to change it. "I had to take [NASA's] complaints and demands back to the board," one of which was that the company get rid of some of the Grumman board members. "It was a tough message. I've still got the scars. But you do what you have to. Let the chips fall."

He delivered the message.

When Buzz Aldrin and Neil Armstrong landed on the moon in July 1969, Grumman worried that the lunar module's engine, which it had subcontracted out, wouldn't work. "We'd been having problems with it. When they were ready to come back, I'll tell you, that's what you call clutch time. They had cameras on it. Everybody in the world was watching. Those were tight times." In fact, he said, "Every mission was an uncomfortable period because of what might happen. I had to be prepared for whatever went wrong. I was always at the boss's [Lew Evans] side. That was the one requirement he had of me. If things went wrong, I was the buffer. His crutch, I guess. I had a real good staff that handled the day to day with the press."

While the relationship between NASA and Grumman was, at times, less than perfect, developments during Apollo 13, after Astronaut Jim Lovell uttered his now famous "Houston, we've had a problem," proved Grumman's worth. Lovell had just heard a jarring explosion in the moonbound spacecraft, and he and fellow crew members, Fred Haise and Jack Swigert, were realizing that their oxygen was spewing snowlike in the cold outside the injured ship and the ship itself was revolving uncontrollably. They were in dire trouble. Later investigation would reveal that one of the large oxygen tanks in the spaceship's service module had exploded, damaging other tanks and systems, each of which began failing. With oxygen and power levels plummeting and their survival in serious question, the crew crawled into the Grumman-built module, named "Aquarius," whose systems had not been damaged in the explosion, and survived there using the LM's lesser power to guide the spacecraft back into an emergency homeward-bound trajectory that ultimately saved their lives.

Butch and Lew Evans, who, by that time, had become president of Grumman, were in mission control when the emergency developed. "It was a somber time, a scary time. I don't think we ever sat down." As the drama unfolded, the seriousness grew. "You could hear a pin drop as they [the crew] made each makeshift move to cope with the problems they were having. You wonder what if we lose this crew in space and never get them home?" As the crew moved into the LM and began battling to return home, NASA began referring to the lunar module as its "lifeboat." Butch: "One of the big concerns was that if they missed the angle of entry into the earth's atmosphere by even a few degrees, they'd bounce off like a flat rock skipping off water and keep going out in space. If they hit it too steep, they'd burn up. Either way, it would be the end."

The reentry in the crippled ship had to be precise.

The smaller LM's power was used to get the trajectory going and then the LM itself was discarded as the astronauts went back into the command module for the final plunge. "That was the crucial time—as they approached earth. I'll tell you, I watched grown men get down on their knees and pray, tears in their eyes. It was very dramatic. You had to be there to really see what was happening."

Butch was at Cape Canaveral or Houston during almost every Apollo mission and received an Apollo Achievement Award from NASA "in appreciation of dedicated service . . . as a member of the team which has advanced the nation's capabilities in aeronautics and space . . ." But in the early 1970s, following Lew Evans's death, Grumman no longer saw a need for his services.

He was fired.

"When Lew died, you had the other faction there . . . Lew hadn't come from within the company. He was a lawyer, had worked in navy contracts . . . He was kind of New School and they were traditional . . . I remember we were standing graveside as Lew was being lowered into the ground . . . We'd been close with Lew, Thea and I. We'd spent a lot of time with him and his family. They had a ranch about ten miles from the cemetery [Manassas National in Virginia], and we were going to go there afterward. I remember a chairman of the board, Clint Towl [one of the original founders of Grumman], waving to me, standing on a mound above the grave site and looking at me. It meant are you coming with me or are you staying here? And, naturally, I was staying. That was it. It was over with."

A few days later he was summoned and given the news. "I remember he [not Towl but another executive] stood looking out the window and said, 'I hate to do this, Butch.' I said fine, no problem. They were cleaning out all of Lew's people." When NASA heard the news, they offered Butch a job. He became assistant to the director of NASA's Office of Industry Affairs, Ron Philips, where he was principally involved with getting universities to develop commercial applications for NASA's space technology and finding private investors to back the development. At first he ran into trouble. "It was a different world than what I had been used to, sitting in front of a fireplace and sipping sherry with a university president. That wasn't my style. I wanted to get more out of them for the money we were paying. I told them quite frankly I was disappointed at their nonperformance, and apparently that wasn't the way it was done."

After being cautioned by the head of NASA, he dropped the sledgehammer approach and devised a competitive grading system that shamed nonproducers without saying a word. It was a written report circulated throughout NASA and other pertinent entities that would list all commercial applications developed by each university. The university itself was required to submit the report regularly. "I told them so with a smile. Now that's the way to get someone's attention. You can be at the top—or the bottom. Up to you. And God and everybody else will see how you are doing."

He spent approximately ten years at NASA. "I adjusted and they did, too . . . It wasn't like shooting down airplanes or flying with the Blue Angels, but I did my job and did it well as far as I know." In 1984 Butch retired, still keeping an office at NASA for consulting work, but eventually deciding to go back to California. "You've got to quit sometime." Thea's mother needed care, and they had a yearning for their roots. "Santa Cruz wasn't what we'd grown up in," so they bought a house south of there, on a forested, often-fog-shrouded Monterey, California, hillside, the ocean, so much a part of their lives, happily nearby.

Reflecting on his civilian career, Butch says, "After I went to work for Grumman, Lew Evans and I were at lunch having martinis or whatever and he asked me, 'How do you develop the camaraderie you had in the service? How can we get that at Grumman?' I said, 'You're never going to have that here, Lew. Aerospace is dog eat dog. Everybody's up your back, clawing. It's a very immoral situation . . . In the navy, there's competition, but the key point is the closeness to death . . . the degree of hazard that you face in the game. That's the basic bonding element. There's real respect and admiration from being in that situation.' He thought about it. In industry, the key element is how do I get a raise? How do I get ahead? How many benefits or days off do I get? Entirely different. And that was that."

No question about which career Butch liked better.

Retirement didn't mean inactivity. Butch began speaking to various groups, including kids, about his life and lessons learned with the same unadorned, sometimes humorous, matter-of-fact style he's used all his life. "We weren't flamboyant, hair-on-fire types," he likes to say about his World War II generation. "Just went to work, and the work was war." In his lifetime, he'd participated in almost the entire history of aviation, from the early biplanes to futuristic moon shots. There is no more. He was in the biggest war of all time, World War II, and at one of its darkest, most violent stages, the early struggle for the Pacific. He became an ace. He'd been deeply involved in the advancement of carriers and carrier aircraft, which today are the vanguard of military might and the calling card of the United States Navy. Most of all, he'd created the aerial demonstration team best known in the United States and around the world—the navy's crack Blue Angels, unequaled ambassadors of American preeminence in aviation and innovation, a testament to what can be achieved when skill, daring, and courage are combined with unflinching teamwork built on trust and a burning desire to be the best at what one does.

The Blue Angels would always honor Butch, as would newspapers in stories around the country when he would speak or appear, especially in conjunction with air shows, which he continued to attend. From time to time his advice would be asked on matters of importance to the team, such as when he was asked to evaluate a leader to determine if he was competent or not. He'd love to fly the Blue's current jet, the F/A-18 Hornet. The twin-engine fighter-bomber "has got all the thrust and power you'd ever want. If you go back to the prop days, we had less power, less control." The last jet Butch flew was the Vietnam era F8U Crusader which had heavy hydraulic controls. The Hornet uses electrical "fly-by-wire." Electrical impulses move the jet's controls faster and with less effort. "That's why the accident rates today are much lower than we had. Quicker response. Better control. From everything I hear, [the Hornet] is an absolute delight to fly. It's got the power and energy to do things we couldn't." Like starting a show with a takeoff. "We had to be airborne to build altitude and energy. They can just about sit there on the runway and almost go straight up.

In contrast to Butch's fifteen- to seventeen-minute shows, today's Blue Angels are in the air for three quarters of an hour and, on a good day, perform up to thirty different maneuvers. But all the moves are built on the basic rolls, loops, Cuban eights, inverted passes, entries, exits, echelon rolls, and breaks that he and the originals introduced. Today's Blues now use six jets in their shows, four in the basic diamond and two solos who join the others in a six-plane delta formation as extra wingmen for several of the maneuvers. Butch thinks air shows are an obligation. "The public deserves to see what we've got. Just like you had visitors' days when I was a little kid. We'd go down to San Pedro and go out on the battleships and look at our forces. Today, we have open houses at the bases. There has been an increased emphasis on bringing the military together with the surrounding community. The people have the right to see our airplanes and judge what we're doing with them."

What lessons did he learn from a life spent largely in the air?

"First, to do everything to the best of my ability. That was number one. I didn't believe in second place. I have to go back to the word 'discipline.' To be a pilot with the Blues you've got to be able to put that airplane exactly where it's supposed to be. If you don't, somebody might die. To me, that's discipline. To some it's easy to let themselves drift. They don't have the discipline. But in a demonstration team, if you don't have that striving for perfection, you shouldn't be up there."

How do you get it?

"You freeze your mind. You grit your teeth and put it there, and you hold it there. Nothing stops you. Upside down. Right side up. Whatever. The concentration has to be absolute."

And you have to have control. "Like control of fear."

How do you get that?

"It's mental. Understanding the situation and knowing there's a capacity for busting your ass every time you get in the airplane. But to stay ahead of that mentally and not let it degrade your performance. Fear is debilitating. A lot of people can't get fear out of their mind. Consequently, they can't cope. I've been afraid. Show me anyone who says he hasn't and I'll tell you he's a liar. You have to believe in yourself, believe it's not going to be you. It's going to be him. I never thought of myself going out there and busting my butt."

Anything else?

"How to tie my shoes . . . No . . . Let me think . . . Keep your eye on the big picture. In other words, support your superiors and their objectives. In one of my fitness reports I was considered a 'tremendous' strength to my superiors. I always thought their objectives were my objectives."

Does that mean that the mavericks are wrong?

"No, there's a little bit of maverick in all of us. I tried to sell positions that were a significant change in the way things were done. That's maverick. But they weren't off the top of my head. They were well thought out."

There really wasn't much more to say. Butch doesn't like pontificating. Like most fighter pilots, he prefers action to words. He'd rather his past speak for him.

That certainly has happened.

In 1993, he was honored as one of fifteen world aviation pioneers comprising the US Air Force's Air Command and Staff College's annual "Gathering of Eagles" program. The program, at Maxwell Air Force Base, Alabama, brings aviation greats to the college's graduation class ceremonies so they can see and hear first-hand the heritage of the field they are about to enter. Since the program's 1982 inception through 2003, 287 distinguished aviators from twenty-five nations around the world have been brought to Maxwell to speak, have their portraits painted, and be recognized for their outstanding contributions. Air force general Charles "Chuck" Yeager was among the fifteen in Butch's class, joining such previously honored Eagles as Buzz Aldrin, Gunther Rall, Curtis LeMay, Saburo Sakai, Jimmy Doolittle, Robin Olds, Adolf Galland, Jose Larious, Randy Cunningham, and G. Leonard Cheshire.

In 2000, the passenger terminal at NAS Jacksonville, where he'd started the Blues, was renamed in Butch's honor. A bronze plaque telling what he did was put inside with a display and outside at the entrance a fighter with his name on it was parked. In 2001, he was given a special recognition award by the International Air Show Hall of Fame in appreciation of the patronage he's brought to their shows. In 2002, in perhaps the honor he most appreciated, he was inducted into the US Naval Aviation Hall of Honor, along with Admiral Ernest King, commander of the US Fleet during World War II, Admiral Joseph Reeves, an early aviation pioneer and catalyst for carrier development, and Kenneth A. Walsh, a marine aviator and World War II Corsair pilot who won the Medal of Honor for attacking and destroying a large number of Japanese fighters single-handedly. The hall is at Pensacola and in it he joins his mentors, Butch O'Hare and Jimmy Flatley, Admirals Mitscher and Schoech, under whom he directly served, and pilot greats and friends, Jimmy Thach, Marion Carl, Joe Foss, and Pappy Boyington.

In 2003, still going strong despite ailments that had him walking shakily, he was grand marshall of Seattle's annual Seafair Parade, riding and waving in a new Cadillac near where he'd performed so many years before with the fledgling Blues. Sadly, later that year, Thea, who had developed a heart ailment, died, certainly a blow to Butch after more than fifty-five years of marriage. But he has carried on, continuing to speak before groups and willingly granting press interviews whenever asked. At eighty-four, tall and smiling, always quick to move to the crowds seeking his autograph, who know him as "father" of the Blues, he still enjoys the sight and sound of jets as they roar overhead, especially the Blue Angels in their Hornets. "I wish I could go up and do it again. I wouldn't change a thing." In his own stout heart, and in the hearts of those who know him, he will always be "First Blue," the flyer who started it all.

This biography was written primarily from taped interviews with Butch and people who knew him. In my research, I accumulated thirty-eight tapes with approximately 114 hours of transcribed interviews. The interviews were supplemented with records and memorabilia Butch and others kept and with official navy records obtained through the Freedom of Information Act and the Privacy Act. In addition, a variety of books, articles, and other documents were used. In addition to Butch, the following is a list of most of these sources:

INTERVIEWS

Boudreaux, Robert N., original Blue Angel mechanic
Burrows, Ken, VF-113 pilot
Cunningham, Mel, VF-191 pilot
Edwards, Jill, Butch's daughter
Elder, Bob, VF-191 skipper whom Butch followed in a number of jobs
Feightner, Edward L. "Whitey," VF-10 pilot, Blue Angel, admiral, ace
Gillcrist, Paul T., VF-191 pilot, FAGU instructor, admiral
Gordon, Don, VF-10 pilot, ace
Hoover, Bob, army pilot, air show pioneer
Hopper, Phil, Pratt and Whitney engineer
Horton, Bob "Sport," VF-113 pilot
Kanze, Bob, VF-10 pilot
Klapka, E. J., VF-113 pilot
Nothhaft, Henry "Hank," Butch's son-in-law
Nothhaft, Randie, Butch's daughter
Olson, Lyle, VF-113 pilot
Quiel, Dick, VF-113 pilot
Rees, Joe, navy F-111 manager

Reiserer, Russell L., VF-10 pilot, ace
Rhodes, Raleigh E. "Dusty," VF-10 pilot, Blue Angel skipper
Scheuer, Dave, Grumman Blue Angel representative
Slaiby, Ted, Pratt and Whitney engineer
Taddeo, Al, original Blue Angel pilot
Vejtasa, Stanley "Swede," VF-10 pilot, ace
Vincent, E. Duke, Blue Angel pilot
Vineyard, M. W. "Tex," VF-2 pilot, ace
Voris, Bob, Butch's brother
Voris, Dick, Butch's brother
Voris, Thea, Butch's wife
Weisner, Maurice "Mickey," pilot, admiral
Whisler, George, pilot, Crusader skipper
Williamson, Ron, NAS Jacksonville historian
Wolf, John T. "Mike," VF-2 pilot, ace
Young, Rob, historian, National Air Intelligence Center, Wright-Patterson AFB

BOOKS

Bergerud, Eric M. *Fire in the Sky: The Air War in the South Pacific.* Westview Press, 2000.
Chant, Chris. *Aircraft of World War II.* Dempsey-Parr, Bristol, U.K. 1999.
Clark, Sydney. *All the Best in Hawaii.* Dodd, Mead, 1949.
Cunningham, Walter. *The All-American Boys: An insider's candid look at the space program and the myth of the super hero.* Macmillan, 1977.
Ewing, Steve, and Lundstrom, John B., *Fateful Rendezvous: The Life of Butch O'Hare.* Naval Institute Press, 1997.
Foss, Joe, and Brennan, Matthew. *Top Guns: America's Fighter Aces Tell Their Stories.* Pocket Books, 1991.
Gillcrist, Paul T., *Feet Wet: Reflections of a Carrier Pilot.* Pocket Books, 1990.
Great Campaigns of World War II. J. B. Davies, co-ordinating editor; Phoebus Publishing Company, London. 1980.
Hammel, Eric. *Carrier Strike: The Battle of the Santa Cruz Islands.* Pacifica Press, 1999.
Hoover, R. A. "Bob," with Mark Shaw. *Forever Flying.* Pocket Books, 1996.
Hoyt, Edwin P. *McCampbell's Heroes.* Avon, 1983.
Johnston, Stanley. *The Grim Reapers.* Dutton, 1943.
Kernan, Alvin B., *Crossing the Line: A Blue Jacket's World War II Odyssey.* Blue Jacket Books, Naval Institute Press, 1997.
Long, Eric F., and Avino, Mark A. (photographers). *At the Controls: The Smithsonian National Air and Space Museum Book of Cockpits.* Smithsonian Institution Press, 2001.
Lundstrom, John B., *The First Team and the Guadalcanal Campaign.* Naval Institute Press, 1994.
Marshall Cavendish Illustrated Encyclopedia of World War II, Vol. 19. Marshall Cavendish, 1972.
McGuire, Jim. *A Pictorial History of the Blue Angels.* Squadron/Signal Publications, 1981.

Mersky, Peter. *The Grim Reapers: Fighting Squadron Ten in World War II.* Champlin Museum Press, 1986.

Miller, Thomas G., Jr. *The Cactus Air Force.* Bantam, 1981.

Morrison, Wilbur H., *Pilots, Man Your Planes! The History of Naval Aviation.* Hellgate Press, 1999.

Morrissey, Thomas L. *Odyssey of Fighting Two.* Privately published, 1945.

NASA. *Chariots for Apollo: A History of Manned Lunar Spacecraft,* by Courtney G. Brooks, James M. Grimwood, and Loyd S. Swenson, Jr., 1969, HTML revised December 5, 1996.

Oriskany cruise book staff. *Into the Wind.* 1955 Far East cruise, privately published (Voris collection).

Parrish, Thomas, ed. *The Simon and Schuster Encyclopedia of World War II.* Simon & Schuster, 1978.

Prados, John. *Combined Fleet Decoded: The Secret History of American Intelligence and the Japanese Navy in World War II.* Random House, 1995.

Preble, Christopher. "Joint Strike Fighter: Can a Multiservice Fighter Program Succeed?" December 5, 2002. www.cato.org/pubs/pas/pa460.pdf.

Rausa, Rosario. *The Blue Angels: An Illustrated History.* Moran Publishing Corp., 1979

Shapley, Deborah. *Promise and Power: The Life and Times of Robert McNamara.* Little Brown, 1993.

Sherrod, Robert. *Tarawa: The Story of a Battle.* Duell, Sloan and Pearce, 1944.

Sommerville, Donald. *World War II Day by Day: An illustrated Almanac, 1939–1945.* Dorset Press, 1989.

Spector, Ronald H., *Eagle Against the Sun: The American War with Japan.* Free Press, Macmillan, 1985.

Stafford, Edward P., *The Big E: The Story of the USS Enterprise.*

Sunderman, James F., (ed.) *World War II in the Air: The Pacific.* Van Nostrand Reinhold, 1981.

Tillman, Barrett. *Hellcat: The F6F in World War II.* Naval Institute Press, 1979.

———. *Hellcat Aces of World War II.* Osprey Publishing, London, 1996.

———. *Wildcat: The F4F in WWII.* Naval Institute Press, 1990.

———. *Wildcat Aces of World War II.* Osprey Aerospace, London, 1995.

Treadwell, Terry C., *Ironworks: The Story of Grumman and Its Aircraft.* Tempus Publishing, London, 2000.

Veronico, Nicholas A., and Fritze, Marga R., *Blue Angels: Fifty Years of Precision Flight.* Motor Books International, 1996.

Whelan, James R. *Hunters in the Sky: Fighter Aces of World War II.* Regnery Gateway, 1991.

Wilson, Randy, "The Clash of the Carriers: US and IJN carrier air power in early 1942," The Dispatch, Spring, 1996, via the Confederate Air Force Web site

ARTICLES

Associated Press, "O'Hare Shot Down in the Pacific; Comrades Describe Night Fight," *New York Times,* December 11, 1943.

Banke, Jim, "What Caused the Apollo 13 Disaster?" Space.com, 13 April 2000.

Barker, Mary, "First 'Blue Angel' Recalls the Early Years," *Monterey County Herald,* October 13–19, 1994.

Batten, Richard, "Buzzard Brigade at Guadalcanal, US Navy Office of Public Relations, 1943, obtained at USS Enterprise Web site, www.cv6.org/company/accounts/rbatten/.

Billotte, Bill, "Fellow Aviators Grimly Carried On, Knowing Comrade Had Died in Crash," *Evening World-Herald* (Omaha), n.d. but presumably July 20, 1946.

Birmingham (Ala.) *News*, "That Flash You See May Be a Blue Angel," November 16, 1952.

Black, Steve, "Russ Reiserer—'Turkey Shoot' Ace-in-a-Day," sent to me by Russ Reiserer.

Brown, Nettie Cardoza, series of articles entitled "The Blue Angels: A history of the Navy's Flight Demonstration Team," *Imperial Valley* (Calif.) *Weekly*, 1973.

Caldwell, Joe, "Thirty-five Years Ago Today, Precision Flying Team Made Its First Appearance over Craig Field," *Florida Times-Union,* June 15, 1981.

Cantrell, Susan, "Butch Voris: 'Gladiator in the Sky,'" *Monterey County Herald,* December 26, 1999.

Cleveland News, multipage special section on the 1946 National Air Races, August 30, 1946.

Cleveland Plain Dealer, "Angels Give Hapless Jap the Devil," September 1, 1946.

Corpus Christi Caller-Times, "Navy Newcomers Report Abroad," March 16, 1952.

Corpus Christi Times, "Blue Angels Give Preview For Press," June 16, 1952.

———, "NAS Blue Angel Dies in Crash," Corpus Christi Times, July 7, 1952.

———, "Veteran Jet Pilot Joins Blue Angels," September 29, 1952.

Courier (Ottumwa, Iowa), "Blue Angels, in Navy's Fastest Planes, Ace Act at Sunday Show," September 12, 1946.

Craib, Ralph, "Oriskany's Pilots See 'Just Another Job' Ahead," *Oakland Tribune,* February 11, 1955.

Crawford, Bruce L., "An Obscure U.S. Navy Fighter Did Yeoman Duty When Times Were Toughest Early in World War II," *Aviation History,* May 1996.

Foley, Bill, "1946 Show at Craig Heralded the Jet Age," *Florida Times-Union,* n.d. Post-1986 since that date is mentioned as past.)

Fritz, John, "46 Angels Took Off into the Blue," *Florida Times-Union*, October 25, 1996.

———, "Even Naming Blue Angels Took Skill," *Florida Times-Union,* October 25, 1996.

Geary, Frank, "Today Marks Birth of Blue Angels," *Jax Air News,* May 9, 1996.

Goodwin, Dave, "Best Recruiting Poster Ever Designed," *Pensacola Journal,* November 12, 1981.

Gordon, Bill, "Blues Brought Tight Precision and Skill Through 8 Aircraft," *Pensacola Journal,* November 12, 1981.

Grumman Plane News, "Navy Stunt Team Picks Bearcats," August 14, 1946.

Handke, Paul, "Navy's Blue Angels to Give Thrill Show," *Parkersburg Sentinel,* September 7, 1946.

Hartshorne, James D., "Fulton Wins Sohio Race at 353 M.P.H.," *Cleveland Plain Dealer,* September 1, 1946.

Jacksonville Journal, "Navy Crash Victim Here Is Identified," September 15, 1948.

Jax Air News, "Formation Flying," May 2, 1946. (Photo with caption.)

———, "Naval Flight Team to Star in Jax Air Show," June 13, 1946.

———, "Flier Who Downed 8 Japs Leads Air Show Navy Aces," June 27, 1946.

———, "Contest to Name Navy Flight Team Proves Popular," July 4, 1946.

———, "Winner of Flight Team Contest to Be Announced Next Week," July 18, 1946.

———, "Blue Angels Will Star in Air Show at Jax Craig Field," April 17, 1947.

———, "Crash During 'Open House' Claims Life of Flight Team Ace," October 3, 1946.

Jet Journal (Miramar, Calif.), "Command Changes Bring New CAG-5, VF-141 CO's," January 24, 1958.

Jet Journal, June 27, 1958. (Front page pictures of Butch.)

———, "Former Blue Angels Leader 'Butch' Voris Relieved as ComCVG," December 12, 1958.

Johnson, John W., "Blue Angels Will Be Ready to Take to Air Next Week," *Corpus Christi Times,* November 7, 1951.

———, "Supersonic Salesmen Open Up Drive for Young Navy Fliers," *Corpus Christi Caller Times,* June 17, 1952.

Kansas City Star, "12,000 See Speed," July 5, 1946.

Kirby, John F., "Get It Up, Get It On, Get It Down," *Naval History,* June 1996.

Knott, Richard, "US Naval Aviation at 90," *Aviation Week & Space Technology,* April 9, 2001.

Lacouture, John E., "Maui Aviation: A Brief History of NAS Puunene . . . ," *Wings of Gold,* Spring 1989.

Lincoln (Neb.) *Sunday Journal and Star,* "Precision Jet Fliers Perform Today," November 2, 1952.

———, "30,000 Spectators Watch as Navy Planes Cavort in Aerial Maneuvers," November 3, 1952.

Long Island Commercial Review, "Grumman PR chief: Voris," August 3, 1966.

Manley, Victoria, "Blue Angels Start to Arrive," *Californian,* September 29, 1999.

Marolda, Edward J., "The U.S. Navy in the Cold War Era, 1945–1991," Department of the Navy Naval Historical Center, www.history.navy.mil/wars/coldwar-1.htm

Memphis Commerical Appeal, "Jesters," June 20, 1952. (Photo with caption.)

Memphis Press-Scimitar, "Navy's Top Fliers to Appear Here," June 17, 1952.

Miller, Harry L., "Record Throng Sees Airport Event; History's Worst Meat Famine Near," *Parkersburg* (WVA) *News,* September 9, 1946.

Nakkula, Al, "50,000 Rain-Soaked Spectators on Hand for Finale of Air Show," *Rocky Mountain News,* August 26, 1946.

NASA Special Publication 4009, The Apollo Spacecraft: A Chronology, Vol. IV, "Preparation for Flight, the Accident, and Investigation," n.d., Obtained on the Web at www.hq.nasa.gov/office/pao/History/SP-4009/v4plc.htm.

Naval Aviation News, "Blue Angels," August 1955.

———, "Angel Album: Nostalgic, Historic Presentation of the Navy's Flight Demonstration Team, December 1961.

Oakland Post-Enquirer, "110,000 See Air Show Here," October 14, 1946.

Pensacola Journal, "Pensacola Salutes," November 12, 1981. (An 18-page special supplement devoted to the Blues.)

———, "The Roster of Blue Angels," November 12, 1981. (From the special section.)

Pifer, Bette, "Cdr. Voris of Clairemont Recounts How It Is to Fly with Blue Angels," *Clairemont* (Calif.) *Sentinel,* December 31, 1958.

Porter, R. Bruce, "That First Night Trap," *Hook,* Fall, 1986.

Scheuer, Dave, "The Birth of the Blues," *Foundation,* vol. 17, no. 1, Spring 1996.

Sisler, George, "Navy Blue Angels to Show Mastery of Jets at Fete," *Commercial Appeal* (Memphis), June 17, 1952.

Taylor, Theodore, "Turn On the Lights," from *The Magnificent Mitscher,* reprinted in *Brassey's Air Combat Reader,* edited by Walter J. Boyne and Philip Handleman (Washington, 1999).

Thompson, Warren, "Show Time," *Airpower,* May 2000.

Tozer, Lindsay, "'Once a Blue, Always a Blue," *Florida Times-Union,* November 1, 2000.

Treen, John, "They Know the Ropes, but Don't Call Them 'Acrobats,'" *Detroit News,* August 30, 1952.

USS Hornet Museum, "The Hornet during WWII." Obtained on Web at www.usshornet.org/history/ww2.asp.

USS Hornet Museum, "Ship's Log." Obtained on Web at www.usshornet.org/history/ships_logcv-12.html.

Weathersbee, T., "'Faded' Angels: Memories Soar," *Pensacola Journal,* November 12, 1981.

Willard, John, "From the Wild Blue Yonder . . ." *Quad-City Times,* July 11, 1982.

Youngman, Lawrence, "Fair's Air Show Is Held Despite Morning Rain," *Evening World-Herald* (Omaha), July 19, 1946.

———, "Navy Bearcat Pilot Killed in Crash at Aviation Fair," *Evening World-Herald* (Omaha), July 20, 1946.

———, "100,000 May Attend Air Fair Today, Crowds Stimulate Top-Notch Flier," *Sunday World-Herald* (Omaha), July 21, 1946.

———, "80,000–120,000 Attend Final Program of Aviation Fair; Crowd Sets Record," *Evening World-Herald* (Omaha), July 22, 1946.

DOCUMENTS

I estimate I received over 300 official navy documents, many of them formerly classified, concerning Butch's naval career, everything from travel orders to fitness evaluations to awards to after-action reports. Almost all were helpful, if not in supplying direct information, then in helping to establish dates and his whereabouts. In addition, I located documents on the Web or in repositories such as the Naval Historical Division in Washington and the National Archives. It would be too tedious and voluminous to list every document. The following are the most pertinent.

Chief of Naval Operations, April 2, 1946, directive beginning, "It is desired that a flight exhibition team be organized . . . ," RG 38, Records of the CNO, Box 1172, National Archives and Records Administration, College Park, Md.

Davison, Rear Admiral Ralph, April 18, 1946, reply to CNO that flight exhibition team is established at Naval Air Advanced Training Command, National Archives Branch, Fort Worth, Tex.

Flatley, J. H. "Jimmy," VF-10 after-action report, November 21, 1942, "Battle for Guadalcanal: Report of participation in the actions which repulsed an attempt by the Japanese to recapture Guadalcanal," multiple pages, obtained from Naval Historical Division, Washington, D.C.

Flight Logs, R. M. Voris, four volumes, from August 1941 through November 1960, totaling 3,405.7 hours.

Guadalcanal Journal, US Marines, obtained on the Web at http://users.erols. com/jd55/guadalcanal2.html.

Investigation into the death of Lieutenant Ross F. Robinson, Chief, Bureau of Aeronautics. Multiple papers and photos dated from June through September 1948, released to the author by the Judge Advocate General, Department of the Navy, Washington Navy Yard, D.C.

Investigation into the death on July 7, 1952, of Lieutenant (j.g.) Dwight E. Wood Jr. Multiple papers and photos, obtained from Department of the Navy, Judge Advocate General, Department of the Navy, Washington Navy Yard, D.C.

Pratt & Whitney releases on the J42 and J48 jet engines, Pratt & Whitney Archives.

Spangenberg, George A. "Brief History and Background of the F-14, 1955–1970." Obtained from the Spangenberg Web site at http://gasoralhistory.hom.att.net/ vfl.htm.

———. "F-111B Status," February 5, 1964. Obtained from Spangenberg Web site at http://gasoralhistory.home.att.net/vf4.htm.

———. "Lessons from the F-111 Program," March 13, 1967, Spangenberg Web site at http://gasoralhistory.home.att.net/vf6.htm.

TFX 1962–1967—A System Out of Balance, John Boochever, November 4, 2003. Obtained on the Web at www.sais-jhu.edu/programs/ir/strategic/courses/docs/TFX%.

USS Enterprise Deck Log, October 25–26, 1942. Obtained on the Web at www.cv6.org/ship/logs/log19421026.htm.

USS Enterprise Action Report—November 10–27, 1943. Tarawa and Makin. Obtained on the Web at www.cv6.org/ship/logs/action194311.htm.

VF-2 Aircraft Action Report, June 11, 1944, "VF sweep over Guam." Naval Historical Division, Washington, D.C., multiple pages.

VF-2 Aircraft Action Report, June 18–19, 1944. "Interception of Air Attack Against Task Force, Naval Historical Division, multiple pages.

VF-2 Aircraft Action Report, June 19, 1944, "Interception—Orote Area, Guam," Naval Historical Division, multiple pages.

VF-2 Aircraft Action Report, June 20, 1944, "Bombing, Torpedo and Strafing Attack on Jap Fleet," Naval Historical Division, multiple pages.

VF-2 Aircraft Action Report, June 24, 1944, "Interception of Attack of Task Group," Naval Historical Division, multiple pages.

VF-2 Aircraft Action Report, July 3, 1944, Fighter Sweep and Bombing, Iwo Jima . . . ," Naval Historical Division, multiple pages.